THE STORY
OF THE
URDD

1 Ifan ab Owen Edwards in 1922

THE STORY OF THE URDD

(THE WELSH LEAGUE OF YOUTH)

1922—1972

GWENNANT DAVIES

ABERYSTWYTH
CWMNI URDD GOBAITH CYMRU
1973

First Published - *December 1973*

ISBN 0 903131 08 0

© *Gwennant Davies*

Printed by
J. D. Lewis & Sons Ltd., Gwasg Gomer, Llandysul

To

MEMBERS OF THE URDD

so that they may build on the past

to meet the needs of the future

Contents

List of Photographic Plates

Acknowledgements

The photographs included in this volume were mainly taken by Urdd leaders and supporters who kindly agreed to their publication in Urdd magazines and it was, therefore, assumed that their permission to include them in this book would be just as generously granted. It was not considered necessary to give individual credit in respect of the various plates ; indeed, in some instances, this would have been an impossible task. We know, however, that we are indebted to the following : Prys Edwards ; Elwyn Huws ; Dr. Iolo ap Gwynn ; E. Breeze Jones ; Raymond Daniel ; R. Glyn Pickford ; J. J. Jones ; Ron Davies ; Malcolm Slater ; Anthony David ; Chris J. Arthur ; Studio Jon, Fishguard ; BBC ; HTV ; Hill's Welsh Press ; The London Welsh Association ; *Western Mail.*

In this connection, special credit must be given to Geoffrey Charles (*Y Cymro*), who over the years has taken hundreds of photographs of Urdd events. The Urdd is greatly indebted to him and to *Y Cymro* for generously allowing us to select from their collection.

The Urdd is not only particularly grateful but also deeply indebted to two bodies for their generous gifts towards the publication costs of this volume—the National Union of Teachers (£500) and the Catherine and Lady Grace James Foundation (£300).

Preface

' The Story of the Urdd ' is an attempt to condense the essence of
the three volumes in which R. E. Griffith traces the development
of the movement during its first fifty years, from 1922 to 1972. In
doing so, one tried to follow the same general pattern, and bring
into focus the more important phases in the movement's
progress. Naturally, many of the fascinating and intimate details
included in the Welsh volumes had to be sacrificed in the process.
It is hoped, however, that something of the thrill of the early years
has been retained, as well as the determination that enabled the
Urdd to survive the difficulties of the war years and emerge transformed into a recognised youth movement geared to help its
members to live life more adventurously and more abundantly.
This was achieved by the movement without losing sight of the
ultimate objective of stimulating and encouraging its members to
serve Wales, their fellow-man and Christ to the best of their ability.
In this context, the reader cannot fail to be aware of the Urdd's role
in the language issue. The emphasis throughout has been on
inspiring the members—both Welsh-speaking and non-Welsh-
speaking—to care about the language and its future, for the Urdd
firmly believes that it is the emergence or non-emergence of this
kind of active concern that will eventually decide whether the
language will win or lose the struggle for its existence.

It was impossible within the scope of one volume to make more
than casual reference to the phenomenal amount of voluntary
activity that sustained and invigorated the movement throughout
the fifty-year period. The untold contribution of this host of
voluntary workers is inherent in the story of the Urdd, for without
them the movement would not have survived.

I would like to acknowledge my indebtedness to the many who,
in diverse ways, have helped in the publication of this volume. To
the Officers and staff of Urdd Gobaith Cymru who relieved me of
other duties in order to make writing possible ; to Miss Sulwen
Evans for her patient care in typing and re-typing the printers'
copy ; to Mr. Brynmor Jones for his readiness to undertake the

uninspiring task of preparing the index ; to Mr. Hywel Harries for designing the cover jacket ; and to Gomer Press for taking endless pains to ensure a high standard of printing.

My debt to Mr. R. E. Griffith is greater than I can express, not only for his guidance and advice, but even more so for the endless practical help which was so readily given, even though the task coincided with the preparation of his own third volume, while at the same time being directly involved in all other aspects of the Jubilee celebrations. This, however, is just another example of a lifetime of service to the Urdd and to Wales.

Gwennan Davies.

October 1973.

2   Neuadd Wen, Llanuwchllyn

3   The two Urdd badges—1922 and 1944

4   The camp at Llanuwchllyn

5   Members of the girls' camp, 1930

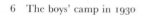

6   The boys' camp in 1930

I N his volume 'The Welsh', Wyn Griffith summarises the contribution made to the life of Wales by Urdd Gobaith Cymru. He refers to it as the movement that sprang into being when a 'moment of vision' came to Ifan ab Owen Edwards in 1922. No student of present-day Wales would deny that January 1922 was truly 'a moment of vision'. But to account for the 'vision', and to understand how Ifan ab Owen Edwards came to accept the subsequent self-imposed responsibility of turning the vision into reality, one must look at the background of the period in terms of Wales, and at the personal upbringing of Ifan ab Owen Edwards himself.

This takes us back to the village of Llanuwchllyn, near Bala, the boyhood home of his father, Owen M. Edwards. Owen Edwards was the eldest of four sons whose parents were endowed with few worldly possessions but who somehow struggled to allow three of their sons to embark upon an academic career. That of Owen Edwards took him first to Bala and then to Aberystwyth ; thence to Glasgow and eventually to Balliol College, Oxford, where, in 1887, he obtained the Lothian Prize and a First Class in Modern History. Two years later, he was elected a Tutorial Fellow of Lincoln College, a position he held until 1907. Two milestones occur in 1891. In that year, he married Ellen Davies of Llanuwchllyn, and in the same year, he launched his monthly magazine *Cymru*. *Cymru* was followed in 1892 by *Cymru'r Plant*—a monthly magazine for children. Both of these he continued to edit until he died nearly thirty years later.

In 1907, he was appointed Chief Inspector of Education for Wales, and this allowed him to return to Wales and to his native Llanuwchllyn. His interest in education, however, was not confined within the periphery of the school. Side-by-side with his official duties at Oxford and later at Llanuwchllyn, he dedicated himself to the task of creating in his fellow-countrymen a pride in their history, their language and their culture. To this end, he wrote prodigiously, and he wrote the kind of books for which the ordinary Welsh-speaking Welshman of his day would be prepared to sacrifice some of his very meagre earnings. His style was lively, his approach personal, and he produced fascinating books of travel, of nature, of history and folklore. Professor W. J. Gruffydd describes how he and his generation revelled in these books ' because they revealed the inexhaustible treasures that existed in the ordinary life of Wales and in the history of its people. For the first time in centuries, reading and writing Welsh had become exciting.'

Ifan ab Owen, the second of Owen and Elin Edwards' three children was born in 1895 and spent part of his childhood at Oxford. But at the beginning of every vacation, as soon as his responsibilities at College were ended, Owen Edwards brought his family to Llanuwchllyn and they returned to Oxford only when the next term was due to begin. This meant that, each term, the children missed part of their formal schooling. But Owen Edwards was convinced that to allow his children to take root in their Welsh heritage was even more important than the best education that Oxford could offer. Ifan ab Owen began his schooling in a Kindergarten at the age of three. Then followed a period at another private school until he was old enough to be sent to The Dragon School. This was a Gordonstoun type of school—with extensive playing fields, gymnasium and swimming pool—which specialised in outdoor activities. With its advanced educational ideas, it made a profound impression on Ifan ab Owen, and its influence remained with him for the rest of his days.

His early life, therefore, was lived in an atmosphere of continuous dualism. Welsh was the language of his home ; English was the language of education. Every vacation was spent at Llanuwchllyn where he was steeped in an exclusive Welsh atmosphere. He often recalled how, during his first vacation from The Dragon School, his mother sent him to Sunday School in his Eton suit, complete with bowler hat ! He was ever grateful to his fellow-members who must have felt a degree of sympathy one would hardly expect from lively twelve-year olds. To their credit, they refrained from mockery and quickly accepted him as one of them.

His days at The Dragon School, however, were destined to be limited, for when his father became Chief Inspector of Education for Wales, the family left Oxford and made Llanuwchllyn their permanent home. In due course, Ifan ab Owen found himself a pupil at the Bala Grammar School. His first shock of disappointment came when he realised that his new school showed a complete disregard for those aspects of education which were considered all-important at The Dragon School. Physical education seemed to be tolerated rather than encouraged, and out-door activities seemed to be un-heard of. Apart from that, there was little new in the atmosphere of the school despite the fact that he was now in the very nerve-centre of Welsh Wales. English was again the medium of instruction. It was true they were given lessons in Welsh, but even this was taught through the medium of English. History was still the history of Britain, and of England in particular. There was no place for the history and culture of Wales even though ninety-five per cent of the boys were native Welsh-speakers. In this respect, however, the Grammar School at Bala was no different from any other Grammar School of the period in Wales.

It is hardly surprising, therefore, that, during this period, Ifan ab Owen was influenced to a far greater degree by the cultural background of his own home, and that of the community at Llan-uwchllyn, particularly that which centred around the chapel, the shoemaker's workshop and the village library. The leaders of the community, even if not well educated in the scholastic sense, were men of substance who had minds of their own about the things that mattered. And in no time, Ifan ab Owen had become part of the community. At the same time, his interest in outdoor activities, awakened and stimulated by The Dragon School, was not to be abandoned. Like the other village lads, Ifan ab Owen swam in the ice-cold waters of mountain streams, and became expert at catching fish with his hands. The greatest thrill of all came when he and two of his pals spent their first night under canvas on a hilly slope in full view of Aran Benllyn.

In 1912, Ifan ab Owen started on a degree course in History at Aberystwyth. Here again, the emphasis was on British and Europ-ean history ; Wales hardly ever came into focus, as though it were just an unimportant corner of this wider entity. He graduated in 1915, but felt that partly perhaps due to his own immaturity he had gained little that was lasting from his sojourn at Aberystwyth.

By that time, the First World War was already in progress, and Ifan ab Owen was soon called for military service. In February

1916, he crossed to Boulogne to begin his overseas service with the artillery at the Battle of the Somme. Two incidents during the war period left their mark on his consciousness. The first was the death at Arras of one of his Llanuwchllyn friends who had shared in his first overnight camping experience near Aran Benllyn. In the second incident, Ifan ab Owen found himself in conflict with a junior officer who was unaware of the fact that letters were permitted to be written in Welsh, and commanded him to rewrite, in English, his letter to his parents. Ifan ab Owen flatly refused and was promptly dubbed ' *a stubborn Welsh pig* '. Needless to say, this led to a counter-retort, with the result that Ifan ab Owen spent the night in detention, and the next day, appeared before the authorities to account for his insubordination. His right to correspond in Welsh was conceded, but the incident had left its mark and had compelled him to orientate his priorities. The result was a new conviction that, to him, Wales and his Welsh heritage were of supreme importance.

In March 1918, it became apparent that the war could not last much longer. Accordingly, Ifan ab Owen wrote to ask his father to send him one or two books that would provide some preparation if he lived to continue his studies at Oxford. Some time later, when, in a lull of battle, he was engrossed in his reading, his Colonel-in-Chief came upon him unawares and could hardly believe that one of his men should be reading Burke's *Civilisation* and Maine's *Ancient Law*. Ifan ab Owen was immediately sent on an officers' course in the Isle of Wight, and when Armistice was declared in November, he was released within a month and caught the first train home to Llanuwchllyn.

In January 1919, he left Llanuwchllyn once more, this time for Lincoln College, Oxford, where his father had been Tutorial Fellow for eighteen years. Whereas he had felt young and immature when he went to Aberystwyth, he now felt much older than his twenty-three years. At that time, ex-servicemen were allowed to take a shortened five-term course, and Ifan ab Owen was glad to avail himself of the opportunity and pledged himself to do all he could to make up for lost time. This did not mean divorcing himself completely from the non-academic side of college life, and he soon became a member of various college societies. One of his first acts, in this connection, was to restore the Welsh language to its rightful place as official language of the *Dafydd ap Gwilym Society*.

He had spent barely three months in Oxford when his mother died suddenly and unexpectedly. Little did he think that in just a year later, in May 1920, he would be called once more to Llanuwch-llyn, this time to his father's bedside. In his unrelenting self-impelling efforts on behalf of Wales, Owen Edwards had burnt himself out.

Ifan ab Owen Edwards returned to Oxford to take his final examinations. One day, as he was sitting in his room preparing for his first paper, a very distinguished-looking Indian knocked on his door. It was Mohamed Ali, Mohammedan leader and friend of Mahatma Gandhi. He explained that coming through Paris he had bought an English newspaper and read of the death of Sir Owen Edwards. Years earlier, he himself had been a student at Lincoln College, and Owen Edwards had been his tutor. When he arrived at Oxford and heard that Owen Edwards' son was a student at his old college, he decided to call on him to offer his condolence. He went on to say that it was Owen Edwards' lectures that first led him to understand the true meaning of Indian nationalism, a matter which later he frequently discussed with Mahatma Gandhi.

The following day, there was another incident quite unrelated to Ifan ab Owen Edwards' academic work. When he returned to his room after his first examination paper, he found that the printed proofs of the next issue of *Cymru* and *Cymru'r Plant* had been sent on to him by the publishers, Hughes and Son, Wrexham. For Ifan ab Owen, this presented more of a problem than his examination papers. He had never in his life corrected proofs and his last Welsh lesson had been at Bala Grammar School. It was, however, work which his father had been unable to complete, and the son could not now shirk his responsibility. So, in between his examination papers, the proofs were corrected and returned to the publishers.

With his examinations over, Ifan ab Owen returned immediately to his home at Llanuwchllyn. In his mail he found a letter from the publishers requesting that the copy of the August number of both magazines should be sent as soon as possible. This was tantamount to assuming that he was to become the new editor, something he had never envisaged and for which he felt he had no qualifications. Moreover, the authorities at Lincoln College had suggested that he should return to Oxford as a research scholar. His friends and relatives favoured the latter course, but he himself felt he should remain in Wales and seek means of serving his country in a more practical and direct manner. In his dilemma, he turned into his father's study. What he found helped him to decide on his course of action. Despite his ill-health during the last year of his life, Owen Edwards had prepared sufficient material for six monthly issues of *Cymru* and *Cymru'r Plant*. Everything was neatly laid out on the table at which he used to work. There was now no choice, and Ifan ab Owen Edwards had made his decision. He would remain in Wales, carry on some of the work his father had left unfinished, and find himself a career based on his father's ideals of service to the Welsh nation and the Welsh language.

Shortly afterwards, he was appointed history and games master at the Dolgellau Boys' Grammar School. It seemed that Providence was on his side. Before he had completed his first year, however, Principal J. H. Davies of Aberystwyth had offered him a post as lecturer in the Extra-Mural Department at the College and Ifan ab Owen Edwards had accepted.

At the beginning of August, before he took up his new post at Aberystwyth, he and his sister, Haf, were at the National Eisteddfod of Wales at Caernarfon. Here he met Eirys Lloyd Phillips, an art student from Liverpool, and thus began a friendship that was to last a lifetime. She had been brought up in Liverpool, and her father, a Montgomeryshire man, had learnt Welsh as a second-language. Her mother's first language, however, was Welsh and she was a descendant of the famous David Charles of Carmarthen. In November 1921, Ifan ab Owen Edwards and Eirys Lloyd Phillips announced their engagement. In the meantime, his work as extra-mural lecturer at Aberystwyth had begun. He continued to live at Llanuwchllyn and travelled regularly to evening classes in the rural areas of Merioneth and Cardiganshire. And in between his academic duties, he devoted his attention to the editing of *Cymru* and *Cymru'r Plant*.

Whenever his extra-mural duties took Ifan ab Owen Edwards to Cardiganshire for two consecutive evenings, he would always spend the night at *Y Pandy*, in the village of Llanarth, and he had good reason for recalling with joy the hospitality he invariably received. One night in October 1921, having returned to *Y Pandy* after his evening class, his mind turned to the January 1922 issue of *Cymru'r Plant* which would soon have to be ready for the printers. What did he have to say to the readers of *Cymru'r Plant* at the beginning of a new year ? Was it possible to give even his young readers some sense of identification with Wales ? The First World War had brought with it a surfeit of power-politics and a renewed interest in the rights of small nations. In Wales itself, almost every section of the Welsh community had for several years been persistently demanding some form of autonomy for Wales within the British federal system. His own father, Owen Edwards, had realised that the Welsh people had long been conditioned to accept a depreciated evaluation of their culture, and he had worked night and day in an effort to awaken in his fellow-countrymen a greater awareness of their nationhood, a greater pride in their cultural heritage. Ifan ab Owen had long since shared his father's ideals, but he was also aware that he did not possess his father's qualifications or his unique position as Chief Inspector of Education and the idol of all Wales. His would have to be a different furrow, his own furrow. He had, however, inherited one potential asset, and that was *Cymru'r Plant*. It could be used as a vehicle for ideals, as a medium to exhort and to encourage his readers to discover for themselves a fullness of life that could be found through their own language and culture.

But how was this to be achieved ? Ifan ab Owen Edwards recalled that his father, as long ago as 1896, had attempted to establish a children's movement—*Urdd y Delyn*—through the medium of *Cymru'r Plant*. With a final membership of nearly two thousand, it lasted just ten years and then faded out. A movement confined within the pages of a magazine could not be expected to last. It needed scope for its activities ; it needed organisation. And already overburdened with the tasks he had set himself, Owen Edwards could not possibly give it the attention that would make it a living force.

There had been another attempt in 1911, again through the pages of *Cymru'r Plant*, but this time instigated by Mallt Williams, a lady of unusual character and personality who lived at Llandudoch (St. Dogmaels) near Cardigan. The movement was named *Byddin Cymru* (The Wales Army). Its aim was to show the children of Wales how best to serve their country, and it emphasised that their first task was to defend the Welsh language. A *Byddin Cymru* Eisteddfod was planned in 1913 but it failed to materialise. There is no doubt that the four-year war period militated against such a movement,

and in 1918, *Byddin Cymru*—like its predecessor, *Urdd y Delyn*—
petered out with a membership of only 1,527.

These recollections offered little encouragement to the young
editor. Was it possible that there was no support for such a movement within Wales ? Or could he avoid the pitfalls that had befallen
both *Urdd y Delyn* and *Byddin Cymru* ? Of one thing he was certain,—
there had never been a time when Wales was in greater need of such
a movement. The language was already facing a crisis of survival
and the Welsh people were conditioned into an apathy of inferiority.
The newly-awakened faith in the values of small nations had to be
nurtured, and as one of the smallest nations, Wales must be helped
to make its own contribution, however small, to the welfare of
humanity. Casting his doubts to the wind, Ifan ab Owen Edwards
turned up the paraffin lamp and began his letter to the children of
Wales. He went on—

> ' Wales' position today is as vulnerable as it ever was. There
> are so many strangers in our midst that even our language, your
> language and mine, the language of your father and mother, is in
> danger of disappearing from the hills and dales of our country.
> What shall we do, we the children of Wales, the hope of our
> country ? What if we join together, determined to do everything
> we can to help our country ? We will form a new *Urdd*, and we
> will call it *Urdd Gobaith Cymru Fach*.'

Then followed brief conditions of membership and the promise
that the names of the members would appear in *Cymru'r Plant*. As a
post-script, he added his appeal to parents, ministers of religion and
teachers for their support in making the new ' Urdd ' a success—

> ' The children are our hope for the future. Our country is
> submerged by the English flood ; we must act now to prevent
> our children being swept away by the tide . . .'

The response of his readers far exceeded his expectations. He
could only afford the space for a limited number of names in each
issue of *Cymru'r Plant* and although 720 names had appeared by the
end of 1922, hundreds were still on the waiting list. Competitions
were set each month, and through *Cymru'r Plant*, Ifan ab Owen
Edwards spoke directly to the members of his young movement. To
continue his campaign for membership, he conceived the idea of
instituting four different ranks to which those with initiative and

dedication could aspire. A member who succeeded in winning six new members was given the rank of *Is-Gapten* (Lieutenant). Another six members, and he became *Uwch-Gapten* (Captain). Yet another twelve members, and he became *Rhingyll* (Major). But he would need to win yet another twenty-six, a grand total of fifty, before he could win the noble rank of *Cadfridog* (General) ! It is obvious that this coveted rank was inevitably restricted to the dedicated few. It may appear strange that Ifan ab Owen Edwards should have chosen military ranks for his ' officers '. Was he influenced by the Boy Scout Movement, or by Mallt Williams' *Byddin Cymru*, or was it simply that, as a result of the war years, he himself and Welsh people generally had become so familiar with military titles ? However, it did not seem to have struck anyone as being incongruous or unacceptable.

Strangely enough, the first two to win the title of *Is-Gapten* were girls, and it was also another girl who became the first ' General '. She was Marian Williams and did not, as one would expect, come from the heart of Welsh Wales but from Treuddyn in Flintshire. Marian also made history by organising her enlisted members into a group that met regularly once a week. And so, without any pressure or even any suggestion from the Founder, the first Urdd Branch or *Adran* came into being. Such an announcement in *Cymru'r Plant* inevitably prompted others to follow suit. Early in 1923 came the formation of the second *Adran*, this time at Abergynolwyn. Penrhyndeudraeth and Llanwrin followed in the same year.

It is clear that during the first two years of its existence, the Urdd was a language movement. Its main aim was to protect and promote the Welsh language. In 1923, however, it became evident that the Founder was also concerned about the fate of the land of Wales. The Corporation of Warrington had cast its eyes on Glyn Ceiriog as a source of additional water supply.

> ' They want to drown the birthplace of Huw Morris and Ceiriog and the land of Alun Mabon ' said the editor of *Cymru'r Plant*. ' What if we talked of drowning Stratford on Avon and the birthplace of Shakespeare ? . . . Can we, the children of Wales, tolerate this ? Are we going to allow outsiders to drown our valleys one after the other ? Let us voice our protest without delay . . .'

So, a petition was initiated and within three weeks, seven thousand children had responded to the call. Glyn Ceiriog was not drowned. Of course, there was strong opposition to the scheme from many public bodies. But it did not pass unnoticed that the names of seven-thousand children, through *Urdd Gobaith Cymru Fach*, were among the list of those who protested.

Not long afterwards, the Founder expressed his patriotism in even more militant terms. In the August issue of *Cymru'r Plant* he wrote—

> ' Should Wales be given self-government ? Should Wales have control over its own affairs or is it right that it should be controlled from England ? Should Wales be granted its independence ? '

For some reason, however, this matter was not pursued further. Did the Founder have second thoughts and decide that he was moving too far into the political arena ? Or was it merely that he discovered that there was a move afoot to establish a Welsh Nationalist Party (*Plaid Genedlaethol Cymru*) with the aim of achieving self-government for Wales and that, for this reason, it was no longer necessary for the Urdd to operate in the political field. Perhaps, too, he realised that the impending economic crisis, already beginning to cast its shadow, would provide the Government with the excuse for shelving the demands for a Welsh parliament and that the time was, therefore, inopportune for such a campaign.

It was not long before the Welsh people themselves found that the struggle for existence demanded all their energy. The vicissitudes of the coal industry during this period are all too well-known. Unemployment and depopulation became the order of the day in the slate-quarrying areas ; woollen mills all over Wales were being closed ; the lead mines came to an end and agriculture was to feel the acute pinch of the lean years. This economic depression was to last until the beginning of the Second World War, and against this background, it is perhaps surprising that even during the long lean years, the Urdd grew, flourished and developed.

Ifan ab Owen Edwards and Eirys Lloyd Phillips were married in Liverpool in July 1923. His sister, Haf, had already left home to be married to David Hughes Parry and Ifan ab Owen Edwards and his bride were now to make their home at Neuadd Wen, Llanuwchllyn.

From the very first, his wife shared his interest in and his concern for the new movement ; shared in his rejoicing and his disappointments. She also readily undertook much of the work entailed in establishing the movement, especially on the secretarial side. When her husband boasted that he had married a wife and a secretary, she would retort that she had married not one man but a whole movement ! It was she who designed the first badge of the movement and the first membership certificate. She also became responsible for many of the illustrations for *Cymru'r Plant*, especially those in the junior section, *Cymru'r Plant Bach*, until she was relieved by W. Mitford Davies, an Anglesey artist, who continued to provide illustrations for *Cymru'r Plant* for a period of nearly forty years.

1924 saw the movement going from strength to strength. More and more members reached the rank of ' Captain ' ; more Branches (*Adrannau*) were formed. But although South Wales had many individual members, there were, as yet, no *Adrannau* and not even one ' Lieutenant '. However, in 1924, came the long-awaited break-through. Contrary to expectations, it did not come in the Welsh areas of West Wales but in one of the mining valleys of South Wales, in Abercynon. The three stalwarts responsible for the break-through were W. P. John, W. O. Barnett and R. E. Griffith. These three, while still in short trousers, became officers of the *Adran* and organised its activities. They even produced a printed programme of events and sent weekly reports to the local press. It is not surprising that W. P. John, Chairman of the *Adran*, soon reached the coveted rank of ' General,' to be followed shortly by his fellow-General, R. E. Griffith. Inspired by letters from the Founder, the officers and members soon decided that they would not confine themselves to running the *Adran* at Abercynon. In their spare time, they visited neighbouring districts and somehow contrived to sow the seeds in places like Ynys-y-bwl, Cilfynydd, Penrhiwceiber and Mountain Ash. Another missionary trek took them to Senghennydd, Abertridwr and Ystrad Mynach, much to the delight of the Founder who took a personal interest in their campaign. And when, in due course, he suggested that they should now consider establishing a *Cylch* (District), they were able to reply proudly that it already existed !

By this time, the flood-gates had been opened wide and week by week brought reports of new *Adrannau* being set up both in South and North Wales. One of the more prominent *Adrannau* was that at Penygroes County School in Caernarfonshire under the leadership of Hywel D. Roberts—already holding the rank of ' General '. The Adran used to meet immediately after school on Fridays and the Headmaster would announce in morning assembly—' Hywel's Brigade will meet in the Lecture Room at 4.00 o'clock '. And then he would add dryly—' And General Roberts, you see to it that the battalion is out by 5 o'clock '.

It is significant that the leaders of the movement were all teen-agers, and Ifan ab Owen Edwards spoke directly and unpatron-isingly to them in his letters and through the pages of *Cymru'r Plant*. In his heart of hearts, however, he knew that he also had the support of the older generation—those parents, ministers and teachers to whom he had appealed in his post-script in the January 1922 issue of *Cymru'r Plant*.

By the end of 1924, there were signs that the Urdd was stepping out of *Cymru'r Plant* and becoming a virile movement operating through its ever-widening system of *Adrannau*. This became even more apparent in 1925 when the movement held its first members' rally. The Founder had decided that the National Eisteddfod at Pwllheli would be a suitable occasion and a chapel schoolroom was booked for the purpose. Long before the meeting was due to begin, however, it became obvious that the schoolroom would be in-adequate and the audience was moved into the chapel. Even so, every seat was taken and many people were disappointed. Until then, most of the members had known Ifan ab Owen Edwards only through the pages of *Cymru'r Plant* and the anticipation of seeing the Founder in the flesh must have added to the excitement of the occasion. Just before the meeting began, Ifan ab Owen Edwards spotted a lad wearing the badge of a 'General', and asked him who he was. ' *Y Cadfridog R. E. Griffith* ' came the reply. Ifan ab Owen Edwards promptly asked him if he would address the meeting, and just as promptly, he agreed ! Neither could have foreseen at the time how close the connection between R. E. Griffith, the Urdd and its Founder was later to become.

1925 was the year in which a link was formed between the Urdd and the Goodwill Message of the Children of Wales to the Children of the World. This was the brain-child of the Rev. Gwilym Davies, a Baptist minister who later decided to devote his life to the cause of international understanding. The idea that the children of Wales might one day call the children of the world in the name of peace and goodwill came to Gwilym Davies in 1918, but it was not until The Welsh School of Social Service had adopted the suggestion in 1922 that his dream began to become a reality. Although it was not addressed to anyone in particular but rather to the children of the world, Gwilym Davies succeeded in getting the Post Office to send out the Message in Morse Code on the morning of June 28, 1922. It was heard by at least one person—the Director of the Eiffel Tower Radio Station in Paris, and at his own expense, he repeated the Message later the same morning. But there was no reply. In 1923, another Message was sent out, but again there was no reply. Then in 1924, the BBC broadcast the Message for the first time. Two replies were received, one from the Archbishop of Uppsala, and the other from the Minister of Education for Poland. From then onwards, the response grew, and replies were received from more and more countries each year. The Message was printed in full in the June 1925 issue of *Cymru'r Plant* and from then onwards, the Urdd was to become a staunch supporter of the Goodwill Message. It is also possible that the two men—Gwilym Davies and Ifan ab Owen Edwards—unconsciously influenced one another, the one becoming more aware of his Welshness and the other conceding that nationalism and internationalism need not be mutually exclusive. Until 1925, the Urdd had been a purely nationalistic movement, aimed at fostering and promoting the Welsh language and Welsh culture. During much the same period, similar youth movements came into being in other European countries, based on the same fervent patriotism, the same dedication to land and language. In some of these countries, however, this dedication of youth became a tool in the hands of those leaders who aimed at political power, based in some cases on a belief in racial supremacy.

Several factors helped the Urdd to avoid such a catastrophe. Wales was a very small country overshadowed by a powerful neighbour ; the Urdd was—and still is—a voluntary organisation, unlike the state-controlled continental movements ; the Founder himself, after his experiences of the war years, was firmly convinced that waging war was not the way to achieve peace. But it is also possible that Gwilym Davies' Peace Message may have added its own influence in introducing a spirit of understanding and tolerance towards people of other races and other ideals. At any rate, from 1925 onwards, a new note could be found in *Cymru'r Plant*. The motto—*Er Mwyn Cymru*—remained, but it was enlarged to read *Er mwyn Cymru, a Chymru er mwyn y byd* (For Wales, and Wales for the world). The aim—*I greu Cymru bur, Gymreig* remained, but was expanded to read *I greu Cymru bur, Gymreig er mwyn y byd a dynolryw*. (To create an undefiled Welsh Wales, for the benefit of the world and of humanity). Not only did the Founder support the Goodwill Message in *Cymru'r Plant*, but he later set himself to devise opportunities for members of the Urdd to meet the youth of other countries.

It was in 1925 that Ifan ab Owen Edwards had to make one of the most important decisions of his lifetime. He was offered a post as HM Inspector under the Board of Education. In the enthusiasm of his first reaction, he sent a telegram accepting the offer. But he was immediately beset with doubts as to the wisdom of his action. What would then happen to the Urdd and to *Cymru'r Plant* ? It was a moment of dilemma. By the following morning, however, he had made his decision. With the full agreement of his wife, he sent another telegram cancelling his acceptance. This was not the only occasion on which he had to choose between personal advancement and loyalty to his ideals, to the Urdd and to Wales. For not only was he regarded as an able administrator, but also as a man capable of academic distinction. In addition to his Oxford M.A., he had already been awarded a Master's degree by the University of Wales for research published under the title *Catalogue of Star Chamber Proceedings Relating to Wales*. But despite his interest in the past history of his country, its future was even more important, and if the Urdd had a contribution to make in the shaping of that future, then his own future was inevitably linked with that of the movement he had founded.

Following the success of the members' rally at Pwllheli the previous year, the Founder announced that the second annual rally would be held at Swansea during the National Eisteddfod week of 1926. But contrary to his expectations, the Swansea meeting did not reach the heights experienced at Pwllheli. This, no doubt, was partly due to the fact that it coincided with the visit to Swansea of the Duke and Duchess of York, and also with the Crowning ceremony at the Eisteddfod pavilion. More important still was the fact that the South Wales miners were now on strike and the effects of the depression were already felt throughout the whole of the area. Nevertheless, it was a disappointment by comparison only, and the five-hundred who attended experienced the same thrill as had been felt at Pwllheli. It was at this meeting that the first Urdd banner was presented, with the promise that individual banners would soon be available for each *Adran*. By the summer of 1927, this promise had been fulfilled, and every *Adran* was able to choose its own combination of colours. Possessing a Branch banner had an immediate effect. It gave the members a greater sense of unity, a new confidence, and a greater feeling of pride and responsibility.

By July 1927, the Urdd had more than 5,000 members in 80 Branches of which half had already obtained banners in their own specific colours. The Founder now deemed the time ripe for a procession. Such a parade would be a visible sign to the man-in-the-street that the Urdd—in more than one sense—was ' on the move '. He decided to link his parade with the annual rally of Urdd members during the National Eisteddfod of Wales at Holyhead. More than a thousand members from thirty Branches arrived by special trains and were assembled behind the Llangefni Silver Band for the procession to the Town Hall. The audience overflowed into a nearby chapel where a second meeting was hurriedly arranged. The rally was a tremendous success. And J. M. Howell of Aberdyfi —first benefactor of the Urdd—not only contributed towards the expenses of the meeting but also paid for the admission to the Eisteddfod of all members under fourteen years of age. The following day, even the English dailies carried reports and pictures and the event almost stole the show from the National Eisteddfod itself.

Just as important was the much smaller meeting which followed. This was a meeting of adult supporters called by the Founder so that he could share with them some of his plans and dreams for the future. He felt the time was ripe for regional meetings in addition to the annual rally. He already had plans in mind for a summer camp to be held in 1928. Moreover, he felt that the movement had grown to such an extent that the *Adrannau* now needed help from their elders. He, therefore, suggested a new rank—that of *Cefnogwr* (Supporter)—adults who would help in the organisation of the movement on local, regional and national levels. The idea was immediately acclaimed, and Ifan ab Owen Edwards returned home a happy man.

It was at this time that the writer, Kate Roberts, suggested that the word *Fach* should be omitted from the movement's title. The Urdd had created a new image for itself and for Wales and should no longer be referred to in sentimental, patronising terms. The Founder readily agreed, and it is as *Urdd Gobaith Cymru* that the movement has been known ever since.

The publication of the Government Report, 'Welsh in Education and Life', in 1927 was an event of considerable importance. In essence, it confirmed the ideals of Sir Owen Edwards in his emphasis on teaching the Welsh language and steeping pupils in the history, literature, and music of their own country. The Report not only served as a stimulant to the schools but it also provided valuable encouragement to a movement such as the Urdd that, although less formal in its approach, was working towards the same ultimate end.

7   Camp leaders in the 1929 boys' camp

8   The pilgrimage to Geneva, 1930

9   Llangrannog Camp—the girls' huts

10   The camp at Porth Dinllaen, 1934

THE annual Urdd rally held at Treorci in 1928 certainly reached a new high-water level. A local organising committee had been established and it was planned to hold the meeting in the Park and Dare Hall under the presidency of J. M. Howell of Aberdyfi. When all the two-and-a-half-thousand seats were taken, hurried arrangements were made to accommodate another thousand in a nearby chapel. While the meetings were still in progress, a message from the Eisteddfod officials was received indicating that the 'Urdd' was expected in the pavilion in fifteen minutes. The three-thousand members were quickly assembled and led by three bands on to the Eisteddfod field and into the pavilion. As they filed into their places, the audience rose and sang *Hen Wlad fy Nhadau* with all the fervour of the Rhondda Valleys. And without fuss or publicity, J. M. Howell paid for the admission of several hundred members whose parents were unemployed and could not afford the price of a ticket, while Sir W. James Thomas paid for refreshments for all the members who attended.

Seven regional rallies were held during 1928—at Abercynon, Corwen, Rhymni, Ton Pentre, Llanrwst, Caernarfon and Liverpool. The largest of these was that at Caernarfon where special trains had been arranged and more than two-thousand members—each *Adran* having its own banner—marched from the station to the Castle. The most important, however, was that at Corwen. Here the main responsibility had been taken by the Rev. and Mrs. T. Arthur Jones, and in expressing his thanks at the close of the meeting, the Rev. Arthur Jones said he foresaw the possibility that the Urdd could organise a national Eisteddfod in which all Welsh children could compete. The Founder immediately took up the suggestion, and invited local *Cefnogwyr* (Supporters) to meet him at Corwen to make preliminary arrangements for such an event to take place the following year. J. M. Howell was elected President, and the Rev. Arthur Jones became Secretary. It was to be a two-day event, with drama competitions on the Friday, followed by a parade and the Eisteddfod competitions on the Saturday. A few trophies were to be awarded in the main competitions, but there would be no money prizes. The detailed syllabus was then left to the Secretary. During the months that followed, the committee met frequently to ensure a worthy reception for the competitors. And side-by-side with the local committee, Ifan ab Owen Edwards and his wife assumed responsibility for all aspects of publicity, and made sure that members were fully informed of the event, urged to take part, and helped with their travelling arrangements.

*　　*　　*　　*

While preparations for the Eisteddfod were in progress, however, another event—equally significant and possibly more instant in its appeal—was to take place. This was the first summer camp for Urdd members, and it was to be held at Llanuwchllyn in August 1928. Of course, it was not the first children's camp ever to be held in Wales. But a holiday camp in the heart of Welsh Wales and run entirely in Welsh was quite another matter, and it was only after much persuasion that those who wished to attend were finally granted permission by their parents. There were to be two ten-day camping periods for boys only—the girls had to wait until 1929 for theirs. The cost was 10/- per person ; 1/- a day ! J. M. Howell of Aberdyfi and Mallt Williams of Llandudoch had each contributed £100 towards the cost of hiring the necessary equipment.

It was the first time for the Northwalian campers to make personal contact with the *Hwntws* from South Wales and the different dialects sounded strange and incomprehensible. But after a few days of sharing in the experiences of camp life, and after the Northwalians had won their soccer game and been well beaten in a rugby game the following day, the barriers between North and South Wales disappeared once and for all. What remained were Urdd members pledged ' to create an undefiled Welsh Wales, for the benefit of the world and of humanity '. By today's standards, the camp facilities and amenities were somewhat primitive, and the stories and reminiscences have assumed saga proportions. Porridge and boiled eggs were the menu for Sunday breakfast and the *Swyddog* (Camp Leader) in charge had calculated with mathematical exactness that if one egg took three minutes, 80 would take

240 minutes. It meant getting up at four in the morning to make sure the eggs would be ready for breakfast !

The Founder and his wife were in charge of the camps and took full advantage of the area's rich potential in history and folk-lore. A visit from J. M. Howell, the Urdd's benefactor from Aberdyfi, was perhaps the highlight of the event. All-in-all, the camps proved to be an unqualified success, and gave to outdoor activities the same prominence as had hitherto been given to cultural activities in the *Adrannau* and the annual rally. The fact that, in chronological order, the camps preceded the Eisteddfod is perhaps a reflection of the influence of The Dragon School. Following the success of these first camps, the Founder made a three-fold announcement—that a camp for girls would be held the following year ; that a uniform for both boys and girls was being devised and would be compulsory wear at camp ; and that an appeal was to be launched for funds to buy the essential camping equipment now that camping was likely to be a permanent feature in the Urdd programme. Needless to say, J. M. Howell and Mallt Williams were again the main benefactors.

Cymru'r Plant in the twenties had many readers in Patagonia, the Welsh settlement established sixty years earlier by Welsh emigrants to South America. These readers were soon to become Urdd members and several Branches were formed mainly associated with the Welsh churches. Like the *Adrannau* in Wales, the Patagonian Branches obtained their banners from the Founder, but there they linked their annual parade with St. David's Day. In the early thirties, the Welsh community suffered a major calamity when floods destroyed the irrigation canals and swept away farmhouses and chapels. By virtue of a tremendous effort, reclamation and rebuilding were undertaken and the settlement began life anew. By this time, however, they were facing opposition from the Argentinian government which was suspicious of an alien people speaking a strange language and having its own youth organisation. The schools too were having their effect and Spanish was already superseding the Welsh language, especially amongst the younger generation. Contact with Wales was already weakened and the limitations of the Second World War were to sever it still further.

During the first seven years of the Urdd's existence, space was found for news of Urdd activities within the pages of *Cymru'r Plant*. But as the movement grew, more and more space was required and this meant that the reading material had to be correspondingly curtailed. A compromise was reached when Ifan ab Owen Edwards decided on a 48-page *Cymru'r Plant* to be sold at 2d, and an identical magazine with a 16-page appendix—*Cronicl yr Urdd*—to be sold to Urdd members at 3d. In his editorial to the first Chronicle in January 1929, Ifan ab Owen Edwards outlined his manifesto.

> ' The aim of the Urdd is to create an undefiled Welsh Wales—not for its own sake, not in any attempt to make Wales superior to other countries, but in order that Wales can play its part in bringing peace to a world which today is too ready to display a spirit of antagonism and of war . . . The Urdd believes that every nation has its own message to give to the world. If Wales is to develop and present its own contribution, it must cherish those elements which are characteristic of the nation at its best—its literature, its traditions, its religion and its language . . .'

*　　*　　*　　*

By mid-May, all was ready for the first Urdd National Eisteddfod at Corwen. No stone had been left unturned, and the whole of Corwen, and indeed of Edeyrnion, was on tip-toe to welcome the children of Wales to their first Eisteddfod. The pavilion was packed for the drama competition on the Friday, and the weather was perfect for the procession which preceded the Eisteddfod session on the Saturday. Members taking part in the parade were assembled on the Recreation Ground and led to the pavilion by the Coedpoeth Silver Band. An enormous pyramid had been erected on the square and three girls representing Poetry, Purity and Peace were enthroned thereon. Above the tableau, the word CYMRU stood out in gold letters.

Forty-two Branches were represented in the stage competitions, all but four of which came from North Wales and Merseyside. Nevertheless, the Llanelli Girls' County School Branch arrived in force, having travelled by special train, and they figured prominently in several competitions. When they were declared winners of the choral competition, someone began singing *Sospan Fach* which was immediately taken up and sung with gusto by the choir. The two

Presidents—Principal D. Emrys Evans of Bangor and Ben Bowen Thomas, both Southwalians—joined in, soon to be followed by the Northwalian audience, and the spontaneous enthusiasm thus created lasted throughout the evening.

No money prizes were offered—a principle which has been adhered to ever since. Successful competitors were given a Gregynog Press certificate by courtesy of Misses Margaret and Gwendoline Davies, a Welsh book, and a star to be fixed to their *Adran* banner. The Eisteddfod proved to be a greater success than anyone had anticipated, and the Founder had nothing but generous praise for the tireless efforts of the Corwen committee and especially those of the Secretary, the Rev. T. Arthur Jones, who proved himself to be not only a dedicated organiser but also one who could inspire others to follow suit.

While preparations for the Eisteddfod were in progress, arrangements were made for the 1929 summer camps. Unlike those of the previous year, they were to be held at Llangollen in the grounds of Plas Tŷ'n Dŵr which had recently been purchased by Hywel Huws of Bogota, Colombia. This was his first contact with the Urdd, and his interest in the movement was maintained until his death in 1970. There were to be three weeks of camping; the first was for girls, followed by two weeks for boys. The Urdd now had its own equipment, and an experienced cook and meals-organiser had been engaged. The success of the Llanuwchllyn venture was repeated at Llangollen, and throughout the period camp songs echoed through Castell Dinas Brân. These included *Hen Domos Siencyn druan, Llanfairpwllgwyngyll,* and the topical parody—

' Draw, draw yn Llangollen, ym mharc Plas Tŷ'n Dŵr
Plant bach ofnadwy sy'n byw,
Plant bach yn llawn o ddireidi a stŵr,
Welsoch chi rioed ffasiwn griw.

Ifan, cofia'r plant,
Ifan, cofia'r plant,
Anfon swyddogion i rannu yr uwd,
Ifan, cofia'r plant.'

And Ifan ab Owen hilariously joined in the fun. Looking back over half a century, who would deny that Ifan did indeed remember the children of Wales ?

J. M. Howell of Aberdyfi became first President of the Urdd in November 1929. He had long been a benefactor of the movement, and even before the Urdd was founded, Ifan ab Owen Edwards had received from him a cheque for £50 towards the cost of publishing *Cymru'r Plant*. The editor felt unwilling to accept such a sum from someone he had never met, and returned the cheque with a note of appreciation. J. M. Howell, however, went personally to Llanuwchllyn and insisted on being allowed to help. It was the first of many examples of his generosity, usually accompanied by a note which said ' you will know best how the money should be spent '. J. M. Howell was a wealthy landowner, a Tory in politics and an Anglican by religion. His own Welsh was not fluent, but he believed fervently that Wales should treasure its language as the only key to its national identity, and he insisted on speaking Welsh on every possible occasion. His financial help—and that of others who followed him—made it possible for the Urdd to step out of *Cymru'r Plant* and develop into a virile movement with its *Adrannau*, its camps, its rallies and its Eisteddfod. It later enabled the Urdd to organise and systematise its activities and to appoint a full-time staff, so that when the Government began to take an interest in youth service and to offer grants towards organisational costs, the Urdd was sufficiently well-established to qualify for the grants available. J. M. Howell deserved the only honour the Urdd had to bestow, and he remained President from 1929 until he resigned in 1944 when he was in his eighties and no longer felt capable of taking the active part which he considered a President should play in the life of a youth movement.

*   *   *   *

The second Urdd National Eisteddfod was held at Caernarfon in 1930, following much the same pattern as that at Corwen the previous year. What was memorable was the fact that there were now three-thousand competitors, and another three-thousand members who had come to the Eisteddfod as spectators. It was estimated that six-and-a-half thousand members took part in the parade through the town. Every one, including the Founder, was completely taken by surprise, and for a whole hour the traffic came to a stand-still. And one can imagine the task of getting through the marathon preliminary tests on the Saturday morning !

But Ifan ab Owen Edwards was not one to be content with repetition, however successful that might be. Having experimented with a scheme, he learnt from his mistakes and made improved plans for the future. Having done that, he was always ready for a new experience. One such innovation was the visit to Geneva by sixteen boys in the summer of 1930. Ever since 1925, Ifan ab Owen Edwards had regularly supported the Goodwill Message and the whole of the May issue of *Cymru'r Plant* was devoted to its promotion. But, for him, it was not enough to send a verbal message from the youth of Wales to the youth of the world, not enough to write about other countries and other people. It was also important for Urdd members to visit other countries and meet their inhabitants. It was a pilgrimage of this nature that the Founder had in mind for the sixteen members who ventured overseas for the first time on a visit to Geneva—the home of the League of Nations. Ifan ab Owen Edwards himself led the group, but their friend and guide in Geneva was the Rev. Gwilym Davies, Founder of the Goodwill Message, and Wales' unofficial representative at the League of Nations. One of the many highlights of the visit was the ceremony of placing a wreath of daffodils at the foot of the statue of Robert Owen of Newtown in the International Labour Office. Altogether, the visit was an unforgettable experience and one which those privileged to take part would always cherish.

The summer camps of that year were again held at Llangollen and attended by some two-hundred girls and two-hundred-and-fifty boys. Parents and teachers had now realised that the Urdd camps had a strange though intangible effect on their children and there was no lack of applicants. It was during these camps in 1930 that it became apparent that Ifan ab Owen Edwards was concerned about those children who were of Welsh parentage but who, for one reason or another, had been denied the opportunity of learning the language. As yet, he had no clear idea of how they could be found a place within the Urdd but he felt that sooner or later a place must be found for non-Welsh-speaking members.

The number of *Adrannau* continued to increase, and their activities were gradually being broadened to include craftwork, first-aid, physical education and dancing. More and more District Committees were also being formed, and these in turn widened the horizons by organising activities on a District level. The Founder could now see the evolution of a more organised system within the movement, and announced that he would like to see it in operation by 1932, particularly in relation to the Eisteddfod. Each *Adran* would hold its own Eisteddfod based on the national syllabus and the winners would go forward to compete at the District Eisteddfod. Competitors on the national level would then be confined to the winners at the District Eisteddfodau. He clearly did not wish to see a repeat of the Caernarfon marathon ! Now that the Urdd had become a truly national movement, the Founder foresaw the need for a system of government and control that would ensure its balanced development and its perpetuation.

One other person who seemed to be acutely aware of the need for organisation was W. J. Williams of Llangystennin, near Llandudno. He was a barrister who had held a responsible post in the Civil Service before being appointed European Secretary to the Kodak Company. When he retired in 1928, he decided to return to Wales and made his home at Llangystennin. It was then that he accidentally came into contact with the Urdd. He happened to be travelling by train from Birmingham to Llandudno Junction. Sitting opposite him was a boy from Ffestiniog wearing an Urdd badge. Intrigued by the badge, he asked the boy to tell him about the movement. Some time later, in response to an appeal for funds to purchase camping equipment, Ifan ab Owen Edwards received a cheque for £50 from someone he had never even heard of—a W. J. Williams from Llangystennin. In the following year, and again in 1930, W. J. Williams visited the camps at Llangollen. He questioned the Founder about the finance and organisation of the movement and looked amazed and horrified as Ifan ab Owen Edwards—in a jocular mood—recalled his experiences. W. J. Williams turned on him in all seriousness—' You have started something big in the life of Wales, and it will grow into something even more important. But you cannot run a movement of this dimension without a governing body, and if you continue as you are now doing, you will soon find yourself in the workhouse '. The outcome of this lecture was that a meeting was arranged between J. M. Howell, Mr.

and Mrs. W. J. Williams and Mr. and Mrs. Ifan ab Owen Edwards.
It was then that W. J. Williams suggested the establishment of an
Incorporated Company under The Companies Act, 1929. It was
agreed that he should investigate the possibilities and later make
recommendations to a meeting of Urdd Supporters. He immediately
took up the task, with much valuable help from Professor D.
Hughes Parry of the London School of Economics and T. Ivor
Jones, a London lawyer who later became Honorary Solicitor to the
Company.

One other decision taken at this meeting at Dolgellau led to the
appointment of a full-time Organiser for North Wales who would
also assist in the organisation of the annual rally, the Eisteddfod, and
the summer camps. No sooner had the decision been taken than
J. M. Howell wrote a cheque for the first year's salary ; Mrs. W. J.
Williams undertook to buy a car for his use, and the Founder said
he would be responsible for his travelling expenses. It was in this
unassuming and unconventional manner that the Urdd began to
build up a staff. The person appointed was J. H. Griffith of Penrhyndeudraeth who had already made a remarkable success of
running his own *Adran* and his own District.

Such an appointment was long overdue. In retrospect, it seems
incredible that one man could have achieved so much on a voluntary
spare-time basis while still a full-time member of the University
staff. Not only had Ifan ab Owen Edwards developed his movement
and organised its activities, but month by month, he had edited
Cymru'r Plant, added *Cronicl yr Urdd*, and in 1930, announced the
publication of a second monthly magazine—*Y Capten*—designed to
cater for his older readers thus leaving *Cymru'r Plant* free to concentrate on the requirements of those under twelve. Time and
again, if a new scheme or new development seemed desirable or
necessary, the Founder hardly stopped to consider its time-
consuming implications. With no thought for himself, he simply
added it to the load he already shouldered. Now there would
be another pair of hands, someone who could devote his whole time
to the movement. No one doubted, however, that it would not be
long before Ifan ab Owen Edwards had other schemes waiting to be
put into operation. He had already decided that the establishment
of a headquarters office would become inevitable, and partly with

this in view, he and his wife decided to leave Llanuwchllyn and make a new home for themselves at Aberystwyth.

*   *   *   *

In 1931, the Urdd Eisteddfod was held at Swansea and it was obvious that Ifan ab Owen Edwards was still searching for an acceptable formula for its organisation.   On this occasion, the festival opened with the drama competition on the Thursday afternoon followed by the official opening of the Arts and Crafts Exhibition.   Friday was devoted mainly to preliminary competitions and, since there were over two-thousand competitors, these lasted until late afternoon and were continued on the Saturday morning.   Friday evening saw two sessions of final competitions for individual competitors,—the one in St. Gabriel's Hall and the other in the Patti Pavilion.   At one o'clock on Saturday, three silver bands led the five-thousand members through some of the main streets and into St. Helen's Ground.   It was here that the afternoon and evening sessions of the Eisteddfod were to take place.   It was hardly a satisfactory arrangement either for the audience or for the competitors, and had it rained it would have been disastrous.   Nevertheless, it was a memorable festival and a truly national one.

1931 was notable for its wet August, and during the summer camps at Llangollen the rain hardly ceased.   Nevertheless the tents stood the test, and the girls flatly refused to be moved into an outhouse of Plas Tŷ'n Dŵr.   The weather seemed to have little effect on the members and the only one who caught a cold was the Founder himself !

For the interim period between the girls' and boys' camps, Ifan ab Owen Edwards had called representatives of the Branches and Districts to meet at Llangollen to consider matters pertaining to the future of the Urdd.   Two-hundred representatives were housed in the town, and another fifty at the camp.   It was at this meeting that W. J. Williams of Llangystennin outlined his proposition that the Urdd should be governed by an incorporated body, and as a result, it was unanimously decided to establish *Cwmni Urdd Gobaith Cymru* (The Welsh League of Youth [Incorporated]).

Thus, on 8 March, 1932, the Company was registered by the Board of Trade under the 1929 Companies Act, and shortly afterwards, published its *Memorandum and Articles of Association*, i.e. the constitution and rules whereby the Urdd would in future be governed. For the first ten years of its existence, the movement had been run on a personal basis and every decision and every responsibility had rested with the Founder and his wife. From now on, others would be elected to share the responsibility and the control, though they would still be guided and inspired by the Founder. Being an incorporated body and, at the same time, an educational Charity would have distinct advantages for the movement and this would not have come about but for the foresight and insistence of W. J. Williams. It is not surprising that he was elected first Treasurer of the new Incorporated Company.

Another matter brought to the notice of the Llangollen meeting was the position of the non-Welsh-speaking children who hitherto were excluded from becoming members of the Urdd. For some time, the Founder had been concerned about the problem, and had come to the conclusion that the Urdd had to find a place for this section of the nation who, for one reason or another, had been deprived of the ability to speak the language. He was well aware of the dangers and the complications of admitting the Anglicised members into a movement that was Welsh in essence and in language, but he felt the risk must be taken. As one would expect, there were two very definite and understandable views on the question, but eventually the majority decided to follow the lead given by the Founder. A new rank would be formed—that of *Dysgwr* (Learner). A *Dysgwr* would not be allowed to attend meetings of the *Adrannau* or the summer camps—lest the use of the Welsh language in those activities should be jeopardised—but arrangements would be made for them to take part in the Eisteddfod. The *Dysgwyr* would have their own badge, but whenever a *Dysgwr* had achieved sufficient mastery of the language to enable him to take part in the work of the *Adran*, he could exchange the badge and enter into full membership.

This new development was accorded a mixed reception amongst Urdd supporters in the field. Some saw only the dangers, others saw it as offering new hope and a new challenge to Anglicised areas. What did happen was that new Branches were formed for *Dysgwyr* only, and the Founder soon had to consider the need for new activities in which the *Dysgwyr* would be on a par with the Welsh-speaking members.

One new scheme which came into its own in 1931 was the Urdd's Football Association. In consultation with the Founder, this was organised by a group of young men from Caernarfonshire and it was not long before the North Wales Branches were training their teams and entering this soccer competition. Response from South Wales was naturally somewhat tardy, since they could not believe that any game other than rugby was worth playing ! Nevertheless, the scheme flourished throughout the thirties, and in 1936, the Association was able to select a team to play against a number of youth teams in France.

Since the boys who had visited Geneva in 1930 had talked about it in such glowing terms, the girls claimed it would be their turn in 1931. So keen was the demand that the group eventually numbered eighty-six. They were accompanied by the Founder and his wife, and once again, the Rev. Gwilym Davies was their guide, counsellor and friend. First on their programme was a Sunday morning service at the Cathedral of St. Pierre—the first time ever that a Welsh service had been held there. Visits to places of historic or scenic interest followed in quick succession, and once again the members returned invigorated by their experience.

Despite the success of these visits, one can understand that Ifan ab Owen Edwards was a little uneasy at the thought that he was taking his members on visits to the Continent without, at the same time, giving them the opportunity of discovering their own country. At any rate, a tour of North Wales was announced for August 1931. It did not, however, have the same immediate appeal, and only a small group accompanied the Founder along the proposed route. Nevertheless, even the bare names of the places visited make exciting reading, and one can imagine how history came alive in the hands of the sensitive historian who led them ' in search of Wales '. When the tour was over, Ifan ab Owen Edwards prepared a set of slides dealing with the history of Wales from the time of St. David. These were then made available for showing to *Adrannau* and members of the public, together with slides of the camps and the pilgrimages to Geneva.

The Founder and his wife had now made their home at Aberystwyth, and it was not long before the decision had to be taken that
some help with the administration of the Urdd was inevitable. The
choice fell on Elsi Williams of Comins Coch, who was just then
leaving Ardwyn Grammar School at Aberystwyth. Young though
she was, she was able to take responsibility and initiative and
considered it a privilege to be working alongside the Founder
and his wife. Little did she think at that time that she would
continue working for the movement for more than forty years.

In formulating the aims of his movement, it was one thing for
Ifan ab Owen Edwards verbally to stress the importance of spiritual
values and human priorities. It was quite another thing to devise
ways of giving practical expression to those values, of giving his
members the opportunity to put that faith into practice. The
Founder knew that most of his members were also members of the
local churches and that on the whole he had the support of the
various denominations. If the Urdd were to organise religious
activities in the same way as it organised cultural and recreational
activities, this might well have the effect of drawing the members
away from their churches, and this was the last thing the Founder
wanted. Nevertheless there was a danger that the absence of any
organised activities might be interpreted as tantamount to being
uncommitted in the religious and spiritual field, and there were
already some who voiced this criticism. The Founder had already
given a great deal of thought to the matter, and although the degree
of co-operation between the various denominations themselves
offered little encouragement, he eventually decided on a course of
action. He urged each Branch to call together the local clergy to
discuss the possibility of organising a special inter-denominational
service every three months—primarily for Urdd members but to
which the public would be welcomed. The services could be held in
the various churches in rotation, and linked with special occasions
such as St. David's Day, Goodwill Day, Harvest Thanksgiving or
Christmas.

The first *Sul yr Urdd* (Urdd Sunday) was held at Swansea in
June 1931. Urdd members crowded into the gallery, and supporters
and other members of the public filled the rest of the chapel to
capacity. It was a memorable service, and the Founder felt that if

the idea were generally accepted, he would have won the support of the religious bodies while still retaining the non-sectarian principle on which the movement had been founded.

*　　　*　　　*　　　*

The Urdd had now lived through the first decade in its history and Ifan ab Owen Edwards was generally acclaimed as a man before his time, as a national leader. In 1931, Gwili, editor of *Seren Gomer*, wrote—

> 'Ifan ab Owen Edwards' success in connection with Urdd Gobaith Cymru is most spectacular. Already the membership is almost 30,000 and we predict that this movement will be one of the greatest in its influence on the continued existence of the language. The Founder's father, Sir Owen Edwards, did more than anyone in his day to bring our literature to the notice of the ordinary citizen but Urdd Gobaith Cymru is likely to contribute even more towards the fruition of his ideals.'

The acclamation, however, was not universal, nor was this surprising in a country like Wales where the language was considered by some to be unimportant, by others an inconvenience and a nuisance. Just about this time, The Boy Scout Movement seemed to be alarmed at the Urdd's growth and the general support it was accorded by the Welsh nation. They could not understand the need for another youth organisation when, as an international organisation, the Scout Movement could offer the youth of Wales the same opportunities as it afforded the youth of other countries. Letters to the press by Lord Swansea, chief officer of the Scout Movement in Wales, prompted comments by the editor of *Y Ford Gron*—

> 'Urdd Gobaith Cymru has now become strong enough to cause Lord Swansea to make derogatory remarks about the movement in the English press. The lengthy correspondence which ensued regarding the movement, its ideals and activities gave Ifan ab Owen Edwards the opportunity of writing two unpretentious letters explaining the facts to those to whom they had not hitherto been known. We believe we can assure the Urdd and its officers that Wales wishes them another year of even greater success . . . In the course of its existence, the Urdd

will meet with criticism, and even antagonism, and will welcome it. It recognises that there are more than one facet to one's character, and more than one means of strengthening it . . . The more criticism it receives the better, as long as it is done openly and arises from a love of Wales ; the Urdd will turn it all into strength and into sustenance for the Welshmen of tomorrow.'

It is noteworthy that *Y Ford Gron* during its brief existence (1930-35) made frequent references to the Urdd, its activities and its development. In an article entitled *Codi Cenedl* the author states—

' Not for centuries has the idea of one country, one nation been conveyed so vividly to the consciousness of Welshmen in both North and South Wales . . . In a century's time, historians will evaluate the renaissance in Wales and will note the date the Urdd was founded as a date to be remembered.'

Nor was the editor unaware of the hard task facing the Urdd in the Anglicised areas of South Wales and the border counties—

' The gap between those cut off from their Welsh background and their fellows must be bridged, and it is the Urdd members, with their songs and their games, who can achieve this.'

The movement had now completed ten years of service to the nation, and all Wales was expecting even greater achievements in the future.

3

1932 was an important milestone in the history of the Urdd. A new Handbook appeared, dedicated by the Founder ' to those young men and women who are prepared to sacrifice some of their leisure hours to lead the Wales of tomorrow '. For ten years, the Founder had sought to formulate an acceptable declaration of his aims. Though basically unchanged, the ' vision ' of 1922 had been broadened and deepened through contact with the Goodwill Message ; it had been pruned and clarified, and now, in 1932, it emerged as a brief, concise statement of the movement's aim, as well as being, at the same time, a declaration of the Founder's own philosophy of life. It was a pledge to be—

> ' loyal to Wales and worthy of my country,
> loyal to my fellow-man, whoever he may be,
> loyal to Christ and his spirit of love.'

The pledge took ten years to emerge, but once crystallised, it remained virtually unchanged for forty years.

During these forty years, the Urdd grew and matured ; it saw many changes and innovations—in ideas, in activities and in methods—but throughout the period, its ideals have remained unchanged. The brief statement of those ideals in the form of a pledge was one that could be adopted by any youth movement in any country—loyalty to homeland and to fellow-man, based on the principles and philosophy of love exemplified in the life of Christ.

The new Handbook did not confine itself to offering guidance to Urdd members. It was also intended as a guide for the newly-formed incorporated body. For the first time, the Founder was able to appeal for financial help from his supporters. It was estimated that the next year's expenditure would amount to £1,200, whereas the income was not likely to exceed £560. At the first meeting of the Urdd Committee held at the University College, Bangor, in April 1932, attention was drawn to the financial aspect, especially in view of the fact that the need for a full-time Organiser for South Wales had been apparent for some time. At the time,

11 The Breton welcome to the Welsh Cruise

12 D. Lloyd George at the Machynlleth
Eisteddfod, 1932

13 The 'Lloyd George Banner'

however, it was felt that the financial situation did not permit making an appointment, and the matter was deferred until the following meeting in two months' time. Following the June meeting held at Llanelli, the Founder reported that the Committee was unanimous that a full-time Organiser should be appointed. ' This step has been decided upon although we cannot at present foresee where the money will come from.' This was characteristic of the Founder throughout his life. He would act in faith, firmly believing that, somehow or other, the money would be found.

The 1932 National Eisteddfod was held at Machynlleth. The most important feature was the graded system of elimination which had been put into operation for the first time. Each Adran had been asked to hold its own Eisteddfod, the winners gaining the right to compete at the District Eisteddfod. The winners at the District Eisteddfod would then go forward to the preliminary tests at the National Eisteddfod, and, finally, the best three competitors in each competition would appear on the Eisteddfod stage. This, naturally, reduced the number of competitors at the national level, but ensured a higher standard, greater flexibility and better organisation. The result was less of a rally but a better Eisteddfod.

A marquee had been erected to seat an audience of 10,000. The marquee itself was not ideal, but it was at least an experiment on which further improvements could be based. Six-thousand members took part in the procession, watched from the balcony of the Wynnstay Hotel by officers of the Urdd and some of the Eisteddfod Presidents, including The Right Honourable David Lloyd George. He was to present to the Urdd a new Eisteddfod banner, to be retained for one year by the District gaining the highest marks in the Eisteddfod. For the next decade this banner—*Baner Lloyd George*—became the Eisteddfod's most coveted trophy, and the first to win the honour was the Cwm Tawe District (*Cylch Cwm Tawe*).

*   *   *   *

Ifan ab Owen Edwards had always stressed the importance of retaining what was best in the life and tradition of Wales. Some of these elements might need to be adapted and developed to meet the needs and interests of contemporary youth, but in essence, they were to remain as an integral part of the Welsh heritage. At the same time, the Founder kept an ever-open eye for possibilities of introducing new interests which in time would become part of the Welsh tradition and eventually form a pattern of full and joyous life for the boys and girls of Wales. Outdoor activities, especially camping, walking and swimming, were among the elements already introduced. During the past year, however, his mind had turned to another field of physical activity, that of the *Mabolgampau* —a combination of athletic competitions and mass gymnastic displays. There was nothing new in these activities ; they had existed from time immemorial. During the ages, however, the primitive rituals of early man had given way to more sophisticated feats of discipline and endurance.

The Founder had been impressed by recent festivals held in European countries, particularly those of Denmark and Sweden, and the Sokol Festivals of Czechoslovakia. He knew he could not hope for a festival of similar excellence and magnitude. He was aware too that there might be opposition from those who would feel that such activities were in direct contradiction to the Puritan pattern of the Welsh background. Furthermore, so little attention was paid to physical recreation, especially in the elementary schools of Welsh Wales. Would the Welsh children have the interest or the expertise that would attract them to take part in such a festival ? And would the scheme be given the blessing and encouragement of the teachers ? He decided to venture. Quite naturally, he focussed his attention on South Wales where the tradition of physical and recreational activities was strongest. It happened that Tom Davies was Physical Education Organiser for Llanelli and district, and it was to him that Ifan ab Owen Edwards first turned. To his delight, he discovered in Tom Davies a man whose enthusiasm for physical activities matched his own, who had already organised local displays and who welcomed the opportunity of experimenting on a wider scale. The more they talked, the more their hopes grew. The *Mabolgampau* would be held at Llanelli. The programme would provide for members under 18 and would be in two parts—athletic competitions and massed gymnastics. For the competitive section, the system would be the same as that of the Eisteddfod. Branches and Districts would hold their own *Mabol-gampau* and only the winners would be allowed to compete at the national level. There would be no money prizes ; the District gaining the highest number of points would win the Games Banner (*Baner y Mabolgampau*) which would be held for one year.

As the date drew nearer, it became apparent that the two men had been over-ambitious, and when the final programme appeared, the events had been considerably curtailed. As the Founder had feared, this kind of activity was so new to the Adrannau that it would be unrealistic to expect spectacular results at the first attempt. Nevertheless, the response was considerable. It was the younger children who had taken to the gymnastic and dancing displays, while the athletic competitions had appealed more to the older boys and girls. But inexperienced though they were, when the hundreds of children entered the field and went on to perform their massed displays to the rhythm of music provided by three or four brass bands, the whole performance became transformed into something exciting and artistic. Reviewing the event, the Founder wrote—

' Words fail us in trying to describe the scene. Tears came into our eyes as we watched a New Wales appearing before us. It was an electrifying experience, and the eight-thousand spectators felt a new pride in being Welsh. It seemed as though a new dawn were breaking.'

Among those leading the procession into the field were the Mayor of Llanelli ; J. M. Howell ; Sir Percy Watkins (Secretary of the Welsh Department of the Board of Education) ; W. J. Williams (Chief Inspector of Schools) and W. J. Williams of Llangystennin. They felt compelled to give public support to yet another campaign by Ifan ab Owen Edwards on behalf of the youth of Wales. Looking back today, it may be that uniforms and parades, banners and bands were things that belonged to a specific period, but it does seem that the Urdd may have lost something of considerable value when these aspects disappeared from the pattern of events organised by the movement.

*   *   *   *

1932 was also a vintage year in the camping calendar. After the first experiment at Llanuwchllyn, and two summers' sojourn at Llangollen, the Founder felt it was time to seek a more permanent home where it would be possible to plan ahead at least for a number of years. He decided to explore the possibilities of finding a site that would be within reach of the sea. Returning from the Eisteddfod at Swansea in the early summer of 1931, the Founder and his wife followed the coast instead of taking a direct route to Aberystwyth. They had reached Cardigan without any luck, and tired and dejected, they decided to call to see D. O. Evans, M.P., at Rhyd-y-Colomennod, Llangrannog. Over a meal, they recalled their fruitless search for a suitable site, and were quite taken aback when D. O. Evans said he thought he could show them the ideal spot. Later, he led them past Cefn Cwrt farm, and on to a large sloping field overlooking Cardigan Bay. Beyond this field was a hilly slope, gorse and heather clad, from the top of which one looked down on Dinas Lochtyn and Cilborth beach. Later, as they returned triumphant to Aberystwyth, the Founder and his wife felt renewed and invigorated, having at last found the ideal home for the Urdd camps. The months ahead were full of activity. A new camp, with a nucleus of permanent buildings, had to be ready to accommodate 150 campers by the summer of 1932. The co-operation of the builders under the direction of E. Glyn Davies ensured that the task would be completed, but even so, it would not have been achieved were it not, once again, for the generosity of J. M. Howell.

Four weeks' camping had been planned—two for girls and two for boys. Each week was full to capacity and the campers quickly came under the spell of Llangrannog and the immediate neighbourhood—especially Ynys Lochtyn, Cwmtudu, Tresaith and Penbryn. And in addition to exploring the immediate neighbourhood, there were expeditions to Llangeitho, Tregaron and Ystrad Fflur ; to Fishguard and St. David's ; to Llandyfri and Carmarthen. The highlight of the 1932 camps, however, was the opportunity given to the girls to share the experience with eighteen girls from Germany, led by Fraulein Harker and Dr. Rudolph Hermann of Bielefeld. This was the first time the Urdd had entertained a group from another country. It had long been a dream in the mind of the Founder but he felt it was worth waiting until the group could be welcomed to a more permanent camp. There was no doubt that the project had made its impact and the friendships formed were to last for many years. In a letter to the Founder, Marga Klaeger of Württemberg wrote—

'Living together in camp is an excellent way of giving the nations a better understanding of one another ... In the evenings, my mind often recalls the evening hymn-singing at camp, and I remember that as we said The Lord's Prayer together, each in his own language, I experienced a strange feeling of reverence. I knew that the Welsh girls had exactly the same feeling, and now, I need only close my eyes to see and feel everything just as it was when we said ' Amen ' together.'

Ifan ab Owen Edwards could well feel satisfied as he looked back at the successful events of the year—the success of the Eisteddfod at Machynlleth, the thrill of the *Mabolgampau* at Llanelli, the establishment of a new camp at Llangrannog, and the experiment in international understanding during the first visit of a foreign group. He felt satisfied that the pledge of loyalty to Wales, to fellow-man and to Christ contained just the philosophy that he would like the youth of Wales to adopt.

The first General Meeting of the new Incorporated Company was held at Carmarthen in August 1932. The first Urdd Council had, of necessity, to be a nominated Council and was to serve only until the 1933 Annual General Meeting, when a new Council would be democratically elected according to the recently published Constitution. The report presented to this first General Meeting ended on an optimistic note—

' We have every hope that the movement will grow not only to be one of the largest of Welsh movements, but also to be one of the most influential in working for the betterment of the nation.'

*　　*　　*　　*

In the late summer of 1932, the post of South Wales Organiser for the Urdd was being advertised. Applicants were required to be familiar with South Wales and its problems, be able to write literary Welsh and be prepared to do editorial work. The appointment would be for one year, at a salary of £200. One of the applicants was R. E. Griffith from Abercynon, who had recently left the University College, Cardiff, bent on a journalistic career. It will be remembered that he was one of the three schoolboys who had formed the first Urdd Branch in South Wales, at Abercynon. He had subsequently reached the rank of ' General ', was at the first Urdd camp at Llanuwchllyn, on the first pilgrimage to Geneva, and had attended every possible event in the Urdd calendar ever since. It is hardly surprising that he was called for interview and appointed. In offering him the post, the Founder proceeded to list the disadvantages. Although they had advertised a salary of £200, they did not, as yet, have the money ! Moreover, it was an appointment for one year only, and unlikely that it could be confirmed ! The applicant's only answer to all this was ' When do I begin ? ' So in October 1932, R. E. Griffith became a member of the Urdd staff. As a matter of fact, the appointment was never reviewed ; perhaps it was one of few things the Founder forgot ! And R. E. Griffith continued to serve the Urdd and through the Urdd, to serve Wales, for more than forty years.

During his first year, he was required to spend one week on field-work and the alternate week in the office at Aberystwyth, helping the editor to fill the pages of *Cymru'r Plant* and *Y Capten*. Working along-side Ifan ab Owen Edwards, he was amazed at the speed with which the editor was able to dispatch his stories. Commenting on this, the editor would explain that when the printers were expecting their copy, there was no time to wait for some illusive inspiration. ' And remember,' he would add, ' that we are not writing for posterity but for next month.'

*   *   *   *

Ifan ab Owen Edwards had heard that the Convent School buildings at Aberystwyth were to be sold. It occurred to him that these might be suitable as future headquarters for the Urdd. But when he and his wife went to inspect the premises, they were depressed by the dark-brown paint, and further discouraged by the size of the property. The schoolrooms themselves would be more than adequate for the Urdd, even if the Aberystwyth Welsh Club, currently looking for premises, might be interested in sharing the building. The dwelling house still remained unaccounted for. They continued to discuss the problem until late that evening without finding any solution. They agreed that a supply of paint and a little imagination would transform the school building. But what could be done with the house ? A glance at his face made Mrs. Edwards

realise that her husband had set his heart on getting the premises
for the Urdd but could not quite bring himself to suggest that they
themselves could live in the house and pay rent to *Cwmni'r Urdd* !
It was quite true—she had married not one man but a whole
movement ! When bed-time came, Ifan ab Owen Edwards had
already obtained the support of the Urdd President and Treasurer,
had telephoned the Roman Catholic authorities in London and
agreed to buy the premises for £2,000. The President, J. M.
Howell, immediately sent a cheque for £200 ' to reduce the debt to
£1800 ' ! The Founder added another £100, and then prepared to
appeal for contributions. By the spring of 1933, the old Convent
School had become the new Urdd Headquarters and Ifan ab Owen
Edwards and his wife had again moved house. By the autumn, the
Aberystwyth Welsh Club had occupied their part of the premises
and had adopted Ifan ab Owen Edwards' suggestion that the Club
be called an *Aelwyd* (lit. Hearth). Thus the Aberystwyth *Aelwyd*
became the first *Aelwyd* within the framework of the Urdd. And
after forty years, it is still functioning as an active community
centre.

*   *   *   *

The Urdd Eisteddfod for 1933 was to return to Glamorgan, for
the second time in five years,—on this occasion to Caerffili. By
this time, the Eisteddfod was beginning to follow an established
pattern which still allowed room for improvement and experiment-
ation. One such innovation was the decision of the BBC to broadcast seventy-five minutes of the Saturday afternoon programme.
Caerffili certainly helped to consolidate the role of the Eisteddfod
in the calendar of Urdd activities and much of its success was due to
the energetic approach of its two Honorary Secretaries—A. Glyn
Lloyd and J. Penri Davies.

The second *Mabolgampau* were held on the Vetch Field, Swansea,
on 23-24 June, 1933. They continued to be under the direction of
Tom Davies and he and one or two of his Llanelli colleagues worked
in close collaboration with the Swansea committee. The event was
organised on much the same pattern as that at Llanelli except for
the addition of swimming competitions. The facilities were better,

more members took part, and in general, the standard of performance was higher. Certainly the organiser and his team, and especially the Adrannau, had learnt a great deal from the experience of the previous year. For the thousands of spectators who watched the event for the first time, it was the same thrilling experience as had been the lot of those who attended the Llanelli *Mabolgampau*.

There were still no participants from Mid or North Wales. Though not unexpected, this was one aspect that, even during the first *Mabolgampau*, had been a disappointment to the Founder. He had, therefore, persuaded the Urdd Council to allow him to buy a camera and projector. If the North Wales members could not be persuaded to come to the *Mabolgampau*, he would take the *Mabolgampau* to them—on film. So while others were entranced with the spectacle, Ifan ab Owen Edwards was concentrating on his camera, intent on capturing some of the skill, the movement and spirit of this unique event. During the weeks that followed, the film was edited and prepared, R. E. Griffith was given brief and hurried tuition in operating a projector and driving a car so that he could take over the task of presenting the *Mabolgampau* to those who had hitherto been reluctant to respond.

Once again the Urdd was invited to hold its annual rally on the children's day at the National Eisteddfod of Wales. At Wrexham, it followed the usual pattern of procession to the pavilion, and an hour's break in the proceedings while Urdd members, under their conductor, sang hymns and folk-songs from the Eisteddfod stage. Despite its success, however, there were some who were beginning to wonder whether this arrangement was any longer necessary, now that the Urdd had its own Eisteddfod at which so much more could be achieved.

As usual, there was a month's camping at Llangrannog—a fortnight each for the girls and the boys. They were memorable days, not entirely due to the programme, the friendships or the fun. It was a period of almost unbroken sunshine and the camp at Llangrannog was a veritable paradise—until the camp well dried up ! A crisis threatened, and the campers had to choose between being sent home and having to carry five-hundred gallons of water

14   The procession at Machynlleth, 1932

each day. One hardly needs to add that they chose the latter ! A small price to pay for idyllic days in brilliant sunshine.

Despite his innate optimism, Ifan ab Owen Edwards was also a realist. He knew that the days of continuous exciting new developments could not last indefinitely, and sooner or later, there would come a more prosaic period of consolidation, which, though less spectacular, was not less important in the life of any movement. It was this warning that he voiced in his report to the 1933 Annual General Meeting at Dolgellau.

> ' We have every faith in the future though we know it will be a difficult period. It will not be a period of spectacular new developments but of consolidating what has already been achieved, gradually moving forward with untiring perseverance. This will be the crucial test of the movement. If we are to succeed, we shall need the heroic effort of all Welsh people. Above all, we shall need their financial support.'

His last statement was corroborated by the Financial Report on the first full year in the history of *Cwmni'r Urdd*. Expenses had risen from £715 in 1931/32 to £1,975 in 1933 and there was a deficit of £348/11/4.

*   *   *   *

During the first ten years of its existence, the Urdd had had remarkable success in winning the support of adults as well as children and young people. These adults were now acting as leaders of the Adrannau and of the Districts. They were also the ones who shouldered the work of organising the Eisteddfod and the Mabolgampau and helped with the running of camps. Was there anything the Urdd could offer them in appreciation of their support, something that would serve to strengthen their ties with the Urdd and with Wales ? Various possibilities were turned over in the Founder's mind, and eventually he decided upon the answer. It was announced that the Urdd would organise a cruise during the summer of 1933. Once again, the idea in itself was not new. But an all-Welsh cruise for Welsh people was something quite different. He proposed to charter the RMS *Orduna* from the Pacific Steam

Navigation Company and cruise along the Norwegian fiords. A brochure was prepared describing the ' adventure ' in glowing terms. The Captain would be Welsh-speaking ; Welsh would be the official language throughout, and the Red Dragon would be flown from the mast. ' This,' said the brochure, ' will be the most important social event of the year as far as Wales is concerned.' Bergen would be the first port of call, then would follow Olden and Löen following which the ship would make its way along Geiranger—one of the most beautiful of the Norwegian fiords. The last port of call would be Trondhjem and then the *Orduna* would sail for Liverpool—and home.

The ' adventure ' certainly captured the imagination and soon five-hundred passengers had booked their passage at fantastic prices ranging from £14.10.0 to £22.10.0. The *Orduna* sailed, and it was not long before the passengers were unanimous that the voyage, the programme, the companionship and the fiords exceeded even Ifan ab Owen Edwards' rapturous promises. One of the passengers was (Sir) Ifor Williams and having obtained a picture postcard of a place called Helle he sent it to a friend in Paradwys, Anglesey,—*Cyfarchion o uffern i'm cyfaill ym Mharadwys* (Greetings from Helle to my friend in Paradise) ! Quite apart from its success as a holiday venture, however, the ' All-Welsh Cruise ' had succeeded in welding the five-hundred passengers into a community, and given them a new sense of identification with Wales and with the Urdd.

Ifan ab Owen Edwards and his wife were now living at ' Neuadd Wen', the name they had given to the old convent house. On Boxing Day, 1933, their first son was born. He was named Owen after his grandfather and great grandfather. During the course of the year, Ifan ab Owen Edwards had left the Extra-Mural Department of the Aberystwyth University College after twelve years as tutor, and had been appointed lecturer in the Department of Education, a post in which he was to spend thirteen very happy years.

*   *   *   *

By 1934, the Urdd had a membership of 50,000, but the rate of growth was already showing signs of abating. The movement was now twelve years old, and Branches had been established almost throughout the length and breadth of Wales. Sooner or later, a saturation point had to be reached. Moreover, Branch leaders were urged to interest their members in a variety of activities and to place greater emphasis on a challenge of standards. Not all members would respond to the discipline demanded by such a challenge and some would inevitably fall by the wayside. To provide greater incentive and encouragement to the voluntary leaders, the Founder was anxious that the Urdd should appoint a team of full-time organisers,—young people who could work alongside the voluntary leaders, and offer guidance and help where it was most needed. He realised that this could not be achieved overnight, but in his mind he was already building up the pattern for future years. The first to be appointed under this scheme was Olwen Williams of Llanelli, one of the early 'Generals', who had experience of camping at Llangollen and Llangrannog and had now completed a degree course at Aberystwyth. In addition to helping with camps and Mabolgampau, she was given special responsibility as organiser for Mid and South-West Wales.

Three years had elapsed since *Sul yr Urdd* was first initiated and in 1934 the BBC agreed to broadcast two special services organised by the Urdd, the first from Cwm Tawe in February and the second— the Goodwill Message Service—from Aberystwyth in mid-May. The Adrannau were entirely responsible for the services held on their *Sul yr Urdd* and many felt they would like some guidance in planning the form and content of such services. To help leaders with this task, the Urdd undertook to publish a handbook of services that would be equally acceptable to the Church in Wales and to the Nonconformist denominations. The services were carefully prepared by a panel of laymen and clergy centred around Aberystwyth and the handbook proved to be a boon to schools and churches as well as to leaders of Adrannau.

*　　　*　　　*　　　*

The 1934 Eisteddfod, organised by a committee based on Old Colwyn, was held in a pavilion erected in Eirias Park, half way between Old Colwyn and Colwyn Bay. Competitors came in strength from South Wales and were accommodated in homes, establishing new links of friendship and helping to break down the part-real, part-imaginary barrier between North and South Wales. The pavilion was capable of seating 8,000 and was full to capacity for every session.

The Mabolgampau returned once more to Swansea. They followed more or less the same pattern as before and once again were directed by Tom Davies and his team of experienced teachers working in conjunction with the Swansea committee. The competitions and displays were of a high standard and the arrangements superb. And on this occasion, many more members from the rural areas of Carmarthenshire took part and proved that, given time, they too were capable of athletic and gymnastic skills.

Perhaps the most significant development in 1934 was in the sphere of camping activities. The Urdd had decided to establish a second camping site, this time in North Wales, not to replace Llangrannog but to keep the numbers accepted within a manageable limit, and to reduce the number who would have to be disappointed. Just as it was D. O. Evans, M.P., who discovered the Llangrannog site, so it was Mr. and Mrs. Hughes Roberts of Edern who suggested the site at Porth Dinllaen, between Edern and Morfa Nefyn. And during the summer of 1934, Olwen Williams took charge of a month's camping for girls at Llangrannog while the boys, led by R. E. Griffith and his team of *Swyddogion* (Camp Leaders), explored the possibilities of the new site at Porth Dinllaen. Comparing notes one evening by telephone, the one complained that some of the girls had been stealing apples and the other offered the doubtful consolation that some of the boys had become experts at finding lost golf balls at the nearby golf-course and selling them to next day's golfers ! A group of twelve boys from the Republic of Ireland joined the boys at Porth Dinllaen for one week, while another guest was Edouard Bachellery, a student of Celtic Studies from Paris who spoke fluent Welsh with a French accent, and soon became a firm favourite with the campers and leaders. The setting up of a second camp at Porth Dinllaen was a considerable financial undertaking for the Urdd, but with his usual generosity, J. M. Howell contributed £250 towards the new venture. One important decision made in

1934 was to allow—for the first time—a limited number of *Dysgwyr* to attend during specified periods. As anticipated, the experiment was not without its linguistic problems, and it was decided that, although the plan must be continued, it would need to be carefully reviewed from year to year.

While the campers were indulging in the joys of Llangrannog and Porth Dinllaen, Ifan ab Owen Edwards was guiding their elders on another all-Welsh cruise, this time to Brittany, Spain, Portugal and North Africa. One highlight of the voyage was the two-day tour of Brittany arranged by a Welsh-speaking Breton, Pierre Mocaer. Everywhere, the official and unofficial welcome far exceeded any expectations and throughout the brief two-day tour, the warmth of the welcome never flagged. From then onwards, each port of call provided its own thrills, from Vigo in Galicia to Santiago de Compostella, to Lisbon and Mont Estoril, to Gibralter and Tangier, —altogether a journey of nearly 2,700 miles.

Beneath its apparent success, however, and despite the warmth of the welcome given to its members in Brittany, Ifan ab Owen Edwards was not without his doubts, especially when he compared the cruise with the first venture the previous year. The number of passengers had increased, and something of the Welsh atmosphere seemed to have been lost. And the Founder felt that, unless this could be safeguarded, there would be no real justification for the continuance of the all-Welsh *Mordeithiau*.

*   *   *   *

Like his father, Ifan ab Owen Edwards had always been a keen photographer, and had experimented in the making of documentary films of Urdd events. He began with a film of the Mabolgampau in an effort to interest members in Mid and North Wales in the displays and competitions. And having proved its effectiveness as a means of propaganda, he went on to film other Urdd events, especially the Eisteddfod, the camps and the cruises. By 1934, he was able to provide a full evening's programme, and decided that the time was ripe for the showing of *Y Sinema Gymraeg* in towns and villages throughout Wales. A tour was arranged and Ap Morris Jones from Llanuwchllyn appointed projectionist. The scheme was

an immediate success and for many months full halls awaited
Y Sinema Gymraeg. But the Founder was still not satisfied. So far, the
films he had made were silent films and the perfectionist in him
would not rest until a Welsh sound-film had been made. He set
himself to study the techniques of sound-filming, and those who
witnessed his determination knew that he would not rest until the
task was accomplished.

As usual, schemes which had earned for themselves a place in the
Urdd calendar had to be continued, and every innovation meant
added responsibility and extra administrative work. It became
necessary to strengthen the clerical side of the staff at Aberystwyth.
They were not only expected to cope with the various additional
tasks at headquarters, but were also responsible for the office
administration at the two camps. At the same time, R. E. Griffith
was promoted Chief Organiser, with responsibility for Headquarters
administration and for supervision of field work. In addition, the
organising of the Eisteddfod came under his special care. His
promotion, however, did not mean that the Founder had lost any
of his interest or had lessened his share of the burden ; it merely
meant that he was enabled to devote more attention to devising new
schemes, and that co-operation between the two men had become
closer and on a new level.

*   *   *   *

Perhaps the most exciting event in the Urdd calendar for 1935 was
the Eisteddfod held at Carmarthen. Preparations had been in
progress for two years, and it was obvious that a record-breaking
event was anticipated. The team responsible was headed by the
Rev. Simon B. Jones as Chairman and Miss E. H. Goodwin and
Ernest Evans as Honorary Secretaries.

It had been decided to add another day to the event to cope with
extra items in the programme. At the same time, the pavilion was
to be extended to seat an audience of twelve thousand,—' the
largest timber-and-canvas structure ever to be erected in this
country' according to the *Swansea Evening Post*. During the
Eisteddfod itself, newspaper headlines reflected its all-round success,
and when, on the Saturday, Ifan ab Owen Edwards appealed for

loyalty to Wales and willingness to sacrifice in the cause of Wales, the twelve-thousand-strong audience rose to its feet and repeated the Urdd pledge of loyalty.

The preceding procession of members also broke all records. Led by five brass and silver bands, ten-thousand members marched through the town. The proceedings of the Assizes at the Guildhall were suspended while Judge Mackinnon stood on the balcony along with J. M. Howell and the poet ' Elfed '. In his astonishment, Judge Mackinnon turned to Elfed saying, ' This is superb '. The following day, even the London dailies carried the headlines, ' A nation on the march,' and ' What is happening in Wales ? ' The event ended with another innovation—the *Cymanfa Ganu*, for which the huge pavilion was packed and thousands more stood outside. All-in-all, the Carmarthen Eisteddfod was a memorable event by any standards.

Soon after the Carmarthen Eisteddfod came the fourth Mabolgampau which were held at Aberystwyth. They were not on the scale of those held at Swansea and Llanelli and even so, groups from South Wales were brought in to reinforce the less experienced teams from Mid and South-West Wales. But a target had been reached, and the Mabolgampau had reached another milestone, *en route* for North Wales !

For some reason the response to the 1935 cruise was less enthusiastic than it had been on the two previous occasions. It is possible that the scheduled route did not have the same appeal, or it may have been that the Welsh-speaking members had been discouraged by the more Anglicised atmosphere of the previous year. At any rate, there were no more than 321 passengers for the cruise along the west coast of Europe from France to Norway. Nevertheless, because of the smaller number and the greater emphasis on the all-Welsh character of the cruise, it seemed to have captured the same friendly atmosphere, the same close companionship as had been characteristic of the first venture.

It was the turn of the girls to make their first visit to Porth Dinllaen in 1935, while the boys returned to Llangrannog. *Dysgwyr* were again allowed to attend during one week at each centre, with the proviso that they already possessed a certain prescribed minimum knowledge of the language. The objective was explained to the Welsh-speaking members and to the *Swyddogion* and it was emphasised that their sympathy and their help were essential if the project were to succeed. With this precaution, and the co-operation of the *Dysgwyr* themselves, a greater measure of success was achieved than had been the case during the previous year. It was now felt that the *Dysgwyr* had earned their place in the future pattern of Urdd camps.

On another week, a group of seven Welsh-speaking Scouts had been invited to spend a week at Llangrannog. Within minutes they had come under the spell of Llangrannog and the camp's friendly atmosphere, and by bed-time on the first evening, they felt as much a part of the community as the Urdd members themselves. A visual expression of their appreciation written on a leather scroll is still cherished as a memento. By the end of the week, both the Scouts and the Urdd members felt they had learnt much from one another.

By the summer of 1935, the Founder was ready to implement his plans for the making of a Welsh sound-film. With characteristic impulsiveness, he wrote to J. Ellis Williams, a schoolmaster-playwright from Blaenau Ffestiniog, asking whether he and his drama group would be prepared to co-operate in the making of a Welsh sound-film, based on a Welsh theme and lasting for at least an hour. Without hesitation and without consulting his group, J. Ellis Williams replied that they would be delighted to comply with the request, even though none of them had any experience in such a field. Having committed himself in this way, J. Ellis Williams decided to buy a book on film-making. His first shock was to discover that a one-hour film would cost £2,000 to produce ! He wrote to Ifan ab Owen Edwards to make discreet enquiries regarding the financial position. Ifan ab Owen Edwards was well aware of this fact, but he was not a man to be discouraged by financial considerations. J. M. Howell had already contributed £500 towards the venture. Already a camera costing £250 had been bought together with £100 worth of film, two projectors and a generator ! He was convinced that the rest of the money would come from the proceeds of showing the film. J. Ellis Williams wisely

15   The Urdd Eisteddfod Gold Crown

16   Cwm Tawe District having won the Banner at Llanelli, 1939

17   Ifan ab Owen Edwards in 1939

18   Pupils of the Welsh School at Aberystwyth

decided to leave the financial side of the project to its initiator !
After further correspondence, it was decided that the title of the
film was to be *Y Chwarelwr* (The Quarryman) and the theme
would depict the joys and sorrows, the struggles and dangers in the
lives of ordinary quarrymen in Blaenau Ffestiniog.

When the task was completed, arrangements were made for the
film to be shown throughout North Wales during the winter of
1935/36, on an average of five nights a week. It was immensely
popular ; Ifan ab Owen Edwards' optimism was justified and there
was no financial loss. Paying tribute to J. Ellis Williams and his
team of actors, to their perseverance, their skill and their dedication,
the Founder added, ' Without them, the film would never have been
made.' This, of course, was true, but it is also true that the venture
would never have come about but for his own passionate crusade to
prove that it was possible to use the Welsh language in all aspects of
day-to-day life.

*   *   *   *

Those who remember the mid-thirties are well aware of the
acute economic depression which had spread throughout the whole
of South Wales during that period. In an attempt to mitigate its
effects, the Government had appealed to all organisations to help
in relieving the poverty and the ensuing mental distress. The
co-ordinating body was the National Council of Social Service
working in close co-operation with the ' Commissioners Fund for
Distressed Areas '. Grants were made available to help organisations
that were prepared to contribute towards relieving boredom,
especially amongst young people. It was in this connection that the
Urdd was given its first grant of £300 by the National Council of
Social Service towards the appointment of a Physical Recreation
Officer for Glamorgan and towards the cost of accommodating
at Llangrannog a hundred children from the distressed areas.
Another grant of £450 followed towards initiating training schemes
and towards the building of huts for Aelwydydd in Glamorgan and
Monmouthshire. Thus, for the first time, the Urdd became directly
involved in humanitarian schemes, and was recognised as an
organisation qualifying for grant-aid. It was now up to the Urdd to
prove that this trust was justified and that a Welsh-language

organisation could make an effective and valuable contribution in new fields. The person appointed as Physical Recreation Organiser was Norah Isaac of Caerau, Maesteg, who had just completed her course at Barry Training College, where she was considered to be one of the most gifted of their students. It is true that she had no specialist qualifications in Physical Recreation but she was vigorous and lively, and no one had a better knowledge of the fortitude, the suffering and the personality of those living in the mining areas of South Wales. The Urdd now had two full-time field workers— Olwen Williams in Mid and South-West Wales and Norah Isaac in Glamorgan and Monmouthshire. Then followed the appointment of R. W. Jones, a young man from Llanberis, as Organiser for North Wales to replace J. H. Griffith who had recently resigned. There were also two film projectionists ; a clerical staff of three, together with R. E. Griffith as Chief Organiser. And for their inspiration, and for the tenacity to persevere in the face of disappointments and difficulties, they all looked to the Founder, Ifan ab Owen Edwards.

It was in 1935 that the King George V Jubilee Trust was founded. The fund raised was turned over to the Trust so that the income could be used to help Voluntary Youth Organisations. When the first list of Organisations which were to benefit from the Trust was published, it was noted with much disappointment that the Urdd was not included. Not only was it felt that the only existing Welsh Organisation had been ignored, but it was taken as an insult to Wales and the Welsh nation. It became obvious that the injustice was generally felt throughout Wales, so much so that the *Western Mail* decided to open a fund to compensate for the apparent neglect of the Jubilee Trust. This brought in a total of £1,102/11/9, a fund that was greatly appreciated by the Urdd. Nevertheless, it was realised that, valuable though it was, it did not compensate for an annual grant. It was, therefore, decided to seek the opportunity of putting before the Trustees the special case of the Urdd and of Wales. Happily for the Urdd, the representatives were given a sympathetic hearing and the Trust decided to contribute £100 towards the cost of the 1935 camps and £500 towards improvements in camp equipment. After nearly forty years, it is a pleasure to report that the happy relationship with the Jubilee Trust has been maintained and that, since 1935, a total of more than £30,000 has been received. Every penny of these grants has been spent for the benefit of the youth of Wales, and the Urdd's contribution to their well-being would be much the poorer had it not been for this continued support.

When the Annual General Meeting was held at Bangor in August 1935, the Treasurer was able to report that the year's income and expenditure showed a balance of £1.0.10, in addition to a fair amount of equipment which was gradually being accumulated. In presenting his own report, the Founder reminded his audience that every tomorrow could improve on every yesterday. Without complacency, they should, therefore, go forward with confidence and determination in the implementation of their ideals.

4

1936 was not a year of spectacular developments. The contagious
enthusiasm of the early years had declined, while on the other hand
the Urdd had not quite reached the status of a recognised and
accepted national youth movement. It was a period of transition
and as such, it had its dangers. True, the national events were
constantly being reviewed and improved, and a system was being
evolved which would ensure a high degree of proficiency. It is also
true that, on the local level, greater emphasis was being laid on
more varied and more demanding activities for the older members
of the Adrannau. Some of these members had already left school
and it was recognised that an entirely new approach was necessary
in planning their activities. So far, the Urdd had operated largely
through school Branches, and owed an immeasurable debt to
those teachers and head-teachers who had sought ways and means
of combining Urdd activities with the more formal school curriculum. It was most important that this aspect of the work should be
continued but it was also essential that the Urdd should grow into
a responsible youth movement capable of catering for the needs of
young people during leisure hours and outside the periphery of the
school. This would be the crucial test for the Urdd during the
coming years.

The first problem was the acute shortage of suitably qualified
leaders who could be sympathetic towards adolescent difficulties and
who could offer activities providing some form of challenge—in
manual skills, in endurance, in cultural or recreational standards, in
community service—all of which could be envisaged within the
aims and objectives of the Urdd movement. In view of the shortage
of persons qualified for this type of leadership, it soon became
apparent that some training would have to be provided to give
potential leaders the skills and expertise required for the task.

The second need was the provision of suitable meeting-places,
preferably outside school premises. The ideal seemed to be a chain
of independent buildings similar to those already owned by the
Uwch-Adran at Penrhyndeudraeth or the *Aelwyd* at Aberystwyth.

But where was the money for such centres to come from ? A beginning would have to be made, however, in dealing with non-school members, even though it meant making use of existing buildings, notably school halls, church schoolrooms and village halls. And here tribute must be paid to the authorities controlling these buildings, and in particular to those churches which, despite their Puritan tradition, opened their doors to admit the exuberance of youth in activities quite unconnected with the usual work of the church.

The National Council of Social Service continued its support in the form of a grant of £200 towards the cost of a week's camping for three-hundred-and-fifty boys and girls from the distressed areas, £350 towards extensions to the Llangrannog camp in readiness for the 1936 season, and another £240 towards the cost of erecting temporary buildings to house youth groups in mining areas, meeting outside school hours and school premises. It was with the aid of these and later grants that huts were erected at Treorci, Maerdy, Ynys-y-bŵl, Caerau, Bargoed, Rhymni, and later at Cwmafan. By present-day standards, these were primitive and amateur, offering only limited facilities and certainly no luxuries. But they were hives of activity at a time when activity of any kind was desperately needed, as well as being islands of Welshness—even if not Welsh-speaking—in an ever-growing sea of Anglicisation. Much of the work of erecting and decorating the huts was done locally, and when the time was ripe, the Adran would proudly invite officials of the local Council, the clergy, education officers and headmasters to the official opening. The real value of these hut-centres was that they made a direct and immediate contribution to a community in need. At the same time, their existence was an indication that the Urdd was beginning to reach out of the schools and that at least some Adrannau leaders were preparing to stand on their feet and face the responsibility of running a ' Youth Club '.

*   *   *   *

So far, the Goodwill Service broadcast annually by the BBC had come from various churches in Aberystwyth. In 1936, however, it was entrusted to one of the most active of Urdd Districts—Cylch Cadwgan, Rhondda. It was held at Treorci and conducted by one of the pillars of the movement, the Rev. T. Alban Davies.

Another broadcast of special interest to the Urdd was made in 1936. This was a feature-programme depicting the growth and activities of the movement devised and produced by T. Rowland Hughes. He spent a few days at Aberystwyth gleaning as much information as possible about the early years from the Founder and Chief Organiser, and he succeeded admirably in presenting the thrill and glamour of the twenties as well as the growing depth and responsibility of the thirties.

* * * *

While J. Ellis Williams, the schoolmaster-playwright from Blaenau Ffestiniog, was devoting much of his leisure hours preparing for the making of the sound-film *Y Chwarelwr*, he was also called upon to act as Chairman of the committee responsible for the eighth Urdd National Eisteddfod which would be held at Blaenau Ffestiniog in June 1936. This was the first time the Eisteddfod had experienced the warmth of welcome found in a slate-quarrying area. No request ever had to be repeated, a whispered suggestion was all that was needed. The Eisteddfod was now R. E. Griffith's special responsibility and when he arrived to join the local committee for the three months prior to the Eisteddfod, he soon realised that it was a pleasure and a privilege to be working side-by-side with the men and women of Ffestiniog and in particular with the Honorary Secretary, Meirion Jones. This policy of joint responsibility and co-operation had been a feature of the Urdd Eisteddfod since R. E. Griffith was appointed Organiser. The arrangement has persisted, and has proved acceptable both to the Urdd Council and the local committees. The Eisteddfod could certainly not be run without the experience and hard work of the local committees, but they warmly welcome the arrival of a staff member who is well-versed in the intricacies of the Eisteddfod system, and is thus able to guide the committee, share the responsibility, and shoulder some of the burden during the last crucial weeks before the Eisteddfod.

Having 'loaned' the Mabolgampau to Aberystwyth in 1935, South Wales was eager to see their return in 1936. By this time, Adrannau in East Glamorgan had become interested, and as Tom Davies was moving to Cardiff, the city seemed to be the obvious choice of venue. The Mabolgampau took place at the Cardiff Arms Park in July, following one of the best organised and most disciplined processions the Urdd had ever arranged. The displays and competitions were of a very high standard, and were watched with enthusiasm by the Lord Mayor, and by representatives of the Board of Education and the Local Education Authorities.

A week later, another Mabolgampau, on a much smaller scale, was held at Machynlleth. Unfortunately, this event was hampered by torrential rains, much to the disappointment of the Adrannau and the organising Committee. The Founder's consolation was to remind them that the most valuable part of the Mabolgampau was the advance training, and that this had not been impaired by the rain. Moreover, the Mabolgampau had now reached Machynlleth, and the Founder predicted that, the following year, they would be held in North Wales.

The fourth all-Welsh cruise in 1936 was less successful than its predecessors. There were fewer applications from Welsh-speaking members, and there was no alternative but to invite applications from non Welsh-speaking passengers. Then, at the last moment, the Spanish Civil War made a change of schedule inevitable. Instead of a cruise to Spain, the Mediterranean and North Africa, calling at Gibraltar, Barcelona, Palma, Algiers and Coruna, the passengers had to be content with Madeira, Casablanca, Lisbon and La Rochelle. Reviewing the event later, the Founder expressed his doubts regarding the advisability of organising a cruise for the following year and, with the approval of the Council, decided that the idea could at least be suspended for a year. But if response to the cruise was disappointing, leaders and older members were pressing for another pilgrimage, and a visit to Geneva and Montreux was accordingly arranged. This was led by Prof. G. A. Edwards of Aberystwyth and it succeeded in recapturing much of the thrill of the early pilgrimages. There was no doubt that these visits had greater possibilities in fostering international understanding than the *Mordeithiau,* and the Founder consoled himself that this was, after all, of greater importance.

Coinciding with these overseas visits were the usual camping activities for younger members. The boys returned to Porth

Dinllaen and the girls to Llangrannog. Grants from the National
Council of Social Service and the Jubilee Trust had made possible
the provision of more huts and tents, as well as other improvements
which contributed to the comfort and well-being of the members.
A total of 701 boys and 765 girls attended camp, three-hundred-
and-fifty of whom were helped by the grant from the National
Council of Social Service. Even so, many families could not afford
to send their children to camp even with the help of a grant,
despite the fact that the cost of a week with four meals a day was
only 17/6d. per person. Nevertheless, there were more applications than could be accepted, and the Founder was already
pointing to the need for a third centre. Visitors from the other
Celtic countries were occasionally received and among the 1936
guests were Seoras Erskine Marjoribanks and Donald Macphail
from Scotland. Following this visit, it was later learnt that a Scottish
Youth Organisation—*Commun na h-Oigridh*—had been founded.

The sound film—*Y Chwarelwr*—did not have the same enthusiastic
reception in South Wales as it had been given in North Wales the
previous winter. It may be that the slate-quarryman was something
of a stranger to South Wales audiences, but the difference in
response was more likely to be due to the fact that South Wales had
already grown accustomed to commercial films and that any
amateur film was bound to suffer by comparison. It was obvious
that future shows would best be limited to the more rural areas of
Wales where the film would have a better chance of being appreciated.

*   *   *   *

On the whole, the events of 1937 were to follow the usual pattern.
One new scheme did, however, emerge. The Welsh Books Campaign
was one of R. E. Griffith's ideas, and one which won the immediate
support of Welsh publishers. It was announced as a new method of
celebrating St. David's Day, and fourteen Adrannau were invited
to take part in the project. Each Adran would receive a consign-
ment of Welsh books from the publishers and were free to conduct
their campaign in their own way. Most of the Adrannau decided
to take the books direct to the homes, some on foot, some on bicycle,

while one Adran was enterprising enough to make use of a pony and trap ! When the returns reached Swyddfa'r Urdd at the end of March, a total of 1,025 books had been sold, and the result was announced with considerable satisfaction.

The ninth Urdd National Eisteddfod was held at Gwaun-cae-gurwen, the first time it had been held in a mining area. It had been arranged that the Eisteddfod should be held during the first part of Whit-week in order to coincide with the miners' holiday. By the time the Eisteddfod was held, however, the greater part of the working population of South Wales had a continuous enforced holiday and eight out of ten of the men in the Aman Valley were without work. One cannot cease to wonder at the determination and sacrifice which enabled the community to meet the expenses of the Eisteddfod and at the same time to offer free hospitality to hundreds of competitors from North Wales. That it was achieved at all is something to be wondered at ; that the Eisteddfod accounts showed a surplus of £400 is nothing short of a miracle.

Close on the heels of the Eisteddfod came the Mabolgampau, this time at Penybont-ar-Ogwr (Bridgend). Once again the standards were high and the organisation excellent. Tom Davies was still at the helm, and Norah Isaac had infused the enthusiasm into every valley. The Mabolgampau were now drawing as much attention as the Eisteddfod. Nor was the interest any longer confined to South Wales. After three years of spade-work—film-showing, coaching and coaxing—interest had at last been aroused, and the first North Wales Mabolgampau were to be held on the Recreation Ground in Bangor just a week after the Penybont event. To add to the thrill of the occasion, the Founder suddenly decided to book a special train to bring in teams from Llanelli as reinforcements. This was characteristic of the impulsive, adventurous manner in which he worked. The result was a spectacular event which thrilled the spectators and surprised even those well-acquainted with recreation-al activities.

Shortly afterwards, the Urdd Council set up a Committee of experts to direct the development of the Urdd's physical recreation activities. Much valuable help was given to the committee by W. Russell Rees and Annie Rogers—two HM Inspectors of Schools specialising in this field. The committee was asked to advise on future mabolgampau, promote an interest in games and dances within the Adrannau, and seek official recognition of the work accomplished by the Urdd in this field. As a first step, it was advocated that the Urdd should appoint two qualified Organisers who would specialise in the field of physical recreation.

There were three expeditions to the continent during the summer of 1937,—one to Lugano and Lucerne led by T. P. Williams of the German Department at Aberystwyth, one to Geneva and Montreux led by W. T. Anthony of Llanelli, and a second visit to Lugano and Lucerne led by Prof. G. A. Edwards. And while these 109 members were exploring parts of the Continent, the Founder led a coachload of young people bent on visiting the homes of some of the famous men of North Wales.

The camps, of course, went on as usual,—the boys at Llangrannog and the girls at Porth Dinllaen. Numbers reached a new maximum of fifteen-hundred. Groups of *Dysgwyr* were again catered for, and in addition, two groups from Belgium and Norway had been invited to attend. The voluntary *Swyddogion* now had years of experience and the contribution of a greater number of Urdd Organisers was already making itself felt. It was no longer necessary for the Founder and his wife to reside at the camps, but whenever they arrived on a brief visit they were given a rousing welcome. The Founder would take the opportunity of discussing the general running of the camp, listening attentively to every suggestion and every criticism. The next minute, he would be wandering around the site making a mental note of the structural improvements or extensions that seemed necessary. He was never satisfied with the *status quo* ; there was always something new or something better to be considered. And later, when advocating these improvements in a Committee or Council meeting, he would often say,—' the question is not whether we can afford them, but whether we can afford to be without them.'

The Urdd was now recognised as one of the primary youth movements in Britain, and as such, was invited to select representatives to be present at Aberystwyth and Caernarfon during the visit of the King and Queen in 1937. Four-hundred members attended at Aberystwyth and five-hundred at Caernarfon. It is unlikely that the Royal visitors had previously known anything of the Urdd, and they caused some anxiety to the organisers of their tour by delaying the proceedings while they questioned the Urdd leaders about the movement, its objectives and activities.

When winter came, the Urdd Cinema was once again on tour. A new and better projector had been procured, new films had been added, some of them in colour. Of course, this only served to make the black-and-white films appear insipid by comparison, but at least it was considered to be a step in the right direction.

Throughout the year, the Urdd Committee and Council met regularly. Both depended a great deal on the lead given by the Founder, and his enthusiasm—and often his sense of humour— would usually win their support. Mrs. Edwards still acted as Honorary Secretary to Cwmni'r Urdd, and although the movement now had a number of full-time staff, a good deal of responsibility still rested on the shoulders of the Secretary. Above all, she—more than anyone—knew the Founder's inner feelings. She was always at his side, usually supporting his plea, at other times exercising a gentle restraint when she felt he was moving forward too quickly.

At the Annual General Meeting held at Bae Colwyn (Colwyn Bay) in October, members could not fail to be impressed by the report on events organised on national and regional levels. The Treasurer noted that the accounts showed a balance of 4/9d, but added that the picture would have been very different had it not been for a gift of £500 from J. M. Howell. Staff changes were reported. Olwen Williams had returned to her native Llanelli to take up a teaching post. Three new Organisers had been appointed, —Beti Hughes of Pontrhydyfen, Dafydd J. Miles of Caerffili and Eunice Roberts of Llanberis. All three had been keen Urdd members, all were University graduates, trained for the teaching profession. With a full-time staff of eleven, the Urdd, according to the report, could look forward with confidence to another year of crowded activity.

*   *   *   *

In 1938, the British Government began to lay a new emphasis on Physical Fitness. This was aimed particularly at young people, and the Government was ready to grant-aid any movement prepared to co-operate in the task of creating a generation that was physically fit. To this end, money for extensive propaganda was made available and the National Fitness Council was set up under the chairmanship of Lord Aberdare. A special Committee of the Council was set up to popularise all forms of physical activities within Wales. On the surface, this interest in promoting the physical well-being of youth was entirely laudable. There were, however, some who feared that the international situation had some bearing on the Government's intensive propaganda and apparent generosity.

There was, of course, ample cause for concern regarding the international situation. Spain was already torn by civil war ; a bitter tension existed between China and Japan ; Hitler had succeeded in creating a strong and militant Germany, while Mussolini seemed bent on seeing the re-establishment of the Holy Roman Empire. The League of Nations already showed signs of disintegrating, while the major European powers were re-arming at an unprecedented pace, competing with one another in the multitude of their armies, fleets and air-forces.

Against this background, it was natural that some members of the Urdd Council were suspicious of the Government's motives in its campaign for fitness. Not that the Government's propaganda, as such, provided any ground for suspicion. And after all, one could argue that health and strength and physical activities of all kinds were already being promoted by the Urdd through its Mabolgampau. Why should the Government not display a genuine interest in and concern for these very same attributes without being accused of an ulterior motive ?

The Urdd had already been recognised as one of the major British youth organisations and had become one of the thirteen original member-organisations of the Standing Conference of National Voluntary Youth Organisations. Of the thirteen, the Urdd was the only organisation having its roots in the soil of Wales. There were, of course, several other organisations operating within Wales, but they were all English—or British—organisations having their headquarters in England. The Urdd, on the other hand, was a

Welsh organisation, founded to promote the Welsh language and
Welsh culture and to serve the Welsh nation.

The National Fitness Council was already aware of the work done
by the Urdd in the field of physical recreation, and it became
obvious that the Council would be prepared to offer substantial
grants towards further developments in this direction. The Founder
himself was prepared to take the Government's interest at face
value and to accept any grants that were available, provided they
were unconditional grants which left the Urdd free to operate
according to its own constitution and ideals. And despite the
uneasiness felt by some members, he was able to persuade the Urdd
Council that it would be foolish to stand aside and fail to take advantage of grant-aid that would enable the movement to offer better
facilities to its members both on a local and national level. Thus
it was that, during the course of 1938, the Urdd received substantial
grants towards the appointment of Physical Education Organisers,
towards a series of training courses and one-day schools, towards
improving camp facilities, and towards the purchase or erection of
Aelwydydd premises where provision was made for an equipped
gymnasium. It was with the aid of these grants that the gymnasium
at Llangrannog Camp was built, as well as premises for some half
dozen *Aelwydydd*. Attempts were made to persuade other *Aelwydydd*
to take advantage of the available grants. It may be that these
leaders shared the suspicion felt by some members of the Urdd
Council, or just that rural Welsh Wales was slow to recognise the
value of physical recreation. Whatever the reason, many *Aelwydydd*
delayed their applications and the opportunity was lost. Before the
end of 1939, the international situation had deteriorated and the
National Fitness Council had ceased to exist.

In addition to developments connected with the Government's
emphasis on physical fitness, it was essential that the usual pattern
of Urdd events be maintained. Thirty Branches were involved in
the second Welsh Books Campaign and, between them, they sold
a total of 3,535 books, more than treble the number sold the previous
year. Authors and publishers were, of course, delighted, but there
were some booksellers who feared that an annual campaign of this
kind would rob them of their regular customers. No formal protest
was voiced, however, and, as it was possible that the reverse might

also be true, it was decided to wait and see whether there was any real cause for anxiety.

The BBC offered the Urdd another St. David's Day appeal and the choice fell on the Rev. Dr. Elvet Lewis, the poet ' Elfed '. The appeal, which was broadcast from Droitwich as well as from the Welsh station, resulted in a total of £1,316/16/9, and no one was more pleased than Elfed himself.

Another BBC programme in which the Urdd was involved was the broadcast of the Goodwill Service arranged by the Twyn Carno Branch, Rhymni, when the address was given by the Rev. George M. Ll. Davies whose admiration for the Urdd had long been manifest.

The Urdd National Eisteddfod for 1938 was held at Aberystwyth. On this occasion, the Urdd Council had decided to limit the stage competitions to group-work in an attempt to persuade the Adrannau to concentrate more on the group and less on promoting talented individuals for whom there were already ample opportunities at local Eisteddfodau. Such a change, however, was too revolutionary, and the reaction of competitors and supporters was reflected in the dwindled audiences at the Eisteddfod.

Another Council decision to which the public reacted unfavourably was concerned with the administration of the Eisteddfod. The Council argued that the administration was on two distinct and separate levels—the Council and its Sub-committees being responsible for one, the other, more local aspect, being the responsibility of the local Committee. This division of labour was accepted in principle, but it was felt that the dichotomy, as defined by the Council, limited the responsibility of the local committee to the more mundane, material aspects of the arrangements. This, it was argued, would sap the enthusiasm of the local committee and lose the support of the general public. The ultimate result was a compromise, and a new pattern emerged which ensured a greater degree of co-operation and less rigid division of responsibility. This revised policy led to a much more effective co-operation in future years.

The Mabolgampau at Pontypridd in July reached another high-water level. Aided by the Urdd Organisers, and drawing on the experience of Tom Davies and the newly-established Physical Recreation Committee, six local committees had shared in the planning and administration. By this time, a system of elimination of competitors was already in operation. Each District within the area held its own Mabolgampau and chose its best swimmers, gymnasts and athletes, while a number of one-day schools for Branch leaders were held in various centres, so that they, in turn, could instruct their members for the massed displays. Pontypridd was an ideal centre for the Rhondda, Aberdâr, Merthyr and Rhymni valleys, and within easy reach of Cardiff, Swansea and West Wales. The procession which preceded the Mabolgampau was assembled at the memorial to the joint-authors of *Hen Wlad fy Nhadau* in Ynys Angharad Park, and it was perhaps natural that the anthem was sung with unusual fervour by participants and spectators during the finalé of the Mabolgampau. Since 1932, the *Mabolgampau Banner* had been won annually by the Llanelli District, but at Pontypridd, they were beaten into second place by the Cardiff District. This in itself gave East Glamorgan a new confidence and provided a new source of enthusiasm.

It also happened that the National Eisteddfod of Wales was held at Cardiff. The Urdd members' rally which had previously been associated with that festival had now been discontinued. Instead, the movement had its own stand on the Eisteddfod ground, largely intended as a meeting-place for Urdd leaders. At Cardiff, the Urdd had also been invited to contribute a fifteen-minute item as part of the children's concert in the Eisteddfod pavilion. It was decided to ask Tom Davies to produce a short ' Health and Vigour Pageant ' (*Pasiant Iechyd a Hoen*) depicting the development of physical recreation within Wales. It was natural that it should be performed by the Cardiff District Branches, the District that had earlier snatched its triumph at the Pontypridd Mabolgampau.

A meeting of some significance was held during the Eisteddfod week. It was convened by *Undeb y Cymdeithasau Cymraeg* (The Union of Welsh Societies), and attended by members of all the various movements that were in some way concerned with the Welsh a nguage problem. Amid considerable enthusiasm, it was decided to organise a national petition to be presented to the British Government calling for official recognition of the Welsh language in law courts held within Wales. A National Committee was set up, together with a smaller Executive Committee. The wording of the petition was entrusted to a panel of experts including historians and lawyers, and it was decided to set up an office at Aberystwyth and to appoint an organiser and a secretary. It was foreseen that the task might take two or three years to accomplish, and a fund was opened to meet the expenses involved.

It was unusual to find such unanimity in Wales as was experienced when the Welsh Language Petition was launched at Cardiff in 1938. Most sections of the Welsh community had declared their support— the political parties, the religious denominations, the local authorities and practically every voluntary organisation which was in some way concerned with the wellbeing of the Welsh nation. It was natural, therefore, that the Urdd should be actively involved in the petition. Leaders of Branches were asked to help in the distribution of literature and in collecting signatures ; the Urdd Council contributed to the Petition Fund, and an office for the organiser and his secretary was made available at the Urdd Headquarters in Aberystwyth.

*   *   *   *

Ten years had elapsed since the first Urdd camp was held at Llanuwchllyn. Much had happened during that period and the Urdd now ran two centres that would compare favourably with any camps in Britain. More than 1,800 attended the 1938 camps— the boys at Porth Dinllaen and the girls at Llangrannog. One factor that caused some concern, however, was the fact that the number of Welsh-speaking campers had diminished while there had been an understandable increase in the number of *Dysgwyr*. Many of them had experienced the thrill of taking part in the Mabolgampau and the camps offered even more exciting possibilities. Moreover, the Council of Social Service continued to grant-aid those boys and girls from the Distressed Areas who would not otherwise be able to attend. The effects of the depression, however, were not confined to the mining areas and there were very many families in the rural areas who could not afford the cost of a week

19 Mass demonstration at the Aberystwyth Mabolgampau, 1935

20 *Dawns Cymru*—part of the Mabolgampau programme

21 J. M. Howell—first Patron and President

22 Sir Eric Skaife

23 The Founder ; the Rt. Hon. R. A.
Butler ; J. M. Howell ; and James Griffiths,
M.P. at the Urdd's coming of age

24 Dr. Rudolf Hermann from
Bielefeld, Germany

at camp, and this might well be the cause of the reduction in the number of Welsh-speaking members. In an attempt to secure help for these members who did not qualify for the grants of the Council of Social Service, the Founder turned to the ' Pilgrim Trust '. The grant received, however, amounted to no more than £30 and the Founder's concern remained. Much as he welcomed the increase in the number of *Dysgwyr*, if it coincided with a reduction in the number of Welsh-speaking members, the whole camp atmosphere would be progressively Anglicised so that it would eventually defeat its own end.

A week's camp at Llangrannog for adults was an entirely new venture. Many of the early campers were now over eighteen and so were excluded from camp except as *Swyddogion*. And although this was a cherished privilege, they felt it would also be desirable if they could have one week to themselves—without the children ! As soon as the request had been made to the Founder, he set about making arrangements for a week's camping for ' men ' at Porth Dinllaen and for ' women ' at Llangrannog. To his surprise, there was no response ! He was even more surprised when R. E. Griffith suggested that it might be worth considering a mixed camp ! An announcement to this effect was made, and almost immediately, applications began to pour in to Swyddfa'r Urdd !

Hitherto, all Urdd camps had been for boys only or girls only and the question of mixed camps had not arisen. Even if it had arisen, it would probably have been argued that more healthy exuberance was possible, more initiative shown and certainly fewer disciplinary problems when the sexes were kept apart. Still, the Founder agreed that co-education had proved feasible and he was prepared to admit that a mixed camp might have its advantages ! As one would expect, the experiment was an unqualified success. That friendships were established—some of which led to life-time partnerships—was only one aspect of its success. It might even prove to be a pointer to a new camping policy.

Grants made by the National Fitness Council had enabled the Urdd to make many improvements and extensions at the Llangrannog Camp. The dining-hut was extended to seat three-hundred and a new kitchen added. Plans were in hand to build a chapel, a gymnasium, a hall, a sick-bay and first-aid post. The camp was to be connected with the main water supply, and the premises were to be lit by electricity. Even with grants, these improvements meant a considerable financial burden, and it was decided to close the camp at Porth Dinllaen so that all effort could be concentrated on Llangrannog. A guaranteed tenancy of twenty-one years had been secured for Llangrannog whereas no lease had been possible at Porth Dinllaen. Nevertheless, it was with heavy heart that the camp at Porth Dinllaen was closed, and the regret was shared by the inhabitants of Edern, Nefyn and Morfa Nefyn, who had come to look upon the camp as part of the community.

While the camps were in progress, another group of adults, led by W. T. Anthony of Llanelli, visited Geneva and Montreux. Despite the success of the pilgrimages, however, there were many who felt the time had come for another cruise. And, finally, Ifan ab Owen Edwards yielded to pressure and agreed to consider a cruise for 1939.

The Welsh Cinema continued its tour and as many as 129 places were visited during the winter of 1938/39. New films had naturally to be included and these were now of a more general pattern, and included documentary films dealing with a wide variety of subjects ranging from ' The National Museum of Wales ' to ' Flights over Everest '.

At the Annual General Meeting held at Tregaron in October 1938, it was reported that the expenditure for the previous financial year exceeded £5,000 and that it was a considerable struggle to make ends meet, despite grants of approximately £1,500. Tribute was paid to the Council of Social Service, the National Fitness Council and the Jubilee Trust for their continued support. Changes in the Urdd staff were also reported. These included the appointment of Elwyn L. Jones of Pontarddulais, a former member of the Adran at Gowerton County School and a University graduate trained for a teaching career. Full of enthusiasm, he took charge of Cardiganshire, Montgomeryshire and part of Merioneth. Two young men who possessed special qualifications in Physical Education—Ieuan Williams of Pontarddulais and T. Maddock Rees from Pontrhydyfen—became Physical Training Officers, to be joined later by Ceridwen Macleod of Bangor. This in itself was an indication of the emphasis laid by the Urdd during this period on the importance of physical recreation.

*   *   *   *

The task of providing challenging leisure-time pursuits designed to help the young to become worthy members of their society was one that faced all recognised British youth organisations in 1939, and the Urdd was no exception. Where the Urdd differed from other organisations was in its interpretation of ' society ', and in its emphasis on Wales as a national entity. It was basically a patriotic movement, pledged to promote the Welsh language and concerned for all that was essential to the life of the Welsh nation—a concern not apparently shared by other youth organisations. From time to time, this emphasis on the nation and its language gave rise to doubts that the Urdd was a politically motivated organisation and some people, even within Wales, found it difficult to understand that a movement could be patriotic and yet non-political. On the other hand, it may be argued that this was the very strength of the movement—that it could attract to its ranks people of different political convictions who were, nevertheless, united in their concern for the well-being of the Welsh nation.

On the local level, the task was twofold. In the first place, it was often necessary to urge leaders to widen their horizons and offer their members a wider choice of challenging activities. There was always a danger that some leaders took too limited a view of the movement. For some, the Eisteddfod was of paramount importance ; for others, the Mabolgampau or the summer camps. Secondly, it was now necessary to emphasise the importance of a varied programme that would cater for the widest possible range of interests and abilities. Equally important was the need to remind leaders that, important though these activities were, one should not allow them to obscure the objective of ' loyalty to Wales, to fellow-man and to Christ.'

The Welsh Books Campaign had now found its established place in the Urdd calendar. Thirty-five Adrannau took part in 1939 and once again, more than three-thousand books were sold. People had now begun to look forward to the campaign, and authors and publishers were greatly encouraged. There were, at that time, no Government or Local Education Authority grants to aid the publication of Welsh books ; the Welsh Joint Education Committee, the Welsh Books Council and the Welsh Arts Council were not yet in existence. It was in this kind of vacuum that the Urdd offered its services to the cause of Welsh publishing. It could well be argued that such a project was outside the scope of the Urdd's function as a youth organisation. Certainly, no one could have blamed the movement for *not* taking any action. But here was a task that needed doing, and it would be the youth of Wales who would suffer if the task were neglected. It might be little that the Urdd could do, but that little had to be done in the hope that the British Government and the Welsh people themselves would eventually awaken to their responsibilities.

*　　*　　*　　*

On the international horizon, dark clouds were gathering. Germany was already in control of Austria, and Czechoslovakia was threatened ; Mussolini had conquered Abyssinia, usurped Albania and was already a threat to France and the Balkans. Russia was believed to be siding with Britain and France, while America seemed bent on maintaining a policy of isolationism. Denied the support of the USA, the League of Nations had largely lost its influence and its disintegration was already imminent. And without the security of the League of Nations, the smaller nations of Europe had ample cause to fear for their very existence.

It was to such a world that Gwilym Davies addressed his 1939 Goodwill Message. It needed a man of faith and courage to express any hope for peace and goodwill in the face of so much enmity, but Gwilym Davies never faltered, although he was probably better acquainted with the European situation than anyone else in Wales at that time. Calling the youth of the world, his Message continued—

' The world is full of suffering, cruelty and strife. And we are told that civilisation may perish. Let us tell the world that civilisation shall not perish.

More than ever, the world needs what we alone can give—the confidence and the comradeship of youth . . . So shall we, millions of us, grow up to be the friends of all and the enemies of none.'

The Urdd, as usual, supported the Message, and the May issue of *Cymru'r Plant* was devoted to presenting the background of some of the smaller countries of Europe. The Founder and Chief Organiser were not without their fears that Europe might be plunged into another war, but maintained that panic and despair would help no one, and that the Urdd should carry on as usual in the hope that the catastrophe could be averted.

The Urdd National Eisteddfod was held at Llanelli at the beginning of June. The silent protest against the decision of the previous year to limit stage competitions to group-work was again apparent, both in the limited support of the Adrannau and that of the public. It was clear that this decision would now have to be reconsidered. Nevertheless, there were notable highlights—the high standard of stage work, especially in the drama competitions, the excellence of the Arts and Crafts Exhibition, and the warmth of welcome—so characteristic of the area—that was shown to competitors from afar.

For the second time, the North Wales Mabolgampau were held at Bangor, and the years of training and exhortation were beginning to bear fruit. More members took part, the standards were higher, and the interest and support of the public had doubled. But another misfortune awaited them. After a month of unbroken sunshine, the rains came, and it was under great difficulties that the organisers and participants carried on. But while the organisers were despondent, the Adrannau were adamant that another Mabolgampau should be held the following year. And this enthusiasm in the face of adversity was like a beam of light breaking through the dark rain clouds.

Fate seemed more kindly disposed towards the South Wales Mabolgampau held at *Castell Nedd* (Neath) during two days of continuous sunshine. The Civic Welcome on the Friday was followed by the Ambulance and First-Aid Competitions, and the evening closed with a *Noson Lawen*. On the Saturday, more than a hundred Branches took part in the procession, while four thousand members, watched by four-thousand spectators, took part in the displays and competitions. The programme concluded with a display by the Welsh Gymnastic Team, trained by Tom Davies and recently returned from their visit to Sweden.

On his way home from the Bangor Mabolgampau, the Founder had travelled via Bala and stopped his car at a spot between Bala and Llanuwchllyn. He climbed over the wall and fought his way through the undergrowth to take a look at Plas Glan Llyn, the property of Sir Watkin Williams Wynn. Twelve years earlier, Ifan ab Owen Edwards had sought to rent the premises as a camp centre and had been refused. When he returned to the car, he said—' That's the place I would like to have for the Urdd. Some day it may be possible.'

The camp at Llangrannog had been greatly improved by the addition of new buildings, especially the gymnasium and the chapel. The first to use the camp in 1939 were a group of boys attending a fortnight's school-camp run in conjunction with the Education Authorities of Cardiganshire and Carmarthenshire. It was a combination of formal classes and environmental studies, together with games, swimming and indoor recreational programmes. In later years, the two Education Authorities were to be joined by Pembrokeshire, until, eventually, Pembrokeshire and Carmarthenshire, having explored the possibilities of school-camps, were able to develop their own camp centres.

The school-camps were followed by the Urdd camps, and in 1939, they began with three weeks' camping for 300 girls. During the first week, a special inter-denominational consecration service was held in the new chapel, the address being given by D. O. Evans, M.P., who had first suggested the camp site to the Founder in 1931. A large white cross had been placed above the chapel doorway, and this led to some criticism, more particularly from Nonconformists who regarded it as a symbol of allegiance to the Episcopal Church, if not, indeed, to the Church of Rome. For the Urdd, on the other hand, it was a symbol that would serve to remind the members of their pledge of loyalty to Christ.

The three weeks for girls were followed by a mixed camp for young people in the 18-25 age group. Once again, it was highly successful and when the Founder was heard commenting on the advantages of a mixed camp, the members felt it would not be long before mixed camps became the pattern for the younger

age-groups as well ! The adult week was followed by three weeks
for boys who were equally thrilled with the improved amenities of
the ' new Llangrannog'.

Plans for another all-Welsh cruise—another *Mordaith*—had long
since been completed. A smaller ship than had previously been
used was chartered from a Yugoslav shipping company. The
passengers assembled in London on August 12, travelled by special
train from Boulogne to Venice and boarded the *Kraljica Maria*.
They cruised along the Dalmatian coast, visiting Rab, Sibenik,
Split and Dubrovnik, disembarking for a coach tour from Dubrovnik to Cetinje, the world's smallest capital. From Dubrovnik to
Greece, spending a day on the island of Corfu where they sensed the
uneasiness of the inhabitants who feared they might share the fate
of Albania. This caused Ifan ab Owen Edwards to consider
whether he should abandon the remainder of the cruise and turn for
home. He decided to wait until they reached Athens. Here, there
was less tension ; the British fleet was anchored nearby and there
was a greater feeling of security. In consultation with the Captain,
Ifan ab Owen Edwards decided to continue the journey. When
they arrived in Sicily, however, they found the port surrounded by
mines and guarded by submarines. The inhabitants were courteous
but not particularly friendly. Here too they learnt of the treaty
signed between Germany and Russia. The *Kraljica Maria* reached
Naples and the passengers visited Pompeii and climbed Vesuvius.
They spent a day in Rome, tracing some of the well-known Roman
remains. From Naples to Monte Carlo which, to their surprise,
they found deserted. It was then that the passengers fully realised
the gravity of the situation. They bid farewell to the *Kraljica Maria*
and its captain, caught a train to Paris where they found the same
atmosphere of fear, amounting almost to panic. They reached
London, tired but relieved, on August 27, just a few days before war
was declared. Despite the difficulties of the latter part of the
journey, the fears and uncertainties, the passengers voted this
to be the best cruise of all. It was, however, destined to be
the last. Even when peace returned in 1945, it was some years
before it was possible to charter a ship for holiday purposes. And
when it did become possible, the cost had more than trebled. And

so, with much regret, it was decided that this chapter was to be closed and that the Urdd should now concentrate on visits and exchanges for smaller groups and for younger members. It was felt that the movement could make some contribution in trying to restore a spirit of goodwill in a world torn by hatred and scarred by war.

5

WAR was declared on September 3, 1939. This was the catastrophe which many had feared but hoped could be averted. Its effect would be detrimental to the life of all concerned, but to the small nations of Europe—Wales included—it could be a disaster. Already, throughout the period between the two World Wars, Wales had struggled to maintain its identity against powerful odds. It had been a period of increasing disintegration. Economic depression in the coal-mining industry ; depopulation in the slate-quarrying districts ; closure of woollen mills and lead mines ; acute poverty in agriculture. As a result, Wales had lost a generation of its youth to England. Hand-in-hand with this general depression came a deterioration in religious interest, in Welsh awareness and in the cultural life of Wales. All this coincided with the Anglicising influence of the mass media—the cinema, press and radio. The Urdd had sought to stem this deterioration ; it had aimed at creating a greater measure of self-respect in the minds of the growing generation of the twenties and thirties. Now the war threatened to undermine all such efforts, and indeed to destroy the very life of the Welsh nation. And the Welsh people themselves were conditioned by press and radio to believe that nothing now mattered but the struggle to win the war ; everything else must be sacrificed to that end.

The first immediate threat was the cessation of Welsh radio programmes. During the previous four or five years, the BBC had appointed a nucleus of Welsh-speaking staff who provided excellent radio programmes in Welsh. The sudden withdrawal of these programmes left a vacuum in Welsh homes and the bastions of Welsh culture were thereby considerably weakened. The second blow was the influx of evacuees from English cities. Faced with a real emergency, the people of Wales were very ready to offer hospitality to these children who, through no fault of their own, were compelled to seek shelter in a strange land. There was no lack of sympathy and no effort spared in answering the call for help.

Nevertheless, it was unavoidable that the effect of the influx on Welsh-speaking homes would be very considerable.

It was obvious, therefore, that the life of Wales was seriously threatened, and it was this that prompted two leading members of the Welsh Nationalist Party—Saunders Lewis and J. E. Daniel—to call for the setting up of an Advisory Committee to watch over the affairs of Wales during the war period. Shortly afterwards the Council of the National Eisteddfod of Wales decided to call a nation-wide conference to consider the danger to Welsh life and culture. It was attended by representatives of many organisations and movements ; an Executive Committee of twelve leaders of Welsh life was formed, and Ifan ab Owen Edwards was one of the twelve.

Apart from its detrimental effect on Welsh life in general, the war soon brought new and immediate problems which the Urdd—like other voluntary organisations—had to face. The first direct threat was contained in a letter from the Government giving a month's notice that all grants would cease, and urging the Urdd to reduce its staff and cut costs to the bare minimum. The Founder felt shattered, convinced that this would be the end of the Urdd, and not even R. E. Griffith could offer any hope or consolation. There seemed to be no way out. Ifan ab Owen Edwards wrote to all members of his staff, with the exception of R. E. Griffith and Elsi Williams, explaining the situation and advising them to seek alternative posts. But it was one thing to dismiss the staff. There were still hundreds of Adrannau all over Wales ; there were new camp premises at Llangrannog ; there were Aelwydydd premises recently acquired or completed. These could not be deleted with the stroke of a pen. But would the Urdd ever hold another camp ? Or another Eisteddfod or Mabolgampau ? It was indeed the end.

A fortnight later a second letter arrived from the Board of Education. The Government had reconsidered the situation. It had realised that the war would bring with it enormous social problems, especially amongst young people, and that the need for youth organisations would be greater than ever. Direct grants would, therefore, be made available, and the Urdd, like other similar organisations, was urged to carry on and to intensify its efforts. The gloom was lifted ; there was new hope ; the Urdd could go on. The Founder's fighting spirit returned ; from now on, the war would be a challenge but not a defeat. The Urdd would need a new slogan that would convey this fighting spirit to leaders of Urdd Branches and to all those who had the future of Wales at heart. It was R. E. Griffith who suggested the motto, *Rhaid i Gymru Fyw* (Wales must live), and the Founder enthusiastically agreed. They were now determined that the war would not be allowed to rob Wales of its heritage.

It was too much to hope that all the dismissed staff would return ; some had already obtained alternative posts. It was thus that the Urdd lost T. Maddock Rees, Ceridwen MacLeod and D. J. Miles. And of those who did return, those within a certain age-group would soon be called for military service. It was obvious that, while the war lasted, the ranks would be depleted and that the Urdd would have to depend more and more on older part-time workers.

*   *   *   *

The Founder's son, Owen, was five years old and ready for school at the end of 1938. His father felt it was important that his education should be through the medium of Welsh and based on Welsh life and Welsh culture. For the first year or two, this would be possible locally since the elementary school at Aberystwyth had a Welsh Infants' Department and it was to this school that Ifan ab Owen Edwards took his son in January 1939. In September, the war came, and hundreds of evacuees from Liverpool arrived at Aberystwyth. It was quite impossible to accommodate these children in existing school buildings and, until additional buildings could be temporarily brought into use, a shift system was introduced. Like most parents, Ifan ab Owen Edwards was not happy with this arrangement and he decided to offer the Director of Education the use of rooms in the Urdd premises for the Welsh Infants' Department. The Director gladly accepted the offer and the move was made. The teachers, however, felt isolated, and at the end of a fortnight, the children were moved back to the local school, much to the disappointment of Ifan ab Owen Edwards. As things stood, there was little hope for the Welsh Infants' Department within the overcrowded situation. Ifan ab Owen Edwards decided that the only alternative was to set up a private class for Welsh-speaking infants. The parents of four other children agreed to join in the venture. And on the Friday, Ifan ab Owen Edwards informed the Director of Education of his plan and said that the class, with at least five pupils, would commence the following Monday. This left him just two days to prepare his classroom and find a teacher ! The teacher problem was quickly solved. Norah Isaac was one of the fifteen staff who had recently been dismissed and, so far, had not found alternative employment. She had four years' experience as Organiser for South Wales, sharing in the organisation of camps and Mabolgampau. She was trained for the teaching profession and was obviously gifted in this direction. The choice was obvious.

During the weekend, Ifan ab Owen Edwards got down to the task of providing improvised furniture and equipment that would make-do until more suitable alternatives could be found. With a ruler in one hand and a saw in the other, and with Owen as his model, he cut down tables and chairs to the measurements required by five-year olds. And so, with a total of seven pupils, his ' school ' opened on the Monday afternoon.

All this happened within a period of three weeks, and within the very period in which Ifan ab Owen Edwards had experienced his greatest despair when he felt that his movement was collapsing at his feet. But even in his moment of despair, he did not lose sight of his vision, and the man of action was not averse to the manual work that was necessary to turn his vision into reality. To most people in Aberystwyth at the time, he was a determined and obstinate man, a Welsh extremist, and his infants class, was derisively referred to as the 'Ifan ab School'.

The experiment was quick to establish itself, and more parents expressed a desire that their children should join the original seven. Ifan ab Owen Edwards decided that some organisation was needed. A meeting of parents was called, and it was decided that representatives of the parents and of the Urdd, together with a number of educationists, should act as Governors, with Ifan ab Owen Edwards as Chairman, I. C. Jones as Treasurer, and R. E. Griffith as Secretary.

It was in this kind of mad rush that *Ysgol Gymraeg Aberystwyth* (the Aberystwyth Welsh School) came into being. There were two reasons for its formation. The first was Ifan ab Owen Edwards' conviction that a child living in his own country should be taught through his mother tongue and that his education should draw its inspiration from the nation's own culture and tradition. The second reason lay in the circumstances arising out of the war crisis and Ifan ab Owen Edwards' personal predicament regarding his son's education. These were the circumstances which gave him the opportunity—indeed compelled him—to follow his conviction, come what may. Would he have acted as he did had it not been for these circumstances ? This is a question that cannot be answered. But Wales has cause to be grateful that he grasped his opportunity, without realising, at the time, that he was causing a revolution within the education system, and in effect, founding a new Welsh ' movement '.

*   *   *   *

Despite the restrictions imposed by the circumstances of war, the Founder was able to report to the Annual General Meeting in October that the Urdd was facing up to the challenge. The motto *Rhaid i Gymru Fyw* (Wales must live) had provided the right kind of inspiration to the Branches and the leaders. It was expected that the Government would honour its promise of grant-aid, and, to tide over the interim period, J. M. Howell had contributed £500 to Urdd funds. There was also a gift of £100 from Dr. Erie Evans of Bangor and numerous lesser contributions from well-wishers from all over Wales. It was realised that, because of restrictions, it would not be possible for the Council to meet as frequently as before, and to counteract this, it would be necessary for the Executive Committee to assume greater responsibility. To facilitate this, it was decided that a nucleus of members be elected to the Council who were within easy reach of Aberystwyth.

One effect of the war was the sudden requisitioning of buildings for the Government's own use. This was the fate of the newly built Urdd centre at Aberystwyth towards the end of 1939. In response to a demanding knock on her door, Mrs. Edwards opened to find a beribboned army officer who announced that the army was taking over the Urdd premises. In her surprise, Mrs. Edwards said ' But what about the little Welsh school ? ' ' Little Welsh school be damned ' came the reply, ' dont you know there's a war on ? ' And he turned on his heel and marched into the building.

Fortunately, the school classroom and the offices of Swyddfa'r Urdd were not suitable for the army's purpose and these were spared. The Aelwyd, however, lost its premises and it was three years before this part of the building was restored to its original use.

One of the Founder's characteristics was his ability to react quickly to changed and varied situations. And during the early war years, the Urdd benefitted from this ability whenever it became necessary to act swiftly in response to one new development after the other. On November 27, 1939, Circular 1486 was sent to Local Education Authorities by the Board of Education urging them to set up a committee dealing especially with the problems of youth. This was the important document which led to the establishment of the 'Youth Service' in England and Wales. Previously, most youth work had been accomplished by voluntary organisations with very little government support. It had been left to the voluntary bodies to recognise the need and to pioneer. The Government now realised that this service was the foundation on which to base the provision of leisure-time activities for young people and that the experience of the voluntary organisations should not be lost. At the same time, it was recognised that they could not be expected to carry on during the restrictions of the war situation without substantial financial aid, and that even with such aid, they could not meet all the necessary demands. Circular 1486, therefore, sought to set up a partnership between the Board of Education, the local education authorities and the voluntary organisations. This co-operation between the statutory bodies and the voluntary organisations was to be the basis of the new 'Youth Service,' offering opportunities to boys and girls in the 14-20 age-group. The Board of Education would give direct grants to voluntary organisations, and the local education authorities were expected to do likewise within their own area, as well as to set up youth centres where there were gaps in the provision made by the voluntary organisations. A Welsh Youth Committee, under the chairmanship of James Griffiths, M.P., was set up to co-ordinate the scheme.

This development brought new hope to the voluntary organisations which had long struggled against great odds to provide leisure activities for their members. Now the Government was to acknowledge their efforts and offer its support in their future contribution. They now had to consider whether they could accept this patronage without sacrificing their ideals or their independence. This was the criterion on which the Urdd examined the possibilities. The Board of Education lost no time in fulfilling its promise of financial aid. The Urdd was given a grant of £750 for the period up to the end of March 1940, and assured of a further grant during the following financial year. Its immediate task was to close the ranks of its staff, re-appointing those who were still available, and replacing those who had already taken alternative appointments. Elwyn Jones was recalled as Organiser for South Wales, and Dafydd Jones of Maenan, Llanrwst became Aelwydydd Organiser for North Wales, thus sharing some of the burden resting on Eunice Roberts. Margaret Parry of Machynlleth was appointed Organiser for Mid-Wales with special responsibility for girls' activities.

One result of the issue of Circular 1486 was that it led to the formation of a new link in the Urdd's administrative system. Previously there had been Branch Committees, District Committees, and the Urdd Council with its Executive Committee. Now that it was necessary to co-operate more closely with the county education authorities, it became necessary to establish another link—the Urdd County Committee. The Founder and Chief Organiser attended meetings of leaders in each county, advising them regarding the constitution of the new body and its function within the Urdd's administrative system. Soon these County Committees were to become virile bodies, not only working in co-operation with the local education authorities, but also supervising and stimulating Urdd activities within their respective territories.

*   *   *   *

It was not easy to maintain the usual programme of events in the face of ever-growing restrictions. Nevertheless, 44 Branches joined in the Welsh Books Campaign and between them sold 3,545 volumes. More surprising still was the fact that the Goodwill Service survived and, in 1940, was broadcast from Bethesda in Caernarfonshire. But perhaps the greatest achievement was the Urdd National Eisteddfod which was held at Rhyl during the war's darkest hour—Dunkerque week. Of course, the Eisteddfod was not on the usual scale. There was no curtailment of the sections in which the work could be completed at home, in the Arts and Crafts Exhibition, the drama or the ambulance competitions. But stage competitions had to be limited to one day and therefore restricted to group-work only. The customary timber-and-canvas pavilion had to be abandoned and the Eisteddfod held in a smaller but permanent Pavilion. What caused the greatest surprise was the fact that so many competitors from South Wales had overcome seemingly insurmountable difficulties and found their way to the Eisteddfod.

A brave attempt was also made to run the summer camps as usual, despite the inevitable restrictions. Erection of tents at Llangrannog was forbidden, which meant that the number of campers was confined to the 150 that could be accommodated in the huts. Foods were rationed, and although campers had to hand in their coupons for the week, camp appetite being what it is, it needed imagination and resourcefulness to satisfy their needs ! Petrol too was rationed and special transport was difficult to arrange. And when darkness fell, every light had to be carefully concealed—no small feat where 150 unthinking and high-spirited youngsters were concerned. Sometimes, even the Swyddogion would unwittingly cause embarrassment. The story is still told of the night ' Bobi Gordon ' led a number of his fellow-Swyddogion for a moonlight swim, when the sound of the voices from the beach brought the villagers from their beds firmly convinced that the Germans had landed at Cilborth !

*   *   *   *

One of the Urdd's most prominent Leaders in Cardiff during the thirties was W. C. Elvet Thomas, teacher of Welsh at the Cathays High School for Boys. He soon established an Urdd Branch in the School and in a very short time had registered a hundred members, the great majority of whom were *Dysgwyr*. He was intent on getting as many as possible of his pupils to be Welsh-speaking, and he found that the Urdd activities could be a valuable supplement to formal class-teaching. He, therefore, took advantage of all Urdd events, but particularly the Mabolgampau and summer camps. By the end of the thirties, the Cathays High School had achieved such prominence that it was ' adopted ' by the Lord Mayor and permitted to use the title *Adran yr Arglwydd Faer* (Lord Mayor's Urdd Branch).   In

25 Owen and Prys Edwards in the mid-forties

26 Team games at Llangrannog Camp

27 The Aelwyd at Maerdy in the Rhondda Valley

28 Home of the Swansea Young Wales Club

November 1938, a special religious service was held in the Cathedral at Llandâf to commemorate the Seventh Jubilee of the publication of the Welsh translation of the Bible. During the opening hymn, three boys in Urdd uniform, members of the Lord Mayor's Urdd Branch, walked up to the altar and presented the Welsh flag, receiving it back again at the close of the service. It was a symbol of offering to God, in the Cathedral in which Bishop William Morgan had officiated, the future of the Welsh nation.

This act may have given Elvet Thomas the idea for another pilgrimage in 1940. He planned a pilgrimage from Cardiff to St. David's, taking with him three boys chosen to represent the Adran. The Lord Mayor gave them a letter to present to the Dean and Chapter of St. David's Cathedral and asked them to represent the City of Cardiff as well as the Adran. The night before they left, the four pilgrims attended a special service in Eglwys Dewi Sant, conducted by the Vicar, the Rev. R. M. Rosser. Time was not the all-important factor, and Elvet Thomas had planned their route so that together they could explore and discover as much as possible of South Wales, with particular reference to its historical background. In due time, they arrived at St. David's Cathedral, tired but immensely satisfied with their achievement.

With this kind of association between Elvet Thomas and his members, it is little wonder that many of them were determined to master the Welsh language. One need only name a few of the notable pupils inspired by him, men like Dr. R. M. (Bobi) Jones, Edward G. Millward, Rowland Lucas, Alan Greedy, W. H. Raybould, Gilbert Ruddock, Alan Parsons and Gareth Crandon. These and many more became fully bilingual at a time when there was no language-laboratory and no established schemes of second-language teaching. Even today, many teachers would like to know the secret of Elvet Thomas' success.

*   *   *   *

Financial aid for voluntary organisations was already available. The Board of Education gave grants towards headquarters administration and towards the purchase and adaptation of club premises ; the local education authorities offered grants towards maintenance of clubs, while the Carnegie United Kingdom Trust was prepared to give financial aid towards the cost of books, furniture and equipment. By and large, it was obvious that the Government was generous in its support of the newly formed ' Youth Service '. The Urdd decided that the opportunity should be grasped and that it should aim at setting up a chain of Aelwydydd throughout Wales. And from 1940/41 onwards, the Aelwydydd Campaign was given priority and its organisation entrusted to the Chief Organiser.

With the establishment of Aelwydydd, the Urdd became aware of the need for some form of leaders' training. The technique of dealing with teenagers, meeting in independent premises, was entirely different from working with Adrannau linked with schools. The planning and co-ordinating of this training was entrusted to Margaret Parry, Organiser for Merioneth and Montgomeryshire, and it was she who pioneered in this field. These courses were weekend or vacation courses, and did not in any way constitute a comprehensive scheme of training. They did, however, provide the opportunity for studying the leisure-time needs of youth, as well as the methods of presenting various activities that were likely to appeal to this older age-group no longer prepared to accept the regimentation of school and classroom.

One outstanding personality who came into contact with the Urdd during this period was Eric Ommanney Skaife, an Englishman, and a soldier by profession who had reached the rank of Brigadier. He had been taken prisoner during the First World War, and during his years in prison, he began to learn Welsh and Russian. When peace returned, he found himself at the head of the Royal Welch Fusiliers and applied himself with even greater vigour to the learning of Welsh. It was in this context, through *Cymru'r Plant*, that he first came into contact with the Urdd. When the time came for him to retire from the Army, he decided to make Wales his permanent home, and he first settled at Crogen, near Corwen. It was he who opened the Aelwyd at Llandrillo in 1940, and in doing so, he claimed that it must be the first time that an Englishman in military uniform had opened an Urdd Aelwyd ! Shortly afterwards, he became a Vice-President of the movement, and no-one was ever more faithful to Urdd meetings and events ; no-one was more forthright in his support of the Urdd when occasion demanded ; no-one more determined to make use of the Welsh language whenever possible—even to the extent of putting native Welsh-speakers to shame. He died in 1956, and was buried at Brithdir with the military honours appropriate to his rank, but the burial was preceded by a Welsh service at St. Mary's Church, Dolgellau. The church was crowded, and many could not be accommodated. It was the tribute of the nation to one who had chosen to become a true adopted son of Wales. For the epitaph on his unpretentious tombstone, he had chosen words which, translated, mean ' My heart belonged to Wales ; in its soil lie my remains.'

> *Yng Nghymru yr oedd fy nghalon,*
> *Yn ei thir hi mae fy ngweddillion.*

*   *   *   *

In common with many young men of similar convictions, R. E. Griffith was aware that he would soon have to face a personal crisis. He was a pacifist and a conscientious objector. He was not concerned about any effect this might have on his personal future, but he was worried lest this unpopular conviction might have an adverse effect upon the Urdd, especially in official circles and in the eyes of those authorities whose support was so important to the future growth and development of the movement. Naturally, he discussed his problem with Ifan ab Owen Edwards who, although he did not share his conviction, at least sympathised with him in his dilemma, and understood and appreciated his concern for the movement. When the time came for a decision to be made, it was agreed between them that the Founder should discuss the position with the Executive Committee in R. E. Griffith's absence, informing them that the Chief Organiser would resign his post before being called to appear before the Tribunal as a conscientious objector. The Committee, however, was just as sympathetic as the Founder himself, and he was asked, as Chairman, to write to the Court in support of R. E. Griffith.

A fortnight later, R. E. Griffith appeared before Judge T. Artemus Jones and the Tribunal at Caernarfon. He had already informed the Clerk to the Court that he wished to conduct his case in Welsh and that he did not propose to prepare a written statement in advance. He was given every opportunity to present his case, and the Judge then asked whether he wished to call any witnesses. R. E. Griffith replied in the negative. Looking around the court, the Judge asked, ' Is there no-one in court who knows the appellant ? ' A moment later, Hywel D. Roberts, one of the Urdd's early ' Generals ', moved forward to speak on behalf of his friend and fellow-' General '. R. E. Griffith then handed the Judge a letter from Ifan ab Owen Edwards. The Judge read the letter to the court, and then announced an adjournment. When the Bench returned, R. E. Griffith was surprised to hear the Judge make an eloquent speech in support of the Urdd and its service to Wales. He picked on the phrase *Rhaid i Gymru Fyw*. 'And so,' he went on, ' if Wales is to live, Urdd Gobaith Cymru must live, and for this reason, we release you from military service on condition that you continue to serve the Urdd side-by-side with Ifan ab Owen Edwards.'

For the moment, the clouds had dispersed. Like other conscientious objectors, however, R. E. Griffith had now to live with his conviction. It was to be expected that opposing views would be held by some members of the staff and by many Urdd leaders, but the fact that the Founder and Chief Organiser were able to co-operate although holding conflicting views on this issue made it easier for others to accept that it was possible to respect the other person's view although not necessarily being able to share it. And R. E. Griffith knew well that those who took up arms were just as conscientious in their decision as he himself had been in his. He knew that they looked forward to the time when they could be back in Wales, playing their part in the work of the Urdd movement.

*   *   *   *

In October 1940, two publications were issued by the Urdd. The first was *Gwasanaeth Ieuenctid yng Nghymru* (Youth Service in Wales), a pamphlet which attempted to review objectively the youth situation with special reference to Wales, indicating the pioneering work of the voluntary organisations and tracing the help received from various bodies, particularly the Council of Social Service and the National Fitness Council. It referred to Circular 1486 and the implications of the new partnership advocated by the Government. It gave advice on the setting up and running of Aelwydydd, and indicated the various sources from which help could be obtained.

The pamphlet was, therefore, a handbook for leaders as well as a review of the current Youth Service situation. It gave the new Aelwyd leaders the background information which enabled them to see their work in the context of the Youth Service in general, and also as a significant link in the development of the Urdd from being a children's movement to being a youth movement recognised as such by the Government. The Urdd realised, however, that the pamphlet in itself was not enough. Some means must be devised of providing a more permanent link between the Aelwydydd and one another, and between them and the Urdd as a movement. It was this need that gave rise to *Yr Aelwyd*, a monthly news-letter which first appeared in October 1940.

For its first year, it was a twelve-page duplicated news-letter, distributed free to Aelwydydd and members of the Urdd Council. The task of compiling the news-letter was something R. E. Griffith eagerly looked forward to, but since the extra work of typing and duplicating a monthly bulletin would be too much for the already burdened clerical staff at Swyddfa'r Urdd, R. E. Griffith undertook the task himself, and most of the work involved in preparing the news-letter was done during all-night fire-watching duties. *Yr Aelwyd* was destined to continue for thirty years, but perhaps it is natural that those first duplicated issues meant more to the editor than the more professional-looking magazine which followed in later years.

When the first Annual General Meeting of Governors and Parents of *Ysgol Gymraeg Aberystwyth* was held in October 1940, the year's work was reviewed with satisfaction. Professor Idwal Jones, Dr. Gwenan Jones and R. L. Gapper were now among the educationists on the Board of Governors, and the number of pupils had increased to seventeen. In his report, as Chairman, Ifan ab Owen Edwards expressed his belief that the school had opened a new chapter in the history of education in Wales which could have a far-reaching effect. In the initial stages, it would demand perseverance and sacrifice, but an experiment of this nature was well worth the effort. The school had already, even during its first year, given the pupils a new confidence and self-respect ; a pride in being Welsh and in speaking the language.

*   *   *   *

The Aelwydydd Campaign met with opposition from some of the churches. Early in 1941, the Rev. R. S. Rogers, Editor of *Seren Cymru*, the Baptist weekly, wrote as follows—

> ' It would be a great misfortune if youth of 14 years and over were to concentrate their interest on centres such as the Aelwydydd, where religion is never mentioned.'

The Rev. R. S. Rogers was no doubt alarmed at the obvious success of the Urdd in attracting young people in the 14-20 age-group, and the possible effect on attendances at week-day church meetings. The Urdd, however, felt that his criticism of Aelwydydd as ' centres in which religion is never mentioned ' was unfair and unfounded, and in the April issue of *Yr Aelwyd*, the editor replied to the criticism by referring to the three-fold pledge of the Urdd, and the efforts made in encouraging members to respond to that pledge, which called for loyalty to Christ and his spirit of Love. He also referred to the dilemma the Urdd was facing in trying to encourage its members to adopt a Christian attitude to life, while, at the same time, avoiding unnecessary duplication of religious services and intrusion into spheres best catered for by the churches themselves. If Urdd Branches were to organise their own religious services, they could well be in competition with existing arrangements within the churches. If they refrained, they were accused of being secular. The problem for the Urdd, therefore, was to encourage its members to accept Christian principles, to be positive in their response and their allegiance to Christ without infringing on the existing arrangements of the local churches.

It is fair to note that the editor of *Seren Cymru* was not the only one who feared the effect which the Aelwydydd Campaign might have upon the churches, and partly in an attempt to allay such fears, *Yr Aelwyd* included an article entitled *Aelwydydd yr Urdd ac Eglwysi Cymru* (Urdd Aelwydydd and the Churches of Wales). This referred to the difficulties facing the youth of Wales as a result of the war crisis and the contribution the Aelwydydd could make, provided they were given the support of local community leaders. The article made a special appeal to the churches—

> ' In this crisis, the premier youth movement of Wales has a plan to offer . . . In the wilderness of today, a voice calls "Wales must live"—the language of Wales must live, the culture of

Wales must live, the religion of Wales must live. This is a challenge to the nation to return to the true values of life, to save the soul of Wales. It is a call from the hearts of the leaders of Wales' own national youth movement, a call to all the churches to stand firmly behind this attempt to guide the rising generation into being good Welsh citizens and good Christians. Will the churches respond to the call ? Will they co-operate ? Will they forget minor differences in order to achieve this major aim ? We do not ask this for the sake of the Urdd. The Urdd is but a medium. We ask this for the sake of Wales, with a view to the future of our towns and villages, for the benefit of our society, and for the advancement of religion in the Wales of tomorrow.'

The article went on to suggest ways in which the churches could co-operate and emphasised that the Urdd wished to succeed, not in competition with the churches, but with their aid and their co-operation.

The appeal was discussed in many religious circles with varying response. In many instances, loyalty to one's own denomination or one's own church militated against possible co-operation either with one another or with the Urdd. In other instances, it was hailed with enthusiasm and ministers took up the challenge, either offering their services in the leadership of an existing Aelwyd, or, where no such arrangement existed, taking the initiative in forming an Aelwyd, not only for members of their own church, but for all the youth of the neighbourhood. One notable example was the Rev. James Humphreys, a Rhosllannerchrugog minister who, with the support of his congregation, made premises available, organised Aelwyd activities, and succeeded to such an extent that it eventually became necessary to purchase independent premises and appoint a full-time Warden. To a lesser degree, the same kind of story could be told of the efforts of other clergy throughout Wales, individuals who realised that the Urdd and the churches were, in reality, facing the same problem, and that nothing could be lost and a good deal gained by co-operation.

In March 1941, it became possible to enlist the help of the new Aelwydydd in the Welsh Books Campaign, and as many as 59 Branches took part, selling a total of 7,584 volumes. It seemed as though the war crisis had spurred members and leaders into greater activity and that there was a thrill of satisfaction in being able to overcome the difficulties and restrictions that arose from the war situation.

The same kind of enthusiasm characterised the training schemes during this period. Forty-two Leaders' Courses covering a wide variety of subjects were held during the year. Financial help was received from the local education authorities, and the Urdd was urged by the Board of Education to continue this aspect of its activities. The Board made available a grant of £1,250 towards central administration and with the additional grant of £500 from the Jubilee Trust, it was possible to appoint new staff to relieve a little of the pressure on existing members. On the other hand, it was becoming increasingly difficult to retain the services of young men as full-time staff, and the Urdd had to depend on the part-time help of older men, or men who, for other reasons, were exempt from military service.

It had been intended to hold the 1941 Urdd National Eisteddfod at Treorci. When preparations were begun during the autumn of 1939, enthusiastic Rhondda committee members were hopeful that the war would be over before Whitsun 1941. They, therefore, got down to the task of preparing a syllabus for a full three-day festival, including stage competitions for individual competitors, a feature that had been omitted from the Eisteddfodau of 1938, 1939 and 1940. By the autumn of 1940, however, it became apparent that it would not be possible to hold the national event in 1941, and the Treorci team gallantly handed over their prepared syllabus to the Urdd, and offered to start afresh as soon as hostilities were ended. But although it was not possible to hold the national event, there was no reason why the District Eisteddfodau should not be held as usual, and so the Treorci syllabus was adopted as the official syllabus for the 1941 District Eisteddfodau. It was most encouraging to find that the District Committees responded with enthusiasm, even though competition was to end on the District level. Once more it proved that all need not be lost, and that difficulties can indeed be a spur to greater effort.

It was not without much effort and many worrying moments that arrangements were completed for the 1941 summer camps at Llangrannog. The greatest problem was that of obtaining the necessary permit and petrol to convey the campers to and from Carmarthen station. Eventually, James Griffiths, M.P., Chairman of the Welsh Youth Committee, intervened, and a permit was received just a fortnight before the camps were due to open. The food situation also presented difficulties, and at the last moment, the military authorities declared that camping at Llangrannog would not be allowed. Frantic calls to superior officers were made, permission was granted, and the camps went ahead. Nevertheless, it was now apparent that the difficulties were mounting and that it was doubtful whether camps could again be held at Llangrannog until the war was over.

Without the National Eisteddfod, the Mabolgampau, the cinema, overseas visits and cruises, the war years might indeed appear to have been lean years. But this was not really so. It is true that the publicity and the inspiration derived from these special events was lost. On the other hand, the situation enabled the Urdd to concentrate more on local activities, on District schemes and on the Aelwydydd Campaign, and all this would be a valuable asset when the time came to embark once more on the major national events.

*   *   *   *

Although *Ysgol Gymraeg Aberystwyth*—now a two-teacher school— was making good progress from an educational standpoint, it was, nevertheless, disappointing to have to report to the second Annual Meeting of Parents and Governors that the number of pupils was no higher than 19, an increase of only two pupils. Not only was it disappointing that Welsh-speaking parents were slow to support the school, but it was also clear that the school could not be financially self-supporting without a minimum of 25 pupils. At the same time, the status of the school had been given considerable boost through the publication of a prospectus tracing the origin of the school, its aims and objectives, and including pictures of the pupils at their work.

The prospectus also included comments by three eminent persons who had visited the school—Professor T. Gwynn Jones, Ellen Evans, Principal of Barry Training College, and Professor R. T. Jenkins. All three paid special tribute to the school—its staff and its pupils. It may be sufficient here to quote, in translation, from R. T. Jenkins' comments—

' It is obvious that the children are happily engaged in their lessons. It is also clear that the latest and most interesting teaching methods are employed—and this through the medium of Welsh. I hope that this school will be an example to others in other areas of Wales, while awaiting the day when each one of our local authorities will have awakened to their responsibility, and seen, from the success of *Ysgol Gymraeg Aberystwyth*, that Welsh education through the medium of Welsh is possible without any neglect of English and without sacrificing any of the ' advantages ' which, unfortunately, have been more important in the eyes of many a Welshman than the fostering of his mother tongue.'

One could hardly wish for a better tribute to the school at the end of its first two years. If Aberystwyth parents were somewhat tardy in their support of the scheme, it was obvious that some of Wales' prime educationists were agreed that this little school had opened a significant new chapter in the history of Welsh education.

*   *   *   *

The Aelwydydd Campaign had reached its climax by the autumn of 1941. When the May number of *Yr Aelwyd* appeared, it contained a map of Wales showing the location of the Aelwydydd—83 in number. By the beginning of December, the number had risen to 98, and there were more to come. This development put a heavy strain on the Field Organisers—particularly Elwyn Jones, Eunice Roberts and Margaret Parry—who had to maintain personal contact with the Aelwydydd, guiding them in their first eager but faltering steps. It also increased the work of the staff at Swyddfa'r Urdd, since there were applications for grants, insurance policies, etc. to be dealt with. In addition, when the Aelwydydd Campaign was first launched, the Urdd had undertaken to contribute £5-£10 to each new Aelwyd, to tide them over the period until they could obtain help from the LEA. It had not been evisaged that, within a period of eighteen months, over £500 would have been paid. Even by the winter of 1940, the Aelwydydd Fund was exhausted and a fresh appeal was made for contributions from well-wishers. With his usual generosity,

J. M. Howell was the first to respond. Contributions were also received from well-established Aelwydydd ready to help those who had not yet found their feet. By the end of 1941, another £750 had been received into the Aelwydydd Fund.

The acquisition of premises and equipment meant new and additional responsibilities both for Cwmni'r Urdd and for the Aelwydydd Committees. Insurances had to be arranged and, naturally, the war had increased the hazards. The Aelwyd premises at Brynaman were damaged during bombing raids on Swansea and before the end of 1940 the Aelwyd at Fforest-fach suffered the same fate. A letter from the Aelwyd leader read—

> ' It is only a few weeks since the Aelwyd at Fforest-fach was declared open. Today it is even more open than ever ! The windows and doors were destroyed during the latest *blitz* on Swansea. Still, you will be glad to know that we are not despondent, and the good work goes on.'

At the end of 1941, *Cymru'r Plant* was on the threshold of its fiftieth birthday, and in the December issue of *Yr Aelwyd*, the editor drew attention to the fact that *Cymru'r Plant* had appeared without a break since January 1892. In his birthday tribute to *Cymru'r Plant*, R. E. Griffith said—

> ' It was *Cymru'r Plant* that brought the Urdd into being, and the Urdd, in turn, brought the Aelwydydd into being. Wales is therefore greatly indebted to the yellow-covered magazine and its two editors. What if Sir Owen M. Edwards had not started *Cymru'r Plant* ? It is possible that Ifan ab Owen Edwards would not then have founded the Urdd. Close your eyes for a moment, and try to imagine Wales without the Urdd.'

Early in 1941, the War Office and its departments had begun to exert pressure on the voluntary youth organisations. They sought their aid in training boys and girls of 16-18 years in preparation for service in the Air Training Corps and the Women's Auxiliary Air Force. The Urdd took pains to explain to the Ministry of Aviation what kind of movement it was, pointing out that it did not agree with a policy of conditioning the minds of boys and girls under 18 to techniques of destruction, but that it would willingly encourage its members to give social and humanitarian service within their locality, and to take part, where necessary, in civil defence. This argument was accepted, and no further pressure was exerted for some months. However, on December 20, 1941, the Board of Education issued its Circular 1577, ' Registration of Youth ', in which it outlined the policy of the Government under which boys and girls in the 16-18 age-group were required to register and join either one of the recognised youth organisations or one of the pre-service organisations such as the A.T.C. or the Army Cadets. There was also a suggestion that the registration of the 14-16 age-group might follow. The aim was to ensure that every boy and girl would be associated with some recognised organisation which would enable them to give service of some kind during the war crisis.

The Urdd was quick to see that some action was necessary. As one of the recognised youth movements referred to in the Circular, it felt that every Welsh-speaking person within the specified age-group should at least be given the opportunity of joining a non-military organisation. For the Urdd, this meant winning new members and establishing new Aelwydydd.

It was a challenge to the Urdd ; it was also a challenge to church leaders and to teachers to ensure that the opportunity was within reach of every boy and girl. Ifan ab Owen Edwards and R. E. Griffith prepared a Declaration which was put to a special meeting of the Urdd Executive Committee. It was readily accepted and immediately circulated to the Board of Education, to Aelwydydd, to churches, to secondary schools, and to the press. The Declaration indicated that the aim of the Urdd was to foster Welsh Christian citizenship amongst the youth of Wales, and that it would continue to concentrate its efforts on community service, leaving any other provision the Government considered necessary to the authorities concerned. It outlined the basic demands that would be made on the young people who wished to register as Urdd members under the Government Registration Act, and it appealed for the support and co-operation of the entire nation in providing for the youth of Wales the opportunity it needed and deserved.

6

THE 1942 Urdd Eisteddfod was to have been held at Corwen, and just as the stalwarts of the Rhondda had hopefully prepared a syllabus for the previous year, so too the men and women of Edeyrnion prepared for 1942. They knew, of course, that if the war continued, the Eisteddfod could not be held, but since the syllabus had to be ready well in advance, they could only hope and be prepared. At the turn of the year, however, it became apparent that peace was still a long way off, and once again, it was regretfully decided that the National Eisteddfod would have to be postponed.

The syllabus, however, was adopted as a scheme of work for the Branches, and as usual, more than sixty District Eisteddfodau were held. For the first time, special competitions for Aelwydydd were included. This proved not only to be an incentive to greater activity on the club level, but also helped to strengthen the liaison between the Aelwydydd and one another and between the Aelwydydd and the Urdd as a national movement. Occasionally—due in part to travel restrictions—there was a tendency for some Aelwydydd to see themselves as local clubs only, but on the whole, there was ample evidence of a sense of identification with the Urdd and with Wales. It was this sense of ' belonging ' that made so many of them join the Adrannau in the Welsh Books Campaign for 1942, so that, together, ninety-nine Branches sold a total of 17,378 volumes, an increase of ten-thousand, and this despite the growing restrictions imposed by wartime conditions.

One noticeable feature in the Aelwydydd Campaign was the fact that it was so much easier to establish an Aelwyd where a flourishing Adran was already in existence. Time also proved that the Aelwydydd which graduated from existing Adrannau were also the most stable and the ones most easily and strongly linked with the Urdd as a national movement. These were the Aelwydydd which survived the exigencies of war, and were able to carry on into the post-war period when they were no longer restricted by the demands of compulsory registration. This realisation brought home to the Urdd the need to maintain the work of the Adrannau, side-by-side with the Aelwydydd Campaign, despite the emphasis which the Government had already begun to lay on the older age-groups.

By the end of March, the effect of the appeal to the churches was beginning to make itself felt. The entire nation had been roused by the Registration Act, and when the churches saw that the declared aim of the Urdd was ' to promote Welsh Christian citizenship ', and that this was acceptable to the Government, there was a flood of applications from churches wishing to set up Aelwydydd, sometimes within a single church, but, more often, a community Aelwyd run by a group of churches working in co-operation. The second was, of course, the more acceptable as there was a danger of a one-church Aelwyd becoming no more than a church-society assuming the title of an Aelwyd for the sake of convenience.

Three months after the publication of Circular 1577, the number of Aelwydydd had more than trebled, from 109 to 362. This sudden growth-trend was not so obvious in the case of ' English ' voluntary organisations operating in Wales, and it was certainly not true of voluntary organisations in England. The response in Wales caused considerable surprise in government circles and served to emphasise that there were important differences in the reactions of the two nations. In England, the pre-service units were far more popular than they were in Wales and even brought about a drop in the membership of some of the voluntary organisations. In Wales, on the other hand, especially in the Welsh-speaking areas, whatever views people held on the war itself, the majority supported the Urdd in its disapproval of pre-service military training. And although the Government was surprised at this attitude, the Urdd was given every encouragement to carry on according to its own policy.

It was natural that the new Aelwydydd which sprung into being with mushroom suddenness during the first half of 1942 did not have the same stability as those established in 1940 and 1941 when committees were urged to think in terms of independent premises in which the Aelwyd could meet on two or three evenings a week for a variety of activities. Such conditions would obviously not be immediately practicable in the case of the two-hundred-and-fifty Aelwydydd which were launched within a period of a few months. Most of these met once a week in any available premises. It is true, however, that many were gradually spurred to greater activity and came closer to the image which the Urdd had in mind for its Senior Branches.

In the 1942-43 financial year, the Jubilee Trust grant of £500 was renewed, and the Board of Education increased its headquarters grant from £1,250 to £1,850. Grants were also made to Aelwydydd by the Board of Education, the local education authorities and the Carnegie U.K. Trust. The Urdd ' Aelwydydd Appeal ' had raised another £1,000, and altogether, the financial position was fairly satisfactory. Three staunch friends of the Urdd during this period were Sir Wynn Wheldon, Permanent Secretary of the Welsh Department of the Board of Education ; H. E. Melvin, Youth Secretary in the Welsh Department, and James Griffiths, M.P., Chairman of the Welsh Youth Committee. It was on them that the Urdd depended to interpret the movement and its aims to the Board of Education ; and it was to them that the Urdd turned when the War Office and its departments made threatening noises. In any difficulty, the Urdd knew it could turn to these three, confident that its plea would fall on sympathetic ears.

The movement also had good friends among the local education authorities of Wales—Councillors, Directors of Education and Youth Organisers. Generally speaking, they were well aware of the contribution made by the Urdd long before they themselves were called upon to co-operate in the establishment of the Youth Service. Both the statutory bodies and the voluntary organisations realised that the corner-stone of the partnership envisaged by the Board of Education was co-operation rather than competition, though it was difficult to see how the LEA's could set up their own system without militating to some extent against the interests of the voluntary organisations. It was natural that both partners would be anxious to promote their own schemes, and that some tension would inevitably occur. Even during 1942, it was already apparent that it would not always be easy for the voluntary organisations to maintain their independence of action while, at the same time, co-operating with the statutory bodies to the extent envisaged by the Board of Education.

It was not surprising that the language problem should again be raised—this time in connection with the Aelwydydd. The Urdd had already decided that *Dysgwyr* should be accepted into full membership of Adrannau, and should be incorporated into the system both on the local and national levels. In initiating the Aelwydydd Campaign, it was natural that the Council should consider what place should be given to the non-Welsh-speakers in the older age-group. Should the Urdd set up Aelwydydd which were Welsh in atmosphere though the language was English? While this was under consideration, however, the Youth Registration Act came into force, and in the turmoil that followed, the question of the *Dysgwyr* had to be left in abeyance. It was not long, however, before the matter was settled by the non-Welsh-speakers themselves. They pressed for the immediate establishment of a counterpart to the Aelwydydd, and it was thus that the 'Young Wales Clubs' came into being. They would have the same ideals as the Aelwydydd; the traditions and history of Wales would be their inspiration, and service to Wales would be their aim. As one would expect, the call for the establishment of such clubs first came from Glamorgan, and it was fortunate that the Urdd had, in Elwyn Jones, an organiser in full sympathy with this new development. Once the scheme was launched, the next step would be to produce an English-language magazine that would act as a link between the clubs as well as a vehicle for information and ideas. To aid this new development, a sub-office at Pontardawe was placed at the disposal of the Organiser.

The camp at Llangrannog had to remain closed during the summer of 1942, much to the disappointment of Urdd members. But just as they were bemoaning this fact, Elwyn Jones discovered a small camp at Llanmadog on the Gower peninsula which could be made available to Aelwydydd members during one week in August. For the 22 boys, 14 girls and 9 leaders who attended, it was a week to be remembered—the very first camp to be organised for members of Aelwydydd, mostly young people at work and within the 17-20 age group.

The magazine *Yr Aelwyd* had only reached its second birthday in the summer of 1942, when the authorities responsible for the conservation of paper supplies decreed that the necessary paper for its continued independent existence could not be made available. Faced with this crisis, it was decided that *Cymru'r Plant* should take it under its wing, and that the available twenty-four pages would be shared equally between them. Despite the curtailment on regular publications, there seemed to be no such restriction on *ad hoc* publications. Taking advantage of this, four new Urdd publications appeared during the autumn. The first was *Llyfr o Wasanaethau Crefyddol ar gyfer Ieuenctid Cymru* (Religious Services for Welsh Youth). Eight years had elapsed since the first handbook of services appeared and six-thousand copies were sold. The previous handbook had largely been intended for Adrannau, and now those children's services were incorporated in the new handbook, with the addition of twelve services for Aelwydydd. The publication of this new handbook, under the editorship of the Rev. Principal G. A. Edwards, did much to convince the churches that the Urdd was justified in maintaining that its aim was ' to foster Welsh Christian citizenship ', with the result that still more churches were ready to offer their co-operation.

*   *   *   *

It was now obvious that the Urdd National Eisteddfod could not be held until the war was over, and it was not fair to allow local committees, one after the other, to draw up a scheme of competitions, even though the material could be used as a syllabus for the District Eisteddfodau. Some feeling of frustration was bound to remain, despite the promise that the Urdd would turn to them again as soon as possible after the war was ended. It was, therefore, decided to set up a panel of experts who would draw up an annual scheme of work appropriate to the demands of various ages and interests. The scheme was published in booklet form, entitled *Awgrymiadau* (Programme Suggestions) and each District Committee was free to base its own Eisteddfod syllabus on these suggestions.

It was in October 1942 that *Dyddiadur Tomos Bifan* (Tomos Bifan's Diary) first appeared in *Yr Aelwyd*. It was intended simply as a means of bringing a little light relief into an otherwise serious magazine, Tomos Bifan being an imaginary simple character living in an imaginary village in Anglesey. He was a grocer, active in the work of the chapel, and a shrewd observer—and commentator —on the Welsh scene in general. With his humour and his lively comments, he became so popular a character that the monthly diary lasted for twenty-one years !

*   *   *   *

1942 was a successful year in the history of *Ysgol Gymraeg Aber-ystwyth*. For no apparent reason, though it was no doubt partly due to the publication of the prospectus, the number of pupils rose from 19 to 32. Perhaps it also had something to do with the fact that a number of professional people had sent their children to the school, not because it was a private school—for there were already two good private schools in the town possessing much better facilities—but because they felt that this was the school that provided the kind of education they wished their children to receive.

Thirty-two pupils meant two classes of reasonable proportions and Mrs. R. E. Griffith, an experienced infants' teacher and a former student of Barry Training College, was appointed to take charge of the infants, leaving Norah Isaac free to concentrate on the juniors. The older pupils were now fluent in Welsh and English, and Norah Isaac decided to introduce French as a third language. Lessons in harp-playing too were given by Alwena Roberts (Telynores Iâl) to those interested in instrumental music. Perhaps the most interesting project, however, was the production of the school magazine, *Dail Gwanwyn* (Spring Leaves). It was entirely the unaided work of the pupils, typed by eight-year old Owen Edwards, and duplicated and assembled by other 5-8 year olds. At Christmas, the first school concert was given, and this, together with *Dail Gwanwyn*, was sufficient to prove—to anyone who still had any doubts—that the school was capable of giving each child the opportunity to develop his or her own skills and personality.

At the Annual General Meeting of Parents and Governors, Ifan ab Owen Edwards was elected first President of the school, and his place as Chairman was taken by the Rev. J. E. Meredith. It was announced that the Board of Education was keenly interested in the Welsh School experiment. One of the Board's Inspectors had spent some time at the school, but although he had made a very favourable report, it was learnt that the school could not be officially recognised until it had 30 pupils in the 7-11 age-range, more space, and better facilities. There were now more parents who wished to send their children to the school, but the school was confined to two classrooms of limited size, so that no further expansion was possible. Even when the military authorities relinquished the hall which had been requisitioned in 1939, it could not be used as a classroom as it would be needed for Aelwyd activities in the evenings. Discussing the problem with R. E. Griffith, Ifan ab Owen Edwards remarked ' The little Welsh school is becoming a big school. The only way it can expand is for us as a family or Swyddfa'r Urdd—or both—to move out'. And it was not long before he announced that they as a family—now with the addition of their younger son, Prys—were looking for a new home.

During the winter of 1942, another attempt was made to consolidate the field staff. New appointments were made, including Beryl Owen as Organiser for Merioneth and Montgomeryshire, Muriel Evans as Organiser for Cardiganshire and North Pembrokeshire, and for the first time, an Organiser for Brecon and Radnor in the person of W. R. Jones. In all, the Urdd once more had a staff of 16, with combined salaries of over three-thousand pounds. Even so, it was felt that each region was too large to be effectively covered by one person, particularly at a time when petrol rationing, of necessity, limited travelling distances. To ease the situation, a number of part-time Organisers, people well-acquainted with the Urdd and its activities, agreed to help within their own areas. They did so because of their dedication to the movement and were well aware that their financial remuneration would be very meagre. They made a valuable contribution, especially during the upsurge following the Registration Act when the Aelwydydd were springing up in such numbers.

When the Annual General Meeting of *Cwmni'r Urdd* was held at Aberystwyth in October 1942, the Founder was in high spirits as he reviewed the development of the past year and recalled that the Urdd now had nearly four-hundred Adrannau and another four hundred Aelwydydd or *Uwch-Adrannau* (Senior Branches). After ten years as Treasurer, W. J. Williams of Llangystennin resigned and his place was taken by Prof. D. Hughes Parry of the London School of Economics. W. J. Williams, Rachel Davies and Brigadier E. O. Skaife were elected Vice-Presidents, and Dr. Gwenan Jones took over from Rachel Davies the duties of Vice-Chairman.

*   *   *   *

The leading article in the January issue of *Yr Aelwyd* appeared under the title *Teyrnged* (Tribute) and in it, R. E. Griffith paid tribute to the Founder on the occasion of the Urdd's twenty-first birthday.

> ' Twenty-one years ago, on the first of January, 1922, Urdd Gobaith Cymru was founded . . . Today we pay tribute to our leader. We rejoice with him, and thank him for the heritage handed on by him to the youth of Wales. He taught us to love Wales with an inextinguishable love ; he inspired us to serve our country without counting the cost. He did so, not by preaching at us, but by living his life as he would like the youth of Wales to live. What will last will not be anything he said or anything he wrote, but what he accomplished.'

Plans for celebrating the event were already in hand although they had to be tailored to fit the restrictions inevitable in war conditions. The first of these plans was the publication of *Yr Urdd : 1922—1943*, a booklet written by Ifan ab Owen Edwards tracing the development of the movement during the twenty-one years of its existence. In the last chapter, he wrote—

> ' I am now growing older, and it is the young who should lead a youth movement . . . Wales is your heritage, to be cherished and handed on to the next generation as we handed it on to you. The task of creating the new Wales, the Wales of tomorrow, is yours.'

In the preface, Ifan ab Owen Edwards pays tribute to his wife and lists the many ways in which she had helped him ever since the Urdd was founded. He went on,—

> ' Above all, she patiently suffered her husband's impatience when he was tired and fatigued, and it was she who invariably urged him to follow his ideals at the expense of personal advancement.'

The first celebration was naturally held at Llanuwchllyn on the 1st January, where there was a gathering of Adrannau in the afternoon and of Aelwydydd in the evening.

Most papers and magazines in Wales had agreed to include an article on the movement some time during the first quarter of 1943. Forty different articles by forty writers duly appeared and, but for paper restrictions, these would have been published later as one volume.

The restrictions, however, did not prevent the printing of *Gwasanaeth o Fawl a Diolch* (Service of Praise and Thanksgiving), prepared by the Revs. G. A. Edwards and Gwilym Owen of Aberystwyth. The leaflet was in immediate demand by Adrannau and Aelwydydd and the ten-thousand copies were sold within a few weeks. Scores of religious services based on the leaflet were held at the end of February and the beginning of March.

A special Twenty-First Fund had been given a target of £2,000 and after J. M. Howell—who had himself, from time to time, contributed more than £10,000 to the Urdd—had broadcast his appeal, a total of £2,431 was received in contributions.

The main event, however, was the national meeting held at Aberystwyth on the 5th March. Representatives of all Adrannau and Aelwydydd had been invited, and the King's Hall was filled to capacity. The Chair was taken by Ifan ab Owen Edwards and the two guest speakers were The Rt. Hon. R. A. Butler, P.C., M.A., M.P., President of the Board of Education, who spoke in English, and James Griffiths, M.P., Chairman of the Welsh Youth Committee, who spoke in Welsh.

In the midst of the celebration when all Wales was paying its tribute to the Urdd, one dissentient voice was heard. It appeared in a *Penguin Special* entitled ' Young Citizen ' by Dr. A. E. Morgan—

' In these days, when the world needs wider horizons and a breaking down of nationalist barriers, it is unfortunate that Welsh youth should be subjected to the influence of a body which is based on such a narrow foundation. Its leaders will doubtless rebut the charge and claim that on the basis of Welsh patriotism it is possible to build citizenship of the world. The question remains why it is necessary to have an organisation peculiar to Wales. Within the Scout and Guide movements everything that the Welsh League of Youth believes in could find scope, with the great advantage that they are organisations with international affiliations and an outlook which is bounded only by the utmost brotherhood and sisterhood of humanity . . . The League is certainly doing valuable work among its members, but in the interests of concerted and economical effort for youth as a whole it is to be regretted that particularist organisations should compete in a field where so much remains to be done and the utmost co-operation is needed.'

Instead of replying to his criticism, the Urdd decided to send Dr. Morgan a copy of three tributes, two of which were paid by The Rt. Hon. R. A. Butler, M.P., and James Griffiths, M.P. That of R. A. Butler concluded with the words—

'If you develop your activities along original lines, you may well provide England with an example such as the Welsh nation has done in secondary education. We in England may need your Celtic imagination to enable us to cope with the world problems of the future. Do not be afraid of being patriotic.'

James Griffiths came to a similar conclusion.

'During the twenty-one years of its existence, the Urdd has made three unique contributions : it has helped to keep alive the Welsh language in a period of great difficulties ; it has fostered a healthy and safe patriotism ; it has created a youth organisation which, in many ways, is an example of what a youth organisation ought to be.'

The third tribute was paid in his leading article by the Editor of the *Times Educational Supplement,* following the Aberystwyth meeting—

'The occasion proved as moving and inspiring as it was significant and historic. It was a remarkable demonstration of unity and of the successful development of a great youth movement . . . The central purpose of the Urdd is to foster a truly Welsh citizenship based on the Christian religion and ethos. In pursuit of this aim, it keeps entirely free of political affiliations and sectarian ties, but stresses the international aspect of citizenship and seeks by all possible means to strengthen the bonds of friendship between the youth of Wales and those of other lands. . . . The Urdd has captured the imagination of young Wales as no other movement of this century has done, and the surging tide of its progress shows no signs of having reached high-water mark. It has shown itself capable of wise expansion and beyond doubt is capable of yet more, linking up, as it has done in the past, with other organisations in pursuit of the same ideals. Wales is unique in these islands in having brought to birth a spontaneous national youth movement ; not to allow that movement fully to mature would be to lose a great opportunity.'

Nothing more was heard from Dr. A. E. Morgan.

At the height of its preparations for the celebrations, Swyddfa'r Urdd was in the throes of moving home. More space was needed by *Yr Ysgol Gymraeg*, and the Executive Committee had authorised Swyddfa'r Urdd to search for alternative premises. In January, new premises were found in the town centre, and a month before the national celebration meeting, staff and equipment were moved to new quarters.

*   *   *   *

The panel's *Awgrymiadau* (Programme Suggestions) were published and were adopted for the 1943 District Eisteddfodau. This time, however, there was another new feature. Some of the County Committees were persuaded to experiment with a County Eisteddfod. In these cases, winners at the District Eisteddfod went on to compete at the County Eisteddfod. The move was well received, and this saw the beginning of a new link in the Eisteddfod system which could well be adopted when the time came to reinstate the Eisteddfod on the national level. In the meantime, it was decided that all County Committees would in future be urged to make arrangements for a County Eisteddfod.

Having sold 17,375 Welsh books in 1942 through the efforts of 99 Branches, it did not seem unreasonable that the Urdd should raise its target for 1943 to 20,000. By St. David's Day, 188 Branches had agreed to take part, and with the sale of 39,625 volumes, they almost succeeded in doubling the target. There was now no doubt that the Welsh Books Campaign had become an important factor in Welsh publishing and it was decided to call a conference of Welsh Publishers to discuss its significance and to see whether any changes appeared to be necessary. Having outlined the role played by the Urdd Campaign and the arrangements made for the following year, the conference went on to discuss the advisability of establishing an Association of Welsh Publishers and Booksellers and setting up a national centre for the distribution of Welsh books. Representatives of the Urdd and of the publishers were elected to prepare a memorandum for the next meeting. Ifan ab Owen Edwards was more than satisfied, and on the way home, he remarked to R. E. Griffith— ' We have embarked on something important today. It will take years, but a beginning has been made.'

During the winter of 1942 /43, efforts were concentrated on establishing Young Wales Clubs in the Anglicised areas of South Wales. In Glamorgan and Monmouthshire, even where the language had largely disappeared, there was still a strong element of Welsh awareness. This was not true to the same extent of Brecon and Radnor. In Breconshire, although there were still areas that were entirely Welsh-speaking, English was the language of three-quarters of the population. In Radnorshire, less than 5% of the population could speak Welsh. In these two counties, W. R. Jones found that he had to struggle against considerable ignorance and prejudice regarding all matters having a Welsh bias. Many thought the Urdd was a political organisation, some that it was a Non-conformist organisation, others that it was a secular, Fascist organis-ation similar to Germany's *Hitler Jugend*. Nevertheless, with characteristic patience and determination, W. R. Jones gradually succeeded in making a break-through and, within a period of two years, a whole network of Young Wales Clubs were formed in places such as Brecon, Builth Wells, Talgarth, Llandrindod, Llanbedr-Castell-Paen, Trefyclo (Knighton), and Llangynllo. They were English in speech, but as time went on, they became progressively Welsh in atmosphere and in conviction.

Another 1943 development was the setting up of *Adran y Merched* (Girls' Section). This was not an attempt to segregate the sexes but an acknowledgement of the fact that there were activities of partic-ular interest to girls, and that more attention would be paid to these activities when they did not have to compete with other attractions! Regional committees were set up, as well as a National Committee with Mrs. Ifan ab Owen Edwards as President, Dr. Gwenan Jones as Chairman and Margaret Parry as Secretary. Weekend courses were organised, suggestions drawn up of activities for girls in Aelwydydd and Young Wales Clubs, and a lending library of reference books for leaders made available. Another facet of their activities was the effort made to maintain contact with Welsh girls doing wartime work in Wales and the Midlands. Un-fortunately, however, *Adran y Merched* lost its main-spring when Margaret Parry left to be married after four years of very notable service, as county organiser, as training officer, and as Secretary of *Adran y Merched*.

It was obvious that it would not be possible to make use of the camp at Llangrannog during the summer of 1943, and this had to be accepted as inevitable. Moreover, the War Office had cast its eye on the premises and had made enquiries regarding the possibility of purchase. The Urdd Committee, however, decided to resist any attempt to purchase the premises, though it was prepared, if pressed, to allow its use for civil defence. This would at least make it possible for the Urdd to return as soon as the war was over.

The experiment at Llanmadog in 1942 had opened up further possibilities for 1943 and arrangements were made to hold three weeks of camping there in late August and September. Because of travel restrictions, it was decided to confine the camps to members from South Wales, one week being reserved for Young Wales Clubs and the other two for Aelwydydd. It was the first time that a camp for Young Wales Clubs had been held but, to everyone's surprise, it was even more successful than the Aelwydydd weeks. For the North Wales members, the Aelwyd at Caernarfon was turned into a hostel for the whole of August. There were expeditions in Snowdonia, to Llŷn and Ynys Enlli (Bardsey Island) and across Menai to Anglesey.

The third residential scheme was a fortnight's summer school for sixty older girls and leaders held in a school hostel at Dolgellau. It was the first major course organised by *Adran y Merched* and there were lectures and group-practice in craftwork, folk-dancing, folk-songs and *cerdd dant*. By 1943 many of the local education authorities were organising their own courses for youth leaders. It was an opportunity for the leaders of all organisations to share experiences and skills, and to discuss plans and problems. Many Urdd leaders attended these courses at Bangor and Bala, while 25 attended a course organised by the Board of Education at Borth. All these were welcome additions to the camps and courses organised by the Urdd itself, but it was felt that nothing could make up for the loss of the camps at Llangrannog and both members and leaders eagerly awaited the day when they could return to their own precincts.

Altogether, 1943 seemed to be a year of new projects and experiments. One of these was *Senedd yr Aelwydydd* (Youth Council) arranged by the Meirionnydd County Committee at the instigation of Margaret Parry. Five topics were submitted for discussion by the

Aelwydydd, and each Aelwyd was then asked to send two representatives to the Youth Council held on May 29 at the County Hall,
Dolgellau. Two members opened the debate on each topic, and
these were followed by speakers from the floor. All the members
were in the 16-21 age-group and they took their task seriously and
debated in earnest. They were very conscious of the defects in their
society and of their own responsibility in any effort to create a ' new
world '. Listening to their discussion, and observing their
earnestness, R. E. Griffith looked forward to the day when every
county had its Youth Council, which might conceivably lead to the
formation of a national Council of Youth.

Another development arose from the new interest in mountain-
rambling, especially in North Wales. The absence of national
events seemed to act as a spur to greater activity on the District
and County levels, and fell-walking seemed to provide a substitute
for the challenge of the mabolgampau on the one hand and the
social recreation of the camps on the other. On Whit Monday,
twenty-six members of the Penfforddelen Aelwyd climbed Snowdon,
and on the same morning, sixty-seven members from Meirionnydd
and Maldwyn (Montgomeryshire) set out to climb Cader Idris, the
one from Dolgellau and the other from Talyllyn, planning to meet
on the summit. The Meirionnydd contingent duly arrived, but there
was no sign of the Maldwyn group. Assuming that the Maldwyn
climbers had turned back because of misty conditions, the Meirionnydd group set off on the return journey. They had almost
reached the foot of Cader Idris when they heard the Maldwyn
climbers singing at the summit ! Undaunted, they made it an
excuse for planning another expedition at a later date.

But perhaps the most memorable event was the hundred-strong
three-county expedition to the summit of the Berwyn range. The
Meirionnydd group were led from Llandderfel by Bob Lloyd
(*Llwyd o'r Bryn*) while the Dinbych and Maldwyn groups set out
from Llangynog led by Robert Richards, M.P. This time, the groups
met according to plan, and immediately began to prepare a hearty
meal, food coupons forgotten ! Then, after a brief devotional
service, there was an interlude of verse and song, interspersed with
stories recounted by the inimitable Bob Lloyd.

' With due respect to the mountains of Wales,' wrote D. Tecwyn Lloyd in the early summer, ' we of Llawr-y-betws Aelwyd are off on a scout to Scotland.' This was a group of boys bent on real mountain-walking in the Grampians and the Cairngorms. Led by Tecwyn Lloyd and Islwyn Pritchard—then a Youth Leader in Dundee—they covered an average of 20 miles a day, spending the nights in Youth Hostels.

During the spring of 1943, the Urdd was informed that the Army would be vacating the Aberystwyth Urdd premises at the end of June. This meant that *Yr Ysgol Gymraeg* would have the use of the hall during the day, while it would be available to the Aelwyd in the evening. By this time, however, the ranks of the Aelwyd were seriously depleted and it was decided to experiment with a bilingual youth club. The LEA and the Town Council gave their ready support, and since the registration of the 16-18 age group was still in force, there was no lack of members. This called for the appointment of a full-time Warden, and I was offered the vacancy. I gave up my teaching post at *Ysgol Sir Aberteifi* (Cardigan County School) and launched into a new career at the beginning of September. This was not the only appointment of its kind made by the Urdd during this period and a team of full-time club Wardens rapidly followed.

Ysgol Gymraeg Aberystwyth had now become popular, even respectable, and all Wales knew of its existence. With the additional premises made available through the departure of Swyddfa'r Urdd, it could now aim at a total of 50-60 pupils. By September, the school already had 45 pupils on its register, and Mary Vaughan Jones had been appointed as the third full-time teacher.

The Urdd Annual General Meeting was held at Pontypridd. In recounting the events of the year and commenting on their success in the face of wartime difficulties, Ifan ab Owen Edwards said—

' And this is as it should be in the year in which the Urdd comes of age. It is encouraging for us, who saw the founding of the movement, to realise that the Urdd is not growing old as it grows older.'

It was the Rev. George M. Ll. Davies who rose to move the adoption of the report, and the young men and women who had been with him at Llanmadog Camp a month earlier gave him a rousing welcome. A public meeting followed, attended by large numbers of Aelwydydd and Young Wales Club members. They were addressed in English by Rhys Hopkin Morris, Controller of the BBC in Wales, and in Welsh by Ben Bowen Thomas.

By mid 1943, the pattern of the Youth Service was emerging more clearly. The statutory bodies were organising leaders' courses and these were intended for LEA club leaders and for leaders of voluntary organisations. Urdd leaders were urged to participate in these courses and to benefit by sharing basic training with leaders of other organisations. At the same time, the voluntary organisations still felt the need for their own courses, dealing specifically with those activities in which they specialised, and at the same time, providing the inspiration to work together for the ideals which had first brought them into the movement. It was not always easy to persuade some LEA's that voluntary leadership could be a valuable asset within the pattern of the Youth Service. With the financial means at their disposal, several Authorities began to set up their own clubs and either appoint full-time Wardens or offer financial remuneration to teachers who were prepared to act as part-time leaders. The Urdd, on the other hand, though lacking the financial and material resources that the statutory bodies could provide, set great store on voluntary work, on ideals and inspiration. The danger of competition, instead of co-operation, became apparent whenever the authorities set up LEA Youth Clubs, instead of Youth Centres in which the voluntary organisations could freely share the amenities. The result of this policy was to force the Urdd to continue its campaign to purchase or erect independent premises, even though it was realised that, despite grants, such a policy placed a very heavy burden both on the Urdd Council and the Aelwyd Committees. It was one of the problems that the voluntary organisations had foreseen—and feared—when the Government first proposed the setting up of the Youth Service.

7

1944 saw the introduction of a new Urdd Gobaith Cymru badge. The first badge had been designed by Mrs. Ifan ab Owen Edwards before she was married, and had been used for over twenty years. It was not without a good deal of nostalgia that it was finally decided to introduce a new and entirely different badge, designed by R. L. Gapper of Aberystwyth. When he first showed his design to the Executive Committee, he explained—

> ' A badge is a symbol, and as such, the simpler the better. My task is to design a symbol that will denote membership of the Urdd. If you can see your ideals expressed in the symbol so much the better, but that is a matter for the individual.'

Generations of Urdd members have since cherished the triangular badge, and the three coloured bands—green, red and white—have become a symbol of their pledge of loyalty and service to Wales, to fellow-man, and to Christ.

By 1944, many hundreds of Urdd members had spent two, three or even four years in the armed forces, some in Britain, but many more overseas. Being away from home under war conditions was in itself a burden on their spirit, and the Urdd was anxious that their fellow-members at home should do what they could to ease that burden. Aelwydydd were urged to keep in touch with the absent members and to send them news of what was happening in their own Aelwyd, in the Urdd as a movement, and in Wales. The National Library of Wales had undertaken to send free parcels of books, periodicals and records to young Welsh exiles, and Urdd members were asked to raise money towards the cost of the project. At this time too, a large number of Welshmen were stationed in the Middle East and had formed Welsh Societies, some of which were registered as Aelwydydd. These Societies were linked with one another and with Wales through their newspaper *Seren y Dwyrain* (Star of the East) edited by T. Elwyn Griffiths of Llandybie. The production of this paper—printed in Welsh in Cairo and distributed free to more than fifteen-hundred Welshmen—was something of a miracle. Having heard of the venture and of the need to extend the service, the Urdd appealed for funds towards the cost of producing and distributing the journal to an ever-growing membership of Welsh Societies in exile.

It was in 1944 too that the Urdd was privileged to play a part in adding the Welsh version of the Lord's Prayer to the existing versions in forty-one languages which already adorned the walls of the *Pater Noster* Church on the Mount of Olives. In the early summer, Richard Hughes, President of the Jerusalem Welsh Society, wrote to Swyddfa'r Urdd saying that hundreds of Welsh soldiers had visited the church during the past years, and many had expressed their disappointment that the Welsh version was not included. Did the Urdd think that Wales could do anything to remedy the situation? Without even waiting for a committee decision, Ifan ab Owen Edwards and R. E. Griffith agreed to write to Richard Hughes saying that the Urdd would be responsible for the cost if he could make the necessary arrangements. Without delay, Richard Hughes chose a favourable spot inside the church, obtained the necessary permission, and commissioned the best craftsman in Jerusalem to do the work. While this was going on, the Urdd appealed to every member, through Adrannau, Aelwydydd and Young Wales Clubs, to contribute personally towards the cost of the project. The response was excellent, and it was the shillings and sixpences of the members themselves that helped to make the dream a reality. Later that year, Richard Hughes wrote to say that the work was completed to their satisfaction. Strange as it might seem, the first person to visit the spot just as the craftsman was carving the last letter was a Welshman and a former Urdd member—Emyr Currie-Jones of Caernarfon, now Honorary Solicitor to the Urdd, living in Cardiff. It was thus that the youth of Wales became responsible for ensuring that, henceforth, Welsh pilgrims to the Mount of Olives would have the pleasure of reading the Lord's Prayer in their own language at this distant and sacred spot.

Welshmen ' in dispersion ' could, of course, be found much nearer home, and their numbers were increased in 1944 when the Government decided to direct young men into the coalmines instead of into the armed forces. They were first sent for training at the Oakdale Colliery in Monmouthshire. Many came from Welsh-speaking rural areas, and it was a considerable wrench to be suddenly transplanted from rural Wales into an Anglicised industrial society. Many were also Urdd members, and the Urdd felt it had a responsibility to help them become acclimatised to the unfamiliar atmosphere in which they found themselves. Fortunately, there were a number of Welsh people in the Oakdale area who were equally anxious to help, and were prepared to co-operate with the Urdd, *Undeb Cymru Fydd* and other interested bodies. The idea of setting up an Aelwyd for the ' Bevin Boys ' was welcomed, and the Urdd Organiser, Elwyn Jones, and the Rev. T. Alban Davies of Ton Pentre were among the prime movers. The training period was relatively short and the ' Bevin Boys ' were then directed to work in various coalpits for the duration of the war. The Urdd urged its Aelwydydd in mining areas to seek out the ' Bevin Boys ' who might be in their area and to welcome them into their midst.

*   *   *   *

By now, consolidation—rather than expansion—was the key word in the Urdd policy in connection with its branches. In addition to its four-hundred Adrannau, there were now 411 Youth Branches, 386 being Welsh-medium clubs. Of these, 251 were Aelwydydd in the true sense, meeting at least twice a week, many in their own premises, and some having the service of part or full-time Wardens and receiving grant-aid from the education authorities. The remaining 135 Youth Branches were termed *Uwch-Adrannau*. They met once a week in hired or borrowed premises and their programmes were less ambitious and more superficial. Now that the Registration panic had receded, Urdd Organisers were able to concentrate more on improving the quality and variety of activities offered.

There were now 25 'Young Wales Clubs', ten in Breconshire, four in Radnorshire, six in Glamorgan, three in Monmouthshire, one in Montgomeryshire and one in Cardiganshire. Out of the duplicated news-sheet initiated by Elwyn Jones in 1941 grew the printed magazine—*Young Wales*. Elwyn Jones was acutely aware of the serious lack of publicity material available in English, and set himself the task of producing a special handbook for ' Young Wales Clubs '. He argued that much more should be done in this direction if the Urdd was to retain the interest of the non-Welsh-speaking section of the community. Even today, one feels that this problem has not received the serious attention it deserves and needs.

*   *   *   *

A target of 45,000 had been set for the 1944 Welsh Books Campaign, although one realised that saturation point must soon be reached—if indeed it had not been reached. The final result surprised even the more optimistic and showed that a total of 54,043 volumes had been sold. The fantastic growth of this Campaign during the eight-year period was illustrated in the figures which appeared in the press.

1937	1,025	1941	7,584
1938	3,545	1942	17,378
1939	3,063	1943	39,625
1940	3,545	1944	54,043

An editorial note in the June issue of *Yr Aelwyd* tried to analyse the driving force that impelled the members to achieve such fantastic results. It was not just a case of reaching a target ; it was not for competition or for personal fame or gain. It was just that members saw in this project a means of putting something back into the Welsh community, at a time when so many other channels were closed to them by war-time restrictions.

The Campaign had grown so suddenly and reached such proportions that its very success was becoming a problem to those responsible for its administration. They consoled themselves that the growth could not continue for ever, that saturation point must eventually be reached, and that when the war was over, other avenues of service to Wales would be open, and some of the energy now devoted to this work would be channelled into other directions. More important still was the hope that those readers who had supported the Campaign would eventually become regular customers in Welsh bookshops. If this happened, it would have served its real purpose.

The second Welsh Books Campaign Conference was held at Shrewsbury in June. The Urdd had been aware that the scheme was being organised in direct co-operation with the publishers, but without any contact with the booksellers. During the first few years, this would not have constituted a serious intrusion into the book-trade, but now that the project had assumed the proportions of 50,000-60,000, it was a different story. And some of the booksellers were beginning to voice their complaint. The matter was discussed at the Shrewsbury Conference and it was decided to call a further meeting in July, and to invite forty established booksellers to attend. Of those invited, seven were present, four sent their apologies and the other twenty-nine were apparently not interested. Nevertheless, it was decided that, in future, the booksellers were to be represented at each meeting and a suggestion that a Publishers and Booksellers' Union be set up was unanimously adopted. R. E. Griffith was asked to prepare a draft constitution to be considered at the next meeting.

Ifan ab Owen Edwards and R. E. Griffith were delighted at the progress made, and justifiably proud of the part played by the Urdd in this new development. Not only had it established the Welsh Books Campaign, but it had also been instrumental in bringing together the publishers and booksellers, and they were now moving towards the formation of a Union of Welsh Publishers and Booksellers. Some might raise doubts whether these activities were really the province of the Urdd. Could the time and energy devoted to such work be justified when the Urdd was neither publisher nor bookseller, when its main responsibility was to provide youth service activities for its members ? There was but one answer. The Urdd's loyalty to Wales could not exclude the fate of the language and literature of Wales. The publication and sale of Welsh books was essential to the life of the nation ; if Wales was to live, Welsh literature must live, and it was left to the Urdd to put into action the machinery that would make this possible.

*　　*　　*　　*

Based on the annual ' Programme Suggestions,' the District Eisteddfodau were held as usual, and in several instances, they were followed by County Eisteddfodau. These larger events added to the excitement of competitors and made them look forward with even greater eagerness to seeing the National Eisteddfod re-instated when the war was over.

During the Easter holidays, R. Gordon Williams (Bobi Gordon) of Penygroes, Caernarfonshire, led a group of boys on an expedition through South Wales, having planned their route so that they could be given hospitality and overnight accommodation at various Aelwydydd. From Aberystwyth they trekked to Swansea, Llanelli, Cwmafan, Pontardawe, Cardiff, Pontypridd and Brynaman. They returned tired but jubilant, convinced that differences between the people of North and South Wales were no more than an illusion, an early-morning mist that quickly disappeared in the warmth of hospitality.

In the January issue of *Yr Aelwyd*, R. E. Griffith had nostalgically recalled the joys and virtues of Llangrannog. He went on to bemoan the loss suffered by those who were denied the experience of camping—

> ' It is not merely the loss of a holiday, it is the loss of an experience that, more than anything else, prepares young people to become worthy citizens and leaders of their community.'

Without fully realising the difficulties that would be involved, he made a rash promise that camps would be held at Llangrannog the following summer. The premises had been used by the Home Guard for weekend training, and a great deal had to be done before they would be habitable for campers. There were staffing difficulties as well as food and petrol problems, and at times, it seemed an impossible task. However, a promise had been given and it had to be kept. Seven weeks' camping were planned, two for members of Adrannau in the 11-15 age-group, one for Dysgwyr of the same age-group, two for members of Aelwydydd in the 15-20 age-group and two for members of Young Wales Clubs. For the first time, they were all mixed camps—the camps at Llanmadog and Caernarfon having already paved the way. More than a thousand members attended, over six-hundred of whom were in the 15-20 age group. Naturally, it was not possible to forget that Britain was still at war, and it may be that this heightened rather than detracted from the inspiration which both campers and leaders derived from the experience. Members of the Aelwydydd and Young Wales Clubs especially were found to be mature and responsible young people. Many had lost relatives in the war. They sincerely believed that only one thing could save the world from disaster and barbarism, and that was the spirit of love and tolerance based on the teaching of Christ.

In April, Ifan ab Owen Edwards and his family had moved out of Neuadd Wen, and were now living at Bryneithin, a country house about three miles from Aberystwyth. Their departure opened up possibilities of further expansion for *Yr Ysgol Gymraeg*, and it came just at the time when it was most needed. It was the first time that pupils of the school had taken the ' Scholarship ' examination and the eight who faced the ordeal in 1944 passed with ease. This was a triumph for the principle of education through the medium of Welsh ; it proved that it was possible to give pupils a thorough background of Welsh culture whilst at the same time safeguarding their academic standards. This was the proof that turned the scales in favour of the school in the eyes of those parents who had previously been unwilling to ' sacrifice ' their children in the experiment. The number of pupils rose to 56 and a nursery class was added to those already established.

At the Urdd Annual General Meeting held at Machynlleth in October 1944, J. M. Howell insisted on resigning from being President. He felt that a much younger man should be elected to take his place, and that such a man should not be difficult to find. It was with much regret that the meeting accepted his resignation. With exceptional altruism, he had befriended and supported the movement from its infancy, and had watched with pride and interest as it grew into a powerful organisation. Without his financial and moral support, the Urdd would not have been able to develop as it had done. Such men are rare. Later that afternoon, Ifan ab Owen Edwards was elected to follow J. M. Howell as President. Everyone present felt that Ifan ab Owen Edwards had now come into his inheritance. Nothing could be more natural than that the Presidency should fall to the man who had created the movement and led it for twenty-three years. He could accept the office knowing that the Urdd was firmly behind him, and that the people of Wales were firmly behind the Urdd.

At the Machynlleth meeting, the County Committees were given their official status within the Constitution. From now on, representatives to the Urdd Council would be elected by the County Committees rather than the District Committees. The meeting also confirmed the establishment of a number of Sub-committees, with special responsibility for Finance, Buildings, Staffing, International Affairs, and Girls' Activities. Dr. Gwenan Jones was elected Chairman of the Council and her place as Vice-Chairman was taken by Professor R. I. Aaron. Professor D. J. Llewelfryn Davies was elected Honorary Counsel, a post he was to hold for twenty-five years.

In November 1944, the Ministry of Education issued its Circular 13, dealing with leisure-time provision for schoolchildren. It urged local education authorities to consider how the Youth Service (now catering for the 14-20 age-group) could be extended to provide for the 11-14 year olds. After five years of concentrating on the senior members, the Ministry was beginning to show concern for the younger boys and girls. And it acknowledged that the voluntary organisations possessed valuable experience which should not be overlooked in dealing with this age-group.

> ' The assistance which voluntary organisations can render should be fully enlisted. Many of the organisations associated with the Youth Committees have done much for children of 11 to 14 and have developed a technique which seems to meet their psychological needs . . . Local Education Authorities should therefore consider whether they can assist such organisations, financially or otherwise, so as to enable them to extend their work among children of school age.'

This was a field in which the Urdd had pioneered for more than twenty years. The Circular was, in effect, an acknowledgement that the Urdd and similar voluntary organisations were ahead of their time.

Circular 13 did not have the same impact as its predecessor, Circular 1486, issued by the former Board of Education in 1939. One reason for this was the fact that it was content to urge without exerting pressure. The local education authorities were free to act or not to act, and most chose not to act. It was very rarely that Urdd Adrannau dealing with the age-group indicated in the Circular received grants towards their work, although a few authorities had grant-aided groups taking part in the Eisteddfod, or in camps and courses. These, however, were rare exceptions, and even today, most education authorities choose to consider the work of voluntary organisations with younger children as being outside the scope of the Youth Service, and not eligible for grant-aid.

1944 was a year of re-organisation and consolidation as far as Urdd staff were concerned. The aim now was to appoint an Organiser for each County (eight had already been appointed) and a Warden for each Aelwyd or Club that possessed its own premises (nine had already been appointed). Until this aim could be achieved, the staff would be aided by a team of part-time Organisers and part-time Club Wardens. At Swyddfa'r Urdd, there were constant changes among the younger clerical staff, but Elsi Williams remained Chief Clerk and there were several experienced secretaries who had years of excellent service to their credit. The employment of a full-time staff of 32, in addition to part-time workers, meant that much time had to be spent on fund-raising, despite the fact that the Ministry of Education grant had been increased to £2,750, and that the Jubilee Trust continued its grant of £500. Without these, it would have been impossible to retain the staff that had become necessary to deal effectively with developments in the mid-forties.

*   *   *   *

Early in 1945, it became obvious that the war would be over within a few months. At its May meeting, the Executive Committee felt confident that plans could now be made to reinstate the National Eisteddfod the following year, and it was decided that the Edeyrnion District in Merioneth be asked whether they could act as hosts. They agreed with enthusiasm and Swyddfa'r Urdd offered every possible help. It was realised that some changes in the pattern were necessary. Competitions for Aelwydydd would have to be included, and County Eisteddfodau would have to be a compulsory link in the Eisteddfod system. Much had to be accomplished in a short time, and to facilitate the arrangements, Swyddfa'r Urdd undertook to prepare a syllabus and publish the schedule of competitions, leaving the Eisteddfod Executive Committee free to concentrate on local preparations. By September 1945, the war was over, the schedule of competitions made available, and the entire Eisteddfod machinery put into action.

Having sold over 54,000 Welsh books in 1944, it was natural though perhaps over-optimistic to raise the 1945 target to 60,000. This time the target was not reached, and the number of books sold was 43,678. Many factors could be cited as possible explanations, and possibly all contributed to the decline. First, there was an acute shortage of new books, and of those published in 1944, only limited editions were available due to paper shortage, and these were barely sufficient to supply the regular booksellers who must, naturally, be given priority. Secondly, eight years of campaigning had exhausted the publishers' accumulated stocks of old works. Thirdly, one hoped that the Campaign had served its purpose and helped to create the interest in reading that would make people buy regularly at established bookshops. After all, the Campaign was not an end in itself, but a means of strengthening and boosting the official book-trade. When this was achieved, the Urdd would have cause to rejoice that its task in this particular field was over.

In mid-summer, the draft constitution for the Union of Welsh Publishers and Booksellers was accepted by the Conference, which included representatives of eleven publishers and fourteen booksellers. A Council of twelve was elected, with Ifan ab Owen Edwards as Chairman, Howell Evans of Liverpool as Vice-Chairman, Megan Hughes of Aberystwyth as Treasurer and R. E. Griffith as Secretary. The Union would not only direct the Welsh Books Campaign, but also devise and operate any other plans that were deemed necessary to promote the book-trade in general.

*   *   *   *

As in 1944, fund-raising claimed much time and effort. The annual turnover was now in the region of £8,000 towards which the Ministry of Education had increased its grant to £3,150 and the Jubilee Trust grant of £500 came with its usual regularity. J. M.

Howell continued his £500 covenant subscription, and in 1945, the Urdd received its first grant from a local education authority towards the salary of a County Organiser. This, incidentally, came from the Cardiganshire Education Authority thus disproving the traditional belief that the *Cardi* is tight-fisted ! About this time, a number of writers and poets had begun to transfer to the Urdd the financial remuneration which accrued from the publication of their books. These authors included R. T. Jenkins, W. J. Gruffydd, T. Rowland Hughes, T. I. Ellis, T. Ifor Rees, Leslie Harries, and particularly I. D. Hooson who transferred to the Urdd most of the royalties from his works.

It was in 1945 that the Ministry of Education agreed to recognise Urdd Organisers and Wardens as eligible under the Teachers' Superannuation Scheme. This was something that Ifan ab Owen Edwards had striven for during the previous twelve months, and he was more than pleased when he finally succeeded. He was well aware that the Urdd could not compete with statutory bodies in the salaries paid to staff members, but when they were also deprived of the security of a superannuation scheme, it meant considerable sacrifice on their part. No one appreciated this more than the Founder, and no one was more anxious to improve their conditions of service.

Young lads were still being directed to work in the coalfields, and in 1945, the Rev. J. Haines Davies set up an Aelwyd for ' Bevin Boys ' at Treharris, with T. Napier Williams as Secretary. Other Aelwydydd that were outside the usual pattern were those set up over the border. Five of these were on Merseyside, one in Crewe— chiefly for young Welsh people doing war work in the area—one in Birmingham, one in Oswestry and one in Chester. The Chester Aelwyd was one of the earliest of Urdd clubs and it has continued for thirty years, thanks largely to the efforts of J. F. Owen and his daughter, Edna Owen. One has only to recall the activities of two other members of this family, Beryl Owen of Dolgellau and Ivor Owen of Llanuwchllyn, to realise what a notable contribution the family has made to the Urdd and to the life of Wales.

To hold or not to hold the camps at Llangrannog in 1945 was never in question. ' Peace ' had returned to Europe and shortly after the camps had opened, the war with Japan also came to an end. Many of the shortages and restrictions naturally remained ; it would be too much to expect a return to normality overnight. But it was ' peace ', and this had a psychological effect ; it was like sunshine after prolonged rain. More than a thousand boys and girls from Adrannau, Aelwydydd and Young Wales Clubs attended during the seven-week period. And as always, there was ample evidence that these camps have a tremendous effect on the young campers, far more than one would expect from a brief one-week stay. Whenever the time comes to bid farewell to camp, the boys are unusually silent and many of the girls in tears. All vow that they will return as soon as they are allowed to—if not next year, then some day. Sentiment ? Possibly, but even when the tears are dried and the vows forgotten, something still remains ; some inspiration gleaned from the community spirit, an inspiration that, one day, will lead to greater service to Wales and to humanity.

The Southwalians were not to be outdone by their compatriots in the North. Having read of the inter-county expeditions to Cader Idris and the Berwyn range, they decided to plan a four-county rally to Nantstalwyn, a mountain-farm nine miles from Tregaron, nine from Llanwrtyd and nine from Rhandirmwyn. It was here that the Aelwydydd and Young Wales Clubs of Cardiganshire, Carmarthenshire, Brecon and Radnor arranged to meet on a Saturday in July. The weather was perfect. It was a glorious opportunity to ' discover ' this isolated part of Wales ; it was also an excuse to meet fellow-members from other counties.

Long before the war had ended, the International Relations Committee had been active under the chairmanship of the Rev. Gwilym Davies. The Urdd support of the Goodwill Message had not ceased throughout the war, nor did the BBC once fail to broadcast the Message. And although the Urdd Goodwill Service which originated in 1933 and which had been broadcast by the BBC had to be discontinued during the later war years, the May issue of *Cymru'r Plant* and *Yr Aelwyd* were invariably devoted to the cause of peace and goodwill. In 1945, a series of monthly articles *Cymru a'r Byd* (Wales and the World), dealing with countries such as Switzerland, Denmark, Sweden, Czechoslovakia and Iceland, were designed to draw readers' attention to the life and problems of other small nations. When the war was drawing to its close, however, the Urdd felt that some contribution of a practical nature should be made. Plans to hold an international camp at Llangrannog were considered, but it was too soon for young people from Europe to be allowed entry. Plans to co-operate with the Friends Ambulance Corps in their efforts to alleviate some of the suffering in Europe also had to be abandoned. Eventually, it was decided to organise a Christmas appeal to be transferred to The Save the Children Fund as a gift from the people of Wales. This appeal to help the needy and homeless children of Europe went straight to the heart. Three months were given to a publicity campaign through Urdd Branches, churches, press and radio. A total of £3,924/17/7 was raised, and every penny sent to The Save the Children Fund.

It was decided that the money be spent on providing and distributing food, clothing and medical supplies in those areas where the need was greatest, and that the gift be sent direct in the name of Wales. Eight large vehicles were purchased as mobile clinics or canteens. The first went to Poland, the second to Belgium, one to Hungary, two to Yugoslavia and so on. On one side of each vehicle was painted the Red Dragon ; on the other, an inscription in Welsh and in the language of the country that received it. In Welsh, it read, for example—

Rhodd Cymru i Blant Poland
trwy Urdd Gobaith Cymru
mewn cydweithrediad â Chronfa Achub y Plant.

With the remaining fund, tons of food, clothing and medical supplies were despatched to The Save the Children Fund centres in the various countries. At the time, a number of young people from Wales—some of whom were former Urdd members—were working in Europe with humanitarian organisations, and one can imagine their glow of pride as they read of the response of the people of Wales. To one Urdd member came the privilege of driving one of the vehicles across Europe to Yugoslavia. He was Alwyn Griffith of Pwllheli.

This was one way of putting the Goodwill Message into practice ; it was a practical expression of the Urdd pledge of loyalty to fellow-man, whoever he may be. There could be no better way of celebrating the peace.

*   *   *   *

In June 1945, Circular 51 was issued by the Ministry of Education, setting out the revised arrangements for grant-aiding voluntary youth organisations in the post-war period, taking into consideration the provisions made under the Butler Education Act, 1944. Henceforth, the Government would draw a distinction between national and local needs. The Ministry would offer direct headquarters grants towards administration and training, but grants to local clubs would henceforth come mainly from the local education authorities—

' The time has come for the Local Education Authorities to assume in full measure their responsibility for giving such assistance as may be necessary to enable the local youth organisations within their respective areas to function effectively.'

About the same time, the report of the Welsh Youth Committee, ' Post War Youth Service in Wales ' was published, pointing very much in the same direction.

The Urdd continued its policy of purchasing premises that would serve as Aelwydydd centres. Grants were received towards the cost of purchase, and it was thus that the Urdd bought premises at Swansea, Llanelli, Corwen, Manod (Blaenau Ffestiniog) and Newport, Pembrokeshire. But although purchasing arrangements and applications for grants were made by *Cwmni'r Urdd*, the move would not have come about had it not been for the enthusiastic efforts of individuals who saw the need and were prepared to work towards a solution,—people like Mildred Hughes in Newport, Olwen Williams in Llanelli, the Rev. H. E. Jones and J. Griffith Jones at Corwen, and Dr. Annie Owen in Swansea.

*   *   *   *

Discussions had been going on throughout the year regarding the possibilities of extending *Ysgol Gymraeg Aberystwyth* to include residential facilities. This idea was mooted by Ifan ab Owen

Edwards, and if he could find suitable premises for such a school, he proposed to use them in a dual capacity, turning the school into a camp and training centre during school vacations. When ' Lluest ', a small mansion on the outskirts of Aberystwyth, suddenly came on the market, Ifan ab Owen Edwards, after brief discussions with his fellow-officers, went ahead and purchased the premises for £3,000. The officers estimated that it would take another £10,000 to adapt and equip the premises, but their immediate problem was to find the £3,000 to repay Ifan ab Owen Edwards as soon as it could be arranged. There was nothing to be done but to launch another appeal. Within six months, £1,500 had been raised, and it was not long before the remainder became available. It was thus that Lluest was purchased, a building that was to figure prominently in the history of the Urdd, and indeed in the history of Welsh education.

When the Parents and Governors met for their Annual Meeting in October 1945, it was natural that Lluest should be the main topic of discussion, and Ifan ab Owen Edwards outlined his plans for the future. He would like to see the school move to Lluest in April of the following year. In another six months, he would like provision to be made for fifteen boarders—this in response to requests from parents in other areas who were anxious that their children should attend the school. He realised that such a project could not be accomplished without considerable effort and sacrifice. It would mean an initial outlay of £4,000. The Urdd had already spent £3,000 on purchasing the building ; it was now up to the parents and governors to play their part in giving the school the opportunity it deserved.

As usual, his pioneering spirit was irresistible, and this enthusiasm made the impossible appear practicable. By now, the pupils numbered 71. Six more children had successfully taken the ' Scholarship ' examination ; two others had been accepted for entry into public schools. There was no longer any doubt regarding the school's academic standards. It attracted more than its share of visitors and observers, both from Wales and from overseas, especially educationists from abroad who were themselves wrestling with bilingual or multi-lingual problems. The Ministry of Education continued to observe its development and School Inspectors made frequent unofficial visits.

Continuing his report to the Annual Meeting, Ifan ab Owen Edwards emphasised, however, that it was not intended to urge other Welsh towns to establish a Welsh independent school on the pattern of *Ysgol Gymraeg Aberystwyth*. Without the support of an organisation like the Urdd, such a task—financially and otherwise— would place too heavy a burden on any parents' association. The aim should now be to stimulate the Local Education Authorities in Wales to set up schools on a similar pattern, based on the traditions, culture and life of Wales, and using the Welsh language as the main medium of education, and the one medium of inspiration. The experiment at Aberystwyth was a heavy drain on the Urdd and on the parents and governors, but it was a price that had to be paid, not only to prove that the experiment in itself was practicable, but in order to win the right for Welsh parents everywhere to obtain for their children the same kind of education at State expense. Ifan ab Owen Edwards disclosed that he and the Headmistress were already planning to meet groups of Welsh parents in various towns and would support them in an effort to persuade their Education Authorities to establish a Welsh State School, in accordance with the 1944 Education Act. This would be their main aim during 1946.

*   *   *   *

It was at the Annual General Meeting at Llanelli that Mrs. Ifan ab Owen Edwards asked to be relieved of her responsibility as Honorary Secretary. She had held the office since the establishment of *Cwmni'r Urdd* in 1932, and during the previous nine years, she had worked alongside her husband as unofficial secretary. Her place as Honorary Secretary was taken by Hywel D. Roberts who, for twenty years, had been a keen supporter of the movement. Dr. Gwenan Jones continued as Chairman, and Professor R. I. Aaron's place as Vice-Chairman was taken by Dr. Iorwerth Hughes Jones, a pillar of strength in the Welsh life of Swansea. He had been on the first Urdd Pilgrimage to Geneva, at the first ' Senate ' at Llangollen, on the first Welsh Cruise in 1933, as well as being one of the officers of the Mabolgampau held that year at Swansea.

Writing in 1945, Ifan ab Owen Edwards reviewed the growth and development of the Urdd since 1922. He referred to 1937 as a milestone in that it was the year in which the Urdd first received grant-aid from The National Fitness Council. From 1940, grants were also received from the Board of Education and the local education authorities. Referring to the post-war period, he said—

' It is most important that we should realise the importance of the Adrannau. These are the cornerstone of our movement. Through the efforts of hundreds of patriotic teachers, these Adrannau are the means of introducing into formal education an awareness of Wales and its culture. We should aim at maintaining a balance between the Adrannau and the Aelwydydd, and ensure that the fundamental ideals of the Urdd continue to be the inspiration of all our Branches.'

It was thus that the Urdd went forward into the post-war period. In peace, as in war, the motto would be the same—' RHAID I GYMRU FYW ' (Wales must live).

8

THE Urdd survived the 1939-45 War largely because Ifan ab Owen Edwards and his colleagues had accepted the crisis as a challenge that must be overcome. 'Wales must live' was their motto and they believed that, if the life of the nation was to flourish, the Urdd had an important contribution to make and could not be allowed to become a war casualty. In the struggle to survive, no effort was spared and there was no counting the cost in time and energy. As a result, the war was a purgatory from which the Urdd emerged as an experienced and mature movement.

1946 was naturally a year of transition ; a stock-taking period. The Urdd had a total of 817 Branches made up of 409 Adrannau, 376 Aelwydydd and 32 Young Wales Clubs. But the counting of heads was not the only criterion by which the movement could be judged. Behind the Branches was a vast network of local committees, of District and County Committees, linked to an incorporated body which had fifteen years' experience in guiding the movement. On the one hand, the movement had the support of *y werin*, ordinary folk who believed the Urdd to be one of the greatest forces—if not the greatest force—in the life of the nation. On the other hand, it had the support of the State through a Government that recognised it as a movement eligible for grant-aid enabling it to continue its work on behalf of the youth of Wales. In such a secure position, the movement could confidently face a period of peace. The immediate question was where to begin. So many projects had been suspended during the war and had to be re-instated. Many new ideas were waiting to be put into operation. But after six years of war conditions, the first priority must be to ensure that existing schemes were put on a secure basis. One of these was *Yr Ysgol Gymraeg*.

The idealist in Ifan ab Owen Edwards believed in thinking big and aiming high. But he was realist enough to know that there were times when it was necessary to cut one's coat according to one's cloth. He once said to R. E. Griffith, ' Always ask for a whole loaf, but make sure that, if the worst comes, you can live on half a loaf.' Such was their experience with regard to Lluest. In his first enthusiasm, Ifan ab Owen Edwards had envisaged a four-fold purpose. It was to be the new home of *Yr Ysgol Gymraeg* ; it could have a residential wing for a small group of pupils living outside the area ; it could be an additional camp-centre during the summer months ; and it could serve as a training/conference centre during the Christmas and Easter vacations. Events proved that this was too ambitious a scheme. The first, however, was already within reach. By Easter, the premises were almost ready for their new occupants, transport arrangements had been made, and the House Committee was planning a garden féte to raise funds towards the additional costs involved.

With the exception of the nursery class which, as a temporary measure, was left in the old premises, the school moved to Lluest on 1 May, 1946. The new surroundings opened up endless possibilities, and the Governors knew they could depend on Norah Isaac and her staff to take full advantage of the opportunities. Nothing came of the proposed residential wing, mainly because it would involve building new classrooms, and the Urdd could not afford the permanent buildings which were demanded by the planning authorities. This was a disappointment for Ifan ab Owen Edwards, but he was the first to admit that there was still plenty of scope in developing and improving the day-school.

*   *   *   *

It was no easy task to re-establish the National Eisteddfod so soon after the war, but the inspiration inherent in such an event had been lost since 1940, and the delay of another year was unthinkable. During the gap of five years, two developments had taken place that would affect the Eisteddfod. The Aelwydydd had come into existence, and the County Committees had become a new link in the Eisteddfod system. The national event would now draw its competitors from winners at a dozen County Eisteddfodau instead of some sixty District Eisteddfodau. This would mean fewer competitors and supporters, but a big step towards raising the standards and simplifying the preliminary tests and accommodation arrangements. The Eisteddfod was to be held in the Corwen Pavilion, the same building that housed the first Urdd Eisteddfod in 1929. Nothing could be more appropriate.

The Corwen Eisteddfod Committee lost no time in getting down to the task of solving their local problems, the first of which was to persuade the Ministry of Food to relinquish their claim on the Pavilion in which hundreds of tons of sugar had been stored during the war. No sooner was the building cleared than it was discovered that the floor had sagged under the weight of sugar and was declared unsafe for any large gathering. It was not easy to find builders who could undertake the renovating work, especially as an emergency measure, and the problem of obtaining the necessary timber seemed equally insurmountable. At the eleventh hour, a family of builders from Wrexham came to the rescue, and the task was accomplished.

Almost as difficult was the task of obtaining food permits for the numbers envisaged. After lengthy correspondence with the Ministry of Food, R. E. Griffith was asked to meet a Ministry official to plead his case. His story told, the official thanked him in English and then went on to say in Welsh, ' I too am a member of the Urdd. As a boy I went to the Urdd Camp and competed in Eisteddfodau. Dont worry about food ; I'll see that there is enough for everyone ! ' R. E. Griffith left the building walking on air.

Many difficulties, however, still remained. Had the Urdd known in advance what problems were ahead, it is doubtful whether even the most sanguine would have considered the Eisteddfod to be feasible. In the event, T. Gwynn Jones' famous line, ' *Boed anwybod i'r byd yn obaith* ', could have been an expression of their faith. Ignorance is bliss when it allows room for hope. Even seemingly insurmountable problems were eventually resolved and, in retrospect, the difficulties only added to the sense of achievement.

Thirty-four groups competed in the drama section—a marathon task for the adjudicator, Nan Davies of the BBC. The same enthusiasm was apparent in other sections. It may be that the pre-war Eisteddfodau—with their processions, banners and bands—were on a larger scale, but if there was now less show, there was probably more substance. One of the Presidents was the Rev. T. Arthur Jones who had been primarily responsible for initiating the first Urdd Eisteddfod at Corwen in 1929. The other was Ben Bowen Thomas, who, as Warden of Coleg Harlech, had been President in 1929, and now, as Secretary to the Welsh Department of the Ministry of Education, was invited to return.

29 At the entrance to St. David's Cathedral

30 One of the mobile ambulance units in Poland

BRYNEITHYN,
LLANFARIAN,
ABERYSTWYTH.

Annwyl Gyfeillion, 1. 1. 47

Aeth chwarter canrif heibio er pan sefydlwyd Urdd
Gobaith Cymru. Cymdeithas hapus o gyd-weithwyr a lafuriodd
i osod ei egwyddorion ac a greodd ei delfrydau. bryfder y mudiad
heddiw ydyw ein bod hwy yn parhau yn gefn iddo.

Ymunodd cenedlaethau o blant yn yr Urdd oddyma hyn,
tyfasant yn fechgyn ac yn ferched ynddi ac yna datblygu'n
bobl ieuainc. Gwelyn heddiw hwy ydyw ail do ei harweinwyr.
Etifeddasant y delfrydau a greasom ni, manteisiant ar ein
profiad ni, a diogyn yn adnoddau a groglesom ni i'w dwylo
hwy. Y mae ganddynt, wrth gwrs, anawsterau na wyddem
ni amdanynt, ond, o'u gwylied mewn adran ac aelwyd a
gwersyll, teimlaf yn ffyddiog fod dyfodol yr Urdd yn ddiogel
yn eu dwylo. Tristwch i ni fyddai ocdau bod y mudiad y
rhoesom gymaint o'n amser a'n llafur erddo i ddarfod gyda
ni; llawenydd inni ydyw gwybod y pery'r Urdd trwyddynt
hwy i wasanaethu ieuenctid Cymru.

Ar ddechrau ail chwarter canrif, gan hynny, carwn
ddiolch i weithwyr y cyfnod cyntaf am eu ffyddlondeb a'u
teyrngarwch, a dymuno pob bendith a llwyddiant i weithwyr
y cyfnod newydd, camys bugeiliaid newydd fydd ar yr hen
ffyngyllosedl hyn.

Ar drothwn cyfnod newydd un deisyfiad a geisiwn,—
bydded i bob aelod o'r Urdd lynu wrth yr Addewid,—

BYDDAF FFYDDLON I GYMRU, I GYD-DDYN, I GRIST.

Parhaed yr Addewid hwn yn sylfaen yr Urdd; ysbrydoled
ni ac uned ni yn y dyfodol megis yn y gorffennol ——
'ER MWYN CYMRU.'

Yr eiddoch yn ddiduyll,
Ifan ab Owen Edwards

31 Letter written by the Founder for *Y Llinyn Arian* in 1947

It was the winning County rather than the winning District that won the ' Lloyd George Banner ' on this occasion. By now, however, the banner had become too fragile to be presented, and it was an imaginary trophy that was won by the home-county, Merioneth. And so, after five long years, the National Eisteddfod had been re-established and could once more become a force in the life of the Urdd and in the life of Wales generally.

*   *   *   *

Early in 1946, the Urdd received a valuable gift from Ald. William George of Cricieth and his son, W. R. P. George, in the form of two combined terrace-houses in Cricieth which could serve as a home for the local Aelwyd for the greater part of the year and be used as a small residential hostel during holiday periods. It was officially opened in July, and a fortnight later, a five-week camping period began. It was, of course, very different from Llangrannog with its large camp-field and the freedom of the open country, and it was not easy to curb the high spirits of forty teenagers so as not to impose undue inconvenience upon the neighbours. Nevertheless, it had its compensations. Full use was made of the nearby beach and every opportunity taken to explore the rich potential of the sur-rounding countryside. Expeditions were made to Llanystumdwy ; to Betws Fawr, home of Robert ap Gwilym Ddu ; to Y Garreg Wen and Cwm Pennant.

Another benefactor was Dr. Griffith Evans of Caernarfon. The Urdd had already purchased premises in the town which provided a home for the local Aelwyd, and occasionally for national activities as well. The main defect of the premises was the lack of an assembly hall. A site for such a building was available, and Dr. Griffith Evans offered to pay for the erection of a new hall, as soon as building materials could be released for the purpose. In the meantime, £3,000 towards the cost was handed over to the Urdd so that the interest would be available towards other expenses. This was not the first nor the last example of Dr. Griffith Evans' generosity towards the Urdd and towards the Aelwyd at Caernarfon.

It was at this time too that the Urdd received two donations of a different nature. Brigadier E. O. Skaife's choice was a gift of five harps to be used in promoting the art of harp-playing among the youth of Wales. The other gift took the form of two paintings, the work of Margaret Lindsay Williams. They had won great acclaim when exhibited at the Royal Academy and the Paris Salon in 1917 and 1918, and one of them was voted ' painting of the year ' at the Academy. They were subsequently sold and remained separated until bought and reunited by Sir Alfred T. Davies, first Permanent Secretary to the Welsh Department of the Board of Education. The paintings were purchased from him in 1946 by Mr. and Mrs. J. R. Jones of Liverpool, not for themselves, but as a gift to the Urdd, to be hung in the movement's newly-acquired centre at Borth.

Here, of course, we must refer to D. J. James, then a wealthy London business-man, originally from Pontrhydfendigaid in Cardiganshire. He had already contributed generously to religious causes and to Welsh institutions in London and elsewhere, but hitherto he had no contact with the Urdd and did not seem to be aware of its significance. The Founder decided it was time to approach him and attempt to enlist his support for the movement. An appointment was arranged and Ifan ab Owen Edwards put his case to him. He explained his ideals and how those ideals had been crystallised in the Urdd Pledge. He described the activities of the movement, and how the members responded to those activities. He indicated how the Urdd was hampered in its development through lack of finance and what could be achieved if funds were available. All this time, D. J. James listened attentively. Speaking later to R. E. Griffith, he said he had been amazed that a man of Ifan ab Owen Edwards' ability and position should be prepared to devote his leisure-time wholly to labour on behalf of the youth of Wales. He was further impressed by the fact that a man who had achieved so much should be so modest in describing his achievements. His concluding remark was ' I just couldn't resist the man ! '

Shortly afterwards, Ifan ab Owen Edwards accompanied D. J. James around Wales looking at available mansions and hotels. He had decided to help the Urdd, not with a gift of money, but by providing a centre, preferably in Mid-Wales, where the Urdd could intensify and expand its activities. Most of the places visited were considered by him to be too small. D. J. James was bent on obtaining something bigger and better, and dismissed the idea that maintenance of such a place might be a burden on a voluntary organisation. Returning to Aberystwyth via Borth, they came to the Grand Hotel, and D. J. James immediately decided that this was the place. Built in 1870, soon after the opening of the Cambrian Railway, under the illustrious title ' Borth Hydropathic Establishment,' it later became the ' Grand Hotel ' and could accommodate a hundred guests. It was now bought by D. J. James for £16,000 and would be made available to the Urdd in a year's time as unlicensed premises. Once again, the name was changed and the ' Grand Hotel ' became known as 'Pantyfedwen', the name of D. J. James' old home at Pontrhydfendigaid.

*   *   *   *

Whenever youth organisations were invited to attend special functions arranged by the 'Establishment', the Urdd would be among those invited. And although such an essentially Welsh movement sometimes held views that were different from those of the authorities and did not hesitate to express those views when the need arose, it nevertheless accepted that the inclusion of Youth Organisations in special functions attended by representatives of recognised Welsh bodies was reasonable and appropriate. One such event was the visit of King George VI and Queen Elizabeth to Caernarfon in July 1946. On this occasion, the invitation involved a dozen leaders from Caernarfonshire, led by Hywel D. Roberts, then Honorary Secretary of Cwmni'r Urdd.

*   *   *   *

No-one doubted that applications for camp in 1946 would far exceed the fifteen-hundred members who could be accommodated in an eight-week period at Llangrannog. Plans were accordingly made to accommodate an additional two-hundred at Cricieth and another two-hundred at Lluest. The Cricieth venture has already been referred to, but in the case of Lluest, it was a very different story. Amid great excitement, everything was ready to receive the first lot of campers. Then just two days before the camp was due to open, the whole scheme had to be cancelled.

Aberystwyth was struck by a typhoid epidemic. For the same reason, the Girls' Summer School that was to follow the camps also had to be abandoned. ' The best-laid schemes o' mice an' men gang aft agley.'

Llangrannog, however, had an ideal summer. Many members who had spent years in the forces were among the camp leaders. They were now mature men. One of these was Dafydd Morris Jones, of Aberystwyth, who later described his impressions in *Yr Aelwyd*—

> ' Throughout the period I spent in the Navy, I would often recall the happy times I spent at the Urdd camps from 1936 to 1941, and I longed to be able to return . . . I shall never forget the last night of the 1941 camps when it was feared that Llangrannog would have to be closed for the duration. During that last epilogue, the light in the chapel lamp began to grow dim. As the service drew to a close, we watched the flame slowly disappearing. Then the *Pennaeth* said that if the light at camp was to be extinguished, it was important that we should keep the flame burning in the Aelwydydd. And this, through the efforts of many men and women, has been achieved.'

The 1946 camps will also be remembered because of the international element introduced. We had been asked by the British Council to receive a small group of young men from the Gold Coast and Nigeria and these were warmly welcomed. Songs were exchanged ; differences in customs and traditions were discussed ; problems were shared. It was obvious from letters received after their return that their visit had meant as much to them as it did to us. It was a small but valuable contribution towards international understanding. Peace had now made this possible, and the Urdd was eager to grasp the opportunity.

The Goodwill Message too had received a new impetus. During the war years, it had lost most of its overseas contacts although the BBC never once failed to broadcast it on Goodwill Day. Gwilym Davies, however, did not lose courage. He took up the broken threads and re-established his contacts. One of the first replies in 1946 came from Baden in Germany. It read simply—' Are you still in existence ? How it grew dark ! '

*   *   *   *

The Aelwyd at Rhosllannerchrugog reached a new level in 1946. Largely through the untiring efforts of the Rev. James Humphreys, a flourishing Aelwyd had been established in the early war years. It met in chapel premises but opened its doors to all young people and gained the support of the people of Rhos generally. It was able to offer its members a variety of activities including choral-work, drama, discussion-groups, the use of a library and canteen, as well as indoor and outdoor recreational activities. With its large membership and comprehensive programme, it had already outgrown the original premises, and it was not surprising that the local press referred to ' Rhos Aelwyd bursting at the seams '. Faced with this situation, James Humphreys persuaded Cwmni'r Urdd to purchase the old Public Hall. Bought for just £1,000, it was foreseen that another £4,000-£5,000 would have to be spent on renovating and furnishing. However, the Urdd felt confident that the scheme would be eligible for grant-aid, and there was no doubt that the people of Rhos would be firmly behind the venture even though the task might take a number of years.

While Rhos was engaged in its new venture, another hive of industry was emerging at Aberporth in Cardiganshire. The Rev. and Mrs. Tegryn Davies had been running a very successful Adran for more than five years and were anxious to see the establishment of an Aelwyd for those who had grown out of the Adran. A small plot of ground had been bought in 1944, and in 1946, the Aelwyd— already firmly established—erected a timber hut which would henceforth provide an independent home for Urdd activities in the village. Their main interest lay in cultural activities, and even at the Corwen Eisteddfod in that year, it became clear that Aberporth was rich in talent, and that much more would be heard of them in future years.

Olwen Griffith relinquished her post in *Yr Ysgol Gymraeg* and her place was taken by Gwen Tomos, a gifted teacher with specialist qualifications in art. Both staff and pupils were quick to settle down at Lluest. For the Governors, the greatest problem was still the financial one ; even though no rent was charged by Cwmni'r Urdd, it was still difficult to make ends meet. The main source of income was the fees paid by parents, and this was insufficient to pay the salaries of the four teachers, leaving nothing for caretakers' wages, heat, light and general maintenance. Nevertheless, Cwmni'r Urdd felt it was right that it should contribute as much as possible, within its limited resources, towards an experiment that was so important to Welsh education in general. At the same time, the parents too felt that they had their part to play, and their first fund-raising scheme was a garden fête held at Lluest, bringing in a total of £875.

When the seventh Annual Meeting of Governors and Parents was held in October, the Headmistress was able to report that the school now had 81 pupils and that the rural surroundings had given them an entirely new outlook and opened up exciting possibilities. E. D. Jones took over as Chairman from Professor Idwal Jones, and Tom Lewis, a lecturer in Mathematics, became Vice-Chairman. Ifan ab Owen Edwards, I. C. Jones and R. E. Griffith continued in their respective offices.

About this time, the governors and parents were beginning to wonder how long the school could remain an independent school in view of ever-rising costs. Some were in favour of asking the local education authority to adopt it as a state-aided school, while others argued that it was essential that it should remain completely free and unfettered. After some months' deliberations, it was decided to appeal to Cwmni'r Urdd to increase its financial support in order to guarantee the school's independent status. The Urdd Council agreed, on the understanding that the parents themselves undertook some annual fund-raising schemes. It would mean an effort for both bodies, but it was an effort that must be continued until education authorities could be persuaded to provide their own Welsh-medium schools, so that pupils who so desired could obtain free education through the medium of their home language. Indeed, by 1946, there were already signs that things were at last moving in this direction, first at Llanelli, Carmarthen, Maesteg, Cardiff and Bae Colwyn and later at Aberdâr, Cwm Rhondda and Wrexham. Public meetings were held to which were invited parents, teachers, local councillors and education officers. The speakers at these meetings would include Ifan ab Owen Edwards and Norah Isaac, and before they left each meeting, they ensured that a local committee was set up to pursue the matter further. It was thus that most of the Welsh Schools established between 1947 and 1951 were initiated.

Perhaps it was natural that there should be a number of staff
changes now that war-time restrictions were relaxed. It was not
unusual for young graduates to leave posts of greater security in
order to give their service to the Urdd at a much lower salary,
simply because they believed in the movement and its ideals. It
was thus that the Urdd gained the services of Gwyneth Evans, Lili
Thomas and Henry Evans. Muriel Evans was the only Organiser
who left the staff at this period and she had already given the Urdd
three-and-a-half years of dedicated service. Elwyn Jones continued
to supervise the work in South Wales with special responsibility for
the Young Wales Clubs in Brecon and Radnor ; and Dafydd Jones
returned to Denbighshire and Flintshire as soon as he was released
from obligatory agricultural work. There were also considerable
changes in the ranks of the Club Wardens, and new members
included George Rees, Alwyn G. Thomas and Elfyn Jenkins. Emyr
Humphreys took over as Warden of the Caernarfon Aelwyd from
W. R. Jones who returned to the teaching profession ; Nan Davies
left the BBC to become Warden of Tregaron and Pontrhydfendigaid
Aelwydydd, and Tom Parry from Blaenau Ffestiniog became
Warden of the Aberystwyth Youth Club when I was appointed
Deputy Chief Organiser at Swyddfa'r Urdd. There were changes
too in the clerical staff at Headquarters. Evelyn Christian Jones
left after nine years and Janet Kyffin after seven ; both had given
exemplary service to the movement during difficult war years. They
were replaced by Margaret Williams and Nan Jones.

Before the end of 1946, Swyddfa'r Urdd was able to return to its
old home in Llanbadarn Road, now that *Yr Ysgol Gymraeg* had
moved to Lluest and the Founder and his family had moved to
Bryneithin.

*   *   *   *

At the beginning of 1946, *Yr Aelwyd* and *Cymru'r Plant* were able to
part company once more. Ifan ab Owen Edwards had now
completed twenty-five years as editor of *Cymru'r Plant,* and for the
first time, the magazine was given a two-colour cover. *Young Wales*
continued to appear as a twenty-four page quarterly. Its
contributors came from the ranks of the non-Welsh-speaking
members, and most of the editorial work was left to Aled Rhys

Wiliam of Swansea. *Meirionnydd*, bi-monthly magazine of the
Merioneth County Committee, which for three years had appeared
in duplicated form, now became a printed magazine.

A boon to the activities of many Adrannau was the publication of
Caneuon Actol yr Urdd, the work of three teachers who had long
pioneered in the field of action-songs—Olwen Lloyd of Cwm
Rhondda, and Tillie and Agnes Thomas of Clydach. Copyright
was given to the Urdd and the three-thousand copies were quickly
sold.

Officially, the responsibility for the Welsh Books Campaign now
rested with the Union of Welsh Publishers and Booksellers, but in
practice, the work was still administered through the Urdd. The
number of books sold in 1946 was 26,570, and many Branches taking
part were now obtaining their books direct through local booksellers.

At the evening concert following the Annual General Meeting of
Cwmni'r Urdd held at Bae Colwyn in October, Ifan ab Owen
Edwards ended his remarks with the words—*Pan na bydd mwy ohonof
ar y ddaear hon, os cofiwch fi am rywbeth, cofiwch fi am Addewid yr Urdd*.
(When I am no longer with you, if I am remembered for anything,
let it be for the Urdd Pledge). And now, more than twenty-five
years later, the Pledge remains unchanged as the basis of the
movement's activities and inspiration.

*   *   *   *

1947 was the Urdd's twenty-fifth birthday and was, therefore,
celebration year. As in 1943, when the Urdd came of age, it was
natural that Merioneth should steal a march on other counties and
call the clans together to a function at Llanuwchllyn on New Year's
Day. This was originally planned as a county rally, but two coach-
loads of young leaders, who had assembled at Cricieth for a post-
Christmas course, arrived unexpectedly and gave it the air of a
national gathering. Despite food shortages, the organising committee had somehow contrived to provide enough refreshments for all,
including a huge birthday cake, and at the meeting that followed,
members were able to share in the reminiscences of two first-
generation members—R. E. Griffith and Hywel D. Roberts.
Listening to these reminiscences, one caught a glimpse of what the
Urdd had already contributed during its first quarter-century, and

how bleak would have been the lives of the young people of Wales during that period had it not been for the activities initiated by the movement.

Celebrations in other counties followed, and few people in Wales could have been unaware of the fact that the Urdd had reached its twenty-fifth birthday. A Jubilee Fund was opened and a radio appeal by Ifan ab Owen Edwards on March 2 brought in a total of £1,200.

*　　　*　　　*　　　*

While the celebrations continued, it was essential that the usual programme of events should not be forgotten. The people of Cwm Rhondda had been denied the opportunity to act as hosts to the National Eisteddfod in 1941 and now were anxious to make good the loss. For the Rev. T. Alban Davies, this had long been a cherished dream. And just as Cadwgan of old had called the men of Rhondda to arms, so now Alban Davies called upon them to open their doors and their hearts to receive the 1947 Urdd Eisteddfod. And he did not call in vain.

The Aelwydydd had already been brought into the Eisteddfod system at Corwen, and now, at Treorci, it was decided to include competitions for Young Wales Clubs. However, like the younger *Dysgwyr* Branches, they were expected to compete in Welsh, but unlike the *Dysgwyr*, who naturally were able to get more help from the teachers in their schools, the language seemed to prove too great a barrier for the Young Wales Clubs, and the response was disappointing.

One of the main problems at Treorci was to secure a marquee that was large enough to accommodate the expected audiences. The largest available marquee could only seat two-thousand, and was obviously too small for the *Eisteddfodwyr* of Cwm Rhondda alone. Two other marquees were therefore added, one on either side, and between them, they could now seat four-thousand. Even so, it was hardly a satisfactory arrangement and it was obvious that this was a problem that would need urgent attention in any future planning.

The interest in drama seemed to be at a premium. Fifty groups had entered and between them they performed 62 plays. The onerous task of choosing the finalists was undertaken by Mary Lewis of Llandysul, and when one recalls the severe winter conditions of 1947, one cannot but be amazed that she should have somehow succeeded in completing her marathon task. At the final competitions at Treorci, she was joined by Irene Edwards and J. D. Powell, and for the audience it was a feast of dramatic performances.

The Treorci Committee had decided to revert to the pre-war arrangement of a three-day festival, and even so, each session had a capacity audience. There were more competitors from North Wales than in any previous Urdd Eisteddfod held in South Wales, and more than a thousand were given free hospitality in Rhondda homes. Denbighshire had the honour of being the winning county, despite valiant efforts by East Glamorgan who were competing on home ground. The Eisteddfod had cost well over a thousand pounds but, even without the advance fund, it would have been a viable proposition thanks to the response of the people of the Rhondda, and to the enthusiastic Eisteddfod Officials,—its Chairman, the Rev. T. Alban Davies, its Treasurer, the Rev. W. E. Anthony, and its Honorary Secretaries, Bessie Evans and the Rev. Emrys Ebenezer. They, however, would be the first to acknowledge their debt to W. P. Thomas, who would—and could— move mountains in order to ensure a smooth passage for the Eisteddfod proceedings.

The severe weather conditions in early 1947 clamped down on the Welsh Books Campaign. Even so, 149 Branches took part, and between them, sold a total of 17,115 volumes. What was encouraging was the growing co-operation between the Branches and local booksellers, and the fact that more and more of the latter were seeking to become members of the Union of Welsh Publishers and Booksellers.

*   *   *   *

In June 1947, it was announced that Ifan ab Owen Edwards was among those to be knighted in the King's Birthday Honours in recognition of twenty-five years' service to the youth of Wales. It was a distinction he deserved and an honour widely acclaimed by the people of Wales. Ifan ab Owen Edwards accepted the Knight-

hood, not as a tribute to himself but as a recognition of the movement he had created and a tribute to the hundreds of leaders who
had devoted their time and energy in the implementation of the
Urdd's ideals, and who had done so without expecting any reward or
remuneration.

The new title rested easily on Ifan ab Owen Edwards' shoulders.
There had always been a dignity in his appearance, in his manner
and even in his gait. It was part of his personality. Although always
a *gwerinwr*, he was also at ease with the aristocracy. He could walk
with the famous and the humble on equal terms. He often expressed
his regret that Wales had lost the leadership of its aristocracy when,
in their bid for wealth and power, they had denied their Welshness
and rejected the Welsh language. He would add, ' Wales must now
create a new aristocracy to lead the nation, an aristocracy that
speaks the language and treasures the culture of Wales.' At the
same time, he was not without hope that some of the old families
that had once played a significant part in the history of the nation
might one day acquire a sense of identification with Wales, and be
led back to discover their own roots. This was partly the basis of his
interest in the establishment of a Welsh-inspired residential school.

By this time, the Founder's two sons, Owen and Prys, were sturdy
lads—Prys was at Lluest School, while Owen had spent three years
at Ardwyn Grammar School, Aberystwyth. His father would have
liked to send him to a Welsh residential school, but since none
existed, he decided on a Quaker school—Leighton Park, Reading—
whose Headmaster had been a fellow-student of his at Lincoln
College, Oxford. Owen joined the Leighton Park School in September 1947, and it was here that he was to spend the next five years
of his scholastic career.

One special facet of the Jubilee celebrations was the publication
of a souvenir volume entitled *Y Llinyn Arian*. This was entrusted to
an Editorial Board with E. D. Jones, of the National Library, as
Chairman. A selection of poets, writers, musicians, scientists,
architects and artists were invited to donate an example of their
work as a gift to the Urdd on this special occasion. They responded
readily and the result was a substantial volume printed, for Cwmni'r

Urdd, by the Brython Press, Liverpool. The cover and title-page
were designed by R. L. Gapper.

The highlight of the 1947 celebrations was the function held at
Borth, Cardiganshire, on Saturday, July 19. It was to be a combined
garden-fête, open-air public meeting and social event. Throughout
the week, the weather had been ideal. On the Friday, however,
there was a thunderstorm that persisted throughout the night.
Next morning, there was still no sign of abatement and Pantyfedwen looked like an enormous Noah's Ark floating on the
waters. The marquees erected for the garden-fête looked like
sailing-boats tossed mercilessly by the wind. By mid-morning,
the crowds were already arriving by train, cars and coaches,
to be greeted only by torrential rain. Then at mid-day, when
even the most optimistic was in near despair, the miracle happened ; the rain ceased, and the sun took over. Stall-holders, still
in Wellington boots, worked frantically to be ready for the official
opening. It still seemed incredible that at one o'clock the
Llanidloes Silver Band would lead guests and members of the Urdd
Council towards the stage specially erected on the promenade.
However, the impossible became possible. In brilliant sunshine,
the Rev. H. Elvet Lewis led the devotional service. The Panty-
fedwen deeds were handed to Sir Ifan ab Owen Edwards by the
donor, D. J. James. The two main speakers were Ben Bowen
Thomas, Permanent Secretary to the Welsh Department of the
Ministry of Education, and the Right Hon. James Griffiths, M.P.
The official fête-opening followed, and the Chairman, Cynfab
Roberts, paid tribute to the dedicated efficiency of the organiser,
Mrs. Richard Phillips, and to Urdd workers all over Wales who had
made the fête a truly national event.

Later, when the feeding of the five-thousand had been accomplished, the crowds lingered on, reluctant to leave the happy atmosphere
of re-union which had been created. At the end of the day, the
Urdd was richer by more than £1,760, but a great deal richer in the
inspiration gleaned from working together, from new friendships,
and from a sense of triumph in the face of threatening disaster.

*   *   *   *

It was this contact with the Urdd and his gift of the Pantyfedwen centre that made D. J. James generally known to the people of Wales. He was already well-known in London-Welsh circles, and, of course, in Cardiganshire. He had followed his father into a grain business in London and later became interested in the film industry. In addition to land estates, he became the owner of Studios 1 and 2 in Oxford Street. The family were already known for their generosity to religious and other worthy causes, and D. J. James was to follow in their footsteps, with gifts to churches and hospitals as well as to his native Pontrhydfendigaid. Pantyfedwen was not his only gift to the Urdd. Having learnt of the movement's interest in organised games, he presented the Urdd with a solid silver cup which had cost £850 and was heavier and bigger than that of the Football Association of Great Britain ! Later, he established two Foundations—the Catherine and Lady Grace James Foundation, designed, *inter alia*, to benefit the Urdd National Eisteddfod, the National Eisteddfod of Wales and other Eisteddfodau still to be established, and the John and Rhys Thomas James Foundation designed mainly to help smaller and more local Eisteddfodau. Sir David James died on 7 March, 1967, and was buried in his beloved Ystrad Fflur in Cardiganshire.

Pantyfedwen opened immediately as a holiday centre for Welsh families. This was an experiment to discover whether such an arrangement could compensate in some measure for the loss of the popular Welsh cruises. The glorious summer days of 1947 were ideal for beach activities and for exploring the surrounding countryside, while in the evenings, social activities were organised by the guests with the help of the management. Well-deserved praises were showered on the Manager, Maldwyn Jones, and his staff, and the Urdd was implored to continue with the experiment.

While the families extolled the glories of Pantyfedwen, Urdd members were, as usual, enthralled with Llangrannog, Cricieth, and Caernarfon, and although more than three-hundred would-be campers had to be disappointed, more than two-thousand were given a week's holiday at one or other of the three centres, including some overseas groups. To Cricieth and Caernarfon came parties from Holland, Norway, Denmark, Finland, Czechoslovakia and

Java, while Llangrannog welcomed groups from Brittany, Czechoslovakia and West Africa. They brought with them their songs, and these were quickly included in the *repertoire* of the Welsh members, who sometimes substituted Welsh words, but more often adopted both the words and the melody. In this way, the camps would echo with such songs as *Gin gan gwli* and *Slavoni, slavaravoni slavak*. In 1946 and 1947, these overseas groups were usually invited separately and the experience gained in these camps later led the Urdd to embark on its International Conventions. Following their stay at camp, the overseas members of 1947 were invited to spend a further period in homes at Pontycymer, Pontyberem, Brynaman and Bala.

Writing on his return to Czechoslovakia, after a month's stay in Wales, Emanuel Kobosil wrote as follows—

' The youth of Wales may well feel proud of their heritage. They have a movement which has realised that barriers and misunderstandings can only be removed through personal contact, through living together in friendship and sharing one another's problems. This cannot be said of many organisations in the world today, and to my mind, this ideal of international friendship is the most important of all Urdd ideals. At the same time, the movement has a strong patriotic element, a healthy nationalism that arises from love of the homeland and its language, and aims at improving the life of the nation, without any jealousy and without becoming a threat to any other nation— as has happened so frequently in Europe. You in Wales are indeed fortunate.'

Whilst the Urdd was making its own small contribution towards fostering better understanding between the nations, there was a movement afoot to achieve a similar aim through the medium of music. Harold Tudor was a journalist from Coedpoeth serving the British Council. Government representatives from various overseas countries were already being welcomed at the National Eisteddfod of Wales, and Harold Tudor felt it would be even more valuable if the Eisteddfod could open its doors to admit competitors from overseas, especially in the choral competitions. He put his plan to W. S. Gwynn Williams of Llangollen who, among his other commitments, was Chairman of the National Eisteddfod's Music Committee. An approach was made to the Eisteddfod

Council, but although sympathetic, the Council was unable to agree to the suggestion since the essential aim of the Eisteddfod was to promote Welsh culture and the Welsh language. Harold Tudor accepted and understood the Council's decision, but undaunted, he suggested to W. S. Gwynn Williams the possibility of a separate festival, an International Eisteddfod. They visited several towns,— Cardiff, Aberystwyth, Rhyl, Caernarfon, Llandudno and Corwen, but everywhere there were difficulties ; sometimes lack of facilities, at other times, lack of faith and enthusiasm, and everywhere the lack of a suitable building. Then W. S. Gwynn Williams considered the possibilities of a marquee, similar to that used for the Anglesey County Eisteddfod. This could be erected anywhere, so why not at Llangollen—his own home town ? He won the support of the local Council. Naturally, there were doubts. Would groups and choirs be prepared to face heavy expenses and travel hundreds of miles to compete in a small township of three-thousand inhabitants on the Western fringe of Europe ? That would remain to be seen. The doubters were proved wrong, and the faith of W. S. Gwynn Williams was more than justified by the success of the very first International Eisteddfod of Music and Dance held at Llangollen in June 1947. Forty overseas choirs and groups took part, in addition to those from Britain. And when a German youth choir walked on to the stage, conscious of the fact that they came from what was recently regarded an ' enemy ' country, they were overcome by the fact that they were given the same warm welcome as had been given to other countries, and they turned and wept. By today, Llangollen has twenty-seven International Eisteddfodau to its credit, and it has done more than anything to put Wales on the world map. And for that world, the organisers chose, as their motto, words by T. Gwynn Jones— *Byd gwyn fydd byd a gano* (Blessed is a world that sings).

*   *   *   *

On St. David's Day, 1947, the Llanelli Welsh School was officially opened—not as an independent school, but one for which the local education authority was directly responsible, and where pupils could receive free education through the medium of the Welsh language. After seven-and-a-half years of pioneering by the Urdd, one local education authority had accepted the basic principle.

There was almost as much rejoicing at Aberystwyth as there was at Llanelli ! And the fact that the Headmistress was Olwen Williams, a product of the Urdd and a former member of staff, was an additional source of satisfaction.

Lluest now had a total of 90 pupils and their various successes were reported to the Annual Meeting of Governors and Parents in October. The nursery class had now joined the main school at Lluest and a fifth experienced teacher had been appointed in the person of Gwenhwyfar Ellis Williams. The Ministry of Education had been asked to arrange for a full inspection with a view to possible recognition of the school. Cynfab Roberts succeeded E. D. Jones as Chairman and his place as Vice-Chairman was taken by Humphrey D. Roberts. The other officers remained as before.

The Urdd Annual General Meeting was held at Swansea on 18 October. As usual, there were very favourable reports from the President and Chairman, but the Treasurer was rather despondent. Despite an increase in the Ministry of Education grant from £3,150 to £3,500, and an increase from £500 to £1,000 in the Jubilee Trust grant, the accounts for the financial year showed a deficit of £2,326. Thus when 1947—the Jubilee Year—drew to its close, the Urdd was rich in all but material wealth. In this respect, the prospects were not bright.

32   Sir Ifan ab Owen Edwards in the fifties   33   Lady Edwards

34   Lluest—home of the Aberystwyth Welsh School, 1946-51

35   Pantyfedwen, Borth—gift of D. J. James

36   D. J. James presenting the Pantyfedwen deeds to Sir Ifan

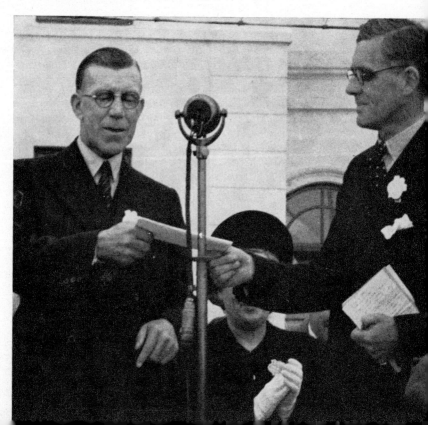

9

1947 had been a year of reminiscences ; 1948 was forward-looking and enterprising. It was the opportunity to lay the foundations of the second quarter-century ; to consolidate the movement's position on the threshold of a new period. The Urdd had more than eight-hundred Branches, all but a few of which were the responsibility of voluntary leaders. Sir Ifan ab Owen Edwards and R. E. Griffith were deeply conscious of the contribution made by these voluntary workers and wished it were possible to appoint more full-time staff to support and encourage them, to share the burden of county administration, and to develop still further activities on District and County levels. Such a move, however, was hampered by financial considerations.

It was while discussing this problem that Sir Ifan disclosed his intention of resigning from his post at the University. It was just two years since he had been appointed Director of Extra-Mural Studies and he had enjoyed the work immensely. Nevertheless, he was aware that as long as he held a post that demanded his full-time attention, he could not contribute as much as he would have wished to the work of the Urdd. One or the other would eventually suffer. He had, therefore, decided that he must devote the remainder of his life to the movement he had created. It would mean that he would no longer receive a salary but, as he explained in jocular mood, he had long discovered the existence of the Stock Exchange, and to his adventurous spirit the loss of a regular salary was of secondary importance !

The news that the Founder proposed to devote all his time and energy to help in the development of the Urdd was a source of great encouragement to all who were connected in any way with the work of the movement. That he was prepared to do so in a voluntary capacity and without remuneration of any kind was an even greater inspiration. This was not the first time that Sir Ifan had placed the Urdd before personal considerations, but this was perhaps his greatest sacrifice. No one appreciated this more than R. E. Griffith, who looked forward eagerly to working in still closer association with the Founder.

As part of their plan to lay a firm foundation for the work of the next decade, they decided on a pattern of re-organisation at Swyddfa'r Urdd aimed at giving more immediate help to those working in the field. Four departments were to be created, each with its own specific responsibility. Firstly, the Appeals Department would have its own committee, with Jenkin Alban Davies as Chairman. Nan Davies was appointed Head of the Department and she would have the assistance of two regional officers. Jenkin Alban Davies was anxious that the department should have every opportunity to succeed and he had himself contributed £5,000 towards its establishment. It was, later, a matter of considerable disappointment to him that this plan did not materialise to the extent that he would have wished.

Secondly, there was to be a Programmes Department, and thirdly the Training, Camps, and International Relations Department which was already in operation and for which I had been given special responsibility. Finally, the Administrative Department which had been the special concern of the Chief Organiser for more than fifteen years. With a clearer definition of responsibilities at Head Office, and with County Organisers acting as direct liaison between Swyddfa'r Urdd and the voluntary leaders in the field, it seemed reasonable to hope that the Urdd's contribution to the life of Wales could be increased and improved.

*   *   *   *

Though the Welsh Books Campaign came under the umbrella of the Union of Welsh Publishers and Booksellers, the scheme continued to be operated by the Urdd. 117 Branches took part in 1948, and 17,326 books were sold. Sir Ifan ab Owen Edwards resigned from the chairmanship of the Union and his place was taken by Howell Evans of The Brython Press, Liverpool, with Kate Roberts of *Gwasg Gee*, as Vice-Chairman.

By 1948, the Goodwill Message had regained much of the ground lost during the war years. It was a source of great satisfaction to his many friends that Gwilym Davies had been awarded the C.B.E. in recognition of his services to the cause of peace, and especially his part in the establishment of UNESCO.

A new experiment initiated through the Urdd in 1948 was the home-to-home exchanges that took place within Wales during the Easter vacation. The idea was for children showing an aptitude in learning Welsh as a second-language to spend part of their holiday in Welsh-speaking homes in Welsh-speaking areas. Under this plan, a group of boys and girls from Cardiff and Barry were accommodated in homes at Penygroes in Caernarfonshire, while a group from Llansawel (Briton Ferry) were accommodated at Llansawel in Carmarthenshire. The result was sufficiently encouraging to warrant developing and extending the scheme, and further experiments did in fact take place. The project was full of possibilities, and teachers in many areas were eagerly pressing for its implementation. Systematically organised, with the possibility of term-time extension, it could have made an enormous difference to the teaching of Welsh as a second-language. But the administration of such a scheme would be more than a voluntary organisation, already overburdened, could achieve, quite apart from the fact that it needed the full co-operation of the education authorities and should, therefore, come under the jurisdiction of the Welsh Joint Education Committee. An effort was made to interest the WJEC in the project, but without success, and a great opportunity was lost which could have revolutionised the teaching of Welsh during the past twenty-five years.

* * * *

In 1948, for the first time ever, the Urdd National Eisteddfod was held in Anglesey. It followed immediately after *Eisteddfod Môn* and by using the same ground and the same marquee, both bodies were able to save time, energy and expense. It was a far cry from Treorci in 1947 to Llangefni in 1948. There were no coal-pits, no narrow valleys like those of Cwm Rhondda, and it needed imagination to believe that the gently sloping hills of Anglesey could be called ' mountains ' ! In contrast to the Rhondda, there were romantic white-washed farmhouses and cottages, and innumerable sandy beaches. The Eisteddfod Fund had a target of £500. When the first two-hundred had been raised, an unexpected contribution of £100 from J. M. Howell, the former President, provided a new impetus and the remaining two-hundred was quickly raised. The Eisteddfod itself was so well supported that, with all expenses paid, there was still a surplus of £741.

Perhaps the biggest surprise was the support given by competitors from South Wales. Over a thousand youngsters travelled to Anglesey, few of whom had previously been further north than Aberystwyth. They were enthralled by the breath-taking views of Cader Idris, Aberglaslyn, Snowdon, Llyn Ogwen and Nant Ffrancon. And when the fleet of coaches arrived at their journey's end, the people of Llangefni looked astounded. They had not anticipated such an invasion. The journey had cost the South-Walians two-thousand pounds. That they should have been able to raise the money was something of a mystery. What was even more incredible to those unaccustomed to their enthusiasm was the fact that all competitors knew in advance that, even if they were among the finalists, they would not get a penny-piece towards their expenses. They came, not for personal gain, but for the sheer joy of competing and the possibility of gaining honour for their Adran or Aelwyd. And what a welcome awaited them ! Months earlier, the Hospitality Committee had visited homes within a given radius of Llangefni appealing for free accommodation for competitors from afar. It was understood that members would bring with them those foods that were still rationed. The parents had, of course, seen to it that this was done and the rations were duly handed over to the hosts on arrival. The hosts, however, had saved for the occasion. There was food in plenty, and when the time came to bid farewell, the rationed food-parcels were returned—unopened.

Six African guests attended the Eisteddfod and although they understood not one word, they sat entranced from beginning to end, amazed at the high standard of the competitions. Today, one tends to remember occurrences quite unconnected with the Eisteddfod programme. There was, for example, the committee member who realised that the Eisteddfod field adjoined the grounds of the Llangefni Sanatorium and decided to connect the Eisteddfod public address system to a loud-speaker in the Sanatorium so that the patients could hear the entire proceedings. Then there was a group of some two-hundred Aelwyd members from South Wales who had been unable to gain admission to the drama competition in the Town Hall. They assembled on the square and began singing, and soon they had become the nucleus of a *Cymanfa Ganu* conducted by Gwynn Tudno Jones of Llanelli. A collection was taken and presented as a gift to the Sanatorium. It was this kind of spirit that prevailed during the three-day festival and it was this that won the hearts of the people of Anglesey and prompted them to extend to their guests a welcome worthy of the title *Môn, Mam Cymru*. It was this too that made Wales one during those three days, all boundaries forgotten. But it was Caernarfonshire that won the ' Lloyd George Banner ' !

Following the successful experiment in 1947, it was not surprising that Pantyfedwen should be in great demand by Welsh families during the month of August. There was obviously a place for a homely hotel in which families could meet in the friendly atmosphere of a Welsh community. And the special provision for young children was, of course, an added attraction.

For the older children, however, Pantyfedwen was no substitute for camp life. And since no more than 1,500 could be accommodated at Llangrannog and Cricieth, it was decided to turn the Aberystwyth Aelwyd premises into a hostel for the accommodation of another fifty per week. One fortnight of the period, however, had to be reserved for an International Camp. The Foreign Office and the Ministry of Education were anxious that the Urdd should receive a group of young people from Germany. This was agreed, and in addition to the Welsh members selected to act as hosts, it was decided to invite groups from France, Holland, Denmark, Sweden and Czechoslovakia.

It is not easy for the youth of today to realise how much bitterness and hatred existed between the nations who had known war at first hand, on their own soil, as did the nations represented at this first International Camp at Aberystwyth. Europe had suffered so much at the hands of the Germans that it was difficult to forget or to forgive. The challenge to the Urdd was to bridge the gulf between them, and restore a faith in humanity that had been destroyed through the atrocities suffered by victors and vanquished alike.

We had asked the Foreign Office to allow Dr. Rudolph Hermann to act as leader of the German group. It was he who had brought the first German group to Llangrannog in 1932 ; during the war, he had himself suffered at the hands of the Nazis. He was, moreover, a teacher of modern languages and spoke fluent English. He was delighted to receive the invitation while we, for our part, knew that in him we had one who understood the Urdd and would help us in our task. We decided that the Germans should arrive before the other groups, and the Welsh contingent met them at the station. The Germans looked bewildered as the Welsh members closed around them, helped them with their luggage and, singing lustily, led the way to the hostel. Later, Theresa Rettler recalled their experience and wrote—

' It was difficult to imagine what kind of welcome would be given to us, the youth of Germany, the country that had been responsible, to a great extent, for the tragic world situation. But when we arrived at Aberystwyth station, our fears were drowned by the welcome we were given. Even before we came to know the Welsh members individually, we knew we would feel at home in their midst. This welcome at the station was the camp's first great success ; it began to create the friendly atmosphere which lasted throughout.'

Another wrote—

' We had been taught to hate other nations. We had lost the war, and we believed everyone hated us. We came here afraid of that hatred. But it does not exist in Wales. Here, there is not malice but kindness, not revenge but sympathy, not hatred but love. For the first time ever we experienced true happiness.'

The real test, however, was still to come. When the other groups were due to arrive, we made sure that the Germans as well as the Welsh members were at the station to greet them. For a moment, the Germans remained in the background, uncertain of their reception. Then without a word, they moved forward and helped with the luggage. Bent Svendsen of Denmark later said—

' I doubt whether we, the Danes, would have been able to make friends with the Germans, had it not been for the example set by the Welsh members. No other nation could have succeeded to the same extent.'

During the same period, at the request of the Ministry of Education, the Urdd was host to Harald Harlinghausen, a journalist who was also a youth leader in Totmos in South Germany. During his stay at Aberystwyth, he spent one evening at the International Camp. Speaking of the problems of Europe, he did not avoid referring to the war and its tragedy. 'The war' he said, 'is something that we in Germany must always remember, but which the rest of the world must try to forget.'

In the end, the barriers were broken down and much praise was due to the Urdd members who, aided by Tomi Scourfield and other staff members, created an atmosphere in which hatred and bitterness could not exist. The venture did not end when the groups left Aberystwyth, for it had been arranged for them to spend a further period in Welsh homes, accepted as members of the family. This too was an experience they would never forget and for which they would be ever grateful.

Gwilym Davies was delighted that the venture had succeeded, and that the Urdd had put into practice the ideal he had annually tried to express in the Goodwill Message of the Youth of Wales. And no one could be more pleased than Sir Ifan ab Owen Edwards ; another of his dreams had now become reality.

But the summer of 1948 was not without its sorrow. Following the visit to Llangrannog of a group of young people from Brittany the previous summer, a return visit had been arranged for the summer of 1948 at the invitation of the Mayors of some Breton towns. One of those who went to Brittany was sixteen-year old Ann Richards from the Garw Secondary School, Pontycymer, whose home was at Brynmenyn, near Bridgend. She and her friend, Valerie Davies, were guests of Monsieur Guillou, Deputy Mayor of Treguier in North Brittany. On Saturday evening, the family accepted the invitation of a friend who was captain of a fishing fleet and wished them to join him on a boat-trip in the bay. A sudden storm threatened, and they decided to return home. Before they could reach land, however, the boat capsized, and of the thirteen people aboard, eight were drowned, including Ann Richards and Monsieur Guillou. It was his daughter who helped to keep Valerie Davies afloat until they were rescued. Ann Richards was buried at Llansanffraid Church, near Abercynffig, on the very day that she would normally have returned from her holiday. A wreath, in the form of the Urdd badge, was placed on her grave. It said simply, ' With the sympathy of Urdd Gobaith Cymru '.

*   *   *   *

The Urdd had long been aware that its greatest asset lay in its voluntary leaders. Whatever its declared aims, the man-in-the-street judges the movement by what he sees and hears of the neighbouring Adran or Aelwyd. And what the Adran or Aelwyd achieves depends very largely on its leaders. Many Urdd leaders had now given years of voluntary service and it was important that the Urdd should continue to be able to attract a sufficient number of new leaders from its own ranks. Equally important was the quality of leadership. They needed to possess the basic skills of youth leadership and know the value and the possibilities of various activities that might appeal to their members. It was with this in mind that a series of weekend courses were held at Cilgwyn, Newcastle Emlyn, designed to train young leaders in music, *cerdd dant*, drama, mime, choral-speaking, craft-work, etc. Programme planning, the responsibilities of club officers, and committee procedure also came under consideration. But the weekends at Cilgwyn were able to offer a great deal more than formal tuition. The informal discussions, the atmosphere and the companionship were in themselves an inspiration that stimulated new effort.

*   *   *   *

1948 was an important year for *Ysgol Gymraeg Lluest*. At the request of the Governors, the Welsh Department of the Ministry of Education agreed to an inspection, and a team of HM Inspectors arrived at Lluest in February. It was six months or more before the eagerly awaited report was received. It began by tracing the circumstances that had led to the formation of the school in 1939, and its development during the interim period up to 1948. It noted that, at the time of the inspection, there were 94 pupils, 69 of whom were Welsh-speaking when they entered school, 8 had some knowledge of Welsh, and 17 were non-Welsh-speaking. The pupils generally were of above-average ability, and came from professional-class homes.

The buildings and equipment were generally satisfactory. Where improvements were considered desirable, plans already under consideration were indicated. There were warm tributes to the staff, and the report continued—'The Head Mistress is quite exceptional in her practical skill as a teacher, in her breadth of vision and in her general influence upon the school.'

The report referred to the aims and objects of the school, and outlined ways in which those aims were being implemented. The most important section was that which assessed the educational standards attained by the school. After indicating the sound foundations laid in the infant and junior classes, the report specifically mentioned the achievements of the older children—

> ' The culmination of the sound basic training is to be seen in the top class where the teaching is of a very high order, and the standard of attainment in Welsh and English, in oral and written work, is particularly good. The teaching of Arithmetic is also sound. A striking feature is the extent of the children's general knowledge and their range of ideas. They have a quite remarkable knowledge of the Bible; of Welsh poetry which they speak well, with feeling and understanding ; of Welsh traditional literature in proverbs, in legends, in *penillion telyn* and in folk songs. All these they enjoy in an intelligent and lively manner.'

There were comments too on the children's mastery of English, and their exceptional interest in History, Geography, Nature and Art. Referring to the pupils who had no knowledge of Welsh when they entered school, the report said—

> ' What causes perpetual surprise to anyone coming in contact with the school is the speed and efficiency with which the non-Welsh-speaking section of younger pupils attain a good working knowledge of Welsh, and the facility with which they speak, read and write Welsh before they leave school.'

The concluding paragraph was a tribute to the vision and perseverance of Sir Ifan ab Owen Edwards and his supporters, to the inspiration of Norah Isaac, and to the dedicated efforts of her staff—

' To sum up, the School successfully reflects in the classrooms and in its general activities the ideal set out by the founders. That ideal is the belief in the value of rich spiritual and cultural education based on Welsh life and language as the best means of releasing the Welsh child to full capacity. With this ideal in mind, the teachers help the children to live the Welsh life joyously. Their growth is marked ; they are stimulated to a desire for knowledge ; their whetted appetites are satisfied and their memories are stored with treasures of Welsh lore, poetry, song and legend. The atmosphere is one of a lively Welsh community living together in freedom, joy and activity, learning to grow richly from their own native soil, and later branching out to embrace a knowledge of English language, literature, song and story, and to some understanding of the way of life of people of other lands.'

Through this report, the Ministry of Education was, in effect, indicating its full approval of the experiment carried out at Aberystwyth, suggesting that it might be ground that would yield a fruitful harvest to any Education Authority that had the vision to follow the lead given by this independent school. Henceforth, Lluest School would be included ' in the Ministry's list of efficient schools '.

With such a report, it was no longer necessary for the Urdd to proclaim the virtues of *Ysgol Gymraeg Aberystwyth* in any attempt to persuade education authorities to adopt a similar policy. All that was now required was to let the report speak for itself. Welsh schools had already been set up at Llanelli, Cardiff, Llandudno, Y Rhyl, Mold and Holywell. No persuasion had been necessary in the case of the three last named. They were established by Dr. Haydn Williams, Flintshire's progressive Director of Education, without any pressure from the Urdd or from parents.

Recognition of Lluest as an ' efficient school ' did not mean that it became state-aided ; it continued to be an independent school which meant that the parents and the Urdd still had to share the financial burden. Despite the financial concern, however, it was decided that the teachers' salaries should henceforth be based on the Burnham Scale and that they should be brought into the Teachers' Superannuation Scheme. The number of pupils had increased to 108 and a sixth teacher was appointed in the person of Gwenda Rees (now Black), a graduate of the University College at Aberystwyth.

At the end of 1948, it was decided that the School Committee should henceforth be a standing committee of Cwmni'r Urdd. This meant that the Treasurer of Cwmni'r Urdd would also be the Treasurer of Lluest School. As President of the Urdd, Sir Ifan ab Owen Edwards would continue to be President of the school, and as Chief Organiser, R. E. Griffith would continue to act as Secretary. The Committee's Chairman was Humphrey D. Roberts.

1948 saw more changes in the ranks of Organisers and Club Wardens. The Appeals Department was further staffed by the appointment of W. O. Jones and Evan L. Isaac as Regional Organisers, with Ann Lloyd as Secretary. Huw Cedwyn Jones, with four years' experience as Club Wardenand as Organiser, was appointed Administrative Assistant to the Chief Organiser with special responsibility for the National Eisteddfod. Tom Bevan became Pembrokeshire's first full-time Organiser. The appointment of a Physical Recreation Officer was long overdue, and in the person of Teifryn G. Michael was found a man of outstanding qualifications and ability. Meirion Powell became full-time Warden of *Aelwyd y Rhos* and Beti Edwards, a graduate with experience in social work, was appointed Warden of *Aelwyd Tycroes* in Carmarthenshire.

Naturally, there were losses too, and the resignation of two of the Urdd's most experienced Organisers was a severe blow. Beryl Owen had given six years of dedicated service in Merioneth, and Elwyn Jones, who now returned to the teaching profession, had been a member of the Urdd staff for ten years. He had been responsible for establishing many of the Aelwydydd and Young Wales Clubs, and was an invaluable asset in all Urdd activities. To lose a man of his calibre was to leave a gap that was not easily filled.

The Annual General Meeting of Cwmni'r Urdd was held at Wrexham in October. Whereas the co-operation between the Urdd and the Ministry of Education was very satisfactory, it was obvious from the reports of the Chairman (Dr. Gwenan Jones) and the Treasurer (Prof. D. Hughes Parry) that some tension existed between the Urdd, as a voluntary body, and some local education authorities. It was this that led Dr. Gwenan Jones to comment—

' We are prepared to co-operate with the education author-ities, but a movement needs to be free if it is to co-operate in the right spirit. Like all other youth organisations, the Urdd is concerned with the leisure of young people. But the Urdd is more than a youth organisation in the usual connotation of the term—it is a means of preserving, developing and enriching the Welsh way of life. To do that, the movement needs to be free of all fetters.'

At this meeting, Dr. Gwenan Jones was among those elected Vice-Presidents and her place, as Council Chairman, was taken by Prof. D. Hughes Parry, with Cynfab Roberts as Vice-Chairman and Chairman of the Executive Committee. Jenkin Alban Davies became Treasurer, and E. Morrice Job took over from Hywel D. Roberts as Honorary Secretary. Two days after the Annual General Meeting, I. D. Hooson, solicitor and poet, died. He had left a legacy of £10,000 to the Urdd, in addition to royalties from his books, *Cerddi a Baledi* and *Y Gwin a Cherddi Eraill*. Another legacy of £1,000 was left to the Urdd in the will of Dr. Erie Evans, of Bangor.

The Annual General Meeting at Wrexham was followed by a concert, and *Adran Ysgol Ramadeg Pontardawe* had been invited to be responsible for the programme. They had abundant talent and their constant training meant that they could present a full and varied programme of high standard. The person directly responsible was Agnes Thomas but, as usual, she was supported by her sisters, Tillie and Sarah, who shared her interests and were motivated by the same loyalties. It is doubtful whether any movement has received such devoted and unselfish service as the Urdd has been given by this Clydach family over a period of forty years.

*　　　*　　　*　　　*

Beneath the satisfaction of knowing that the Ministry of Education had paid *Ysgol Gymraeg Lluest* a glowing tribute in the report issued in 1948, there lay the gnawing concern about the school's financial position. It is true that the school had never been a viable proposition. This was accepted from the very beginning. Its income was derived solely from fees paid by parents, reinforced by occasional money-raising, schemes. This was barely sufficient to pay the teachers' salaries, leaving nothing for other equally essential expenses. The Urdd Council had undertaken to close the gap as far as this was possible within its limited resources. The school was envisaged, however, as an experimental and pioneering scheme that would be continued only until the principle of Welsh-based education was accepted by the Ministry of Education and by the local education authorities.

During the first few years, the Urdd Council had been only too ready to contribute the £300-£400 required annually to meet the deficit in the school's accounts. But when rising costs brought the deficit to £700 in 1947 and to £1,000 in 1948, with the likelihood that it would reach £2,000 in two or three years, the Urdd Council was forced to give the matter serious consideration and decree that, in addition to any capital expenditure, its annual contribution would henceforth have to be limited to £400. By this time, a number of Welsh state-schools had been set up, and similar schemes were under consideration in other Anglicised areas. But despite the unqualified success of the Urdd experiment and the lead given in the provision of state-schools in other areas, there was no move in this direction at Aberystwyth. It seemed as though the very existence of Lluest was detrimental to such a move. It was, there-fore, proposed that pressure should now be brought to bear on the Cardiganshire Education Committee to set up a Welsh School under the jurisdiction of the Authority. This proposition was approved both by the Lluest Committee and the Urdd Executive Committee, and a sub-committee was set up to consider how the decision should be implemented.

It was sheer coincidence that four members of the school staff should resign while these discussions were taking place. Arrangements to fill these posts were made, and then came another blow. Norah Isaac had been invited to take up a post as lecturer at the Barry Training College. It was a difficult decision for her to make, and a major blow for Lluest. She had been a member of the Urdd staff for fourteen years and it was she—above all others—who had made the dream of a Welsh School come true. No one felt the loss more keenly than the Founder, but he knew, in his heart, that Norah Isaac had even more to contribute to the cause of Welsh education and that, in a Teachers' Training College, she would be able to impart to others her experience, her enthusiasm and her vision.

Amidst all these difficulties, Lluest had a total of 112 pupils and a Parents' Association not easily discouraged. It was recognised that the example and stimulus of Lluest was still necessary to parents in other areas struggling to persuade their education authorities to set up a free school based on the same educational principles. Such a struggle was currently in progress at Swansea, and it is doubtful whether the parents there would have succeeded without the support given by Sir Ifan and the Urdd Council. The Swansea Education Authority eventually agreed to set up a Welsh school but declined to pay for the transport of pupils and demanded a three-year legal agreement that these costs would be met by the parents. On behalf of the Swansea parents, Cwmni'r Urdd guaranteed a sum of £500 per annum for a period of three years. The necessary transport costs were, in fact, paid by the parents, and Ysgol Lôn Las soon developed into a school of which the Education Authority could well feel proud.

One highlight of 1949 was undoubtedly the Pontarddulais Urdd National Eisteddfod. It was in fact the combined effort of Hendy and Pontarddulais under the chairmanship of John S. Davies, with T. Glyn Nicholas as Secretary. In an area so rich in cultural tradition, there was no difficulty in assembling a team of one-hundred-and-fifty as members of the various sub-committees. An advance fund of £750 was raised, and free hospitality given to two thousand competitors from afar. The standard of competition was high and, as one event followed the other without delay, a London press correspondent described the festival as ' a non-stop variety show, exciting and breath-taking.' So great was the enthusiasm in the home county itself that no one was surprised that the ' Lloyd George Banner ' went to Carmarthenshire. Perhaps the climax of the whole week, however, was the pageant *Molawd Cymru* (In Praise of Wales) staged in the marquee and produced by Nan Davies, with T. Haydn Thomas as Music Director. It was a miscellany of choral-speaking, drama, mime, music and dance, linked by the narrator into a coherent and artistic presentation.

With a total attendance of more than twenty-thousand people, the Pontarddulais Eisteddfod could not fail to be a financial success. Indeed, there was a surplus of £1,141, the highest on record.

In April, Princess Elizabeth and the Duke of Edinburgh visited Merioneth, and the Urdd Council agreed to the request of the Merioneth County Council that a deputation of Urdd members should join those assembled to welcome the Royal visitors at Harlech Castle as part of their tour of Wales. The occasion at Harlech had none of the pomp usually associated with visits of this nature. On the contrary, it was characterised by the warmth and spontaneity of its welcome. The Urdd contingent was led by R. E. Griffith and Meirion Jones who took the opportunity of explaining to the Royal couple the aims and activities of the movement.

May 18 was Goodwill Day and, as usual, the Message was given full coverage in the May issue of the Urdd magazines. The annual Goodwill Service, initiated in 1933, had been suspended during the war years. It was now re-instated and on this occasion, it was held at Cardiff and organised by W. C. Elvet Thomas and the Cardiff District Committee.

In August of that year, W. J. Williams of Llangystennin died at the age of 86. It was he who had been primarily responsible for establishing Cwmni'r Urdd as an Incorporated Body in 1931/32, and ever since he first came into contact with the Urdd, his interest in and his concern for the movement had never ceased.

*   *   *   *

The appointment of Teifryn Michael as Physical Recreation Organiser had already meant a resurgence of interest in recreational activities. Evening classes and one-day schools had been arranged ; county sports were re-established and the Urdd Football Competition was revived after a gap of ten years. Together with a greater emphasis on outdoor activities at camp, all this helped to restore the balance between cultural and recreational activities in the Urdd programme.

It was during this period too that the Urdd first saw the possibilities of folk-dancing as a recreational activity. Folk-dancing had long found a place in the Urdd programme, both in the Eisteddfod and in the Mabolgampau, but so few Welsh dances were available and so little known about the dance tradition in Wales—mainly due to the religious revivals—that there seemed to be little that could be offered apart from the ' Llanofer Reel '. In 1930, Mrs. Lois Blake, an English lady from Liverpool, already well-versed in the folk-dances of England and of the continent, came to live at Corwen in Merioneth. She began to ponder on the dearth of information

regarding Welsh dances. W. S. Gwynn Williams of Llangollen had
already published his 'Welsh Folk Music and Dance' which
included the Llanofer Reel, and had discovered the manuscript of
the Llangadfan Dances. He solicited Mrs. Blake's help in interpreting the dance notation in this manuscript and, as a result of
their combined effort, these dances were published in 1936. Further
research by Mrs. Blake led to the publication of 'Welsh Morris
and other Dances' and 'Welch Whim'. Then the war came, and
the work had to be suspended. But in 1948, Mrs. Blake was invited
to a Christmas course held by the Urdd at Pantyfedwen, and this
was her first contact with the movement. It struck her that here
was just the movement that could instil the breath of life into the
dances that hitherto had been no more than dead bones. In 1949,
Cymdeithas Ddawns Werin Cymru (The Welsh Folk Dance Society)
was formed, and from the very beginning the Urdd co-operated
with the Society in the task of restoring to the youth of Wales a part
of their lost heritage.

As a result of these developments, we were now able to add
physical recreation and folk-dancing to the cultural content of Urdd
training courses. Weekend courses were held at Cilgwyn (Newcastle
Emlyn), Cilfro (Kilvrough) in Gower, Coleg y Fro at Rhoose,
Bodfach near Llanfyllin, and Plas y Nant, the Christian Endeavour
centre at Betws Garmon. Other centres followed ; our programme
was extended, and the effect was reflected in the work of the
Aelwydydd—both in the variety of activities and in the standards
achieved.

*   *   *   *

The demand for places at camp increased each year, and in
order to accommodate the two-and-a-half-thousand applicants, it
was necessary to make use of the four centres—Llangrannog,
Cricieth, Aberystwyth and Pantyfedwen. Of these, Llangrannog
was the only true camp ; the others were hostels without the freedom
of isolation, and even though a smaller hostel meant closer companionship, it also placed considerable strain on those responsible for
restraining the high spirits of young people so as to avoid complaints
from neighbours.

Following the successful experiment at Aberystwyth in 1948, the International Camp had to be continued. On this occasion, however, it was held at Pantyfedwen, Borth, and was more of a study-convention than a holiday camp. Pantyfedwen was ideal for this purpose. Borth itself was within easy reach of Aberystwyth so that we could draw on the resources of the University for our programme of lectures. There was a superb beach on the doorstep of Pantyfedwen, and Borth was centrally placed for excursions and expeditions to places of scenic and historic interest. The hostel had its own managerial staff so that we were relieved of any need to worry about material arrangements.

To join the strong band of Welsh members, we had invited groups from Norway, Sweden, Germany, Austria, France and America, as well as a small group of refugees from the Baltic countries— Estonia, Latvia and Lithuania. There was not quite as much tension as there had been the previous year, though there were moments when we felt we were skating on thin ice, and the Welsh members had to be on their toes, sensitive to any statement that could cut to the quick or be capable of misinterpretation. Each day ended with an epilogue in which everyone voluntarily joined. Sometimes the whole company would linger on, singing and chatting, and even when *Nos Da* had been said, we would again assemble on the stairs or lean over the banisters, singing Welsh songs and hymns, invariably ending with Idwal Jones'—

> *I bawb lluddedig yn ein gwlad,*
> *Nos da, nos da.*

As in 1948, the most important contribution made by the International Convention was that it helped to restore, to those who had experienced the horrors of war, some faith in humanity, some reorientation of values, qualities that war invariably destroys. As one of the Estonians wrote on his return—

> ' After the hard knocks of the last ten years, we found it almost incredible that such kindness and such friendship should still be possible.'

Following three glorious weeks at Pantyfedwen, the overseas members were accommodated in homes, some at Bala, others at Glanaman.

Nor was this the only gathering with an international flavour planned for 1949. To join a contingent of Welsh members at Pantyfedwen, we had invited representatives of the other Celtic territories for the Easter vacation. They came from Brittany, Cornwall, Ireland, Scotland and the Isle of Man. The affinity between us was obvious ; it was a family gathering. There were talks and discussions—official and unofficial. There were visits to places of cultural and historic interest. We stood together at the grave of T. Gwynn Jones at Aberystwyth ; a Welsh hymn was sung, and a wreath placed on the grave by one of the Bretons while *Ffarwel y Telynor* (The Harpist's Farewell) was played on the harp by Tom Bevan.

We learnt one another's songs ; we danced one another's dances. Joining in the Irish dances proved to be a stimulus to our newly-found interest in our own dances and made us more determined than ever that they should be restored. Gradually we became accustomed to the melancholy tones of the Scottish and Aeolian pipes, and our ears became attuned to the nasal half-tones of the Irish and Scottish folk-songs. When the time came to leave Pantyfedwen, we felt we were bidding farewell to our own kin, and it was obvious that the other Celts felt the same.

In addition to welcoming young people from other countries to Wales, arrangements were also made for groups of young Urdd leaders to visit other countries. Three group-visits were organised in 1949, one to the South of France, one to Ireland and one to Germany. The visit to Ireland was greatly enhanced by the fact that we now had friends there who did not spare themselves in an effort to make us welcome. Prime among these was Oscar Mac Uilis, an ardent Irishman and Secretary to the Gaelic League. He had learnt Welsh and had been at the Inter-Celtic Convention at Pantyfedwen. For as long as we were in Dublin, he was our friend and guide. We were taken to places of historic interest in the city ; we visited the Abbey Theatre ; and there were excursions to Drogheda and the Boyne Valley, to Swords where Gruffydd ap Cynan had been born, and to Monasterboice and Tara. And in the evenings there were *Ceilidh* where we met other Pantyfedwen acquaintances and made new friends.

For the latter part of our stay, we travelled to Galway and were met by Thomas ó'Máille. He was Professor of Celtic at Galway University where it was possible to take a degree course entirely through the medium of Irish. Unexpectedly, we were joined for a few days by Ambrose Bebb, who knew the *Gaeltacht* as he knew Wales, and it was a privilege to have his company. Our most lasting memory was of the boat journey to the Aran Isles and the opportunity to mingle with peasants who seemed literally to perform the miracle of turning stones into bread.

The group heading for Germany was led by R. E. Griffith and had Bielefeld as its destination. Here our contact was Dr. Rudolph Hermann who had brought the first group of girls to Llangrannog in 1932, and led the German groups to Aberystwyth in 1948 and to Borth in 1949. The Welsh members were accommodated in homes and this in itself meant lasting friendships. The first thing that struck the Welsh members as they wandered through the town of Bielefeld was the effort and energy invariably put into a day's work. Half the town had been destroyed during the war, and now, four years later, it was practically rebuilt. In another year, the work would be completed.

During the visit, an unexpected request was made to R. E. Griffith by the German members who had been to Wales. They wanted to set up a Welsh-German Aelwyd within the youth centre to which they belonged. And on the last evening, the ceremony of establishing the Aelwyd was part of the farewell programme. The members pledged themselves to serve their country, to serve their fellow-man whoever he might be, and to be true to Christ.

Arrangements for the third group were made through a travel agency. There was no advance contact at Chamonix or Hauteluce ; it was intended primarily as a sightseeing holiday. As it happened, they were unfortunate in their accommodation, and this naturally detracted from the enjoyment of the tour. Nevertheless, there were exciting excursions to Annecy, to Geneva, to the St. Bernard Pass and Col de Saisies. At Hauteluce they mingled with the inhabitants whose life was simple and plain, and where all the colour seemed to have been concentrated in the churches.

*   *   *   *

By the end of 1949, thirty-five Aelwydydd possessed their own premises. In some cases, maintenance costs were later found to be prohibitive and the premises had to be sold. Others were more venturesome and decided to undertake major reconstruction work. It was no mean achievement to shoulder this financial burden while at the same time continuing the normal activities of the Aelwyd.

As always, there were staff changes, both among the County Organisers and the Club Wardens. The heaviest blow was the loss of Eunice Roberts who had been a pillar of strength in North Wales for eleven years, and who now left to be married. Nan Davies, after three years on the Urdd staff, returned to the BBC and Ann Lloyd joined Maldwyn Jones to share in the managerial duties at Pantyfedwen. Mair Richards, who had joined the Urdd staff five years earlier with a diploma in youth service, left to take a Teachers' Training Course. And Lili Thomas, who had led Carmarthenshire to victory at the Pontarddulais Eisteddfod, returned to the teaching profession.

The Annual General Meeting of Cwmni'r Urdd was held at Caernarfon. It was an opportunity to pay tribute to Dr. Griffith Evans in his home town for his generosity both to the local Aelwyd and to the Urdd as a movement. Despite the encouraging reports on the year's activities, no one could feel complacent when the Treasurer reported that there was a deficit of £4,514 on the accounts of the previous financial year. He explained that this was partly due to the fact that a salary scale for staff members had been adopted, while at the same time, the Urdd had aimed at the appointment of a full-time Organiser for each county. There had been a deficit of more than £1,500 in the Lluest accounts, and a loss of £500 on camps, largely due to expenses connected with the International Convention. The total deficit of £4,514 had occurred despite a Ministry of Education grant of £5,200 and a £1,000 grant from the Jubilee Trust. The Treasurer warned that £10,000 would have to be raised within the next six months if the Urdd was to avoid a deficit on the 1949/50 accounts. The seriousness of the situation was not lost on the members present, and the Council and its Committees were asked to take whatever measures they considered necessary to rectify the position as soon as possible.

Sir Ifan ab Owen Edwards was doubly concerned about the financial position. This was no time to disclose that he had a new scheme in mind, a costly and ambitious project that would temporarily increase rather than reduce the movement's debt. He was confident, however, that this would be the right course of action, that the opportunity should not be lost, and that, somehow or other, ways and means would have to be found to implement this new scheme.

10

Having spent much of his childhood at Llanuwchllyn, Sir Ifan ab Owen Edwards had maintained close contact with the neighbourhood, and even after twenty years of living at Aberystwyth, he would speak of Penllyn in the same glowing terms as his father before him. He, therefore, longed to anchor the Urdd to this part of Merioneth, a district that was thoroughly Welsh and rich in tradition and folk culture. This was partly why he chose to hold his first camp at Llanuwchllyn. Even at that time, he had attempted to persuade Sir Watkin Williams Wynn to allow him to rent Glan Llyn for that purpose, but such an idea was abhorrent to Sir Watkin. However, Sir Ifan kept his eye on the spot, firmly believing that the opportunity would come—some day. And it came in 1949/50.

At one time Plas Glan Llyn had been among the most famous of Penllyn mansions. It had once belonged to the monks of Cymer Abbey, but after the Dissolution of the Monastaries, Dr. Elis Price had appropriated Glan Llyn for himself. Later it became part of the Wynnstay estate, property of the Wynn family. In the mid-nineteenth century, it was used as a shooting-box by the then Sir Watkin Williams Wynn, and on one occasion Queen Victoria was among his guests.

Gradually, however, heavy taxes curbed the spending of the aristocracy ; Glan Llyn ceased to be inhabited and soon fell into disrepair. By the 1930's the Glan Llyn Estate had been acquired by the Treasury in lieu of death duties, and was controlled by the Agricultural Land Commission. In the early forties, the War Office was granted the use of Plas Glan Llyn and it soon showed further signs of wear. By 1949, the Welsh Agricultural Land Sub-Commission was anxious to find a tenant for the mansion, a tenant who would respect both the natural beauty and the Welsh tradition of the locality. Naturally, Sir Ifan ab Owen Edwards had his ear to the ground and lost no time in preparing his case, making an application for the tenancy on behalf of the Urdd. He was asked to meet members of the Sub-Commission to enlarge on his proposals.

Had they rejected his application, he would, no doubt, have been heart-broken ; instead, it was just the proposition the Sub-Commission were looking for, and they were more than ready to grant the Urdd the tenancy of Plas Glan Llyn at an annual rent of £100.

And so, despite the financial difficulties facing the Urdd at this period, the Council readily agreed to support Sir Ifan ab Owen Edwards in embarking on this new scheme. Together, the Founder and Chief Organiser got down to the task of turning Glan Llyn into a camp centre in readiness for the summer of 1950. Urgent repairs were undertaken by the Sub-Commission, and the Ministry of Education gave a grant of £2,500 towards the cost of furnishing and equipping. The remaining expenses came from the I. D. Hooson legacy, and nothing would have pleased the poet-solicitor more than to know that, in the case of Glan Llyn, the youth of Wales had taken over from the aristocracy.

*   *   *   *

It was no easy task to find someone of the right calibre to take over the headship of Ysgol Lluest from Norah Isaac. By good fortune, however, the Urdd was able to appoint Hywel D. Roberts whose name was as well-known as that of Norah Isaac. He had been prominent in Urdd circles since his schooldays and, in later years, he had been a member of the Council and Honorary Secretary of the Company. He was a graduate of Aberystwyth, and had taught in primary and secondary schools before being appointed Further Education Officer for Flintshire. It was felt that he had an important contribution to make to the future of Ysgol Lluest and his appointment was hailed with rejoicing.

By this time, there were ten Welsh Schools under the control of local education authorities. It was now ironic that pupils in these schools obtained their schooling free while the education of Lluest pupils continued to be a burden on their parents and even more of a burden on Cwmni'r Urdd. A memorandum was submitted to the Cardiganshire Education Authority in May, but without response. The school had 125 pupils, five more than the considered optimum for the available building and equipment. The new Headmaster brought with him a wealth of ideas and enthusiasm. And it was a welcome experience for the pupils to have a man on the staff !

Despite fund-raising efforts, the school's financial difficulties continued. There was a deficit of £890 in the 1949/50 accounts and no prospect that this would be reduced in 1950/51. The school had no one to turn to but Cwmni'r Urdd, and since that body was itself in financial trouble and already contributing more than the promised maximum towards the upkeep of the school, the Executive Committee was forced to consider how long the present situation could be allowed to continue. Some parents argued that the experiment had already been proved, that other education authorities had accepted the principle and had already set up Welsh-based state schools. They saw no reason, therefore, for perpetuating Lluest as an independent school. Others held that the battle was not yet completely won, and that Lluest should continue yet awhile. But the question had to be faced—how could the school be financially maintained ? The deficit was already more than the Urdd could afford to meet, and was likely to increase in 1951/52 when the Burnham Scale of salaries for teachers would be upgraded, resulting in additional costs of £600 at Lluest. Furthermore, the Headmaster and his Committee were pressing for an extra teacher, which would mean another £500. This would add yet another £1,100 to the present deficit of £900. The parents were not prepared to pay more ; the Urdd could not afford to meet the deficit. In the dilemma, the Executive Committee, at its December meeting, decided that a resolution be put to the Urdd Council in early January.

*   *   *   *

The Urdd National Eisteddfod at Wrexham in 1950 was a brave attempt at bringing an essentially Welsh festival to an Anglicised border town. No effort was too great for the organising committee. The advance-fund had a target of £750 and a total of £1,000 was reached. Had it not been for this fund, the Eisteddfod would have been a financial loss. More than nine-hundred competitors were given free hospitality and this was offered readily and generously. But the task of projecting the Eisteddfod to the local population was not easy, and had it not been for the devotion of the Officers and their committee members, the Eisteddfod might have been a dismal failure. Wrexham was an Anglicised town and seemed to lack the right atmosphere for a wholly-Welsh festival. It was also a large town, and many of its inhabitants seemed totally unaware of the Eisteddfod's existence. The festival failed to make the kind of impact it had made at Pontarddulais where it meant everything to everybody. This must have been discouraging for those who had struggled for two years against such odds. Great credit was due to the Chairman, Ald. Cyril O. Jones, the Vice-Chairman, the Rev. James Humphreys, the two Honorary Secretaries, D. T. Morgan and T. H. Evans, and the Treasurer, K. Harris Hughes.

Audience attendances were disappointing. Nevertheless the standards were, as always, consistently high, and it was surprising that competitors were able to perform with such zest when faced with a half-empty marquee. But while everyone else bemoaned the lack of local response, Charles Atkinson of the BBC (London) was busy throughout the week recording the competitions and gleaning information about the Eisteddfod and the Urdd for an overseas broadcast. He was more than satisfied, and within a week, his programme had been relayed to France, Germany, Belgium, Sweden, Norway, Denmark and Romania.

* * * *

Two books dealing with Wales were published in 1950. One was ' A History of Modern Wales ' by David Williams, Professor of Welsh History at the University College, Aberystwyth. Dealing with the period 1485-1939, he assessed the Urdd's contribution in the inter-war years as follows—

' A remarkable development in the inter-war years which helped to counteract social disintegration was the growth of the Urdd. It was founded in 1922 and, in time, became over 50,000 strong, in addition to adults who acted as leaders and advisers. Without any political affiliation, the Urdd has sought to develop a healthy national life by instilling into the youth of Wales an interest in their own tradition, together with a sense of their kinship with other countries, and engraining in them a devotion to the service both of Wales and of humanity. By its own national eisteddfod and its *mabolgampau* (olympic games), it has provided the youth of Wales with a stimulus to healthy mental and physical recreation, and has brought together north and south, rural and industrial Wales, English-speaking as well as Welsh-speaking, into a close unity of purpose.'

The other volume was 'The Welsh' by Wyn Griffith. This was not intended as a history book, but rather as a study of Welsh environment and culture, as expressed in our literature, our arts, our politics and our religion. It was an attempt to interpret the Welsh to their English-speaking neighbours. Writing of the Urdd and its place in the life of the nation, the author had this to say—

' In 1922 a moment of vision came to a young man, son of a father who had himself rendered great service to Wales. The new movement—Urdd Gobaith Cymru—catered for body and mind, and much of its initial and continuing success is due to the determination of the founder that it should not be an indoor affair. For Welsh children who did not belong to the Scout movement, this was something new ; holiday camps, hostels, trips abroad, games of all kinds cultivated a pride in fitness that was never allowed to dominate other activities.

Being Welsh, it naturally has its Youth Eisteddfod, a thoroughly healthy and uncommercialised affair, stimulating their minds and helping the arts . . . It serves all and quarrels with no one, and if all the youth movements in the world followed its example, nationalism might acquire a new meaning . . . It is the one movement in Wales which can be praised without qualification, even by a Welshman ; it has done nothing but good and it has quietly brought its idealism into the daily lives of scores of thousands of Welsh children and young people. To its founder, Sir Ifan ab Owen Edwards, Wales owes a debt which, although it can never be repaid, the country is prompt to acknowledge. He has done more for Wales than any man living: more, indeed, than any man for many generations. He has shown us a way of being Welsh, of being true to the country's traditions, without stirring hatred of any other country . . . The success of this youth movement shows clearly that it is possible, given inspired leadership, to turn into solid practical form that widely disseminated and un-organised love of country which is characteristic of the Welsh people. The Urdd commands a loyalty that cuts across religion, politics and social distinctions, and it avoids antagonism of every kind ; it bridges the gap between those who speak Welsh and those who do not . . . It is vitally important to Wales that it should flourish and expand, and that it should do so untrammelled by politics or by officialdom.'

About the same time, the BBC invited a number of prominent Welshmen to take part in a series of talks entitled ' The Future Looks Back.' Each speaker was asked to indicate what event in the half-century 1900-1950 had had the greatest effect on the life of Wales.

The first speaker was Wyn Griffith, and he stated unequivocally that the founding of Urdd Gobaith Cymru in 1922 was by far the most important event of the period.

*   *   *   *

Changes in the Urdd staff meant several interesting appointments. Alice E. Williams, a lively young Caernarfonshire teacher who had been at the very hub of Urdd activities both on a county and national level, was appointed Organiser for Caernarfonshire. W. O. Jones was asked to combine the duties of North Wales Appeals Organiser with those of County Organiser for Anglesey. After four years as Warden at Cwmafan, Tomi Scourfield was appointed Organiser for Carmarthenshire. He was already prominent in all Urdd activities, and particularly gifted in public relations, especially in dealing with young people. A young man of kindred spirit was Alwyn Samuel who was appointed Organiser for Glamorgan and Monmouthshire. Aneurin Jenkins-Jones was appointed to assist with *Cymru'r Plant* and other publications, and to lend a hand in the Training, Camps, and International Relations Department. He was a graduate, a man of high ideals and a wealth of talent. Elsi Williams was promoted Financial Secretary. There were also several changes among Club Wardens, which included the appointment of R. Wyn Jones to take over from Tomi Scourfield as Warden of *Aelwyd Cwmafan*. After courses at Harlech and at Elsinore in Denmark, he had taken a Youth Leaders' Diploma at Swansea and had three years' experience as LEA Club Leader. John Roberts became Warden of *Aelwyd Caernarfon* as it moved into its enlarged premises. He had been eminently successful as Warden of *Aelwyd Llanelli*, in addition to his contribution to the work of the movement in general.

*   *   *   *

In July, *Gwersyll Glan Llyn* was ready for its first campers. It was quite different from the Urdd's other centres. Sufficiently isolated to allow the freedom demanded by the exuberance of youth, it would certainly appeal to the older age-group ready to accept the challenge of lake and mountain. A nucleus of boats had been acquired which included a ship's life-boat, *Y Brenin Arthur*, canoes and skiffs, as well as solid rowing boats for the less experienced.

In his heyday, Sir Watkin had succeeded in getting his own private railway station established on the opposite side of the lake. This halt was now re-named ' Glan Llyn ' and from there, *Y Brenin Arthur* would convey across the lake those campers who arrived by train. There were nine weeks' camping in the summer of 1950, and we were fortunate in being able to draw upon the experience of Teifryn Michael, our Physical Recreation Organiser, and W. O. Jones who had long experience in the handling of boats not only along the Anglesey coasts but on rough seas during the war years.

The mountains too played a big part in the weekly programme, the favourite, perhaps, being Aran Benllyn. It was of Aran Benllyn that O. M. Edwards once said ' Were I a pagan, I would worship the Aran.' Within reach too were Castell Carn Dochan, Moel Migennau, Y Berwyn, Aran Fawddwy, Arennig and Cader Idris. And all around, there were ancient churches and homes of famous men. It was quickly realised that Glan Llyn was situated in a neighbourhood that was not only unique in natural beauty but also rich in history and tradition. There was not the slightest doubt that Sir Ifan ab Owen Edwards had been right in maintaining that even though the Urdd could not afford to establish a new centre, it certainly could not afford to miss this opportunity at Glan Llyn. Even then he was not content ; it was not within his nature to be satisfied. And before the summer was over, he was already listing the improvements he considered necessary.

It was natural that Glan Llyn should perhaps overshadow the other camps during its initial year. Nevertheless, as always, the other centres abounded in the joyousness always associated with camp life. There were seven weeks' camping at Llangrannog, six at Cricieth and two at Pantyfedwen. Operating four centres simultaneously meant a considerable strain on staff resources and it was obvious that the facilities at Llangrannog and Glan Llyn would soon have to be extended in order to eliminate the need for smaller, less suitable centres.

Training schemes continued throughout the year and by now included a leaders' course at Pantyfedwen and at Cricieth during the Christmas vacation. In addition to the cultural side, increasing attention was paid to physical recreation, with evening classes and weekend courses, expeditions and county sports. It was during this year that Aelwyd Aberystwyth began presenting feature programmes based on the work of Welsh men of letters. It was R. E. Griffith who initiated the idea, inspired by the heroic struggle of T. Rowland Hughes who, despite prolonged suffering, was a brilliant novelist and poet. The programme devised meant two months' preparation for sixty members of the Adran and Aelwyd. It was initially envisaged as an isolated project, a tribute to T. Rowland Hughes, but such was its success that this kind of programme became an annual event from 1950 to 1956, with feature programmes based on the works of Idwal Jones, T. Gwynn Jones, I. D. Hooson, J. J. Williams, W. J. Gruffydd and R. Williams Parry. The Aelwyd was fortunate in being able to draw on a team of talented leaders, and what was equally important, it found in J. E. Meredith, Cassie Davies and Hywel D. Roberts a team of narrators who could link the varied items and media into a coherent whole, thus completing the picture it was intended to convey.

*   *   *   *

On the international side, our first event was the Inter-Celtic Convention at Pantyfedwen during the Easter vacation. It was now possible to build on the experience of the previous year, and members of all the Celtic territories were grateful for the opportunity to meet, to learn, to give and to receive.

No sooner had our fellow-Celts departed than we were welcoming a youth choir from Bielefeld in Germany. Our contact, naturally, was Dr. Rudolph Hermann, and the conductor was Friedrich Feldmann. The choir was to spend a month in Wales, based on Llanelli, Aberystwyth, Corwen and Caernarfon, and accommodated in homes. In all, they gave seventeen public concerts, and thrilled their audiences with the quality of their performances which included classical and religious music, folk-songs and instrumental items. They won the hearts of their hosts, and a week at each centre was far too short a period. For the guests, it was an unforgettable experience ; for many, their first visit overseas.

The International Convention had now become an established feature in the Urdd calendar. Reports of previous years had filtered through and there was no lack of applications from Urdd members. It was not just the fun that attracted them, but the opportunity to meet young people from abroad, to listen to their experiences, discuss their problems and discover how they lived and thought. The programme itself was geared to this end, and apart from lectures and discussions, one learnt from personal contact and through working together on a specific project. This interest in the International Convention continued until the end of the decade, by which time travel restrictions had been relaxed, and the opportunity to travel abroad became virtually unlimited.

In 1950, we were able to welcome representatives from Belgium, France, Germany, the Baltic countries, Spain and America. Altogether, about a hundred members were assembled and the first task was to weld them into a single community. It was our first experience of a Spanish group. When the Welsh contingent met them at the station, it was a shock to discover that they had practically no English and Tomi Scourfield decided he might as well speak Welsh ! The last to disembark was Tomas, a ' mountain of a man ' as we would say in Welsh. As he stepped from the train, he introduced himself as ' Elephanto Espaniola ' and for a moment I hardly knew whether or not to treat the introduction seriously until I saw the twinkle in his eye ! It was fortunate for us that we could depend on Gareth Alban Davies of Ton Pentre as our interpreter throughout the period.

After three weeks at Pantyfedwen, the overseas members left for homes in Swansea, Hendy, Cwmafan and Betws. Each year, the influence upon them of their stay in Wales was manifest from correspondence received after their return. An example of this was a picture-postcard of the United Nations building in New York, which arrived during the 1950 Convention. It was sent by two American girls who had been at Pantyfedwen the previous year. It read—' We are here thinking of Pantyfedwen and recapitulating our experience of last year, knowing full well that such movements as the Urdd make the United Nations possible.'

The last event in the Urdd international calendar for 1950 was the visit of a group of 23 members and leaders to South Germany. We would always remember the breath-taking beauty of the

German/Swiss border, of Lake Constance and its vast waters (dare we again mention Bala lake ?) and of the Bavarian Alps. But the highlight of the journey was the Passion Play at Oberammergau, which with brief wartime interruptions had been performed regularly every ten years since 1634. For us, it was a unique and moving experience ; for the actors, it was obviously an act of worship. It seemed incredible that a village of three-thousand inhabitants could find seven-hundred performers for such an ambitious undertaking and that they could present their pageant with such brilliance. It is a miracle of the ages ; it is Oberammergau's gift to the world.

*   *   *   *

By 1950, Sir Ifan ab Owen Edwards had completed thirty years as editor of *Cymru'r Plant*. Indeed, he had surpassed his father's record of twenty-eight years. He had been responsible for 360 issues amounting to almost 15,000 pages, two thirds of which were his own creation, the equivalent of fifty average-sized volumes ! Admittedly, he always maintained that he was not writing for posterity but for next month. But the pages had to be filled and the material had to be written. One must remember too that it was done in his very limited leisure hours, and that he received not one penny for his labour. In fact, it often cost him dearly in money as well as in time and energy. Naturally, *Cymru'r Plant* had seen many changes since 1920. New features had been introduced and, throughout the years, Sir Ifan succeeded in keeping his magazine— as he kept his own mind—flexible enough to adapt itself to the needs of an ever-changing age. He never hesitated to pioneer. To him every experiment was an adventure.

Paying tribute to him in *Yr Aelwyd*, R. E. Griffith remarked—

' . . . We have endless admiration for an editor who has kept on for thirty years in the face of all difficulties, bringing out—on time—one issue after the other, and this in addition to all kinds of other work and responsibilities. We have lived close enough to him to know that he was often weary and sometimes despondent but the next issue of *Cymru'r Plant* would appear as usual, and once more the editor would have a smile on his face.'

*   *   *   *

1950 was 'development year' in the history of several Urdd centres. *Aelwyd Caernarfon* was one of these, where the enlarged and renovated premises were opened in September by Dr. Griffith Evans. Linked by a new canteen to the existing building, a hall had been built at a cost of more than £4,500 which was paid in full by Dr. Griffith Evans. A Ministry grant had been received towards equipment, and the local education authority continued its generous contribution towards the salary of a full-time Warden. It was to ensure that members should derive maximum benefit from the new scheme that the Aelwyd Committee had appointed John Roberts to that post.

It was at this time too that the Urdd came into full possession of its property at Ystalyfera. These premises, with hall, canteen, library and group-rooms, would provide an ideal centre for the Aelwyd. It is a sad fact, however, that the local branch of the Labour Party harboured the idea that the Aelwyd was a Welsh Nationalist Party centre, and consequently refused to lend support. This caused a rift among the inhabitants, made the work of the Aelwyd impossible, and the Urdd members were the ones who suffered.

There was no such tension at Felinfoel where the Aelwyd had flourished since 1942. After seven years as tenant, Cwmni'r Urdd was able to purchase the building for the Aelwyd and to obtain a grant from the Ministry of Education. It was officially opened in October, and already the Aelwyd, under the leadership of Harold Lloyd and his colleagues, had raised the balance of the purchase price so that the club was free of debt.

In December 1950, after four years of hard work, the old Public Hall at Rhos was opened as the new Urdd centre. It had a fully-equipped concert-hall seating six-hundred, a number of smaller rooms with facilities for group-work, canteen, indoor games, etc. The adaptation had cost three-thousand pounds, but it was well worth the money to give the young people of Rhos the opportunity they deserved. No one was more pleased than the Rev. James Humphreys, and it was readily admitted that none of this would have happened without his determination and perseverance.

1950 was also vintage year for the Urdd centre at Swansea. Throughout the 1930's, the Urdd had many Adrannau at Swansea, mostly attached to schools and churches. In 1941/42, a number of leaders decided that some provision should be made—in the name of the Urdd—for young people who had earlier been members of the Adrannau. Few of these were Welsh-speaking and it was decided that the new centre should admit any non-Welsh-speaking members who wished to identify themselves with the Urdd and with Wales. Thus, the Swansea Young Wales Club came into being, meeting initially in church premises. Then in 1943, they moved into a building in Mount Pleasant Drive, and R. Islwyn Pritchard was appointed full-time Club Warden. It was not long before the Club had again out-grown the premises and Cwmni'r Urdd was persuaded to purchase Cae Beili at a cost of £2,000, towards which a Ministry of Education grant was received. The members undertook the task of renovating and equipping the premises, most of the work being done voluntarily. The Club soon became one of the finest in the borough, and such was the demand that membership had to be confined to young people who had already left school. Due attention was paid to physical recreation, both indoor and outdoor. The Club ran its own summer camp at Porth Einon in Gower. There was also ample provision for cultural and educational activities which included drama, music, arts and crafts. They published their own magazine and laid stress on ' discovering ' their own locality, visiting coalmines, factories, docks and other industrial concerns. The Club was open on Sunday evenings for talks, discussions and epilogues, all organised by the members themselves. After giving the Club excellent service, Islwyn Pritchard left in 1947 and was replaced by W. G. Ewart Thomas. When he, in turn, left in 1953, a part-time Warden was appointed.

The Club's Chairman was Dr. Annie Owen, and its success was largely due to her dynamic leadership. It was she who campaigned for an extension to the premises, a new hall where members could meet together for plays, concerts or dancing. The land was available and Dr. Annie Owen was not discouraged by the fact that the scheme would cost £7,000. With a £4,000 grant from the Ministry of Education, her own generosity, the Club's money-raising efforts and the help of Cwmni'r Urdd, Dr. Owen achieved her aim. She would be the first to share the credit with her colleagues, especially T. G. Jeffreys Jones, lecturer in Youth Service at the University College of Swansea. But it would certainly not have been achieved without her enthusiastic leadership.

The story of the Swansea Young Wales Club is told at some length because it was here that the Urdd came nearest to being able to run an ideal Young Wales Club. Unfortunately, the disappointment too must be recorded. The Cae Beili Club declined, not because of any lack of effort, but because the maintenance of independent premises became too heavy a burden for a Branch of a voluntary organisation, especially in competition with the seemingly un-limited resources of clubs run by the Local Education Authority. When Cae Beili had to be sold, it was the end of an era for Young Wales Clubs operating in independent premises. As for the loss to non-Welsh-speaking Wales, who can judge ?

*   *   *   *

The financial position of Cwmni'r Urdd continued to deteriorate. The 1949/50 accounts showed a deficit of £1,906, and the balance sheet disclosed a bank overdraft of more than £6,500. One en-couraging feature was, however, emerging. Cardiganshire Edu-cation Authority was already contributing £300 per annum towards the salary and expenses of a County Organiser. With this as precedent, an appeal was made to other education authorities and by the end of the year, grants had been allocated by Carmarthen-shire, Caernarfonshire, Flintshire, Pembrokeshire, and Denbigh-shire. This timely assistance made it possible for the Urdd to retain its Organisers despite the financial crisis. Incidentally, it also led to a closer co-operation and a better understanding between the Urdd and the education authorities.

At the Annual General Meeting at Aberpennar (Mountain Ash), two new Vice-Presidents were elected—the Rev. Dr. W. T. Havard, Bishop of St. David's, and Dr. T. Ifor Rees, former British Consul and Ambassador, who had retired to his native Bowstreet near Aberystwyth. Despite the many encouraging aspects of the Chair-man's report, the fact that the financial position was becoming serious could not be concealed. The Urdd urgently needed ten-thousand pounds if it were to repay its overdraft and face a new year with reasonable security.

So it was with mixed feelings that we bid farewell to 1950. It had been a year of ebb and flow ; the joy of success in many direct-ions, frustration and disappointment in others. ' Joy and woe are

woven fine ' ; perhaps it would be wrong to expect it to be otherwise.

*   *   *   *

It had been the custom of the Urdd Council to meet twice a year
for a one-day session, usually at Aberystwyth. The Treasurer,
Jenkin Alban Davies, however, felt that this was inadequate and
pressed for a three-day meeting to be held at Pantyfedwen. This
was agreed, and the first residential Council met in January 1951.
It was inevitable that Ysgol Lluest should figure prominently in the
deliberations. A memorandum had been circulated, tracing the
school's development since 1939 and the financial difficulties that
had arisen in recent years. The members had before them a
resolution which recommended terminating the Urdd's sponsorship
of Lluest in July 1952, or earlier should the local education
authority agree to take over the school in the meantime. During
the discussion, Sir Ifan ab Owen Edwards proposed an amendment
to the effect that the Urdd's sponsorship should end in July 1951
rather than in July 1952. He outlined his reasons for the amendment, based mainly on his conviction that a delay of eighteen
months would result in a dwindling in the numbers of staff and
pupils so that the school would linger on in gradual deterioration
instead of being transferred to the local education authority as a
highly successful unit. In the discussion that followed, there were
some who doubted whether six months would be sufficient time to
complete the transfer arrangements and safeguard the position of
the staff. On balance, however, the President's arguments were
accepted and the following amendment was carried—

> ' That we inform the Cardiganshire Education Authority that
> Ysgol Lluest as an independent school will close in July 1951 ;
> that we entrust the pupils and their education to the care of the
> Education Committee, urging the Committee to establish a free
> Welsh School at Aberystwyth, and offering every help the Urdd
> can give in that undertaking.'

The next step was to inform the parents of this decision. A
General Meeting was called at which the facts were outlined by the
Chairman. Sir Ifan ab Owen Edwards explained the reasons for the
decision to end the current arrangement in 1951 instead of 1952 as

previously envisaged, pointing out that this would ultimately be to the advantage of all concerned. He sympathised with the staff who would have to face a period of uncertainty and might possibly have to seek alternative posts, but with the current demand for teachers who could teach through the medium of Welsh, there should not be any real hardship. The case of the Headmaster, however, was rather different and it might not be easy for him to find an equivalent post in so short a time, and the Urdd had, therefore, agreed to offer him a comparable post on the Urdd staff.

Eventually, it was agreed to elect a committee to be responsible for presenting the case to the Education Authority. There were, however, some parents who strongly opposed the decision taken by the Urdd, and correspondence in the local and national press gave the impression that the Urdd had dealt unfairly with the pupils, the parents and the staff. Those who knew the true facts, of course, were not misled by these accusations but the general public could only accept them at face value. In an attempt to end the misinterpretations, the Urdd released a full statement of the facts in June 1951. On the following day, the editorial column of the *Western Mail* drew its own conclusions—

' The Urdd's official statement on the closing of the independent Welsh School at Lluest, Aberystwyth, marks the end of a chapter. The decision to end its private sponsorship and transfer pupils and educational responsibilities to the local authority could not have been made without heartburnings. Indeed, many parents and some Urdd members are strongly opposed to the decision. Yet it is difficult to see what else those in authority could have done in view of their financial burdens. The change is one of responsibility and not of purpose.

For a school to create a tradition within twelve years is something of a miracle . . . By its example, it has inspired Welsh-speaking parents in other towns to press for Welsh schools. The pioneering work of Lluest has been done, the trend is established, and what was once a doubtful experiment has now become accepted practice. Even in this age of centralised control, when individual enterprise is harshly discouraged, all the creative cultural improvements seem to come from the activities of private persons who have the courage to go beyond the book-of-rules and are willing to make sacrifices for the common good. The Urdd has laboured worthily and sacrificed much in order to get the principle of the Welsh School accepted. They have reason for pride in the success that has attended their efforts.'

There is no doubt that the two persons most deeply affected by the decision were the Headmaster, Hywel D. Roberts, and Sir Ifan ab Owen Edwards. For the Headmaster, it was largely a personal problem. He had left a secure post to come to Lluest and now his future seemed to be crumbling around him. He was grateful to the Founder for offering him a post on the Urdd staff, but he did not wish the movement to create a post especially for him, and, moreover, he would prefer something more directly connected with education and a post that would carry greater security than the Urdd, as a voluntary organisation, could offer. He was later appointed Assistant Director of Education at Wigan. Sir Ifan's sorrow stemmed mainly from disappointment at the way a few people, who had received so much from the Urdd, had unjustly condemned the movement by their misinterpretation of the facts.

The education authority gave the matter immediate and sympathetic attention. It was, however, disappointing to learn that the new Welsh ' school ' would not, initially, be an independent unit, but a department of the local Primary School. The Authority would continue, temporarily, to use Lluest premises but those pupils who were under seven years would be incorporated in the local Infants' School. This, together with the fact that some parents decided to send their children to other private schools, meant that only fifty of the original pupils remained at Lluest. These were joined by some twenty others whose parents now opted for free Welsh-medium education.

In May 1952, a petition signed by 90 parents was presented to the Education Committee urging the establishment of a full-status Welsh school at Aberystwyth, and in September of that year, a school of more than 160 pupils was opened in the town. The post of Headmaster was advertised for September 1953, and who should be appointed but Hywel D. Roberts !

While parents at Aberystwyth were battling with their own problem in 1951, parents in other towns were campaigning for Welsh-medium schools. Three of these were opened in September 1951—at Wrexham, Barry and Pontypridd.

*   *   *   *

The Sub-Committee for Religious Affairs had been set up in 1949 under the chairmanship of the Rev. James Humphreys and with Aneurin Jenkins-Jones as Secretary. It had been responsible for publishing a book of carols, and for a series of articles and epilogues that appeared in *Yr Aelwyd*. Discussions on ' Religion and Life ' were also included in the programme of training courses. Members of the sub-committee, however, felt that there was room for greater co-operation between the Urdd and the various governing bodies of the Welsh churches. This was discussed at the Urdd Council meeting in January 1951 and resulted in the passing of two resolutions. Firstly, it was decided to publish an open letter in *Yr Aelwyd* urging members to take an active part in the work of their churches and to see that religion was given its rightful place in the life of their Aelwyd. Secondly, it was decided to appeal to the governing bodies of Welsh churches for maximum co-operation, and to invite their representatives to meet representatives of the Urdd to discuss possible areas of co-operation on local and national levels. The only response came from the Church in Wales, and the help given by its Youth Council was greatly appreciated. The lack of response from the Nonconformist Churches was a disappointment. The Urdd knew, however, that many Nonconformist ministers were already giving their active support to Aelwydydd throughout Wales and it may be that this was more important than the formal recognition of the governing bodies.

*   *   *   *

In his interesting foreword to the Eisteddfod Syllabus for 1951, the Vice-Chairman, D. J. Williams, predicted that nowhere would the Urdd Eisteddfod find a better home than at Abergwaun (Fishguard). And he was to be proved right.

Pembrokeshire's Director of Education was D. T. Jones, a man of many talents whose word was law. The Urdd was fortunate in having him as Honorary President of the Eisteddfod and this, for him, was no empty title. He made an effort to attend every meeting of the Executive Committee and was usually asked to take the Chair. He knew the members personally and when a job had to be done, a wink or a nod was as good as a command. His humour was proverbial and never was so much hard work accomplished amid so much merriment. And between meetings, D. T. Jones would personally keep in touch with the developments. He was a man in a million ; it is little wonder that he and his team of voluntary workers gave us a truly memorable Eisteddfod.

It is difficult to select from the many highlights of the week's programme. The pageant—*Molawd Penfro*—gave us a lively kaleidoscope of the county's history from early times to the days of Rebecca. If one had to choose a single item, the honour would go to the group that revived *Barti Ddu o Gasnewy Bach*, the famous pirate born in 1682. Then there was the all-Irish concert that filled the marquee to capacity on the Friday evening when a choir of sixty young people, together with a group of dancers, came over specially for the performance. They were all members of the Gaelic League, a non-political, non-sectarian movement formed in 1893 by Douglas Hyde for the promotion of the Irish language and culture. Their visit was sponsored by the Government of the Irish Republic, and there to meet them was the Irish Ambassador from London, F. H. Boland. With the performers, came our friend Oscar Mac Uilis who addressed the audience in Welsh. And as Cassie Davies, the evening's President, remarked, the stretch of water separating Cork and Fishguard had shrunk considerably during that evening !

Of the Eisteddfod competitions, the highest praise went to a quartette from *Aelwyd Aberporth*. Only one remark appeared on the adjudicator's sheet—*Perffaith* (Perfect) ! What a tribute to the Aelwyd leader, Mrs. Tegryn Davies. However, it was West Glamorgan who claimed the ' Lloyd George Banner ' and it was realised that this was a county to be reckoned with in future Eisteddfodau.

Without doubt, this was a great festival, thanks to a battalion of workers and their officers, especially W. D. Williams, the Eisteddfod Secretary, and his two assistants, Ruthy James and Olive Jones. Naturally, they would be the first to acknowledge the help received from Huw Cedwyn Jones who joined them for the last three months, and from the County Organiser, Tom Bevan. At the final meeting of the Executive Committee, it was disclosed that this had been the most costly of Urdd Eisteddfodau not, as D. T. Jones said, because they had been extravagant, but because costs had risen so considerably. However, thanks to the advance fund, the good weather and the large audiences, the Treasurer, T. J. Francis, was able to present Sir Ifan ab Owen Edwards with a cheque for a balance of £1,113/6/5.

* * * *

After a gap of eleven years, the Mabolgampau were restored in 1951. For some time, South Wales leaders had been pressing for this, and, with the appointment of Teifryn Michael as Physical Recreation Organiser, it seemed feasible to consider the request. A good deal of preparatory work had been done in evening classes and weekend courses, and it was decided to link the venture with the Cardiff programme in connection with the Festival of Britain in 1951. Tom Davies, organiser of the Mabolgampau in the thirties, was the City's Physical Education Organiser and was closely linked with Cardiff's contribution to the Festival of Britain. His experience and the enthusiasm of Urdd leaders under the chairmanship of Gwyn M. Daniel augured well for the restoration of the Mabolgampau. Before three-thousand spectators, over a thousand members took part in the folk-dancing, the athletic and the gymnastic events. But things had changed. Gone were the mass displays of gymnastics performed to music accompaniment. Instead, we had group exhibitions of free activities. And excellent though these were, they did not provide the spectacle of the old Mabolgampau. The new trend did not seem capable of holding the interest of the spectators ; somehow the thrill was not there. It was obvious that the idea of a large-scale Mabolgampau would in future need careful consideration.

* * * *

More than three-thousand youngsters attended the Urdd camps during the eight-week period in the summer of 1951. Camping had now become an accepted practice, and one tended to take it for granted without fully realising how much was accomplished year by year. The first aim, of course, has always been to give the members an unforgettable holiday. But there is also a plus quality. Through the activities, and through the informal atmosphere of companionship, the leaders strive to instil in the members a loyalty to Wales, to fellow-man and to Christ. To do this, one must have camp-leaders who themselves believe in the ideals and are capable of sharing their conviction with others. And it is a source of great pride to the Urdd that, throughout the years, it has been able to attract camp-leaders of the right calibre.

The second summer at Glan Llyn proved that it had already established itself as a centre for teenagers and young adults. Sir Ifan was a frequent visitor and he invariably returned full of suggestions regarding the improvement of amenities. He was a perfectionist by nature and never satisfied. He would have wished to achieve in two years what has actually taken twenty, due mainly to financial restrictions. When patience was advocated he would say, ' There is so much to be done and life is so short.'

*   *   *   *

The Inter-Celtic Convention displayed the same zest and fervour as it had in the past. New faces appeared, but a few, like Oscar Mac Uilis, made it an annual pilgrimage. What amazed him most in 1951 was the change in the attitude of the Welsh members towards folk-dancing and the new aptitude acquired in mastering an art in which the old tradition had been so completely lost. Mac Uilis himself was an accomplished dancer and a tribute from him was most encouraging. We were optimistic enough to feel that, given another two or three years, we might be able to compete even with the Irish !

There were some who felt that the Inter-Celtic Convention was now strong enough to risk a change of venue and that it would benefit by being held in each Celtic country in turn. The visiting members, however, felt that they lacked a movement that could offer the necessary facilities and organisation to make such a venture practicable in their own countries.

*   *   *   *

Pantyfedwen was again to resound with foreign accents in July, when the fourth International Convention was held. This time, we had representatives from Italy, Germany, France, Estonia and Lithuania, the Netherlands and Switzerland. Our programme included a series of talks on international affairs and less formal talks on various aspects of Welsh life. But, of course, talks and discussions were only part of the programme, and there were excursions to

Llangollen, to Llandrindod, to Glan Llyn and Snowdonia, as well as ample free time for personal arrangements. In this way, the gathering of unrelated individuals became an integrated community, and the community became one big family. Such was Pantyfedwen in 1951.

It was in this year that a mixed choir of fifty voices from *Aelwyd Caernarfon* was invited to take part in a celebration concert in Dublin, organised by the Gaelic League. In co-operation with Swyddfa'r Urdd, the arrangements were made by the Warden, John Roberts, and the choir was trained and conducted by G. Peleg Williams. Representatives of the Urdd and the Aelwyd were received by the President of Eire, Sean O'Kelly, and by the Prime Minister, Eamon de Valera.

Two other overseas visits were arranged, one to a youth camp in Brittany and one to Deva in Northern Spain, home of the Basques. In Spain, our programme included fiestas, bullfights and pelota matches as well as visits to places of historic interest. We visited Bilbao via Guernica, the town which was partly destroyed by German bombers at the instigation of the Franco regime during the Civil War. Here the buttressed remains of an old oak tree, under whose shade the regional leaders used to confer long before their Senate House was built, reminded us of home and of the old oak tree at Carmarthen. (The Basques, however, had taken the precaution of planting an acorn more than a hundred years ago !) We journeyed to Pamplona via Loyola ; to the Monastery of Aranzazu, and to Oñate to visit the 16th Century Basque University which had to be closed at the beginning of this century because it was denied financial support from the Government. Our friend and guide throughout was Simon Bersaluce, a stained-glass artist who had designed windows not only for several churches but also for the main entrance to the Railway Station at Bilbao.

*   *   *   *

In staff changes, we lost the services of Mary Wynne Williams who left after two years as Warden of Llanfyllin Young Wales Club and three as Organiser for Cardiganshire. We also lost Teifryn Michael who, during his three years on the staff, had worked assiduously to develop an interest in physical recreation, and had re-instated the Urdd Football Competition.

Despite a fund-raising scheme of a ' Mile of Shillings ' which brought in a total of £1,880, the financial situation continued to be a matter of considerable concern. Efforts had to be made to cut costs and this included staff curtailment. When vacancies occurred, new appointments would not be made until the situation had improved. As part of this policy, Evan Isaac now combined the work of South Wales Appeals Organiser with that of Organiser for Cardiganshire. It was also decided to postpone the appointment of a Physical Recreation Organiser, and in the meantime some of the more essential responsibilities were shared by existing staff members.

The statement of Income and Expenditure for the financial year 1950/51 showed a deficit of £1,322. This, added to previous deficits, meant that the Urdd was overdrawn by £8,000. The year's overall expenditure amounted to £25,000 and towards this sum, a total of £7,900 was received in grants from the Ministry of Education, the Jubilee Trust and the Local Education Authorities.

It was, therefore, a mixed report of success and failure that was presented to the Annual General Meeting at Corwen in October 1951. The financial situation figured prominently and it was obvious that the Officers were deeply concerned, but at the same time determined to bring the Urdd out of the quagmire. The ending of Lluest School as an independent venture would help considerably since the annual expenditure involved in closing the gap in the school accounts had contributed substantially to the £8,000 overdraft. Nevertheless, Sir Ifan ab Owen Edwards maintained that the experiment—and its expense—was wholly justified in the cause of Welsh Education, and for the ultimate benefit of the people of Wales.

There was no change of Officers on this occasion, but the death was recorded of Gwendoline Davies of Gregynog, who had been a Vice-President since 1932. Four new Vice-Presidents were elected— Sir John Cecil-Williams, the Rev. Gwilym Davies, the Rev. Dr. G. A. Edwards, and Gwynfor Evans. By and large, the Urdd was not sorry to see 1951 drawing to its close. It had been a year of greater worry and anxiety than any since the war had ended. Nevertheless, there were already signs of breaks in the clouds.

1952 was an important year for *Cymru'r Plant* not because it was celebrating its sixtieth birthday, but because of a certain change in policy. Sir Ifan ab Owen Edwards had edited the magazine for thirty years, and throughout that period, the aim had been to provide reading material that was interesting, lively and contemporary. This aim had remained constant, despite changes in size, format and content.

Sir Ifan was aware that he was greatly indebted to those teachers who undertook the voluntary distribution of the magazine within the schools. But it was, after all, a voluntary arrangement, and there were schools where the pupils never had the opportunity of seeing *Cymru'r Plant* unless it was bought by their parents. If the magazine could be distributed direct to schools by arrangement with the local education authorities, it would provide all schools with fresh reading material each month, and it would benefit *Cymru'r Plant* by increasing the circulation. This, in turn, would mean more money to improve the content and appearance of the magazine itself. The editor decided the possibilities were worth exploring.

He wrote to the Directors of Education outlining his scheme and inviting them to meet him to discuss the possibilities in greater detail. The response was encouraging and the invitation was accepted by Directors and their Deputies, HM Inspectors of Schools, college lecturers and school-teachers. In principle, there was general agreement, but some members argued that to be universally useful, the magazine would need to contain some material specifically designed for pupils learning Welsh as a second-language. Sir Ifan agreed that this was a fair request, especially since the Urdd already accepted the need to cater for the *Dysgwyr* in Adrannau, in camps and in Eisteddfodau. With the full backing of the Ministry of Education, the education authorities agreed to give the scheme their support.

Sir Ifan ab Owen Edwards was well aware that the preparation of material for the *Dysgwyr* demanded specialised knowledge and techniques and that he would need the help of specialist teachers in order to fulfil the requirements. But it was a challenge, and a challenge was something he always welcomed. This first meeting in the summer of 1952 established the *Magazines Conference* which has been held annually for the past twenty years, and whose help and advice have been greatly valued.

*　　　*　　　*　　　*

The Urdd had deliberately refrained from publicly celebrating its thirtieth anniversary in 1952. This, however, did not prevent the Council from having a private celebration during its residential meeting at Pantyfedwen in January. The Chair was taken by the Rev. Gwilym Davies, and the speakers, who each dealt with the one aspect of Urdd activities in which they were mainly interested, were Cassie Davies, Meirion Jones, the Rev. T. Alban Davies and R. Gordon Williams. A birthday-cake bearing thirty candles with the words, *Yr Urdd, 1922—1952 ; Cymru, Cyd-ddyn, Crist,* made by Pantyfedwen Chef, Fred Keall, was cut by Lady Edwards.

Two days later, Norah Isaac made a radio appeal on behalf of the movement—

'. . . It must be left to the historians of the future to assess the contribution made by the Urdd to the life of Wales. We who grew up in the movement can testify to the inspiration we received—in an Adran or Aelwyd, in the Eisteddfod and Mabolgampau, in camps and pilgrimages, through the magazines and the Welsh Books Campaign, through religious services and *Cymanfa Ganu,* through a Welsh School and International Camp. All this is part of the Urdd's contribution over a period of thirty years. Thousands of you today are indebted to the Urdd . . . Will you repay a little of that debt now to make sure the Urdd does not have to curtail any part of its service to Wales ? '

As a result of this appeal, the Urdd was richer by £1,372/8/11.

Many of Wales' leading newspapers referred to the fact that the Urdd was thirty years old. Aneirin Talfan Davies in the *News Chronicle* referred to the Urdd as ' a movement that has succeeded in uniting the nation . . . This remarkable organisation is destined to do great things yet for Wales—even greater than has already been accomplished.'

Y Cymro, in its editorial entitled *Er Mwyn Cymru*, said ' This is the most important Welsh movement of the past half-century and without doubt, the most successful.' The Editor, however, foresaw difficult days ahead—

> ' The State is already taking over much of what the Urdd in a voluntary capacity has pioneered . . . In future, the Urdd will have to offer a service that is more specialised and more attractive than that of the statutory bodies. It should not try to compete with them ; it should lead rather than follow. To the degree to which this can be achieved will the Urdd survive the coming years. But whatever happens in the future, Wales' debt to the Urdd and to Sir Ifan ab Owen Edwards is greater than it can ever repay.'

Y Faner referred to the Urdd as ' one of Wales' miracles ' and in the *Liverpool Daily Post*, E. Morgan Humphreys struck the following note—

> ' One asks what Wales today would be like had it not been for *Cymru'r Plant* and the Urdd . . . Sir Ifan ab Owen Edwards and his colleagues have shown what can be achieved where there is vision, energy and faith. One thing is certain, Wales today would show far greater lustre if all of us worked more on behalf of the Urdd and criticised less those who lead the movement.'

Some of this ' criticism ' had appeared in *Y Llan*, the weekly newspaper of the Church in Wales—

> ' Many Churchmen complain that the leadership of the Urdd has fallen into the hands of people who are out of sympathy with the Church in Wales. Overseas visitors on a recent visit to Wales were taken to chapels, but the parish church did not enter into the picture at all.'

Such a misconception could not be allowed to go unanswered and a detailed reply was sent to *Y Llan* and published in *Yr Aelwyd*. It was not difficult to prove that the accusation was completely unfounded and unjustified.

*   *   *   *

In 1952, the Urdd National Eisteddfod visited Machynlleth after a lapse of twenty years. The Chairman of the Executive Committee was the Rev. W. J. Thomas, and although he moved to Ffestiniog long before the Eisteddfod was held, he insisted on completing the task he had undertaken. He knew, however, that he could depend on the co-operation of the two Vice-Chairmen—the Rev. Robert Evans of Llanbrynmair and Lewis Hywel Davies of Machynlleth—and their fellow-officers. And despite the departure later of one of the two Honorary Secretaries, the officers and their team of enthusiasts performed all the many and varied tasks involved in a major undertaking of this nature.

Among the winners at the Machynlleth Eisteddfod were several who have since become well-known in Welsh circles, including James Nicholas, T. Gwynn Jones (Cardiff), R. Alun Evans and Dic Jones. It was at Machynlleth that the Chair and Crown were first offered for creative work. Prior to 1940, they had been awarded to those who had gained the highest marks in literary examinations, but when the Eisteddfod was restored in 1946, the examinations were not continued. Now, at Machynlleth, the Chair was offered for the main poetry competition for those under 25, and the Crown for the main prose competition. It was a great disappointment that no-one was deemed worthy of the Chair. For the Crown, on the other hand, there were 17 competitors and it was won by Catrin Puw Morgan, a 19-year old student from Corwen. The Crowning ceremony was conducted by Islwyn Ffowc Elis, winner of the Prose Medal at the National Eisteddfod of Wales in 1951.

It was at the Urdd National Eisteddfod held at Machynlleth in 1932 that David Lloyd George had presented a banner as trophy for the winning District. Eventually, the banner became too fragile to be used, and for many years the 'Lloyd George Banner', like the Rugby Triple Crown, was an imaginary trophy. For the 1952 Eisteddfod, the Urdd received a new trophy for the winning county, a composite picture painted by Lois Blake incorporating the coats-of-arms of the Welsh counties. It was first won by West Glamorgan which thus became the leading ' County ' for the second year in succession.

The Eisteddfod was not a great financial success. Costs had been high, especially in connection with the pageant and children's concert. Despite the advance-fund, the surplus amounted to only

£217/16/9. The Eisteddfod, of course, was not primarily intended as a source of income, however welcome a profit might be, and the Eisteddfod Committee at Machynlleth could feel proud that they had staged an event that was a source of inspiration for thousands of children and young people. And this was the only criterion that really mattered.

*   *   *   *

The camping pattern was similar to that of 1951, with 1500 campers at Llangrannog, 300 at Cricieth, 700 at Glan Llyn and 100 at Pantyfedwen. The latter was now being used as a students' hostel for the greater part of the year, and by the Urdd for the remaining period. But despite all efforts, it was barely able to make ends meet.

Both the Inter-Celtic and the International Conventions were held as usual at Pantyfedwen. For the Inter-Celtic Convention, an exhibition of 120 photographs had been sent by Eire's Department of External Affairs. From the Isle of Man, we had a group of folk-dancers who thrilled us by their exquisite costumes and graceful movements. The changeable weather during the International Convention made us more appreciative of the brief periods of sunshine. For the first time, two girls from England were among our guests, and the Union Jack took its place among the eight flags that fluttered from the Pantyfedwen flag-pole. The French and German groups came nearer to a harmonious relationship than on any previous occasion, but the fact that the French were mostly girls and the Germans mostly boys may have contributed to the harmony ! A fortnight later, four Urdd groups were to visit Germany—one to Bielefeld and one to Plochingen organised by Swyddfa'r Urdd, and two exchange-visits organised by Aelwydydd —*Aelwyd Llanelli* and *Aelwyd Yr Hendy*—as part of a reciprocal exchange-scheme initiated by T. G. Jeffreys Jones.

It was during 1952 that the name *Travancore* became familiar to Urdd members. Previously, one knew vaguely that there was an Indian province called Travancore, and some might have recalled the popular duet, *Lle Treigla'r Caveri*, in which the name ' Travancore ' figured prominently. And that was all. But in 1952, a member of the Urdd staff had been selected to represent Wales in a

7 The Rt. Hon. James Griffiths, M.P. addressing Urdd members and leaders

38 The Pantyfedwen Soccer Cup—gift of D. J. James

39 Glan Llyn which became property of the Urdd in 1950

40 Members of the Inter-Celtic Conventi[...]
at the grave of
T. Gwynn Jones

41   The Rev. Gwilym Davies, Founder of the
Goodwill Message

World Conference of Christian Youth to be held at Travancore. The selection of Wales' representative was entrusted to the Christian Youth Council of Wales and the choice fell upon Aneurin Jenkins-Jones. He was granted leave of absence and returned two months later stimulated and enriched by the experience. During the following months he addressed meetings in schools, clubs and churches, and shared his experiences with his fellow Urdd members through the pages of *Yr Aelwyd*. The name ' Travancore ' had assumed a new significance for a generation of Welsh youth.

*   *   *   *

During the war years, the formal registration of members by Swyddfa'r Urdd had lapsed ; there were more important things to be done in the struggle to survive. Now, however, the time had come to re-introduce a system of registration for both Branches and members. All listed Adrannau were circularised and some four-hundred replied promptly requesting registration. The new scheme required individual members to register anew each year. For his initial fee, each member received a certificate to which a new membership stamp could be added annually. Within a few months, 15,000 members had enrolled and another fifteen-thousand were soon to follow. Membership was now taken seriously, and Adrannau would hold a brief and simple ceremony to admit new members. Only registered members were now allowed to compete in the Eisteddfod or admitted to camp. Monthly membership lists were published in *Cymru'r Plant*. All this involved a great deal of additional clerical work, and of course, a registration scheme for Aelwydydd was yet to follow.

*   *   *   *

The period 1951-53 was an important one in the field of Welsh publishing and the Urdd played a leading role in the development. The story had begun in 1936/37 when the Urdd initiated its Welsh Books Campaign. Out of this campaign—and on the initiative of the Urdd—grew the Union of Welsh Publishers and Booksellers. By the beginning of the fifties, existing stocks had been well-nigh exhausted and publishers were unable to meet the demands of schools or of the general public. This was no fault of the publishers. There was an acute shortage of paper—the position was even worse than it had been during the war years. At the same time, school requisitions in themselves were not sufficient to justify the cost of new publications. For the public too it was a vicious circle ; so few Welsh books were available that the man-in-the-street had practically lost interest.

The problem was discussed both by the Urdd Council and by the Union of Welsh Publishers and Booksellers. It was obvious that the position was so serious that Welsh publication would cease altogether unless the Government could be persuaded to release an adequate supply of paper, and to offer financial help to Welsh publishers. The survival of the Welsh language depended largely on the availability of literature of a suitable nature and in an adequate supply for the use of teachers and pupils. Faced with a serious crisis, the Union of Welsh Publishers and Booksellers decided to appeal to the Government through the Council for Wales and Monmouthshire. Fortunately, the Council's Chairman at the time was Huw T. Edwards, a Welshman of conviction, who understood the need and welcomed a challenge of this nature. The Council persuaded the Home Secretary, Mr. Chuter Ede, to set up a working party in 1951, under the chairmanship of A. W. Ready—

> ' to examine the present arrangements for the publication of books, magazines and periodicals in the Welsh language and to report as to any measures which are desirable and practicable to meet the needs of Welsh schools and colleges and the Welsh-speaking population of Wales.'

A year later, in October 1952, the Home Office published the report which recommended that an annual sum of £40,000 be made available to ensure an adequate supply of Welsh books for schools.

There was still no guarantee that the Government would adopt the recommendation of the report. Accordingly, the Hon. Society of Cymmrodorion, in co-operation with the Council for Wales and Monmouthshire and the WJEC, agreed to call a special conference at Llandrindod in November 1952 to which all the Welsh Local Authorities were invited, together with national cultural movements and societies. When the case had been presented by R. E. Griffith, the Local Authorities, for their part, pledged their unanimous support. It was left to the WJEC to devise a plan that would enable all the Education Authorities to co-operate in securing a regular supply of Welsh books for their schools.

So far, so good, but the victory was incomplete. The Union was disappointed that the Working Party had confined its attention and its recommendations to the needs of children and of schools, whereas, even according to its own terms of reference, it should also have dealt with the acute shortage of books for adults and made some recommendation in this direction. The Urdd and the Union turned once more to the Council for Wales and Monmouthshire. This was an even more difficult assignment, but after considerable pressure, the Government was persuaded of its responsibilities and the Treasury agreed to allocate a grant of £1,000 per annum to be distributed to the Publishers towards the cost of publishing books of general interest. Such a sum was no more than a drop in the ocean but at least it provided a precedent and left the door open for further pressure. During the past fifteen years, as a result of numerous appeals, this grant has gradually been increased to £25,000 per annum. Big strides have thus been taken since the first Welsh Books Campaign in 1936/37, and it is a triumph in which the Urdd has played a major part.

While this campaign was in progress, Alun R. Edwards, County Librarian for Cardiganshire, decided to identify himself with the struggle on behalf of Welsh publishing. In 1952, he set up his own Welsh Books Campaign in Cardiganshire, not in opposition but supplementary to that of the Union. He won the support of the Cardiganshire Education Authority and its Welsh Books Committee, with the result that it was agreed to allocate a sum of £2,000 to promote the publication of Welsh books. Furthermore, he put to the Union of Welsh Publishers and Booksellers his plan for the establishment of a Publishing Trust towards whose expenses the Government and Local Authorities would be asked to contribute. It was from this idea advanced by Alun R. Edwards in 1952 that the present ' Welsh Books Council ' emerged.

*　　　*　　　*　　　*

Although Lluest School had ceased to exist as an independent school, its influence was still far-reaching and, by 1952, 20 Welsh-medium schools had been established by Education Authorities. From the beginning, the Parents' Societies had played a significant part in the various campaigns, and even when a school had been established, the Society continued to be a link between parents, teachers and Education Authority. In 1951, the Rev. Trebor Lloyd Evans and Ysgol Lôn Las Parents' Society advocated the establishment of a ' Union of Parents' Societies ', which would decide on future policies and voice the opinions of the Societies as the need arose. The Urdd Council was asked to give its approval and support, and it was left to the Rev. Trebor Lloyd Evans and R. E. Griffith to prepare a draft constitution and organise a meeting to take place during the 1952 National Eisteddfod at Aberystwyth. A marquee seating three-hundred was crowded to capacity while another two-hundred listened outside. Sir Ifan ab Owen Edwards presided, and the meeting was addressed by Norah Isaac and Dr. B. Haydn Williams, Director of Education for Flintshire. It was unanimously decided to establish a national ' Union of Welsh Schools Parents' Societies ' and the draft constitution was adopted. A further resolution, even more far-reaching, was agreed upon—

' That this meeting of the Union calls for the establishment of Welsh-medium Secondary Schools in all areas where such a demand exists. It believes that this natural development is essential if the Welsh-medium Primary Schools are to achieve their full objectives.'

The Union formed in 1952 has during the past twenty years had a strong influence on the policies of Welsh Education Authorities. No-one was more pleased with the development than Sir Ifan ab Owen Edwards who saw that the seed sown in 1939 had taken root so firmly by 1952.

*   *   *   *

Prys, the Founder's younger son, was now at Abermâd School, near Aberystwyth. His brother, Owen, however, left Leighton Park School in the summer of 1952, facing two years of National Service. He enlisted in the Royal Artillery and found himself in camp at

Oswestry. In 1953, he was moved to Coulsdon in Surrey to take a course in Russian. In September 1954, he was demobilised, and entered Lincoln College, Oxford, where his father had been a student, and his grandfather a Fellow and Tutor for eighteen years.

*　　　*　　　*　　　*

The Urdd was privileged in 1952 to co-operate with the Council of the National Eisteddfod of Wales in erecting a memorial to the poet-solicitor from Rhos, I. D. Hooson. These were the two movements that had been closest to his heart, and both had benefited from his generous legacies. He had willed that his ashes be scattered on the hills above Llangollen. It was here, therefore, that a granite stone was erected, inscribed by R. L. Gapper with the words *I. D. Hooson, Bardd, Eisteddfodwr, Cyfaill i Blant Cymru.* Prof. W. J. Gruffydd and Alderman W. Emyr Williams, Chairman of the Eisteddfod Executive Committee, spoke on behalf of the Eisteddfod Council, and Sir Ifan ab Owen Edwards and Sir David Hughes Parry on behalf of the Urdd. The unveiling was performed by a group of Urdd members from the Wrexham District.

*　　　*　　　*　　　*

Sir Ifan was still without adequate help in the preparation of *Cymru'r Plant*. Aneurin Jenkins-Jones had found himself fully involved in the work of the Department responsible for Camps, Training, and International and Religious Affairs and thus unable to devote much time to the magazine. A new appointment was called for, and Brynmor Jones of Coedpoeth, Wrexham, a former student of Queen's College, Oxford, was appointed and given special responsibility for *Cymru'r Plant* and the new membership-registration scheme.

During the year, there were several changes in the ranks of the staff, and the Urdd lost the services of three County Organisers— W. O. Jones, Alwena Williams, and Tom O. Bevan, Organisers for Anglesey, Merioneth and Pembrokeshire respectively.

*　　　*　　　*　　　*

The first Annual General Meeting of Cwmni'r Urdd—in 1932—
had been held at Carmarthen, and it was appropriate that it should
return to that town twenty years later. The reports presented to the
meeting showed much the same trend as had been apparent during
the previous years—programme achievements but financial
difficulties. The accounts showed a deficit of £1,693 on the year
1951/52, but the bank overdraft had been reduced from £8,000 to
£6,500. Of the £1,693 deficit on the year's accounts, £1,050 was
due to six months loss on the Lluest accounts. This proved the
wisdom of Sir Ifan's plea that a change of sponsorship should be
made in 1951 and not delayed until 1952. As the Treasurer,
Jenkin Alban Davies, pointed out, ' It was inevitable that Cwmni'r
Urdd should terminate its sponsorship of Lluest in 1951 . . . A new
Welsh School took the place of Lluest ; nothing could have replaced
the Urdd.' He added a warning that we were not yet out of the
woods. Pantyfedwen showed a deficit of £250 in 1950/51 and
repairs and renovations were urgently needed. It had been found
necessary to open Pantyfedwen to a wider *clientele*, reserving only
two weeks in August for Welsh-speaking guests. This change of
policy later led to additional bookings from schools and colleges
from across the border, and in two or three years, Maldwyn Jones
had been able to reverse the financial trend.

The Treasurer explained that the Staffing Committee had been
asked, as a temporary measure, to refrain from making new appointments, wherever possible, when vacancies occurred. In this way, it
was hoped to reduce the overdraft and eventually to maintain an
even keel. So 1952 rolled towards its close—less tempestuous than
the previous year but hardly less critical from a financial standpoint.
Sir Ifan, however, refused to despair. For him, the darkest hour was
the one nearest the dawn.

12

Throughout the ages, man has found that 'necessity is the mother of invention'. And the financial crisis of the early fifties forced the Urdd to devise ways and means of combating the threat. It was R. E. Griffith who proposed holding an annual festival, a function that would yield an annual income of £500-£1,000 towards a debt-redemption fund. Having shared his idea with Sir Ifan ab Owen Edwards, the Chief Organiser set out for Newcastle Emlyn. If only the Cilgwyn grounds could be made available, Newcastle Emlyn would be an ideal centre. Cilgwyn was an old mansion owned by the Fitzwilliam family but leased to the Baptist Missionary Society, and administered by the Rev. J. Clement Davies of Newcastle Emlyn. R. E. Griffith decided to call on the Rev. Clement Davies to explore the possibilities.

Clement Davies listened intently as the proposals were outlined, and long before R. E. Griffith had finished, there was a gleam in his eye that indicated his approval. Yes, Cilgwyn could be made available—both grounds and mansion ; Newcastle Emlyn would be an ideal centre for Dyfed ; it could be a three-county festival. He would call a public meeting at which the project could be outlined. And R. E. Griffith knew that, since the Rev. Clement Davies was enthusiastic in his approval, the battle was as good as won.

At the meeting, the project was readily accepted and a committee set up with the Rev. Clement Davies as Chairman and the Rev. D. L. Trefor Evans as Vice-Chairman. The secretarial duties were to be shared between T. R. Griffiths and W. Haydn Davies, and the Treasurer was no other than Evan Evans who had been a pillar of strength in the planning of the Urdd Eisteddfod at Carmarthen in the thirties, and who had retired to Newcastle Emlyn from his post with the Welsh Board of Health. All were good friends of the Urdd, and with such a team at the helm, the festival was bound to succeed.

What originated as a fund-raising scheme gradually grew into a social, recreational and cultural festival ; more of a *fiesta* than a féte. It provided an interesting scheme of work for the Adrannau and Aelwydydd in the three counties, as well as being a project for the inhabitants of Newcastle Emlyn and district, many of whom had not previously had the opportunity of supporting the Urdd in a practical manner. After months of preparation, all was set for an exciting event. There were two evenings of drama, a *Cymanfa Ganu*, two children's concerts, a *Noson Lawen* and, of course, the fête itself, set in ideal surroundings. While the fête was in progress, a bardic contest took place between the poets of Cardiganshire and Pembrokeshire. Later, the three-day Festival ended in a *Twmpath Dawns* (Community Folk-Dance). As a special bonus, the entire event was blessed with three days of glorious June weather, and despite costs of £300, there was a balance of over £600. Newcastle Emlyn, with the co-operation of the Adrannau and Aelwydydd of Dyfed, had pioneered and established a blue-print for future years.

Planning for the event, R. E. Griffith thought it would add to the festive mood if cartoons and other light-hearted items could be included in the official programme. Discussing this with Aneurin Jenkins-Jones, the latter suggested keeping the official programme to the usual minimum, but producing a separate magazine of the type envisaged to be sold as a festival souvenir. Poets and writers from the three counties responded readily, and Hywel Harries, an art master at Machynlleth, agreed to provide cartoons and illustrations. There was no attempt to create a literary magazine ; *Blodau'r Ffair* was intended to raise a smile, to amuse rather than to edify. The four-thousand copies were sold within a couple of weeks, and it was an instant success.

*   *   *   *

The 1953 Urdd National Eisteddfod was held at Maesteg which, according to Griffith John Williams, was once the hub of the Morgannwg literary tradition. By the fifties, however, the demands of industry and the influx of English and Irish workers had left their scars on the Welsh character of the area as well as on its natural beauty. It was, therefore, to an area heterogeneous in language and interests that the Urdd Eisteddfod was invited, and, in an effort to win the support of the general public, the Committee members had occasionally to overcome prejudice and ignorance. There was, however, a strong team of enthusiasts, guided and strengthened by the gracious spirit of Mrs. George Bowen. It was not idly that she was given the title *Brenhines y Llwyni*.

The Committee's Chairman was Brinley Richards, another solicitor-poet, who today is Archdruid of the Gorsedd of Bards. Under his leadership, the Committee had no difficulty in completing the local arrangements in good time. As for the Eisteddfod itself, there was almost universal praise for the standard of competition— the one exception being the main drama competition where the prize was witheld, the only occasion in the history of the Urdd Eisteddfod on which this has happened.

The one real disappointment, however, was the fact that the Eisteddfod failed to attract the non-Welsh-speaking population to swell the audiences. It was something of a paradox that many of the English-speaking inhabitants had been generous in their contributions to the advance-fund, had vied with one another for the privilege of providing free hospitality for two-thousand competitors, and yet could not be attracted to support with their presence the festival they had supported with material means. It seemed that we had not succeeded in convincing them that the Eisteddfod was something they could enjoy even though they were not Welsh-speaking. As a result, the marquee was never full to capacity, even during the Chairing and Crowning ceremonies. Fortunately, however, this did not deter or discourage the organisers or the competitors. The Chair was won by Desmond Healy, a student at Aberystwyth, and the Crown by Brynmor Jones, newly-appointed member of the Urdd Staff at Aberystwyth.

The Eisteddfod Presidents included Tillie Thomas, representing the hundreds of voluntary workers who gave generously of their time and energy as leaders of Adrannau, and Goronwy Roberts, M.P. for Caernarfonshire. Despite the disappointing public support, the financial report showed a balance of £509/9/3—thanks to the advance-fund of £1,300. More important still was the inspiration derived by the five-thousand competitors, and no-one appreciated this more than the Honorary Secretaries, Morgan D. Jones and Glenys Morris.

*   *   *   *

July and August brought the usual influx of campers to Llangrannog and Glan Llyn. Those who had become strong advocates of Cricieth were, however, disappointed. The centre at Cricieth had been given to the Urdd in 1946 by Alderman William George and W. R. P. George to be used by the local Urdd Branch for the greater part of the year, and as a hostel for activities on a national level during vacation periods. Shortly afterwards, the Urdd became the owner of Pantyfedwen and two years later was given the tenancy of Glan Llyn. Maintenance of four centres was becoming a heavy item at a time when the movement was already in financial difficulties. Furthermore, with the necessary reduction in the number of staff, running four centres simultaneously meant a considerable burden on those who remained. The Urdd Council, therefore, reluctantly decided that the Cricieth premises would have to revert to the donors. They for their part were gracious enough to appreciate the difficulties and were pleased that they had been able to fill the gap until other and more appropriate centres became available.

Pantyfedwen too was a cause of concern. It was being used as a students' hostel during term-time, but largely due to travelling problems to and from Borth, the college authorities were unable to use the hostel to capacity. It was, therefore, found to be more economical to the Urdd that the premises should remain closed for seven months, and the arrangements with the College had to be terminated. At the same time, maintenance work demanding professional expertise needed urgent attention and this would involve an expenditure of £3,000-£4,000.

The Inter-Celtic and International Conventions were held as usual. For the first time, we had to forego the privilege of having an Irish group at the Inter-Celtic Convention. This was a big disappointment, but in fact, its effect was to attract an even greater contribution from the representatives of the other countries. The Cornish delegation had undertaken to prepare a photographic exhibition. We had asked each group to be prepared to deal with some aspect of their culture, which could include folk-songs, folk-dances, or contemporary literature. This proved immensely successful, and despite the fact that current literature had sometimes to be presented in translation, it did not seem to detract unduly from the presentation.

For the International Convention, we were fortunate in having the company of Mr. Jacob Jones, UNA Organiser for Wales, and he was responsible for the series of talks and discussions on the achievements and problems of various UN organisations. Among our overseas groups, we had seventeen students and teachers from Yugoslavia—our first group from a Communist country. There were also groups from France and Germany as well as representatives from Denmark, Syria and India.

Mountain-walking had already become a popular pastime among Urdd members. Apart from regular local expeditions from Glan Llyn, there was in 1953 a combined excursion when members of Aelwydydd in North Wales, and from Oswestry, Chester and Liverpool, gathered at various starting-points aiming to meet on the summit of the Berwyn range. For some, it was recreation ; for others, physical endurance ; for all, it was mental and spiritual therapy.

A new soccer competition for boys under 15 years was introduced in 1953, and in the final match at Porthmadog, the Rhos Adran lost to Cricieth. Rhos Aelwyd were already keen contestants for the Pantyfedwen Cup. Four times they had reached the final, only to find success wrenched from their grasp. But the Rhos spirit was strong enough to bring them back into the fray until they achieved ultimate victory. All these matches were organised by a small group of enthusiasts led by Jonathan Davies of Rhos, T. H. Thomas of Holyhead and Emrys Morris of Abergele, with Dafydd Jones, Organiser for Denbighshire, as Secretary.

*   *   *   *

During the fifties, the film-strip had become a popular visual-aid in schools and clubs. This spurred Sir Ifan ab Owen Edwards to the task of producing a film-strip illustrating the development of the Urdd during its first thirty years. Together with explanatory notes, copies of the film-strip were made available to Adrannau and Aelwydydd, and were particularly useful to County Organisers.

The North Wales Aelwydydd Winter-Rally had now become an annual event, and in 1953, it was held at Hen Golwyn in November.

The guest of honour was O. V. Jones, the eminent gynaecologist from Bangor, and one of the Urdd's early campers.

When Dyfrig Thomas, who had been for five years Organiser for Flintshire, left in 1953, it was decided that the Urdd organisation in Denbighshire and Flintshire be combined under the supervision of Dafydd Jones. This was in addition to acting as Secretary to the Urdd Football Association and his special responsibility as Assistant Organiser of the Urdd National Eisteddfod. This policy of combining duties and linking county to county was far from satisfactory but it was inevitable due to the financial situation. By the end of 1953, it had the effect of combining Merioneth and Montgomeryshire, Denbighshire and Flintshire, Glamorgan and Monmouthshire. Breconshire and Radnorshire were already without an organiser, and Pembrokeshire and Anglesey had only part-time organisers. This meant, in effect, that only Caernarfonshire, Cardiganshire and Carmarthenshire now had full-time organisers. In the same way, duties at Headquarters were shared. Teifryn Michael had not been replaced as Physical Recreation Organiser, and when Brynmor Jones left in 1953, his duties were added to those already undertaken by Aneurin Jenkins-Jones and Huw Cedwyn Jones. These were steps the Executive Committee regretted having to take and the Urdd Officers greatly appreciated the readiness of the staff to assume additional responsibilities in an effort to overcome the crisis. At the end of 1953, it was decided to inform the Council that no further reduction in staff was possible without seriously jeopardising the future of the movement.

At the Annual General Meeting held at Porthmadog in October, the Officers were a little more optimistic than they had been for some time. It was true that the year's accounts showed a deficit of £1,100 but the trend had been reversed and a start had been made at reducing the overdraft. Dr. T. Ifor Rees, Chairman of the Finance Committee, expressed his concern that this had largely been achieved by a curtailment of staff. He urged that more attention should now be paid to increasing the receipts, rather than curtailing costs, since further pruning would in the long run have a paralysing effect on the work of the movement throughout Wales.

*   *   *   *

R. E. Griffith had given twenty-one years' service to Urdd Gobaith Cymru, and in 1953 the University of Wales conferred upon him the degree of M.A. (*honoris causa*), in recognition of his service to Wales. He was introduced to the Vice-Chancellor by one of the Urdd's Vice-Presidents, Principal Sir Emrys Evans. Nor was the Chief Organiser's service allowed to go unheeded by the Urdd itself. The Council and Staff showed their appreciation in a dinner at Pantyfedwen when R. E. Griffith was presented with an inscribed gold watch. Both honours were richly deserved, and he was modest enough, and human enough, to treasure both.

*   *   *   *

At a time when no publishing grants were available and when it was rare for the publication of a Welsh book to be a viable proposition, it might well seem foolhardy for the Urdd to consider publishing a Welsh anthology. When the movement was already in debt, it seemed almost irresponsible. The Chairman of the Finance Committee was Dr. T. Ifor Rees, a man of wide literary interests who was also a shrewd businessman, and it was he who suggested that the Urdd should dare to venture. He maintained that the movement was in a unique position in that it could depend on its own Branches to give the venture publicity and to secure advance subscriptions. The Committee accepted his argument and decided to take the risk.

With Dr. T. Ifor Rees as Chairman, the Editorial Board consisted of Dr. T. H. Parry-Williams, Dr. Thomas Parry, Prof. Thomas Jones, Cassie Davies, Mary Llewelfryn Davies, Dr. J. Henry Jones and R. E. Griffith, with Aneurin Jenkins-Jones as Secretary. They aimed at including selections of some of the best in Welsh prose and verse, with the emphasis on the modern period. The title *Newydd a Hen* (New and Old) seemed to epitomise what they had in mind, and also echoed a verse in the Song of Songs—' And all rare fruits ready at our door, fruits new and old.' For an editorial board whose members were already laden with other responsibilities, it meant a year's project. In the case of early works, it was necessary to simplify some sections and to modernise the orthography sufficiently so that the selections would be understood by the ordinary intelligent reader. The volume should be a classic, but at the same time, readable and interesting.

Newydd a Hen, a 250-page volume, appeared at the end of 1954 and was sold at 9/6d. Two-thousand subscribers had been ensured in advance ; another two-thousand copies were sold within a few months. By the mid-sixties, a further thousand had been sold, and the remainder were sold as paperbacks at 5/-. The publication had, therefore, achieved its aims—it had given the nation a new anthology of its literary treasures, and, despite the odds, it had brought the Urdd a substantial profit at a time of financial need.

At about the same time, Dr. D. Mathew Williams, H.M.I., presented to the Urdd the copyright of three new one-act plays. Of these, *Gwragedd Arberth* and *Peredur* were based on the Mabinogi, while the third, *Ddoe a Heddiw*, dealt with the period of Owain Glyn Dŵr.

By 1954, an ' easy Welsh ' section had been incorporated in *Cymru'r Plant* and, as a result, the circulation increased to 22,500. Sir Ifan ab Owen Edwards, however, was far from satisfied and was already considering the possibility of a separate magazine for those learning Welsh as a second-language. When he put his suggestion to the Magazines Conference at Pantyfedwen, it was accepted with enthusiasm, and from then onwards he was completely engrossed in the idea, and in finding ways and means of putting it into operation.

Still in the field of publishing, it is interesting to note that the Welsh Books Campaign seemed to have gained a new impetus, and 22,281 books were sold in 1954. The fact that Alun R. Edwards, the County Librarian, was organising a similar campaign in Cardiganshire seemed to spur Urdd members to greater activity, and together, the two campaigns were making their impact in more than one direction. Alun Edwards already had plans to try and persuade other Local Authorities to follow the example set by Cardiganshire as sponsors of Welsh literature. If or when that happened, the Urdd could withdraw from the field, knowing that twenty years of voluntary effort on its part had blazed the trail, and paved the way for concerted efforts by Local Authorities.

*   *   *   *

It often happens that when the Urdd is invited to hold its National Eisteddfod in a particular area, the first prod is given by a single individual. He will naturally have shared his enthusiasm with his close associates, and eventually, some committee or organisation will undertake to call a public meeting to consider the matter and ultimately gain general support from the whole area. But nothing would have happened had it not been for that first prod. Meirion Jones, then Headmaster of the Primary School at Bala, was just such a prodder. It was his idea that the twenty-first Urdd National Eisteddfod should be held in Penllyn, with the result that, when his idea had met with unanimous approval, he was elected Honorary Secretary !

Looking back at the 1954 Bala Eisteddfod, no-one now remembers the heavy rains. Unlike Maesteg the previous year, the marquee was full from early morning until late afternoon. The same was true of the evening sessions—the drama and the *Noson Lawen*. Competitors came in their hundreds from all parts of Wales, and it was their presence that made it a national event. Indeed, it was South Wales that made the most determined bid for the County trophy—Carmarthenshire being placed first and Cardiganshire second.

The Presidents on this occasion were R. Gordon Williams of Penygroes, T. W. Jones, M.P. (later Lord Maelor) and Lady Megan Lloyd George. Her address had something of the fervour and eloquence which made her father such a notable Eisteddfodic figure—

' I want the youth of Wales to become Welsh men and women of conviction, proud of their country and of their language. Some people would call this nationalism. That is nothing to be ashamed of. The danger does not lie in that direction, but in the attitude of people who would deny a nation the right to live as a free people, and according to its own will. The Urdd has wide horizons ; it can respect other nations because it first respects Wales.'

Highlights of the Eisteddfod were the Crowning and Chairing ceremonies. The Chair was won by Dic Jones, a 20-year old farmer's son from Blaenporth in Cardiganshire and a prominent member of *Aelwyd Aberporth*. The Crown went to Catrin Puw Morgan of Corwen who had won her first victory at Machynlleth two years earlier.

When the final meeting of the Eisteddfod Committee was held three months later, members of the fifteen sub-committees who had so freely given of their time and energy could well feel satisfied with their achievement, and especially so the Officers,—the Rev. T. Gwyn Jones (Chairman), Tom Jones (Vice-Chairman), G. F. Roberts (Treasurer), and Meirion Jones who had accomplished much more than was expected of him in his role as Secretary. Nor was there any need to ask whether the Eisteddfod had proved a financial success. An advance-fund of £1,500 had been raised and, with all expenses paid, the Urdd was richer that evening by £980.

At the National Eisteddfod of Wales held at Ystradgynlais in August, the leader of the 'Welsh People in Dispersion' (*Y Cymry ar Wasgar*) was W. J. Roberts of Christchurch, New Zealand. In acknowledging the welcome they had received, he said—

'Two months ago, I went to the Urdd National Eisteddfod at Bala and it was truly an inspiration. This was one of the most thrilling experiences of my life, and I can do no better than to urge all of you here, and indeed the entire Welsh nation, to adopt the Urdd pledge of loyalty to Wales, to fellow-man and to Christ.'

*   *   *   *

Armed with the experience gained at the three-county festival at Newcastle Emlyn the previous year, the Urdd felt confident that a festival of this nature could now become an annual event. It did not seem necessary to cast the net as wide as had been done at Newcastle Emlyn and there was much to be said for a concentrated effort within one county. And since the Newcastle Emlyn festival had hardly touched the human or the material resources of North Cardiganshire, it was decided to make Tregaron the centre for the 1954 event. Nor was there any need to look outside the county for participants in the bardic contest (*Ymryson y Beirdd*) ; both north and south Cardiganshire had abundant talent that could be mustered at a moment's notice. This, of course, was only one feature in a varied programme, and as always, the inhabitants of Tregaron were one closely-knit community, ready to move mountains, if necessary, at the beck of the Chairman, Dai Williams. It was this kind of spirit that characterised the festival throughout,

42   Tomi Scourfield at the International Convention

43   Carwyn James instructs budding enthusiasts at Llangrannog

44 Bob Lloyd (*Llwyd o'r Bryn*) casting an expert eye on an exhibit

45 A basket-making group at the Talgarreg Aelwyd

with the result that the sum of £470 was later transferred to the Urdd debt-redemption fund.

Blodau'r Ffair had been such a success the previous year that it was decided to make it an annual publication and to link it with the county in which the Festival was held. Here too there was no need to look beyond the borders of Cardiganshire for contributors, and Hywel Harries had now been given the role of permanent artist. Four-thousand copies were printed and within a fortnight every copy was sold. This meant that no copies were left for the Tregaron Festival for which it was originally intended ! Another two-thousand copies were hurriedly printed and in all, six-thousand copies were sold within a month. There was now no doubt that there was a demand for such a publication.

*   *   *   *

Other major activities followed the usual pattern. The summer camps—now confined to Llangrannog and Glan Llyn—offered seventeen weeks of camping, and accommodated two-thousand members. The Inter-Celtic and International Conventions were again held at Pantyfedwen. For the International Convention we had our second group from Yugoslavia, besides groups from Austria, Belgium and France, and smaller units of two or three from Germany, Sweden, Spain, Nigeria and the USA. Those who wished to spend a further period in Welsh homes were accommodated at Cwmafan and Pontrhydyfen in Glamorgan. Once again these mining communities, with their ever-open doors, had been the first to offer hospitality. They had long since learnt that hospitality, like mercy, is twice-blessed—' it blesseth him that gives and him that takes'.

In mid-August, I had the pleasure of accompanying a group of senior members and leaders to Slovenia, the northern state of Yugoslavia, where we were joined for the duration of our stay by a group of Yugoslavs. Our first week was spent at steel-town Jesenice whose main virtue was the fact that it was within reach of the Triglav mountains and the famous lakes of Bohinj and Bled. From there, we moved to Lubljana, the Capital of Slovenia and a city that completely won our hearts so that we were loth to leave. But we could not return without a brief visit to Zagreb, and to

Postojna to see the twelve-mile cave with its stalagmites and stalagtites so skillfully lit that it was a veritable fairyland. In one huge cavern that had acoustics equal to any modern concert hall, we could not refrain from putting them to the test by singing the Welsh hymn, *Dyma gariad fel y moroedd*, which on this journey had almost become our signature tune.

The one addition to the usual summer activities was the Mabolgampau held at Aberpennar for Glamorgan and Monmouthshire members. The programme was devised by a panel of experts led by two HM Inspectors, Annie Rogers and Emrys Lloyd Davies. Local arrangements were made by a committee with Gwen Williams as Chairman and J. Jenkins as Secretary. The programme included athletics and gymnastics, netball and basketball competitions, archery and folk-dancing. In general, it was based on free activities —group exhibitions of various activities taking place simultaneously. But, as at Cardiff in 1951, this concept did not have the same appeal to spectators as did the old Mabolgampau of the thirties, even though the work was more advanced and the standard considerably higher. But when three-hundred members took their places for massed folk-dancing directed by Alwyn Samuel, something of the old thrill was recaptured.

Three-hundred Aelwydydd members from North Wales went on a pilgrimage to the I. D. Hooson Memorial and nearby Castell Dinas Brân. Not to be out-done, the Adrannau decided on their own rally, and two-hundred young enthusiasts set out from various starting-points determined to meet on the summit of Snowdon. Carmarthenshire Aelwydydd had their own county pilgrimage in September, visiting the homes of famous hymn-writers—Tomos Lewis of Talyllychau, Dafydd Jones, the drover from Caeo, Morgan Rhys of Cil-y-Cwm, William Williams of Pantycelyn and Vicar Prichard of Llandyfri.

*　　　*　　　*　　　*

Staff changes during the year included the departure of Alwyn Samuel who was appointed Headmaster of the new Welsh School at Pontrhydyfen. A native of the village, musically gifted, and with more than three years' experience in youth work, he was an ideal choice for the post. He was followed as County Organiser by Elinor Williams, then a teacher at the Barry Welsh School. The loss of Aneurin Jenkins-Jones after five years at headquarters was another heavy blow. A man of many parts, he had made an outstanding contribution to the life of the Urdd. He left to enter the teaching profession, but as was the case with most staff members who had become an integral part of the movement, his loyalty remained undiminished.

Sir Ifan ab Owen Edwards had again been left without any help with *Cymru'r Plant,* and as he had now undertaken to publish a separate magazine for those learning Welsh as a second-language, an undertaking which demanded a thorough knowledge of the techniques of second-language teaching, it was essential, despite the need for stringent economy, that an immediate appointment be made. The choice fell on Olwen M. Jones, a graduate and an experienced teacher, and she was appointed to give her undivided attention to the magazines.

On the first of June, 1954, J. M. Howell, first President of the Urdd, died at the age of 93. His interest and his generosity had been an inestimable factor in the success of the movement from the early years, and it is doubtful whether the Urdd would have developed as it did, had it not been for the contribution and stimulus of this *uchelwr*—this aristocratic figure from Aberdyfi. It may be that it was his contact with and his respect for J. M. Howell that made Ifan ab Owen Edwards appreciate what Wales had lost when its aristocracy, in search of personal gain, had denied their Welshness and transferred their loyalty to England. It may also have been the ground for his hope that some members of the old Welsh aristocracy could one day be helped to re-discover their roots and identify themselves more fully with the life of Wales.

In the same year, the Urdd lost three of its Vice-Presidents, each of whom had given valuable service to the movement. They were W. P. Thomas of Porthcawl, Captain Geoffrey Crawshay, and Robert Richards, M.P., the unassuming *gwerinwr* who did not deem it improper to join the Aelwydydd in a day's expedition to the summit of the Berwyn.

The end of another triennium meant the election of a new Council and new Officers. Sir Ifan ab Owen Edwards was re-elected President and Lady Edwards President of the Girls' Section. A new policy was adopted with regard to Vice-Presidents. In future, they would be asked to serve for a period of three years, after which they would join the ranks of Ex-Vice-Presidents. Seven new Vice-Presidents were elected in 1954,—the Rev. E. Tegla Davies ; Jenkin Alban Davies ; the Very Rev. Dr. J. C. Jones, Bishop of Bangor ; Sir David Hughes Parry ; Dr. Thomas Parry ; Goronwy Roberts, M.P., and the actor, Emlyn Williams. Dr. Iorwerth Hughes Jones of Swansea was elected Chairman of the Council and E. D. Jones of Aberystwyth Vice-Chairman. Cynfab Roberts became Treasurer and the Honorary Secretaries were Dr. Mary Clement of Aberystwyth and Iolo Francis Roberts of Amlwch.

Reviewing the financial situation for 1953-54, the Treasurer, Jenkin Alban Davies, reported a gradual improvement, thanks to a reduction in costs on the one hand, and additional money-raising schemes on the other, in particular the County Festival, *Blodau'r Ffair* and *Newydd a Hen*. For the first time in many years, there was no loss on the year's transactions ; there was even a balance of £4/17/2 ! In addition, the debt-redemption fund now stood at £1,400. If this trend could be continued, three or four years could see the Urdd out of the crisis. Despite the necessary restrictions demanded by the exigency, it was at least possible to derive encouragement from the fact that the tide seemed to be turning. Sir Ifan ab Owen Edwards, however, was not a man who easily tolerated any imposed fetters. It must have been difficult for him to accept the continual vigilance of the Council and to feel that his wings were being clipped and his freedom curtailed. Outwardly, he was patient and co-operative, but at heart, he was always the individualist, a man of vision and conviction for whom any restriction was a burden on his spirit. He loved to live his life as he drove his car, keeping his foot on the accelerator and using the brake only as a very last resort !

*　　　*　　　*　　　*

In January 1955, the Rev. Dr. Gwilym Davies died. He had devoted his whole life to the promotion of social and political justice and in search of better international understanding. During and after the First World War, he had been closely linked with the League of Nations Union, and later, as a prominent member of the Welsh Council of UNA, it was he who prepared the first draft constitution for UNESCO. The Goodwill Message of the youth of Wales to the youth of the world was only one aspect of his efforts on behalf of world peace, and it was mainly in this connection that he first came into contact with the Urdd. His influence and that of the Goodwill Message on the subsequent development of the movement and on the formulation of the Urdd Pledge has already been referred to. But it is equally true that the Urdd, in its turn, influenced the Goodwill Message and made it speak to and for the Welsh-speaking as well as the English-speaking section of the nation.

Shortly before he died, Gwilym Davies had made provision for the continuation of the Message. He left a legacy of £3,500 towards the cost of preparing and disseminating the Message, and he asked the Urdd and the Welsh Council of UNA to assume joint responsibility for its administration. Fortunately, Mrs. Gwilym Davies had worked alongside her husband for many years, and her interest and knowledge proved an invaluable link with the past. As Chairman of the Urdd's International Relations Committee, Gwilym Davies was followed by the Rev. J. E. Meredith, and about the same time the Rev. Canon Gwilym Owen, also of Aberystwyth, replaced the Rev. James Humphreys as Chairman of the Religious Affairs Committee.

*   *   *   *

The Inter-Celtic Convention was not held in 1955. R. E. Griffith had for some time felt that the Convention itself would benefit by being held alternately in other Celtic countries. While accepting this principle, the Celts themselves doubted whether they possessed an organisation capable of dealing with the administration of such a scheme, or the facilities offered by Pantyfedwen. In the end, however, it was pressure of other work that made it inevitable that the Convention be discontinued. The joint administration of the Goodwill Message had added a new dimension to the work of my Department and something had to be sacrificed to make room for the new responsibility.

The International Convention, however, was held as usual. Shortly after six o'clock one July morning, the staff were at Borth Station to welcome a group of eighteen young people from Yugoslavia. After three days and nights of travelling, all they wanted was breakfast and sleep. But as they walked towards Pantyfedwen, their weariness seemed to evaporate, and they danced for joy when they saw that the sea was just across the road. During the afternoon and evening, groups and individuals arrived from France, Germany, Denmark, Sweden, Holland, India and the Gold Coast. In addition, we were joined by some of the Celts who did not wish to be deprived of an opportunity to visit Wales.

The Mediterranean weather continued throughout the period ; not a cloud in sight, no stormy high tides. And the climate inside Pantyfedwen was correspondingly equable, partly perhaps because so much time was spent out of doors. Occasionally, in conversation, one caught an unexpected glimpse of the concealed tension which the Yugoslavs experienced in their encounters with the Germans. But one also saw the brave effort they made to face the feeling of hatred they had not yet been able to overcome.

When they left Pantyfedwen, the overseas members were accommodated for a further period in homes at Newcastle Emlyn and district. While they were there, we received a letter from one of the Yugoslavs—

'. . . It was only after I noticed that I had unconsciously eliminated some of my prejudice against German people in general that I realised how much does your Convention and the hospitality of the Welsh homes contribute to the fostering of international understanding amongst the young people who come together in this small but inspiring little land of Wales.'

The uninterrupted sunshine was equally welcome at Llangrannog and Glan Llyn. More than £1,000 had been spent on improvements and new equipment. Electricity was connected to Llangrannog and, for the first time, the camp possessed a telephone. For many camp enthusiasts, the discarded storm-lanterns were synonymous with the romantic appeal of Llangrannog, and the introduction of electricity amounted almost to sacrilege! One could sympathise with 'Bobi Gordon', who had not missed a single camping session since 1928, when he produced a new theme-song maintaining that ' the old camp is not what it used to be—long, long, ago ' !

A New Year's reunion-course for campers was held at Panty-fedwen and it was fitting that the programme should include a tribute to the hymn-writer, Ann Griffiths, who had died a hundred and-fifty years earlier at the age of twenty-nine. An illustrated talk on her life and work was given on the Sunday morning, and in the afternoon, a pilgrimage was made to the church of Llanfihangel yng-Ngwynfa in Montgomeryshire, where Ann Griffiths had been married and where she was buried ; to Dolwar Fach, her farmhouse home ; and later, to join the congregation at the Ann Griffiths Memorial Chapel at Dolanog. It was an experience to be treasured, especially as the pilgrimage was led by Sir Ifan ab Owen Edwards who shared with us his knowledge and his enthusiasm.

*　　*　　*　　*

Although its significance was not fully realised at the time, one of the most important events in the Urdd calendar for 1955 was the publication of the first number of *Cymraeg*, the new magazine for Welsh learners. Training in the techniques of second-language teaching was at best rudimentary, and today's facilities in books, tapes, films, language-laboratories etc. were hardly dreamed of. This has to be remembered in order to realise the significance of *Cymraeg* to teachers struggling against overwhelming odds to interest their pupils in learning the language. With this in mind, one can appreciate the far-sighted pioneering efforts of Sir Ifan ab Owen Edwards, always experimenting, pointing the way, and proving that this was a sphere that must be explored if educationists sincerely wished to restore to non-Welsh-speakers their lost heritage.

Thanks to the co-operation of the Education Authorities, there was an advance-order for 15,000 copies of *Cymraeg* and the monthly circulation soon rose to 20,000 and later to 26,000. This spurred Sir Ifan ab Owen Edwards to even greater efforts in trying to find teachers who had a real contribution to make in this field. And the choice was very limited. Sir Ifan had, however, laid his hands on the plough, and to him a challenge was the essence of life. Nor was *Cymru'r Plant* forgotten in the thrill of the new venture. Prior to September 1955, it had a circulation of 23,000. When *Cymraeg* appeared, the circulation of *Cymru'r Plant* fell to 17,000 but the two magazines together reached a record circulation of 43,000. The editor then decided to drop the title *Cymru'r Plant* in favour of *Cymru* (Wales) in order to avoid giving the impression that it was intended for younger children.

R. E. Griffith had acted as Honorary Secretary to the Union of Welsh Publishers and Booksellers since its inception twelve years earlier, and he felt that it was now so well-established that he could be relieved of this office. Ieuan M. Williams, a former member of the Urdd staff, was elected to take his place. R. E. Griffith, however, was not released but elected President—an office he has held ever since.

*   *   *   *

For the Urdd National Eisteddfod at Abertridwr it was a struggle against more than usual odds. One knew, of course, that to hold the Eisteddfod in the Anglicised borderland of Glamorgan and Monmouthshire was in itself a considerable risk. What could not be foreseen, however, was the railway strike on the one hand, and the continuous, relentless downpour of rain on the other. Abertridwr had vied with Amanford for the honour of holding the 1955 Eisteddfod, and despite the fact that Amanford would be more advantageous in many ways, the Urdd Council felt that it had a responsibility to visit the Anglicised areas whenever possible, if only as a tribute to dedicated leaders who, like Mary John of Abertridwr, struggled to run an Adran in the face of seemingly insurmountable difficulties.

During the two years of preparation, the Rhymni Valley stalwarts were untiring and unyielding in their efforts. Although they had fewer workers than usual at their command, the necessary tasks were accomplished in good time, an advance-fund of £1,300 was raised and 2,500 children given free hospitality. It was a near miracle. It was not the Committee's fault that the Eisteddfod had lost the pageantry of the early years. That had been the price paid in a bid for higher standards, a streamlining of the system and more efficient administration. Those who worked within the movement— the voluntary as well as the full-time workers—were satisfied that the Urdd had put first things first. But in the process, something of the spectacle had been lost. And to the man-in-the-street—as to Herbert Davies of the *Western Mail*—the Eisteddfod had lost its impact. So much depends on the eye of the beholder.

It was certainly a disappointment that the Crown was withheld by the adjudicator, Hugh Bevan, even though one agreed that the high standards set by recent Eisteddfodau had to be maintained. For the second time, the Chair was won by Dic Jones of Aberporth for a poem in strict metre entitled *Y Morwr* (The Sailor). Reviewing the Eisteddfod, *Yr Aelwyd* predicted that the Urdd had discovered a poet who would one day be chaired at the National Eisteddfod of Wales. He almost achieved the honour at Newtown in 1965, and the following year, he was chaired at the Aberafan Eisteddfod for his poem *Y Cynhaeaf* (The Harvest).

The Eisteddfod Presidents at Abertridwr included W. D. Williams of Crymych, one of those voluntary leaders who had never been able to say ' No ' to any request from the Urdd, and Ald. Huw T. Edwards who was obviously at home amongst the mining population, and, in his address, recalled his boxing days at Tonypandy fifty years earlier. The Arts and Crafts Exhibition was opened by Wynne Ll. Lloyd, Chief Inspector of Schools, and one who invariably found his way to the Urdd Eisteddfod wherever it was held.

Cardiganshire had made a bold bid for the main Eisteddfod trophy at Bala, and now at Abertridwr, it was their hour of glory. By and large, it was a brave Eisteddfod and a successful one. Despite the odds, there was a financial balance of £730/11/4, but above all else, it had succeeded in showing what could be achieved through courage, dedication and determination.

For the non-competitive annual Festival, it was now time to look beyond Cardiganshire, and this time, R. E. Griffith turned to Corwen. One reason for his choice was the fact that Corwen possessed a pavilion large enough to house such a festival ; the other and even more important factor was Trefor O. Jones. He was already County Secretary ; he had also been Secretary to the 1946 Urdd National Eisteddfod at Corwen, but his shoulders were broad and he seemed to thrive on responsibility. He was a school-master by profession and an organiser and administrator by nature. It was decided to make this a four-county festival, involving the counties of Merioneth, Montgomery, Denbigh and Flint. The programme included bardic contests in free verse and strict metre, a *Twmpath Dawns*, ballad-singing by Bob Roberts of Tai'r Felin, an exhibition of traditional clog-dancing by Hywel Wood, while, as a finalé, the Rev. Huw Jones held an audience of two-thousand spellbound throughout the *Noson Lawen*. The entire function was a two-day feast of cultural, recreational and social events which added another £700 to the debt-redemption fund. The six-thousand copies of *Blodau'r Ffair* quickly disappeared, and people were now beginning to ask why it should be limited to one number a year.

*   *   *   *

After the death of King George VI in 1952, a Memorial Fund had been set up and a Foundation established for its administration. A substantial amount was earmarked for the promotion of youth work, and of this sum, the Urdd was to receive a grant of £6,000 over a period of five years. The money was intended for two purposes— in the first place, to contribute towards the expenses of leaders' training courses, and secondly, to enable selected leaders to study the youth service of other countries, more especially the British Colonies or Dominions. The training grant has proved invaluable in enabling the Urdd to make a small contribution towards the costs of members and tutors taking part in residential courses. As for the grant earmarked for study-travel, it was natural that the offer should go to R. E. Griffith as Chief Organiser, but as he was reluctant to leave the Urdd for a period of three months, both Sir Ifan and he insisted that I should accept the offer. Having agreed, there was very little time for me to change my mind, since, in the meantime, there were camp arrangements to be finalised, a new Youth Council to be initiated, and the International Camp to be run. Eventually, I left for Canada on August 10 and returned towards the end of November. Arrangements for my visit were made by the Canadian Welfare Council, and a very full programme had been arranged which involved visits to camps, conferences and clubs ; discussing their work with scores of leaders and administrators ; making my way from Montreal to Ottawa, Toronto, Winnipeg, Saskatoon and Regina ; seeing a great deal of excellent work and meeting many interesting personalities. It was sometimes exhausting but always fascinating and exhilarating.

One of Canada's current educationists was Dr. Coady and in an article written at the time he said—

> 'We have no desire to create a nation of shopkeepers whose only thoughts run to groceries and dividends. We want our people to look into the sun and into the depths of the sea. We want them to explore the hearts of flowers and the hearts of their fellow-men. We want them to live, to love, to play and to pray with all their being . . .'

He seemed to have expressed just what the Urdd would wish to say to the youth of Wales.

13

THE Urdd had now been in existence for more than thirty years. Those who were children when they first joined the movement in the early twenties were now middle-aged. Many of them had maintained their interest and given years of voluntary service as leaders of Adrannau and Aelwydydd and as camp officers and committee members. They had set a superb example for those who were to follow them. At the same time, it was fair that they should now be allowed to withdraw and that a younger generation be encouraged and trained to take their place. Ifan ab Owen Edwards had always maintained that the leaders of a youth movement should themselves be young ; even if no longer thinking ' the thoughts of youth ' themselves, they must at least be young enough to understand those thoughts—

> ' A youth movement must understand the mind of youth. Though its ideals remain unchanged, it must be flexible enough to accept new ideas and to adopt new methods according to the needs of each generation. The only way this can be achieved is by continually making certain of young leaders. Experience and maturity are important, but no youth movement can flourish unless it also has the enthusiasm, the vigour and the freshness of youth.'

It was from such ideas that *Senedd yr Ifanc* (the Youth Council) emerged in 1955. Such a body was not necessary in the twenties and thirties when the entire membership was young. Now, however, the Urdd was a movement of two generations. It was important that the older should make room for the younger and that the latter should prepare themselves for new responsibilities. It may be natural that, during and after the war years, too much thought was given to ' service to youth ' and too little to ' service by youth'. They needed to be given the opportunity to take part not only in the activities of the movement but in its government as well. It was this policy that brought thirty-five county representatives in the 17-25 age-group to the first Youth Council meeting at Pantyfedwen in

September 1955. It was decided that *Senedd yr Ifanc* should meet twice a year, and it soon became apparent that it would develop into a living force within the movement. During its first ten years, there was a tendency for the *Senedd* to concentrate on introducing new ideas, new activities and new events into the Urdd calendar, but gradually its members began to take greater interest in the government of the movement. Representatives of *Senedd yr Ifanc* were elected to the Urdd Council. The voice of youth was now being heard ; their views were expressed even if they sometimes happened to conflict with those of the ' establishment'.

The first seed of a Youth Council had been sown as early as 1943 when Margaret Parry (later Margaret John) held a county ' Youth Senate ' at Dolgellau. It was sad to think that her life should have ended prematurely in the very year in which *Senedd yr Ifanc*—the National Youth Council—had been initiated. In the same year, the Urdd lost two of its Vice-Presidents—J. R. Jones of Liverpool and T. D. Slingsby-Jenkins of London. It also lost a member of its Council, Dr. Gwyn Williams, a brilliant scientist and a Professor at the University of London. He was the son of W. J. Williams of Llangystennin, and shared his father's interest in the movement. It was later learnt that, in his will, he had left a legacy of £7,000 to the Urdd.

Prys Edwards had been six years at Abermâd School, and was now to follow his brother, Owen, to Leighton Park School, Reading. Staff changes were not as numerous as usual, but it was a disappointment to lose the services of Olwen M. Jones who left to be married after only one year as Assistant Editor of Urdd magazines with special responsibility for *Cymraeg*. It was decided to advertise the post as one of special responsibility, requiring experience in the teaching of Welsh as a second-language. Elinor Williams left her post as Organiser for Glamorgan and Monmouthshire to return to *Ysgol Gymraeg y Barri*—this time as Headmistress. Gwyn Williams relinquished his post as Warden of the Aelwydydd at Dyserth, Rhuddlan and Llanelwy (St. Asaph) to take up an appointment as Youth Leader on the staff of the Merioneth Education Authority.

*   *   *   *

For the first time, the Annual General Meeting was held outside Wales—at Liverpool. Ever since the twenties, Liverpool had a number of Adrannau linked with the Welsh churches. In the early war years, five Aelwydydd were established and these had made a valuable contribution to Liverpool youth of Welsh extraction, and to young people from Wales temporarily resident in the city.

On this occasion, the Treasurer was able to report a slight improvement in the financial position, partly due to the publication of *Newydd a Hen* and the increased circulation of magazines as a result of the direct support of the Education Authorities. Panty-fedwen showed a loss of £600 and this was reflected in the deficit of £1,028/18/4 in the year's accounts. Grants had remained fairly constant at approximately £6,500. Lluest had at last been sold, and this, together with special fund-raising schemes, had reduced the bank overdraft to £3,000. It was no time for complacency but at least we were moving in the right direction.

About this time, Emlyn Williams readily agreed to a suggestion made by Lady Megan Lloyd George that the Urdd should be one of four movements to benefit from his charity performance in London of extracts from the works of Charles Dickens. Arrangements for the performance were made by the London Welsh Association through their Secretary, Peter Lloyd. There was a balance of £1,200 and the Urdd received £300 earmarked towards the debt-redemption fund.

A second gift received was even more unexpected. A letter from a firm of solicitors enclosed a cheque for £500, as a gift from a person who wished to remain anonymous. It was not unusual for the Urdd to receive lesser gifts from persons who did not wish their names to be disclosed, but in such cases, the Urdd knew the identity of the donor. On this occasion, however, not even the officers knew, and it was not until the mid-sixties that the identity of the mysterious donor was disclosed. It was Dilys Jones of Caernarfon, a keen supporter of the movement who had been joint-secretary of *Aelwyd Caernarfon* when it was first established in 1940. Her generous gift could not have come at a more opportune moment.

*　　　*　　　*　　　*

When the Youth Service had become an accepted—though very minor—part in the pattern of further education, and when the contribution made by the various organisations was considered in the context of leisure-time youth activities, there were some who regarded the Urdd as being too selective, largely appealing to the more academic at the expense of the less able. There was, in fact, an element of truth in this criticism. The Urdd had grown from the soil of Wales at a time when any respite that could be snatched from the sheer struggle to exist was devoted to cultural or spiritual activities, and when recreation was something to be tolerated in the very young, but cast aside along with other childish things when the working-class child bypassed adolescence and became adult.

Even in the twenties, Ifan ab Owen Edwards had been aware of this imbalance in the life of Wales—especially in the rural, Welsh-speaking areas—and it was largely in an attempt to restore the balance that he had attached so much importance to recreational activities through the Mabolgampau and the summer camps. At the same time, he recognised that if the Urdd was to make a contribution of any value towards enriching the life of the Welsh nation, emphasis on its language and its culture must, of necessity, be continued.

It was, therefore, possible that by the mid-fifties the statutory bodies, as well as some voluntary movements, were succeeding where the Urdd failed—and failing where the Urdd succeeded. They could well be more successful in the densely populated Anglicised areas where it was possible to concentrate on providing social and recreational activities, and where no specific ideals made demands upon the members. This was a valuable service and it was essential that it should be provided. But it is equally important to realise that the Urdd aims at something more. It is a movement in which ideals matter. It asks its members to identify themselves with Wales, to serve their country to the best of their ability and to promote the language, the culture and the life of the nation. If the Urdd ceased to be inextricably linked with the life of Wales it would cease to have any credibility. Furthermore, members are asked to serve and help their fellow-man, whoever he may be, and to give this service in the spirit and according to the example of Christ. A movement based on these ideals cannot be expected to have a universal appeal. Accordingly, the Urdd is selective because of its ethos and its philosophy. By its emphasis on ideals, it has understandably appealed to the more intelligent and the more thoughtful, to the more Wales-conscious, though not necessarily Welsh-speaking. It is not surprising, therefore, that the Urdd can count so many of the nation's leaders among its former members. Every nation needs able and enlightened leaders, men and women of conviction, of ideals and integrity who are prepared to put the welfare of their country before personal advantage. Today, more than ever, we in Wales need such leaders in every phase of life—in politics, in local government, in education and religion, in industry and commerce. And it is important that the Urdd should continue making this contribution to the prosperity and well-being of the Welsh nation.

*   *   *   *

' If Cardiff was recently made the capital of Wales, Caernarfon will be the capital of Welsh youth during this year's Whit-week '— so claimed the foreword to the 1956 Urdd National Eisteddfod programme. And no-one could deny that Caernarfon was an ideal choice of venue. It was a quarter of a century since the Eisteddfod was previously held in the town, and it seemed as though everyone rejoiced that it had at last returned. Caernarfon had none of the problems that had faced Abertridwr the previous year. Under the chairmanship of Ifor Hughes of Groeslon, and with the help of John Roberts, who readily shouldered the duties of Eisteddfod Secretary in addition to those of Aelwyd Warden, it took little time to form the necessary committees, each with its own field of responsibility, but all co-operating in the task of making the Eisteddfod a memorable experience. One aspect of the Eisteddfod organisation that demands careful planning each year is that of controlling the abnormal traffic and the sudden influx of excited children and high-spirited youth. This is something the public tends to take for granted and to accept as part of the duties for which the police are paid. Those who have worked alongside the police representatives on the Eisteddfod Traffic Committee will know how much planning and preparation lies behind the apparent calm, patience and good humour normally displayed by the officers on duty during the Eisteddfod.

The Presidents at Caernarfon included Meirion Jones of Bala, one who knew from experience what the running of an Eisteddfod involved ; Mansel Williams, Director of Education ; Dr. Thomas Parry ; Dr. Griffith Evans ; and Sam Jones of the BBC. As Guest of Honour, Sir Ifan ab Owen Edwards was introduced by Goronwy O. Roberts, M.P.

Dic Jones of Aberporth claimed the Eisteddfod Chair for the third time in succession ; it was also the third time for Catrin Puw Morgan to win the Crown. Competition from South Wales counties was formidable, but on this occasion, Caernarfonshire took the lead and won the main Eisteddfod trophy.

During the first half of the decade, the monetary side of the Eisteddfod organisation had become increasingly important, partly because of the Urdd's financial situation, and partly because of the ever-rising costs. At Caernarfon, the Finance Committee had raised an advance-fund of more than £1,800, and despite heavy expenses, the Treasurer was proud to be able to hand over to the Urdd a balance of almost £1,320, the highest surplus, to date, in any Urdd Eisteddfod.

*   *   *   *

A month later, the Urdd turned its attention to Llanelli—this time, to the *Gŵyl Sir*, the Urdd County Festival. It opened with a feature-programme in which one caught glimpses of the work of twenty-four Carmarthenshire hymn-writers. That same evening, the county's folk-tales were brought into focus—six episodes of drama, mime, music and dance, presenting *Hen Fenyw Fach Cydweli*, the tales of Llyn y Fan, Llyn Llech Owain, and Twm Sion Cati, as well as excerpts from *Gwilym a Benni Bach* (Llewelyn Williams).

Saturday's programme included the féte: *Ymryson y Beirdd* (Bardic Contest) ; *Pawb yn ei Dro* ; *Pen y Dosbarth* (Top of the Form) ; and ended with a community dance (*Twmpath Dawns*). The financial outcome of all these activities was that a sum of £743 was paid into the debt-redemption fund. Linked with the festival, seven-thousand copies of *Blodau'r Ffair* were printed and every copy sold within a month of issue.

*   *   *   *

In the international field, we were happy to welcome once again the Bielefeld Youth Choir from Germany. It was six years since they made their first visit, and although many of the members had changed, Dr. Hermann and Friedrich Feldmann were still in charge as liaison officer and conductor respectively. Their visit was limited to a fortnight during the Easter holiday, the time being divided between Morriston and Lampeter. Reception Committees were set up in the two centres, and concerts given at Morriston, San Clêr, Cross Hands, Trimsaran, Bridgend, Cwmtwrch, Lampeter, Aberporth, Tregaron, Felindre and Aberystwyth.

June was always a month of anxious anticipation for those of us who were directly concerned with the International Convention. Overseas contacts might have accepted, in principle, an invitation to organise a group to attend the convention, but not until we received a list of participants could we be reasonably certain that their plans would materialise. Even so, difficulties could arise at the last moment, and cancellations could well put the success of the convention in jeopardy. 1956 was one of the anxious years. It was the end of May when we learnt that a group of Upper-School pupils from Bavaria had been refused leave of absence by the education authorities. Then, within a week of the opening date, we were informed that the Czech group—the first since 1947—had been unable to obtain their passports in time. Nevertheless, there were groups from Austria and Norway and a seventeen-strong group from Yugoslavia, besides representatives from Pakistan and Tanganyika. Together with some forty-five enthusiastic Welsh members, we could still hope for an interesting convention. Jacob Jones of Bridgend was again our resident tutor, and it was he who gave the inaugural lecture, entitled ' Looking at the World Today'. He was followed by three specialists from WHO, FAO and UNESCO, one of whom was Dr. Malcolm Adiseshiah of Madras, then Deputy Director of UNESCO. These specialist lectures were, however, only a part of our programme, and the less formal talks and discussions were equally important. So, too, were the even more informal sessions when the colourful Branko of Yugoslavia, who had been a member of the Partisan Movement, and had brought with him a collection of over a thousand unpublished songs, would squat in the corridor, singing to guitar accompaniment and delighting his captive audience till the early hours of the morning ! It is impossible to convey to the uninitiated the spirit of these international gatherings, just as it was impossible for Van from Tanganyika to convey to us the taste of the African mango ! But those who experienced the 1956 Convention knew that it had been one of the best.

Despite a summer of inclement weather and a freak August storm that uprooted half the tents at Llangrannog while the campers were at their Sunday breakfast, compelling the boys to spend one night on ' rebel beds ' in the gymnasium, the camps at Llangrannog and Glan Llyn had another successful year. Indeed, those campers who experienced the storm at Llangrannog looked upon it as an added excitement, another thrill to talk about when they returned home ! For the *Swyddogion*, of course, it meant anxious moments and hard work, but by the end of the week, it had become a saga that they too were proud to relate !

*   *   *   *

It was in 1956 that the Urdd Council accepted the suggestion of its Chairman, Dr. Iorwerth Hughes Jones, that a portrait of Sir Ifan ab Owen Edwards should be commissioned. After much persuasion, Sir Ifan eventually agreed, and the work was entrusted to a Welsh artist, Alfred Janes of Swansea. The portrait was presented to Sir Ifan at Aberystwyth, on September 22, in the presence of Urdd delegates, representatives of political parties, religious bodies, national organisations, youth movements, education authorities and local government. Old and young, Welsh-speaking and non-Welsh-speaking, all joined in paying tribute to one who had done so much to create a united Wales.

It was Lady Megan Lloyd George who unveiled the portrait, paying her own tribute to Sir Ifan ab Owen Edwards as a national leader. In responding, he expressed his particular admiration for the teachers of Wales—

> ' If it was the teachers, with the ' Welsh Not', who almost killed the Welsh language in the last century, it is also the teachers who today are foremost in the struggle to save the language and the soul of Wales.'

In January 1956, a new editor was appointed to be responsible for *Cymraeg*—the second-language magazine whose circulation was already in the region of 26,000. He was Ivor A. Owen of Treharris, who, for the previous eight years, had been head of the Welsh Department at the Quakers Yard Grammar School. During the war years, he had been given a special assignment in teaching English to French and Polish members of the Forces, and having been obliged to experiment with methods of second-language teaching, he had successfully adapted those methods to the teaching of Welsh at his old school. He joined the Urdd staff in April, and Sir Ifan ab Owen Edwards at long last felt that he could shed some of the responsibility he had borne for thirty-five years.

The same period saw the appointment of John R. Lane as Organiser for Glamorgan and Monmouthshire. He had been one of the most active of Urdd voluntary leaders, having held office on District and County Committees and taken a lively interest in all activities organised on a national level. But there were losses too. It was with much regret that the Urdd bade farewell to Alice E. Williams, who returned to teaching after six years as Organiser, first for Caernarfonshire, and then for the counties of Caernarfon and Anglesey. In addition to her work within her own region, she had made an invaluable contribution to the success and development of national events—to summer camps, to training courses, and especially in the field of folk-dancing.

The loss of John Roberts, who had given the Urdd nine years of outstanding service as Aelwyd Warden, first at Llanelli and then at Caernarfon, was another heavy blow. In addition to activities within the Aelwyd premises, he believed in using the centre as a base from which to embark on ' extra-mural ' activities. There were expeditions within Wales ; there were visits to Cornwall, to Brittany and to Dublin, and, alternately, the Aelwyd would act as host to visiting overseas groups. In all these activities, everything would be planned and organised with meticulous care and it is little wonder that John Roberts has since achieved so much success as North Wales Organiser of the National Eisteddfod of Wales.

One result of the curtailment in staff was that R. E. Griffith, as Chief Organiser, was grossly over-worked and over-burdened. Sir Ifan ab Owen Edwards decided that something had to be done to remedy the situation and he brought the matter to the attention of the Executive Committee. As a result, it was decided to appoint an assistant, and the choice fell on J. Cyril Hughes of Ysbyty Ystwyth, who had graduated in Law at Aberystwyth. He took up his post in September 1956, an appointment that was long overdue.

*   *   *   *

The 1956 Annual General Meeting was held at Fishguard. The President referred to the death of three Vice-Presidents—Sir Eric Skaife, the Very Rev. Dr. J. C. Jones, Bishop of Bangor, and the Very Rev. Dr. W. T. Havard, Bishop of St. David's.

Referring to *Senedd yr Ifanc* (the Youth Council), Sir Ifan remarked—

> ' We must always remember that the Urdd is a youth movement and that it needs young leaders and young Officers. *Senedd yr Ifanc* will nurture those leaders, and we, who are older, must learn to give them the opportunity to express their opinions openly, honestly and without restraint—even though they may sometimes amount to criticism.'

The financial report was a little more optimistic in tone than it had been for years. The long-standing debt had almost been eliminated ; Pantyfedwen seemed to have turned a corner and was beginning to show a surplus. Nevertheless, with costs running at £30,000 and grants at £6,500, making ends meet was a continuous struggle and there seemed to be little likelihood that it would cease in the foreseeable future.

*   *   *   *

In recent years, there had been no difficulty in selling six or seven thousand copies of *Blodau'r Ffair*. Like Oliver Twist, the public pleaded for more, and in response to pressure from enthusiastic readers, midsummer and Christmas numbers appeared in 1957. Having sold eight-thousand of the midsummer issue, we ventured on nine-thousand of the Christmas number. One realised, of course, that a saturation point must eventually be reached, but it could only be found by testing the market. And on this occasion, all nine-thousand copies were sold.

Another development in the field of publishing was the re-introduction of *Cymru'r Plant*. The older boys and girls had wel-comed the advent of *Cymru*, but parents and teachers regretted that this had been achieved at the expense of the younger children. Sir Ifan ab Owen Edwards put his problem to the Magazines Confer-ence and it was unanimously agreed that the ideal would be to retain *Cymru* for older boys and girls and to restore *Cymru'r Plant* for the juniors. This would previously have been impossible, but now that Ivor Owen shared the burden, and that Mairwen Lewis, a graduate of Aberystwyth, had been appointed assistant editor, it did not seem to be beyond the realm of possibility. The Conference suggested that the magazines be limited to ten monthly issues coinciding with the school year, thus allowing time for planning and for staff holidays.

The Welsh Books Campaign for 1957 attracted 64 Branches which, between them, sold 10,875 volumes. The top salesmen on this occasion were *Ysgol Frondeg*, Pwllheli, while close on their heels came *Ysgol Gymraeg Nantyffyllon*, *Ysgol Uwchradd Abergwaun* and *Aelwyd Llanrwst*.

*   *   *   *

Following the death of the Rev. Dr. Gwilym Davies in 1955, the Goodwill Message Committee had decided to retain the same Message for 1956. For 1957, however, it was felt that a completely new Message was required. And perhaps the greatest thrill in 1957 was to learn that Radio Moscow had, for the first time, broadcast the Goodwill Message, and this at a time when the iron curtain made political contacts virtually impossible.

Twelve years had elapsed since the end of the war, and in Britain, a generation was growing up for whom the war was no more than a chapter in history. On the continent, however, although much of the material damage had been repaired, the human scars remained. Thousands of refugees had already re-turned to their home areas to begin anew the struggle of building up a livelihood. But there were still thousands of men, women and children who had fled from their homes—sometimes to neighbouring countries—and who now had no homes to which they could return. Having lost all they once possessed, they were allowed to rot away in refugee-camps all over Europe. The young and the healthy among them were encouraged and helped to emigrate to countries prepared to accept them. But there remained a ' hard core ' of unwanted refugees—the old and infirm, widowed mothers and women with illegitimate children. Some had spent more than a decade in overcrowded refugee-camps, gradually deteriorating in mind and body. It was a major problem which the world had been content to forget. To make matters worse, there were new refugee problems in other parts of the world—in India and Pakistan, in Israel and Irak, in Korea, China and Japan. And new refugees from Hungary had recently added to the European problem.

Faced with this situation, UNA decided to make one supreme effort to close the European ' hard core ' camps, placing the refugees in homes or hospitals in the countries in which they were currently accommodated. It was estimated that the scheme would take three years to complete and would cost £18,000,000

Senedd yr Ifanc felt that this was a project in which Urdd members should participate. In an article in *Yr Aelwyd*, they made their plea—

> ' What has "Loyalty to Fellow-man" cost us in personal terms ? If we have achieved anything through visits, exchanges and camps, have we not ourselves gained from the experience ? For thirty-five years we have promoted the Goodwill Message of the Youth of Wales to the youth of the world ; but despite the noble thoughts and the conviction that lay behind the Message, they were expressed in words alone. That may have been sufficient in less troubled times. But today—in a crisis . . . ? '

The result was that Urdd Branches and Committees throughout Wales took up the challenge and either joined in local efforts or sent their contributions via Swyddfa'r Urdd. In the context of such a vast problem, their contribution may have been no more than a drop in the ocean, but it was made with sincerity. And apart from the material help it provided to those engaged in the massive task, it awoke in the members themselves a new awareness of and a new concern for the needs of others. 'Fellow-man' assumed a new and a more real connotation.

Unlike the previous year, there was no cause for concern regarding the number of overseas members attending the tenth International

Convention. They came from Norway, Sweden, Austria, Yugoslavia, France, Belgium and India. We had chosen ' World Population Problems ' as our main theme, and our tutor, Harold Carter from the Geography Department at the University, dealt with three main regions—Egypt, South America, Japan and India. Once again it was Cwmafan that opened its doors to offer hospitality to the overseas members who wished to spend a further week in Welsh homes. Indeed, it had almost become an annual event at Cwmafan and the entire community had come to accept it as a normal part of their pattern of life.

Amanford had yielded the 1955 Urdd National Eisteddfod to Abertridwr, but they felt no bitterness, and returned to bid for the next South Wales Eisteddfod in 1957. Once their request had been granted there was no looking back. The Rev. E. Llwyd Williams was elected Chairman of the Executive Committee and his fellow-officers were Jac Evans, William Davies and Beti Davies. Behind them were a host of willing workers, all determined to make the Eisteddfod a success. Whatever assets Caernarfon could boast of in the previous year, Rhydaman too possessed in abundance. The town's motto, *Hanfod tref, trefn* (Order is the essence of a town), seemed to have been adopted for the Eisteddfod as well. Even the weather responded, and the warmth of welcome given to the three-thousand competitors matched the warmth of the unbroken sunshine. Everything ran with clockwork precision ; competition was keen, standards throughout were high, but no-one could deny that Carmarthenshire deserved to win the main Eisteddfod trophy.

The Eisteddfod Presidents were Iorwerth Howells, Director of Education, Ald. Huw T. Edwards, the Rev. W. Nantlais Williams, J. Clifford Thomas of London, Dr. Ivor J. Thomas of Swansea, and the Rev. and Mrs. Tegryn Davies, joint-leaders of the Adran and Aelwyd at Aberporth. It was Dic Jones, a member of their Aelwyd, who once again won the Eisteddfod Chair, this time for a poem dealing with the farmer's struggle with Nature throughout the ages. The Crown went to Mairwen Lewis who had been placed second at Maesteg in 1953, and who had recently joined the Urdd staff at Aberystwyth.

Strange as it seemed, the Eisteddfod expenses were lower than those of the Caernarfon Eisteddfod, while everything else showed an increase. The advance-fund reached a total of £2,700 and the Eisteddfod proceeds almost balanced the expenses so that the Executive Committee was able to double the surplus achieved at Caernarfon and hand over to the Urdd the sum of £2,651—the highest ever.

Less than a month after the Eisteddfod, the Urdd focussed its attention on the County Festival at Fishguard. Although a much smaller event than the Eisteddfod held there six years earlier, it had been undertaken with the same energy and zest. However, the sudden death of D. T. Jones, Director of Education, cast its shadow over the entire county. Everyone mourned his passing, and together with many others, the Urdd had lost a trusted and valiant friend. A month later, the Festival Committee experienced another blow when T. J. Francis, Headmaster of Goodwick School and Festival Treasurer, died suddenly at the age of forty-eight. Despite these losses, the Festival Committee again closed their ranks determined that the Festival should go on. Geraint Davies, who had already shouldered the duties of Secretary, stepped into the breach and added the Treasurer's responsibilities to those he already carried. The event included a *Cymanfa Ganu* ; *Brethyn Bro* (Home-spun)—a programme portraying the Pembrokeshire of yesterday ; a Bardic Contest between the poets of Carmarthenshire and Pembrokeshire ; Top of the Form ; *Pawb yn ei Dro ; Tri Chryfion Byd*—an Interlude by Twm o'r Nant ; a *Twmpath Dawns ;* a gymnastic exhibition and a *Noson Lawen*. It was an ambitious programme, and proved once again what even a small group of people could achieve with enthusiasm, determination and leadership. Those involved felt it had brought them together in a closer community, while at the same time, creating interesting and exciting activities that brought the Urdd a surplus of £700.

* * * *

Now that the deficit of the early fifties had largely been eliminated, Sir Ifan ab Owen Edwards felt he was justified in putting to the Council a plea for much needed improvements to camp premises. With his usual shrewdness, he argued that it would, in the long run, be an investment ; improved facilities would mean an increase in numbers and hence higher receipts. He raised—and dismissed—

every possible objection, and he knew he had won ! Part of his scheme for Glan Llyn was a new dining-hut with its windows overlooking the lake towards Aran Benllyn, a big improvement on the existing marquee. An unexpected development was the acquisition, on rent, of Glan Llyn Isaf, the estate agent's house a few hundred yards from the mansion and currently vacant. From then onwards the boys could sleep at Glan Llyn Isaf, and an additional forty campers per week could thus be accommodated.

In making his request to the Council, Sir Ifan maintained that a good deal of work at Glan Llyn and Llangrannog could be done by the members and leaders themselves. Work-camps were accordingly held at both centres during the Easter vacation. Most of the voluntary workers were required at Glan Llyn, and Sir Ifan himself was there in their midst, planning, supervising and doing his share of the chores. He was now over sixty years old and no-one expected him to wield pick and shovel with the youngsters, but he knew that his example was appreciated—quite apart from the fact that he enjoyed the experience !

The volunatry work at Llangrannog was directed by Evan Isaac. Here, in addition to the work done by volunteers, contractors were busy erecting two new buildings—a camp-leaders' unit and a chapel. The chapel was built at a cost of £750, and paid for by Dr. Griffith Evans of Caernarfon. Later in the year, while the summer camps were in progress, Dr. Evans formally presented the chapel to the Urdd, and in doing so, he expressed the hope that it would help to stress the importance of Loyalty to Christ. During the ceremony, Dr. Gwenan Jones presented to the Urdd, for use in the chapel, a piano, a lectern and Bible, in memory of Margaret Parry, a former dedicated member of the Urdd staff.

*   *   *   *

Some of the more seasoned campers felt that Glan Llyn and Llangrannog, with their new developments and amenities, could be in danger of losing the sense of adventure and achievement that comes from facing a challenge and overcoming difficulties. It was in *Senedd yr Ifanc* that these feelings were usually expressed and remedies suggested. One result of this was that more hill-walking expeditions were arranged for small groups who carried their requirements in food, clothing and equipment, and slept out of doors or in disused buildings. The first of these expeditions took a group from Aberystwyth to Nantymoch, Cwm Ystwyth, Ffair Rhos, Elan and Claerwen. In addition to the feeling of physical well-being and the thrill of achievement, the members discovered the peace and serenity of the wide-open spaces. It was the first of many similar expeditions—perhaps unspectacular and uneventful, but yet of lasting quality.

When Tomi Scourfield decided to leave the Urdd staff and return to college to take a Teachers' Training Course, it seemed as though one of the brightest stars in the Urdd firmament had suddenly been extinguished. He had been long enough in his post as Carmarthenshire Organiser to have left an indelible mark on the county's administration. He possessed a wizardry that endeared him immediately to campers at Llangrannog and Glan Llyn, and he brought the qualities of a Pied Piper to every international gathering. However, rather than bemoan his departure, we could well be grateful for ten years of service and wish him further success. After a brief period in the teaching profession, he was appointed South Wales Organiser to the National Eisteddfod of Wales. Later, in 1971, he was appointed Secretary to the West Wales Association of the Arts. It was no mere coincidence that the first two Organisers appointed by the National Eisteddfod Council came from the ranks of the Urdd staff. And although they moved to new spheres, their loyalty to the movement remained constant.

Among other staff changes, Margaret Jones, who for ten years had been personal secretary to the Chief Organiser, left in 1957. In the re-organisation that followed, Rita Evans of Llanon was appointed and she has been our cheerful and courteous telephone operator for sixteen years.

By the summer of 1957, Owen Edwards had completed his law course at Lincoln College, Oxford. But instead of continuing his training with a firm of solicitors, he decided to accept a post at the National Library of Wales. Sir Ifan was naturally delighted that his elder son should have returned to Aberystwyth—and to the Urdd.

*   *   *   *

The Annual General Meeting was held at Dinbych in October. Both the President, Sir Ifan ab Owen Edwards, and the Chairman, Dr. Iorwerth Hughes Jones, were unable to be present. Prior to this, Sir Ifan had only once in twenty-five years missed a General Meeting and his absence on this occasion was keenly felt. The annual report was presented by the Vice-Chairman, E. D. Jones. The key-words were development, growth and success. The Treasurer, too, was more optimistic and presented his report with less caution and anxiety than had been the case during previous years. Grants received totalled £6,768—one sixth of the year's outlay of more than £36,000. It was true that there was a deficit of £650 on the year's accounts, but in view of the total expenditure, the reduction in the outstanding debt and the amount invested in improving camp premises, the result was no mean achievement.

1957 was the end of another triennial period, and Officers and members of Council were due for election. The Presidents, Treasurer, Counsel and Solicitor were re-elected. Six Vice-Presidents were chosen—Mrs. Tegryn Davies of Aberporth, Dr. Huw T. Edwards, Norah Isaac, Dr. Iorwerth Hughes Jones, Wynne Ll. Lloyd (Chief Inspector of Schools) and the Very Rev. G. O. Williams (Bishop of Bangor). The Rev. Trebor Lloyd Evans of Morriston was elected Council Chairman, with A. D. Lewis of Aberystwyth as Vice-Chairman of the Council and Chairman of the Executive Committee. Dafydd Morris Jones and Menai Williams became Joint Honorary Secretaries. As 1957 drew to its close, new developments were already on the horizon. Tomorrow was already waiting to be introduced.

14

I T was ten years since the Urdd had first made contact with Lois
Blake. Her experience of English and European folk-dancing
had made her unwilling to accept that there was no such tradition
in Wales, other than the clog-dancing whose sole exponents were
members of the Wood family living in the Bala area. In searching
through dance manuals and other MSS at the National Library of
Wales, she had unearthed fragments of dance notation, pieced
them together, interpreting and filling-in the missing links, until
eventually, in collaboration with W. S. Gwynn Williams, the first
group of Welsh dances were published. The next task was to bring
those bare bones to life, and it was here that a partnership developed
between the Urdd and Mrs. Blake, and later between the Urdd and
the Welsh Folk Dance Society. The dances were taught at Urdd
training courses and became the set-dances at the Eisteddfod. Other
dances were later rediscovered and published, and as dancers
became more proficient, not only were they able to tackle steps and
figures that were more complicated, but they also began to see new
interpretations and discover new meanings in the printed word
which was all that remained of what had once been a living
tradition.

But in addition to teaching team-dances to the enthusiastic few,
it was now necessary to popularise the art of dancing amongst
young people in general. This called for simple, undemanding
community dances that could be performed as social recreational
activities. When not enough such dances were available, they were
compiled, adapted or borrowed, given Welsh titles and danced to
Welsh airs. They were taught at camps and courses and gradually
they spread to the Aelwydydd. It was not long before it was possible
to bring a number of Aelwydydd together for an evening of community dancing and thus the old *Twmpath Dawns* was revived. It
soon became an essential feature in the life of young people, particularly in rural and Welsh-speaking areas. Folk-dancing had become
a cult and a craze. The essence of a *Twmpath* was a good ' Caller '
and almost invariably, they were persons who had learnt the dances

at Urdd camps and courses, and it is to them that we are indebted for maintaining the Welsh character of the *Twmpath*. Music was their main problem, and as no Welsh dance-records were available, Scottish, Irish and English records had to be used until groups of musicians could be formed, and foremost among these was *Band y Gwerinwyr* from Llanon in Cardiganshire. These groups gradually built up a *repertoire* of Welsh tunes so that everything—the dances, the calling and the music—contributed to the Welshness of the occasion. Young people flocked to every *Twmpath* within a radius of 30-40 miles. It was a social and recreational event, and it was open to all who felt energetic enough to participate.

Of course, the *Twmpath*, although originally an activity of the Urdd, was in no way the prerogative of the movement, and soon other societies and organisations realised its value, not only as an activity in its own right, but also as a fund-raising medium. The craze swept through the country, especially West and North Wales. At this intensive pace, it could not be expected to last. But even in a brief period, it had made a significant contribution to Welsh life. Welsh became the language of social and recreational activities and was no longer confined to home and chapel. The *Twmpath Dawns* had given Welsh youth a new zest, and what was more, it restored to them a part of their lost heritage. Incidentally, it helped to make them more aware of their Welshness, and even if the *Twmpath* should later yield to some other, newer form of entertainment, it had proved that it was no longer necessary to deny one's Welshness in order to be ' with it'.

But this was only one aspect of the Urdd's interest in folk-dancing. The *Twmpath* was a social and recreational activity, and high standards of dancing were not the first priority. This did not mean that nothing more was desirable. We already had several groups that competed annually at the Urdd National Eisteddfod and were capable of exhibiting the more complicated Nantgarw dances with grace, vigour and imagination. To experiment still further, a national group was formed and trained by Alice Williams, and in 1957, they were invited to take part in a Folk-Dance Festival at the Royal Albert Hall in London. We then realised that there was no reason why we should not organise our own Folk-Dance Festival in Wales and plans were made to hold such a function in the Corwen Pavilion in June 1958. This was not to be a glorified *Twmpath*

Dawns. Dances had to be selected, teams chosen and trained, costumes designed, music and dance-instructions prepared, an orchestra engaged, and a full-scale rehearsal held in the Pavilion. While a panel of staff members prepared the content of the festival, another team was busy with essential local arrangements. With R. E. Griffith as adviser, they were led by T. Ellis Roberts (Chairman), Mrs. M. Tudor (Vice-Chairman), T. Ifan Edwards (Treasurer) and, of course, the indispensible Trefor O. Jones as Secretary.

On June 14, after a morning rehearsal, we held our breath as we watched the two-and-a-half hour performance : the throb of the music, the kaleidoscope of 300 massed dancers, the exhibition of more complicated dances by experienced groups—all this interspersed with folk-singing and clog-dancing. The afternoon session was followed by a *Noson Lawen* in which the compére, Charles Williams, cast a two-hour spell on his audience of two-thousand. This was followed later by a *Twmpath Dawns* when the Pavilion throbbed with the exuberance of eight-hundred dancers as they responded to the calling of Gwyn Williams of Bangor. The Festival had been a major success. Such a venture, however, involving some four-hundred participants, was inevitably a costly event. This had been anticipated, and to supplement the proceeds of the *Noson Lawen* and *Twmpath Dawns*, an advance-fund of £240 had been raised. It was this that made it possible for the Treasurer to hand over to the Urdd a surplus of £210. Thus a new event had been added to the Urdd calendar, an event that proved to be colourful, spectacular and artistic, while those privileged to participate experienced the thrill of pioneering and the satisfaction of achievement.

*　　　*　　　*　　　*

At this time, the Director of Education for Flintshire was Dr. B. Haydn Williams, an outstanding personality, dynamic and irresistible ; a man with a mind of his own, possessing deep convictions, incredible moral courage and steadfast faith. In Further Education and especially in scientific and technological fields, he was a pioneer. He had also become convinced of the value of bilingual education even in an industrialised and Anglicised county like Flintshire, and had established three Welsh-medium primary schools. Others followed later, and, as a logical development, he set up two bilingual secondary schools. He was, of course, not alone in this pioneering work. He had the support of his staff, together with many enthusiastic teachers and enlightened Councillors. Under his leadership, they created a favourable climate in which Welsh could be taught ; they established a language policy second to none in Wales and this became an example and inspiration to other parts of the country.

Dr. Haydn Williams was well aware of the part played by the Urdd in promoting the language and culture of Wales, and no-one was surprised when he agreed to act as Chairman of the Executive Committee of the Urdd National Eisteddfod to be held at Mold in 1958. The decision to invite the Eisteddfod had already been taken at a meeting organised by a group of teachers who had long been keen supporters of the movement,—such people as J. Caradog Williams of Trelogan, T. Ceiriog Williams of Mold, and D. J. Thomas of Dyserth. And such was their admiration and their respect that they would have none other than the Director of Education as Chairman of the Executive Committee.

As one would expect, Dr. Haydn Williams was brimful of ideas regarding the running of the Eisteddfod. Some of his suggestions were extremely valuable, others proved to be less practicable. It was he who persuaded the Urdd to use the same marquee as that used for the International Eisteddfod at Llangollen, an arrangement that has continued ever since. Furthermore, it was largely due to his lead that the Eisteddfod was given such wholehearted support by the Flintshire County Council and Education Committee.

Of the Eisteddfod itself, one reporter wrote as follows—

> ' The standard was high in all sections. Out of ninety stage competitions, only four fell short of what was expected. This is a tribute to the complete dedication of members and leaders throughout Wales. They can well be proud of the movement's cultural achievements which would stand comparison with those of any youth movement in Europe. And when one considers that it is all done by the self-sacrificing voluntary leaders of a small nation, it is nothing short of a miracle.'

Competition from South Wales was formidable, but no-one could have predicted that West Glamorgan would again win the County trophy, with Carmarthenshire a close second.

46　Hill-walking pioneers in the fifties

47　Ivor A. Owen, Magazines Editor
1956—1970

48　W. Mitford Davies who for forty
years illustrated the Urdd magazines

49 Mrs. Lois Blake

50 Trefor O. Jones and R. E. Griffith with a charming young lady at Corwen

51 Dr. Griffith Evans of Caernarfon

52 Dr. Gwenan Jones speaking at Llangrannog

The Eisteddfod Presidents were Eluned Bebb, Ald. H. R. Thomas, Dr. T. H. Parry-Williams, and Dr. T. I. Davies, H.M.I. This time the Chair went to a newcomer, T. James Jones, one of three talented brothers from Newcastle Emlyn. The Crown too went to a new-comer, Marian Rees of Talyllyn. She had already been placed third at Caernarfon and second at Amanford.

The evening classical concert was another of Dr. Haydn Williams' ideas. A choir of 250 young people from Denbighshire and Flint-shite, together with professional soloists, were joined by the Liver-pool Philharmonic Orchestra in a performance of Verdi's *Requiem Mass*. But excellent though this was, the highlight of the week was a pageant based on the Urdd Pledge and performed by more than five-hundred boys and girls. Devised by Leslie Harries and T. Ceiriog Williams and produced by T. Tudor Jones, it was a superb performance, a thrilling experience and a lasting inspiration.

With these two major performances added to the Eisteddfod, it was not surprising that costs were a great deal higher than usual. Even so, the Treasurer, W. M. Moelwyn Hughes, was able to announce a surplus of £1,515, a figure that only Rhydaman, the previous year, had surpassed.

*   *   *   *

Glamorgan and Monmouthshire had jointly agreed to act as hosts to the sixth annual Urdd Festival. But although the County Committees were to some extent involved, the festival was largely centred on Castellnedd (Neath) and the greater part of the respons-ibility for its organisation was borne by the *Nedd ac Afan* District Committee under the chairmanship of Moelwyn D. Preece. An advance-fund of £500 was raised, and the programme included a *Cymanfa Ganu* and a feature-programme entitled *Cip ar Forgannwg* (a Glimpse of Glamorgan) during which the guest-speaker, Sir Ben Bowen Thomas, stressed the importance of maintaining close links between the schools and the Urdd in the task of promoting the language and culture of Wales. In all, it was one of the happiest of Urdd festivals ; plans were completed without flutter or panic, thanks largely to the Honorary Secretary, T. Glyn John, and the County Organiser, John R. Lane. It was the first festival for which J. Cyril Hughes had been responsible, R. E. Griffith being content with producing another issue of *Blodau'r Ffair* for the occasion. No-one could be more pleased with the result than the Treasurer, Trefor J. Evans, who was able to hand over to the Urdd a surplus of £905, the highest so far in any County Festival.

*   *   *   *

The International Convention took as its theme ' Science and World Society'. We were privileged to have Dr. Glyn O. Phillips as resident-tutor, and he was joined by Dr. Dennis Powell from Harwell, and Dr. Richie Calder whose book, ' Medicine and Man', had just been published. Ieuan John of the Department of International Politics at Aberystwyth was another of our tutors, and he had been asked to analyse the background and the significance of the current Middle East crisis. Lectures, however, were a minor though important part of our programme and sometimes more real contact was achieved through informal discussions, and even through activities as trivial as treasure-hunts. It had now become the custom for Saturday to be a free day, and in advance, groups would get together to plan their Saturday's expedition—some making for the hills around Borth, others venturing as far as Cardiff or St. David's, returning on Sunday full of tales and anecdotes.

In addition to our own International Convention at Pantyfedwen, the Urdd was invited by the Ministry of Education to select six members to represent Wales as part of a British contingent to attend an International Convention at Nivelles, near Brussels. Over fifty applications were received, and from a short list the six were selected by interview.

During the summer of 1958, two-and-a-half thousand members camped at Llangrannog and Glan Llyn. Weatherwise, it was a disappointing summer, and campers and leaders were glad of the improvements and new amenities at both centres. It is surprising, however, how little attention is paid to the weather, especially by Llangrannog campers. It has to be a deluge before they are even aware that it is raining !

Following the experience of the previous year, there were hill-walking expeditions led by two brothers, Iolo and Iwan Williams of Barmouth. Iwan and his group explored the wide-open spaces of mid-Wales while Iolo and his companions set out from the Eisteddfod ground at Glyn Ebwy, aiming first for the Brecon Beacons, then on to Llandyfri and Llanybydder, eventually being given a heroes' welcome at Llangrannog.

*   *   *   *

The Annual General Meeting was held at Morriston, home of the Council Chairman, the Rev. Trebor Lloyd Evans. It was with regret that the President referred to the death of several who had been fervent in their support of the movement. These included Lady Hopkin Morris, former Vice-President ; D. O. Roberts of Aberdâr, a pioneer in the teaching of Welsh and prominent in all movements that aimed at promoting the culture and the life of Wales ; and Carol Lewis, daughter of the Rev. and Mrs. L. Haydn Lewis of Ton Pentre, who died at the age of twenty-three, after a brilliant academic career, and after only one year on the staff of Ogwr Grammar School. Her radiant personality had endeared her to Llangrannog campers and leaders alike and her early death was mourned by all. In memory of D. O. Roberts, a sum of £100 was given to the Urdd by his family, and this, together with £200 contributed by friends of Carol Lewis, was invested in a fund, the income from which would enable deprived children to spend a week at Llangrannog.

In presenting his report, the Chairman outlined the main activities in which the movement had been involved during the year. He had no sooner moved the adoption of the report than he was seconded by Gwyn Daniel of Cardiff who referred to the ' miracle ' performed annually by the Urdd. The movement faced an expenditure of £40,000 receiving barely £8,000 in grants. How this was achieved was something of a mystery, but it was done year after year. This was as good an introduction as any to the Treasurer's report, and although Cynfab Roberts rejoiced that the bank overdraft had at last disappeared, he could not feel complacent. Escalating costs were such that if the Urdd was to continue its work and remain solvent, it would somehow need to increase its income by £5,000 per year.

In closing the proceedings, the Founder recalled how the organisation and activities of the movement had changed over the years. He went on—

' They will change even more during the next ten years—
Senedd yr Ifanc will see to that ! It is a source of great joy to me
that our members are exploring and experimenting with new
activities. But there is one thing that gives me even greater joy,
and this is the fact that none of them wants any change in the
Urdd's ideals.'

* * * *

1958 was the centenary of the birth of Owen M. Edwards. The
idea that the Urdd should take the lead in initiating centenary
celebrations had been mooted in 1956 during a conversation
between R. E. Griffith and Dr. Gwenan Jones. It was perhaps
natural that Dr. Jones should be the prime mover. Herself an
educationist, she was a native of Penllyn, a great admirer of Owen
M. Edwards, and one who had known and collaborated with his
son, Sir Ifan. It was left to R. E. Griffith to put the matter to a
meeting of the Urdd Council. Sir Ifan was informed of the intention,
but naturally felt it would be inappropriate for him to take any
part in the discussion.

The Council enthusiastically agreed that some form of celebration
should be considered. R. E. Griffith was asked to invite a number of
prominent Welsh organisations to elect representatives to form a
steering committee. This body first met in April 1957, later becoming the Centenary Executive Committee with Dr. Gwenan Jones
as Chairman, Cynfab Roberts as Treasurer, and R. E. Griffith as
Secretary. When the Committee was fairly clear on what it
would like to achieve as part of the Centenary programme, a
National Conference was held at Aberystwyth in February 1958.
There were representatives present of more than seventy bodies—
county councils, education committees, national institutions,
colleges, political parties, religious bodies, professional and trade
unions, and voluntary organisations. Chaired by Dr. Gwenan
Jones, the Conference was addressed by Dr. Thomas Parry and
Sir Ben Bowen Thomas. Following this, the Executive Committee
was strengthened and entrusted with the responsibility of carrying
out the schemes outlined by the speakers and approved by the
Conference.

It was anticipated that the plans would cost a total of £8,000 and
it was deemed necessary to set a target of £10,000 for the Centenary

Fund. A Finance Committee was set up, and within a year, more than £9,500 had been raised. One aspect of the celebrations was the reprinting in five volumes of some of the works of Owen M. Edwards. They were edited by Professor Thomas Jones of Aberystwyth and published by Hughes and Son, Wrexham, with whom O. M. Edwards had collaborated closely for so many years.

It was also intended to publish a complete biography of Owen M. Edwards. This task had been begun by W. J. Gruffydd in the thirties, and his first volume, which appeared in 1937, had been out of print since 1948. However, he was unable to complete the work, and the task was then entrusted to R. T. Jenkins. He, too, failed to fulfil the assignment and the biography remained unfinished. The Centenary Committee felt that it was incumbent on them to see the work completed and, this time, it was undertaken by Gwynedd O. Pierce. Unfortunately, he too, was impeded by other obligations, and so far, the full standard biography remains an unaccomplished dream.

Meanwhile, as an interim measure, the Urdd arranged for the publication in 1958 of a short biography by Gwilym Arthur Jones based on a thesis for which he had been awarded a prize at the 1957 National Eisteddfod of Wales. With the ready co-operation of Sir Ifan ab Owen Edwards, the work was extended and published as *Bywyd a Gwaith Owen Morgan Edwards*. An English booklet written by Dr. Jac L. Williams was published by the Centenary Committee under the title ' Owen Morgan Edwards : A Short Biography'. Sir Ifan prepared a film-strip dealing with the life and work of his father, and this was made available to schools, education authorities and libraries. Articles on O. M. Edwards appeared in various sections of the press, and the BBC broadcast a feature-programme by Cynan, a talk in English by Professor David Williams, and a television programme devised by Ifan O. Williams.

The main feature in the celebrations was the national gathering held at Llanuwchllyn and chaired by Cassie Davies. Tributes were paid to ' O.M.' by speakers representing three generations—the Rev. Dr. Tegla Davies, Sir Ben Bowen Thomas and Norah Isaac. The meeting was followed by the unveiling of a statue of Sir Owen M. Edwards. The statue itself was the work of the Welsh sculptor, Jonah Jones, and it stood in a *cilfach goffa*, a recess designed by Dr. Quentin Hughes of Liverpool.

The day's proceedings ended in the Corwen Pavilion with a repeat performance of the Flintshire pageant, first presented at the Mold Eisteddfod. Once again, it was a performance that thrilled the audience. It linked the Urdd Pledge with the ideals on which O. M. Edwards had based his whole life, and it was a performance that 'O.M.' himself would have been proud to witness. And like every other facet of the Centenary celebrations, it aimed at the best. Nothing less would have befitted the memory of so great a man.

*   *   *   *

Since the Youth Service was established in 1939/40, the relationship between the Urdd and the Ministry of Education had been close and harmonious. We were, of course, fortunate in having the unqualified support of the Secretaries to the Welsh Department of the Ministry and the Chief Inspectors of Schools in Wales—men like Sir Percy Watkins, Sir Wynn Wheldon, Sir Ben Bowen Thomas, Dr. W. J. Williams, Dr. William Thomas and Mr. Wynne Ll. Lloyd. It was they who acted as interpreters and as mediators between the Urdd on the one hand, and the Minister of Education, the civil servants and the Treasury on the other. It was often necessary to remind these Government officials in London that Wales was a nation with its own language and culture, which meant that, as in education in general, so in the Youth Service, Wales had some problems that did not exist in England.

It was this standpoint that the Urdd tried to convey to the Albemarle Committee in 1959. This was a body set up by the Minister of Education in 1958 to consider what contribution could be made by the Youth Service in helping young people to play their part in society in view of the social, educational and industrial changes that had taken place since the war ; to review what had been achieved during the 1940's and 1950's, and to consider ways in which the work could be developed during the sixties. The Albemarle Committee was composed of twelve members, but it is doubtful whether any of them understood the Wales that we knew. The Urdd submitted written evidence, and the Founder and Chief Organiser were invited to meet the Committee to put the case for the Urdd—and for Wales. Fortunately, it had been arranged for some members of the Welsh Department of the Ministry of Education to accompany the Committee during its visit to Wales. And it was no doubt due to their influence that a chapter on Wales was incorporated in the Report, and here at least, the unique position that existed within Wales was recognised—

> ' The position is not an exact replica of that in England, for Wales is not an English region . . . Its people are a nation with a culture which, though fertilised and enriched by the mainstream of Western European civilisation, is yet something essentially Welsh . . . The existence of two languages necessitates a different approach to the problems of youth and, at the same time, multiplies them. A bilingual nation needs bilingual provision in the form of youth clubs, no less than in the provision of schools.'

It maintained, rightly, that many Youth Service problems were common to both England and Wales, but nevertheless it concluded—

> ' If the Youth Service in Wales is in some respects similar to that in England, in others it is markedly different. It accordingly merits, however briefly, a separate reference to and a discussion of its own problems.'

When the Government received the Albemarle Report, it adopted the recommendation that the Minister should plan a ten-year development programme acting through an advisory body to be known as the Youth Service Development Council, and that at least two of the Council's twelve members should be familiar with the special problems of Wales. That the Report did not recommend a separate Development Council for Wales was a disappointment. It was too much to expect the two members to be able to persuade the Council to devote adequate attention to the problems of Wales. This fear was later borne out when the Development Council's report—' Youth and Community Work in the 70's '—was published in 1969. This latter report completely ignored the existence of Wales. As a document dealing with England and Wales in general, the Albemarle Report was at least an honest appraisal of the situation. It drew attention to weaknesses that existed ; it gave the Youth Service a new status, and it urged that funds be made available so that statutory bodies and voluntary organisations could accomplish the development envisaged. Hopes in this direction have not been fulfilled. The Ministry's grant to the Urdd in 1959/60 was £5,200, exactly the same as it had been in 1951/52.

Following the Albemarle Report, it was pointed out to the Ministry that to develop its work in accordance with the recommendations of the Report, the Urdd, even at that time, would require a minimum annual grant of £15,000. But even today, thirteen years later, when costs have more than trebled, the total grant still falls short of £15,000. The recommendations of the Albemarle Report, though adopted in principle, have still not been implemented because the Government has not made available the necessary grants.

*   *   *   *

Only once since it was initiated in 1929 had the Urdd National Eisteddfod been held in Cardiganshire. That was in 1938 when it was held at Aberystwyth. And when it was realised that, by 1959, twenty-one years would have elapsed since its previous visit to the county, Urdd leaders in Lampeter decided to invite the Eisteddfod to their town. The Executive Committee had the unusual honour of being led by two women—Sali H. Davies as Chairman, and Mary O. James as Honorary Secretary. With the Rev. T. Burgess Jones as Vice-Chairman, it was as strong a team as any Eisteddfod could have desired. It was this trio, together with their finance officers, who prodded, directed and inspired the two-hundred voluntary workers who created a festival that will long be remembered. Free accommodation was found for three-thousand competitors ; £3,000 was raised as an advance-fund. The marquee was full from early morning to evening.

The Eisteddfod Presidents were Mary Vaughan Jones of Bangor, Jenkin Alban Davies of London, and the Very Rev. G. O. Williams, Bishop of Bangor. Dr. J. Henry Jones, Director of Education, presided at the opening ceremony of the Arts and Crafts Exhibition, and Sir Ifan ab Owen and Lady Edwards were, as usual, Guests of Honour. Dic Jones came back into the fray to win his fifth Chair for a poem in praise of Curnow Vosper's famous painting 'Salem'. This would be his last triumph as he was now 25 years of age and would not be eligible to compete at future Urdd Eisteddfodau. The Crown, however, went to a newcomer, Catrin Lloyd Rowlands of Trawsfynydd. Second and third in this excellent competition were Dic Jones and Eigra Lewis. Cardiganshire could hardly be expected to allow any other county to win the main trophy, and by doubling their efforts they won with a comfortable margin.

One innovation at the Lampeter Eisteddfod was *Clwt y Ddawns*, a folk-evening organised by Evan Isaac, the County Organiser. It included folk-dancing, folk-singing, *cerdd dant* and items by a harp *ensemble*. The other innovation was the *Noson Lawen* contest, not included in the Eisteddfod syllabus, but an *ad hoc* competition confined to Aelwydydd in the counties of Cardigan, Carmarthen and Pembroke. One Aelwyd from each county was selected to appear in the final contest which provided three hours of rollicking entertainment. So successful was the *Noson Lawen* experiment that it was decided to include it in the official Eisteddfod programme from 1960 onwards.

By the end of the fifties, skiffle-songs had become just as popular in Wales as they were in other countries. Light-hearted songs were not new to Wales, but the skiffle had in it a new element. Words and music were original and the group would provide its own accompaniment, rhythm and beat being more important than melody. The result was sometimes crude and the performance, though it could be exciting, was not necessarily pleasing to the eye or the ear. Accordingly, the skiffle could not be included in the main Eisteddfod programme, neither could it be completely ignored, and the *Noson Lawen* gave groups the opportunity to improve their choice of instruments and their mastery of techniques. Gradually, skiffle groups gave way to pop groups that were less concerned with imitating the style of other countries and aimed at creating a Welsh tradition more closely linked with the folk-song and ballad. This was a development that belonged to the sixties, but a beginning had been made at the Llanbedr-Pont-Steffan Eisteddfod.

Success at Lampeter was not confined to the social and cultural fields, but was reflected too in the financial report which showed that proceeds had reached a total of £6,198. Costs had been kept to £2,672 so that there was a balance of £3,526, higher by £875 than the 1957 record held by Amanford. For a small town in a rural area it was something of a miracle, and the Urdd was deeply indebted to the finance officers and to all who had worked tirelessly for two-and-a-half years and achieved such remarkable success.

It was largely at the instigation of the flourishing London Aelwyd, established under the auspices of the London Welsh Association, that winners at the Lampeter Eisteddfod were invited to give a concert in the autumn in the London-Welsh Hall. President of the evening was J. Clifford Thomas, a leading London Welshman who rarely missed an Urdd National Eisteddfod and who had been President at the Rhydaman Eisteddfod.

*   *   *   *

The 1959 County Festival was held at Dinbych. The main burden was borne by Urdd supporters in the town and its immediate surroundings, but for some reason, they did not get as much support from the remainder of the county as they had anticipated. The Festival followed the usual pattern but it had the bonus of two performances, produced by Dr. Kate Roberts, of *Tri Chryfion Byd*, an 18th century Interlude by *Twm o'r Nant*. Financially, the Festival showed a balance of £668, but, of course, its true value could not be measured in monetary terms.

*   *   *   *

Other events followed with the usual regularity. Indeed, one tended to take them for granted. Had it been necessary, for some reason, to cancel the summer camps at Llangrannog or Glan Llyn, it would have been a matter of great public concern, but the fact that two-and-a-half-thousand youth spent a week at Llangrannog or Glan Llyn was not ' news '—except for those privileged to share the experience !

The International Convention too was held as usual, and for the first time, we were able to welcome a group from Poland. There were also parties from Germany and Austria, with smaller units from Norway, France, Hungary and Ghana. Essie Annan from Ghana had travelled alone from London. When she boarded the train at Paddington, two women had already settled in a compartment. When Essie entered, they immediately moved to another compartment. As a consequence, she arrived at Borth somewhat despondent and apprehensive, but soon discovered that there was no apartheid at Pantyfedwen.

On this occasion, the members were given the opportunity to

'discover' Wales. Divided into small groups, they were each given a special assignment. Projects included aspects of education, agriculture, law and order, medical services, history and tradition; and the scheme proved particularly popular and successful. As always, the day's activities were brought to a close in a short epilogue, ending invariably with the evening hymn, *Arglwydd, mae yn nosi* (Lord, the night is falling). One of the overseas members had to leave Pantyfedwen before the others, and the entire ' family ' went to see him off at the station. As they waited for the train, they sang again the camp songs they had sung together, and as the train drew in, the departing member asked them to sing *Arglwydd, mae yn nosi* ! Those listening must have thought it odd that anyone should be singing of nightfall in mid-morning ! But for him who was leaving, the hymn had become a symbol of the Pantyfedwen spirit.

The same kind of spirit prevailed during the exchange-visit arranged by Gwyn Williams, then Youth Officer in Merioneth, between a combined group of Irish dancers from Dublin and *Aelwyd Llanuwchllyn* on the one hand, and a youth group from Baden in Germany on the other. In Germany, the Irish dancers and the Llanuwchllyn folk-singers completely captivated their audiences during the five concerts held in the State of Baden. It was at the end of their concert at Bühl that the Welsh and Irish visitors joined the entire audience to form a torch-lit procession making a midnight pilgrimage to the illuminated ' Cross of Peace', erected on a hill outside the town by soldiers from opposing camps at the end of World War II. The ceremony ended with the presenting of *Y Ddraig Goch*, to be flown along with the other national flags that encircled the Cross of Peace.

In 1957, under the auspices of the Christian Youth Council of Wales, members of an international ecumenical work-camp had joined forces with Aelwyd members at Blaenau Ffestiniog in renovating the Aelwyd premises. In 1959, it was the Aelwyd's turn to be involved in community service. A group of children from one of the ' hard core ' refugee-camps in Europe was invited to spend three months in homes at Blaenau Ffestiniog.

*   *   *   *

In July 1959, Sir Ifan ab Owen Edwards was awarded the degree of LL.D. (*honoris causa*) by the University of Wales. Presenting him to the Vice-Chancellor, Principal Thomas Parry paid him a warm tribute for his service to Wales—

' The University of Wales has done much to illuminate the past in our history, our literature and our language. In awarding an honorary degree to Sir Ifan ab Owen Edwards, it is now helping to illuminate the future, by acknowledging the work of a man who is always one step ahead of his time, ensuring that the next generation will be Welsh in language and in spirit. It is well that this honour should be conferred upon him at Aberystwyth, the centre of his life's work, and home of the National Library of Wales which he has served for many years, and of which he was recently elected President. He, therefore, combines in his person three of our national institutions—the University, the Library and Urdd Gobaith Cymru, and I would readily forgive anyone who would maintain that the greatest of these three is the Urdd.'

It was natural that Principal Thomas Parry should refer to Sir Ifan's service to the National Library. His name is so inextricably linked with the Urdd that his service to other Welsh institutions could well be overlooked. And the National Library was certainly one in which he was genuinely interested. He had been a member of the Library Court since 1931 and of the Council since 1935. He was elected Treasurer in 1950, Vice-President in 1953 and President in 1958, an office he held until 1967. It is little wonder that the Library authorities considered his contribution invaluable.

The Urdd Founder was also one of the Directors of TWW, an appointment he accepted largely because he realised the potential influence of mass-media for good or evil, and the care needed in order to minimise the detrimental effect it could have on the Welsh language. Another of Sir Ifan's interests was the work of the National Parks Commission. He knew Wales well ; he knew its past, and he realised the importance of history if the Commission was to respect and preserve the traditions and amenities of our country.

He was always pleased to be associated with any organisation or institution concerned with promoting the cultural life of Wales. These included the University College at Aberystwyth, the National Museum, the National Eisteddfod Council, the Honourable Society of Cymmrodorion, the Council for Wales and Monmouthshire, the Advisory Council for Education, *Undeb Cymru Fydd*, the Union of

Welsh Publishers and Booksellers and the Union of Welsh People in Dispersion. It was something of a mystery how the completely dedicated leader of a national movement could have found time to help and promote so many other Welsh bodies. This, in itself, is a measure of his energy and his greatness.

*   *   *   *

For some time, the Urdd had been anxious to obtain a portrait or bust of Sir David James to be placed in Pantyfedwen. When it was discovered that a Polish sculptor, Kostek Wojnarowski, was prepared to sell a bust he had made, Sir Ifan wrote to Sir David James to ask his opinion of the bust, explaining that the Urdd would like to purchase it for Pantyfedwen. Sir David replied immediately saying that he was pleased with the sculpture, but if the Urdd wished to have it, he himself would willingly donate it to Pantyfedwen. Shortly afterwards the bust arrived and with it a cheque for £5,000 towards improvements at Llangrannog and Glan Llyn.

*   *   *   *

Ivor Owen had not spared himself during his first two years as editor of the Urdd magazines. *Cymraeg* had maintained its circulation, but *Cymru* and *Cymru'r Plant* still fell short of what was desired, and had it not been for *Cymraeg* it is doubtful whether the Urdd could have continued publishing the other two magazines, despite valiant efforts by the editor to keep abreast of current trends in content and format. Things were further complicated by the almost simultaneous departure of the editor's assistant, Mairwen Lewis, and his secretary. Marion Griffith Williams was appointed assistant, but left in six months' time to take up a post in the BBC. She was replaced by Catrin Lloyd Rowlands of Trawsfynydd who had won the Crown at the Lampeter Eisteddfod. Ivor Owen kept his fingers crossed !

Owen Edwards had by now been a member of the staff of the National Library for two years, and with his wife, Shan Emlyn, lived at Coed-y-Pry, only a few yards from Bryneithin, home of his parents. He took a keen interest in the work of the Urdd and was a member of various committees responsible for its administration. In September 1959, he was invited to appear in a Granada ITV programme and the experience opened up a new sphere of interest. Before long, he was asked to present weekly programmes from Manchester and showed a marked aptitude for this new medium.

His brother, Prys, left Leighton Park School in 1959, and returned to Wales to take a degree course in Architecture. Sir Ifan, who himself had an intense interest in this field, could not have been more pleased. Quietly and unobtrusively, he had done everything he could to encourage the interest Prys had shown in this direction.

*　　*　　*　　*

The Annual General Meeting was held at Blaenau Ffestiniog. In presenting his report, the Chairman, the Rev. Trebor Lloyd Evans, touched on a question that was obviously a source of concern to him. This was the attitude of the churches, and particularly of the officials of some denominational bodies towards the Urdd. He commented—

' The Urdd has no wish to compete with the churches, but rather to co-operate with them. Basically, our problems are the same, and we have much to contribute to one another. As a minister of religion, it grieves me to see some ministers and some churches ignoring the Urdd and rejecting help from a movement that could contribute so much towards their work with young people.'

Sir Ifan ab Owen Edwards and the Treasurer, Cynfab Roberts, turned their attention to financial problems. The movement's annual outlay was soaring towards £50,000 and it still received little more than £7,000 in overall grants. The debt incurred in the early fifties had been eliminated, but with costs rising so steeply, there was a danger that the Urdd could incur a new debt in the sixties. ' It is no time for despair,' said Sir Ifan, ' but neither is it a time for complacency.'

Despite the constant need for economy, it was felt that the Urdd should no longer postpone the appointment of a Physical Re-creation Organiser. No such appointment had been made since the departure of Teifryn Michael in 1951, and the Urdd was laying itself open to criticism that physical recreation was being neglected. Elwyn Huws of Pentrefelin, Cricieth, was accordingly appointed to the post. After a three-year medical course at Edinburgh, followed by two years in the forces, and another two years specialising in P.E. at the Cardiff College of Education, he was well-qualified for such an appointment. His main interest lay in outdoor activities, and this was just what the Urdd required.

For twenty-four years, R. E. Griffith had carried the title ' Chief Organiser', and in 1959, the Council decided that the title of 'Director' would be more appropriate. This did not entail any change in his responsibilities ; it was just that the Council recognised that, in addition to directing the activities of the movement in the field and carrying out headquarters' administrative duties, R. E. Griffith had, for many years, played a vital part in directing the work of the movement through its various committees. The new title was, therefore, more appropriate to and commensurate with the responsibilities he already shouldered.

* * * *

It was January 1960, and the deliberations of the Council in its annual meeting at Pantyfedwen were brought to a close in an epilogue. After the final prayer, the meeting ended, and the members began to disperse. It was only then that those closest to him realised that Sir Ifan ab Owen Edwards was unable to move from his chair. He had suffered a seizure. He was taken to hospital, and for the first few weeks, he was critically ill. Gradually, his strength returned, and some weeks later he was allowed home to face a long period of convalescence, of nursing and physiotherapy. Lady Edwards was a tower of strength in his hour of need and it was fortunate that Owen could help and support them in their affliction. In six months' time, Sir Ifan was again able to walk, slightly hesitant but still erect. When he was urged to use a walking-stick, he laughed loudly and said that he would then feel an old man ! His interest and his spirit returned, but not his energy. He could talk about the Urdd, but he would no longer be able to labour as before. His family and friends felt it was essential that he should be kept informed of all developments within the movement, and even during the summer of 1960, he visited Llangrannog and Glan-Llyn, Swyddfa'r Urdd and Pantyfedwen. The aim was to tell him everything that would cheer him, and hide from him anything that might cause him concern. He was, however, too shrewd to be deceived ; he knew well that there never had been a period when the Urdd had no problems. He was sixty-five years old, but he had made a miraculous recovery, and was still the indisputable leader of the movement he had created in 1922, and which was now stepping confidently into the sixties.

53 Meirion Jones

54 Cynfab Roberts

55 Hywel D. Roberts

56 Aneurin Jenkins-Jones

57   Representatives of some of the Welsh Schools

58   The Urdd Centre at Aberystwyth

15

O NE realised, of course, that the Founder would no longer be able to play the same active role as he had done prior to his illness. But Sir Ifan ab Owen Edwards had taken the precaution of ensuring that the Urdd could carry on even when his active leadership was no longer available. Not only had he created a movement of some fifty-thousand members, but he had also established the necessary machinery for its government. Nevertheless, it was his life, his example and his dedication that provided the inspiration for all others, and those who had worked closest to him missed him deeply. It was R. E. Griffith, however, who felt the loss most keenly. The two had worked closely and intimately over a period of almost thirty years. During Sir Ifan's daily visits to Swyddfa'r Urdd, they had planned, reviewed and assessed, and now those daily conferences had suddenly ceased. R. E. Griffith was deprived of the astuteness, the optimism and the inspiration that only the Founder could provide, and he felt strangely isolated.

Sir Ifan was naturally unable to attend the 1960 Urdd National Eisteddfod at Dolgellau, but he had been able to record a message, and on the Saturday afternoon, the audience listened intently as his familiar voice rang out. He stressed the importance of the Welsh language in the life of the nation—

‘ Britain stands united behind the Queen ; America is united by its flag. Let us in Wales stand united behind our language. The language is our queen, and at Dolgellau, she sits enthroned. But not so at Aberdâr where next year's Eisteddfod will be held. There, the language is fighting for its existence. Will you join us at Aberdâr next year ? Will you who are at Dolgellau today help us to stand united behind our language at Aberdâr ? ’

It was at the Dolgellau Eisteddfod that the 'Royal Prize' was presented to the Urdd. In 1947, a fund had been set up in Merioneth to provide a gift for Princess Elizabeth on the occasion of her marriage. A small balance still remained, and when, in 1959, it was felt that the account should be closed, it was the Queen herself who suggested that it should be given to the Urdd. A new

County Trophy would soon be needed, and Lt-Col. J. F. Williams-Wynne, the Lord Lieutenant, suggested a leather-bound album bearing the Queen's personal crest on one cover and the Urdd badge on the other. The names of the counties that had won the Lois Blake Trophy from 1946 to 1959 were to be inscribed, and from 1960, a page would record, each year, the venue of the Eisteddfod and the name of the winning county. The album was made by craftsmen at the National Library of Wales, inscribed by Huw Cedwyn Jones, member of the Urdd staff, and given safe custody in an oak exhibition-casket specially made by Glyn Rees of Dinas Mawddwy. In the absence of Sir Ifan ab Owen Edwards, the album was presented to Lady Edwards by the Lord Lieutenant.

Another special feature of the Dolgellau Eisteddfod was the introduction of a Science Section into the Eisteddfod syllabus. Those mainly responsible for this innovation were John Williams, E. E. Williams, Dr. R. W. Edwards and Dafydd F. Kirkman, four who felt that those Urdd members whose main interest lay in science and technology should be put on a par with those whose interest lay in literature, arts and crafts. The *Noson Lawen* competition grew to its full stature at Dolgellau, following the successful experiment at Lampeter the previous year. Crymych, Llanbrynmair and St. Clêr were the Aelwydydd that reached the final.

The Eisteddfod Presidents included Ivor Owen of Llanuwchllyn, Iolo Francis Roberts, Alun Oldfield-Davies, and Bob Lloyd (*Llwyd o'r Bryn*). The last named had been associated with the first Urdd Eisteddfod at Corwen in 1929, and was a well-known figure in Eisteddfodic circles. Speaking directly to the Urdd members present, he urged them to speak their language on all occasions. 'Speak Welsh, speak it regularly, speak it well, and speak it loudly.' And those who knew Bob Lloyd knew that he himself did just that !

The Crown was won by John Rowlands of Trawsfynydd, whose sister, Catrin, had gained the honour in 1959. He is one of the few Crown winners who have continued writing, and by today, he has several books to his credit. He was also placed second in the main poetry competition, but the Chair was won by Dafydd Edwards of Ffair Rhos in Cardiganshire, with another Cardiganshire poet, Vernon Jones, a close third.

The honour of being first to win the Royal Prize went to Merioneth, and it was natural that the result was received with loud acclaim. From all standpoints, the Eisteddfod had been a success, and on the financial side, it showed a surplus of £2,141. This was a record for any North Wales Eisteddfod, and only Amanford and Lampeter had excelled on this result.

It was now three years since J. Cyril Hughes had first organised public-speaking contests for Urdd members. This was an activity in which the Young Farmers Clubs had pioneered with excellent results. It was in 1957 that the Urdd entered the field, limiting the competition first to District level and then to County level. Now, however, it was decided to advance a step further with separate competitions for North and South Wales. The enthusiasm shown and the standards reached in these regional contests ensured the competition a place in the National Eisteddfod Syllabus for 1961.

*   *   *   *

The 1960 *Gŵyl Werin* (Folk-Song-and-Dance Festival) was originally planned as a three-county festival to be held at Haverfordwest—hence the title, *Gŵyl Werin Dyfed*; but such was the interest shown that it was eventually opened to the counties of Brecon, Radnor and Glamorgan as well. It even admitted a team from the London Aelwyd, who thought nothing of making the 250 mile journey in order to take part. The Pembrokeshire Education Committee was firmly behind the festival from the start and it had Wynford Davies, Director of Education, as its President. A. G. Rees, Headmistress of Taskers School, Haverfordwest, was Chairman, with Teifryn G. Michael, the County's Physical Education Organiser and former member of the Urdd staff, as Secretary. The Treasurer was another old friend of the Urdd, G. W. John, Headmaster of Camrose South School. With such a team, the festival could not fail to be a success.

Twenty-four groups took part in the massed dancing displays, while eight other teams performed more intricate dances. Owen Huw Roberts gave solo exhibitions of clog-dancing and those who witnessed his skill and agility were not surprised to learn that he was placed first in the solo-dance competition at the National Eisteddfod of Wales held the following August at Cardiff.

It was naturally disappointing not to have the company of Sir Ifan ab Owen and Lady Edwards. We did, however, have the pleasure of welcoming Lois Blake who sat entranced as she watched the three-hundred dancers perform, with zest and abandon, some of the dances she herself had revived. It was one way in which the Urdd could repay a little of its debt to Mrs. Blake.

The dance festival was followed in the evening by a *Noson Lawen* and a *Twmpath Dawns*. It was understood from the first that the *Gŵyl Werin* could not be regarded as a fund-raising event because of the large numbers involved and the consequent high costs. Nevertheless, thanks to an advance fund and generous public support, the financial accounts showed a surplus of £200.

The other 1960 festival was the annual County Festival centred on Amlwch and Llangefni in Anglesey. In addition to the usual ingredients, the Anglesey Committee decided that a carnival would be an effective means of attracting public interest. But while the experiment succeeded in this respect, it seemed to have brought with it an Anglicising influence that doubtless could have been avoided had it been foreseen. The evening events included a ' Pageant of the Nations ' devised by R. Gerallt Jones and Dewi M. Lloyd and produced by Avril Hughes. At the *Noson Lawen*, the final event of the festival, the guest artist was Dr. Meredydd Evans who had just returned to Wales after a sojourn in America. By and large, the officers, under the chairmanship of Handel M. Morgan, could well be pleased with their achievement, and as one result of their efforts, the Urdd profited by £600. Towards this, *Blodau'r Ffair* had made its own contribution and, despite the increase in price, nearly ten-thousand copies were sold.

*   *   *   *

By 1960, the Union of Parents' Societies had been in existence for eight years, and had taken over from the Urdd the responsibility for the promotion of Welsh (or bilingual) Schools. The Welsh Schools' Movement had now come of age, and to celebrate the fact, the Union organised a concert at Aberystwyth, with Owen Edwards, one of the seven original pupils at the first Welsh School, as compére.

In the foreword to the programme, the development of the movement was traced from its unpretentious origin at Aberystwyth in 1939—

 ' Today, some forty Welsh Schools are already in existence, and there have been developments in two other directions. A number of Welsh Nursery Schools have been set up and, at the other end of the scale, two Welsh Secondary Schools have been established by the Flintshire Education Committee. Some of the Training Colleges have already become more Welsh in character and there is talk of a Welsh-medium University College. One sees, therefore, how deep-rooted the seed sown at Aberystwyth twenty-one years ago has become.

 In referring to the Welsh Schools set up in semi-Anglicised towns, we do not forget the scores of natural Welsh schools in rural Wales. They and we are members of one family ; our aims and our methods are identical.'

The capacity audience of past and present pupils, teachers and parents, were addressed by Norah Isaac and Cassie Davies who expressed the Union's gratitude to those who had helped the movement on its way—to Sir Ifan ab Owen Edwards and Urdd Gobaith Cymru, to the Welsh Department of the Ministry of Education, to Welsh Education Authorities, and especially to parents, head-teachers and teachers who had accepted the ideal of bilingual education and proved its practicability.

The thirteenth—and, incidentally, the last—International Convention was held at Pantyfedwen in July 1960, following which the overseas members were given hospitality in Mold homes. Between 1945 and 1960, the European scene had changed very considerably. Post-war travel restrictions had been removed ; economic standards had improved ; travel agencies had multiplied, and overseas visits for families, schools, colleges and youth clubs had become common practice. The International Convention had provided intimate contact between the youth of Europe at a time when it was most needed. It had widened horizons following a period of enforced isolation ; it had helped to bridge the gulf between the youth of ' enemy ' countries ; it had healed some of the wounds and removed some of the bitterness and prejudice resulting from wartime experiences. It had also given Urdd members a new awareness of the problems of other countries, a new concern for people in circumstances less fortunate than their own. They had gained a new outlook, a new attitude which we hoped would be retained. There were now new fields that could be explored, new channels of action that could be followed. If the International Convention had met the needs of the immediate post-war period, and if it had pointed the way to new and extended possibilities, it had more than achieved its aim.

* * * *

It was now five years since the death of Gwilym Davies, Founder of the Goodwill Message. During that period, a genuine attempt was made to carry out his wish that Urdd Gobaith Cymru and the Welsh Council of UNA should share responsibility for the joint administration of the Message. There were, however, serious difficulties. In the first place, having two Secretaries, one operating from Cardiff and the other from Aberystwyth, was not conducive to the smooth efficiency that was required and which both bodies desired. Secondly, the joint-committee was not recognised as an educational charity, and consequently, more than a third of the income from the Gwilym Davies legacy was lost in tax. After careful consideration, the Urdd decided to inform the Trustees that, financially and administratively, the position was not acceptable, and asked them to review the situation and suggest an alternative arrangement.

The Trustees' decision was to ask the Urdd to accept the legacy of £3,529/11/1, with the request that the Goodwill Message should be included amongst its administrative responsibilities for as long as it was considered feasible and necessary. The Urdd agreed to respect the wishes of Mrs. Gwilym Davies and her fellow-trustees regarding the furtherance of the Message. Henceforth the movement would assume full responsibility for its administration claiming, as a Charity, rebate of tax paid on the income from the legacy.

This decision by the Trustees was, understandably, not welcomed by the Welsh Council of UNA, and their first reaction was to suggest that they would produce their own Goodwill Message. Such action would have jeopardised the whole idea of a Goodwill Message from the youth of Wales and could have brought the movement, founded and nurtured by Gwilym Davies, to an ignominious end. Faced with this situation, the Urdd Council decided to appeal to the Welsh Council of UNA to accept the decision of the Trustees and to refrain from any action that would destroy the very movement they sought to support. As a compromise, the Urdd Council further suggested

(i) that two members nominated by the Welsh Council be co-opted to the Urdd committee responsible, among other things, for the administration of the Message ;

(ii) that publications dealing with the Message should indicate that the Goodwill Message was being administered by Urdd Gobaith Cymru in conjunction with the Welsh Council of UNA.

It was two years before this compromise was accepted, but eventually, goodwill prevailed, and the arrangement has since worked harmoniously.

*　　　*　　　*　　　*

Elwyn Huws immediately set himself the task of restoring physical recreation to its rightful place within the Urdd syllabus. The Pantyfedwen Football Cup Competition was re-instated and, largely in response to pressure from South Wales Branches, two rugby competitions were introduced. A series of winter courses in the building and handling of canoes and in mountain-walking and orienteering were held at Glan Llyn. For Elwyn Huws, physical recreation *per se* was invaluable in developing skills, physical resources, self-discipline and a sense of adventure. But within the Urdd, he felt it could be much more, especially when it brought leaders and members together in a residential centre. Under these conditions, it provided opportunities for informal talks and discussions on all manner of topics, and these were often just as valuable as the physical activities themselves.

The announcement of a Ministry grant of £3,800 towards an estimated expenditure of £7,600 at Glan Llyn, including the cost of building a gymnasium and two dormitories, together with the purchase of new recreational equipment, was an additional stimulus, even though the scheme would not be completed for twelve months.

Furthermore, the Ministry of Agriculture decided to grant the Urdd a twenty-one year lease on Glan Llyn and this security of tenure meant that improvements made would not be in vain. Fortunately too, we were on friendly terms with our nearest neighbour, Anthony Pugh, of Glan Llyn Farm. It must have caused him considerable uneasiness at first to know that a camping centre was to be established within a few yards of his property. But despite occasional lapses in the observance of camp code, we were happy to find that we had a sympathetic neighbour, especially since Glan Llyn was now developing into a full-time centre.

Some improvements were also made at Llangrannog. Here, however, we had always been hampered by lack of funds. We had not yet succeeded in convincing the Ministry of Education of the importance of introducing children to recreational camping activities during their pre-youth-service years. For the Urdd, Youth Service is a continuous process of creating new interests, developing new skills, and learning to live together harmoniously as part of a community. At Llangrannog, members were initiated to camp life and prepared for the more advanced opportunities they would find at Glan Llyn. The Ministry, however, had its strict rules, and activities outside the confines of the 14-20 age-group were not eligible for grant-aid. And since the Llangrannog Camp, at least since 1950, had catered almost exclusively for the 10-14 age-group, it meant that no Ministry grant was available towards this centre, and developments and improvements had to be restricted to what could be achieved without government help.

Pantyfedwen too called for attention in 1960; exterior and interior decoration, electrical re-wiring and part-refurnishing meant an outlay of more than three-thousand pounds. Moreover, it would have been very much higher had it not been for the economy measures adopted, and the do-it-yourself attitude of the Manager and his staff.

Branch premises were an even greater problem during the sixties. These were Aelwyd buildings bought with grant-aid to meet the emergency needs of the early war years. In twenty years, the properties had naturally deteriorated in condition and depreciated in value. During this period, Ministry maintenance grants had been reduced and the responsibility placed increasingly on the Local

Education Authorities. Accordingly, Aelwydydd found that energy that should be directed towards providing for the cultural, recreational and social needs of their members, was largely being consumed in fund-raising efforts. It was this that led the Urdd to a policy of gradually disposing of independent Aelwyd premises except where, with available grant-aid, they could be maintained without being an undue burden.

*   *   *   *

As usual, the Urdd had its publicity stand at the 1960 National Eisteddfod of Wales at Cardiff. On this occasion, the Queen and the Duke of Edinburgh had accepted an invitation to attend. After the formal programme in the pavilion, the Royal visitors insisted on an informal tour of the Eisteddfod ground accompanied by the Chairman of the Eisteddfod Council, Dr. Thomas Parry. As they approached the Urdd stand, the Queen remembered the Royal Prize and wondered whether it might be on view. The conversation then turned to other Urdd activities and both she and the Duke were immensely interested in the photographic records of re-creational activities at Llangrannog and Glan Llyn.

In January 1960, *Yr Aelwyd* became more of a news-bulletin and less of a magazine. The new and larger format made it possible to include more pictures, and it was hoped that it would reflect local activities as well as those of national interest. The other Urdd magazines, edited by Ivor Owen, continued according to the prescribed plan. But in addition to the monthly magazines, the editor decided to reprint in book-form some of the series that had proved most popular. It was thus that *Bwmba Bwm* and *Tomos Caradog* by Mary Vaughan Jones were published, together with *Robin Het Galed* and *Ned Dwy Got* by Olwen Bebb Jones.

But perhaps the most important Urdd publication of that year was *Gwasanaethau Crefyddol*, the third selection of short religious services for the use of Adrannau, Aelwydydd, camps and courses. The editorial panel had as its Chairman the Rev. Chancellor Gwilym Owen of Aberystwyth. Several laymen and members of the local clergy were invited to compile services either for special occasions or on particular themes. The result was a collection of

ecumenical services that appealed particularly to older members of
Adrannau and members of Aelwydydd, and the volume has been
found invaluable for use at camps and courses.

The 1960 Annual Welsh Books Campaign resulted in the sale of
11,575 volumes, and once again, the record was held by *Adran
Ysgol Frondeg*, Pwllheli, with the sale of 2,924 volumes to their
credit. *Ysgol Gymraeg Maesteg* had again reached a total of one
thousand, no mean achievement for a primary school in an Anglicised area.

*   *   *   *

There were, as usual, several staff changes. Edith Bott had been
twelve years on the Urdd staff as County Organiser for Merioneth
and Montgomeryshire, and in addition had been responsible for the
hospitality arrangements of the Urdd National Eisteddfod, and
had shouldered the heavier share of the work entailed in organising
the North Wales Winter Rally.

The year 1960 saw the death of several loyal and energetic
supporters of the movement including the Rev. Llwyd Williams of
Rhydaman, Gwyn Daniel of Cardiff, Mary Lewis of Llandysul,
Olwen Mears of Ponciau, John Morgan of Corwen, and George
Davies of Llanwrda. The last named had become a household
name among Llangrannog campers. Few knew his surname—he
was just 'George', and he was everything to everybody. Officially,
he was responsible for kitchen stores and for the camp tuckshop
known as *Siop George*. For the campers, he was some perennial
Peter Pan who could settle all problems. When the 1961 camps
opened, there was a strange emptiness—' George ' was no longer
there.

*   *   *   *

On the financial side, the Urdd was not without its worries.
Running costs amounted to £63,000 towards which just over
£9,000 was received in grants, including £6,500 from the Ministry
of Education and approximately £2,000 from Local Education
Authorities. A £700 grant was received from the Jubilee Trust, and
in the financial report, it was recorded that, during the 25 years

since the Trust was established, the Urdd had received a total of
£16,650.

In 1955, a grant of £6,000 from the King George VI Foundation
was received to be used specifically towards training schemes. A
further £4,000 was received in 1960 earmarked for the same
purpose. Gifts from individuals included £500 from Hywel Huws of
Bogota, Colombia, towards the development of camp-centres, £200
from Dr. Griffith Evans of Caernarfon, and £200 from J. R. Jones, a
native of Llanuwchllyn who had become a high-ranking officer in
the Banking Corporation of Shanghai and Hong Kong.

At the Annual General Meeting held at Aberystwyth, the
Treasurer, Cynfab Roberts, stressed that the Urdd should raise
£50,000-£60,000 per year, in addition to any grants received.
And with costs soaring annually, the position was not likely to
improve. It was at this meeting that Sir Ifan made his first public
appearance since his illness and he was given a rousing welcome.
He and Lady Edwards were re-elected Presidents, and to replace
those who automatically joined the ranks of Ex-Vice-Presidents, the
meeting elected four new Vice-Presidents—Sali H. Davies of
Lampeter, R. Gordon Williams of Penygroes, E. D. Jones, National
Librarian, and the Rev. Trebor Lloyd Evans of Morriston. The
new Council Chairman was Cassie Davies, with A. D. Lewis as
Vice-Chairman and Chairman of the Executive Committee.
Cynfab Roberts was pressed to continue as Treasurer for another
triennium. Owen Edwards was elected Honorary Secretary ; The
Honorary Counsel and Honorary Solicitor were re-elected. Some
members, mostly from the Aberystwyth area, had served on the
Council and its Executive Committee for more than fifteen years.
They had been elected during the difficult war-years and had given
dedicated service ever since. They now felt that they should give
way to younger members, but as some element of continuity was
essential, it was decided that there should be a rota of resignations
over a period of three years. Following a respite, those who had
resigned would be eligible for re-election, and in the meantime, a
number of younger members could be given the experience of
committee procedure in the hope that they too would give the
same unselfish loyalty and service as their predecessors.

*   *   *   *

In a bilingual country, it is natural that the language question should be under constant review. Wales today is far from being a truly bilingual country, and the Welsh language does not enjoy equality of status with English. Nor will this equality be achieved without a determined effort by all who believe in the future of the Welsh nation, whether their first language be Welsh, English or any other language. Those who are non-Welsh but who have adopted Wales as their country may at least be expected to take an active interest in Wales—its problems, its development and its future. For they too have a contribution to make in creating the kind of country we would like Wales to be. Welsh people who have neglected the language, or have been deprived of the opportunity of learning it, must be helped to achieve a greater awareness of their Welshness and, where desired, to learn the language. And those who are able to speak the language, but who decline to use it because they have been conditioned into thinking that Welsh is inferior to English, must be helped to a new outlook, a new pride in the language which, after all, is part of a very rich heritage.

As far as the Urdd is concerned, the language is of prime importance. Loyalty to Wales includes—among other things—promotion of the Welsh language. And the most effective way of promoting a language is to use it. This the Urdd has done consistently, not as a gimmick, but as the natural medium of communication in all its activities—social and recreational as well as cultural.

But whilst the Urdd has never compromised in its attitude towards the language, it has always been sympathetic towards those who, for one reason or another, are unable to speak it. If they are to identify themselves fully with Wales, they must be helped by the Welsh-speaking section of the community. And as part of the Welsh-speaking section, the Urdd has tried to make a positive contribution, within its limited financial resources, and without neglecting its responsibility of providing the Welsh-speaking youth with the means of living a full cultural, recreational and social life.

As early as 1931, Welsh learners were invited to become Urdd members. Gradually, *Dysgwyr* Branches were formed, largely within schools, followed later by Young Wales Clubs for older members. Separate competitions for *Dysgwyr* were included in the Eisteddfod syllabus, and separate weeks designated for them at camp. To help *Dysgwyr* to learn Welsh as a second-language, a special monthly magazine was included among the Urdd publications in 1955. These are some of the ways in which the Urdd has striven to help the non-Welsh-speaking youth to become more fully integrated into the life of Wales. The movement has helped to create an atmosphere in which the *Dysgwyr* could become aware of their Welshness ; it has helped them to realise that there is a contribution that they—and they alone—can make to the future of Wales.

This policy has not been without its critics. There were those who felt that the Urdd had compromised in giving *Dysgwyr* the same opportunities as were offered to Welsh-speaking members. They argued that the position of the Welsh language was so serious that the Urdd's entire resources should be directed towards safeguarding the Welsh-speaking community. More recently, there are those who feel that the Welsh language can survive only if it is given the right political climate, and that this will not be achieved without considerable effort and sacrifice. They maintain—with justification —that the rights of the Welsh language must be fought for, and that time is not on our side. For them, therefore, the Urdd is not sufficiently militant in its approach to Welsh problems. On the other hand, the movement itself believes that the future of the language—and indeed the future of Wales—needs to be safeguarded on more than one level. Constantly working with children in an Adran, or with young people in an Aelwyd, week-in week-out, is neither exciting nor spectacular, but it can be a means of creating a pride in one's Welshness. It is one level on which the Urdd believes its members and leaders can serve Wales, and the movement has adhered to its policy of inspiring its members with a sense of loyalty to Wales, encouraging rather than enforcing, helping rather than condemning.

With this policy in mind, it was necessary that the Urdd should constantly review its methods. Improved facilities, better publicity and more effective communication were always desirable. In 1961, the movement's National Eisteddfod came under special review. Although open to *Dysgwyr*, the Eisteddfod had always been an all-Welsh festival. And since one of its aims was to promote the language and culture of Wales, it was essential that it should remain Welsh in language as well as in spirit. When the Eisteddfod was held in a mainly Welsh-speaking area, there was, of course, no problem. But when it visited an Anglicised area, some would find that they were unable to participate fully in the proceedings ; others would just decide to stay away. Many of them would co-operate enthusiastically in preparing for the Eisteddfod ; they would help in raising an advance-fund and in offering hospitality to competitors. And yet, they felt unable to enjoy the event to the full because their knowledge of Welsh was inadequate. If they decided the Eisteddfod was not for them, the Eisteddfod itself was the poorer for their absence. At the same time, an opportunity to help them to identify themselves with Wales was irrevocably lost. This was one of the problems that occupied Sir Ifan's mind as he recuperated from his illness. And Huw Cedwyn Jones, who shared the Founder's practical interests, was called in to discuss the possibilities. As the first step in attempting to make the Eisteddfod comprehensible to non-Welsh-speakers, it was decided—

   (i) that an abridged English version of the Eisteddfod programme should be published in addition to the main Welsh version ;

   (ii) that score-boards be designed to indicate (a) the stage competition ; (b) the three counties represented ; (c) the order in which they were eventually placed, and (d) the cumulative points won by all counties.

The one disadvantage was that the entire score-board had to be operated manually. An electronic device would, of course, have been far less cumbersome and far more effective, but the Urdd could not afford such a luxury. Even so, the experiment was a big step forward, and was greatly appreciated by the audience when initiated at Aberdâr in 1961.

The Eisteddfod at Aberdâr was a model of efficiency. Not that it was free of problems, but these had been overcome, partly through the wisdom of the Officers under the chairmanship of Idwal Rees, and partly through the expertise that had grown out of a local Eisteddfodic tradition. The one problem that remained unsolved was that of convincing the English-speaking man-in-the-street that competitions confined to youth could still be stimulating. The Eisteddfod no longer had the excitement of bands and processions, and unlike the National Eisteddfod of Wales, it did not have the pageantry of *Gorsedd y Beirdd* or the thrill of massed choral competitions. And in an Anglicised area, high standards and fast-changing media did not seem to be a big enough attraction. It is largely a matter of communication, and the problem still remains.

The Chair at Aberdâr was won by John Gwilym Jones of Newcastle Emlyn, whose brother, T. James Jones, had been the winner three years earlier at Mold. Commenting on the winning entry, the adjudicator, the Rev. J. Eirian Davies, said—' His poem has been poured from the cauldron of his soul. A poet who can write in this manner while yet so young is indeed a rare treasure ; in such a person lies the hope of a nation.' Winner of the Eisteddfod Crown was Eigra Lewis of Blaenau Ffestiniog. She had already been placed second and third at previous Urdd Eisteddfodau, and had won first prize for a novel at the National Eisteddfod of Wales. She has continued to write and is by now well-known for her Welsh prose work.

It was at Aberdâr that Mrs. D. T. Jones of Haverfordwest presented the Urdd with a trophy in memory of her husband, D. T. Jones, Pembrokeshire Director of Education and keen supporter of the Urdd. ' D.T.' was himself a gifted public-speaker, and nothing could have been more appropriate to commemorate him than a trophy for the Aelwydydd public-speaking competition. It was a mace mounted on a decorative oak casket, designed by Huw Cedwyn Jones and made by Glyn Rees of Dinas Mawddwy.

The Eisteddfod Presidents included Trevor Jenkins, Glamorgan's Deputy Director of Education; T. Raymond Edwards, H.M.I.; Irene Myrddin Davies and Dr. Kate Roberts. The Royal Prize at Aberdâr was—not unexpectedly—won by West Glamorgan. The financial result of the Eisteddfod was a surplus of £1,720/18/11, thanks mainly to the advance-fund of almost £2,500. In accepting the cheque on behalf of the Urdd, A. D. Lewis pointed out that those who were struggling to make Wales a truly bilingual country should not despair. He had in his hand the programme of an Eisteddfod held at Aberdâr in 1912. It was entirely in English, and in the music section, there were no more than two test-pieces in Welsh. Though much remained to be done, one could be encouraged by the change of attitude that had taken place in the fifty years since 1912.

*   *   *   *

Owen Edwards had now resigned from his post at the National Library. His weekly journeys to Granada Television continued, and he felt he could not do justice to his work at the Library if he continued spending so much time commuting between Aberystwyth and Manchester. He accepted an unpaid and rather vague post at Urdd Headquarters, dividing his time between duties at Swyddfa'r Urdd, committee work, and publicity campaigns. Sir Ifan, of course, was delighted. Owen could take over some of the leadership he had been forced to relinquish. His hopes, however, were soon to be shattered. Owen, naturally, knew of his father's feelings and he would have been glad to be able to comply with his wishes. But despite his interest in the Urdd, Owen felt he would like the opportunity to prove his mettle in the field of television. The dilemma was ended unexpectedly at the Aberdâr Eisteddfod. As Publicity Officer for the Urdd, he was asked to take part in a *Heddiw* programme dealing with the Eisteddfod. Consequently, he was fur'her invited to act as interviewer, and in another week, he became compére of *Heddiw*, a task he accomplished with distinction for five-and-a-half years. This, however, meant moving to Cardiff, and thus his active association with Urdd Headquarters came to an abrupt end. In 1921, Sir Ifan had seen the possibilities of *Cymru'r Plant*, and had grasped the opportunity of offering his service to Wales through this medium. In 1961 Owen had found a new and different medium. The aims of father and son were identical ; it was only the means that differed.

*   *   *   *

Montgomeryshire became host to the 1961 *Gŵyl Sir* (County Festival). Elwyn Jones, Headmaster of the Llanfyllin Secondary School, was elected Chairman and the function was held on the school campus. The highlight was the Powys Pageant devised by W. J. Jones and E. Ronald Morris, both of Llanfyllin. Its theme was the contribution of Powys to the religious, educational and cultural life of Wales, beginning with the Cloister of Tysilio in Meifod, and including Owain Cyfeiliog and Geraldus Cambrensis ; Owain Glyndŵr and Bishop William Morgan ; Huw Morris and Ann Griffiths, and ending with Richard Mills of Llanidloes. The scenes were presented by members of nine Aelwydydd—young men

59   Evan L. Isaac, Chief Field Officer

60   J. Eric Williams, Principal Officer at Glan Llyn and Physical Recreation Officer

61   On a canoe expedition

62   The ceremony at Y Pandy, Llanarth, in 1961

and women who had little previous experience of acting but who succeeded in making history come alive. President of the evening was J. Lloyd Thomas of Pontardawe, former Headmaster of Llanfyllin Secondary School.

The festival also included a féte opened by Mrs. Jano Clement Davies, while in other parts of the building, there were team competitions to test the skills of members in verse, story-telling, miming, etc. A *Cymanfa Ganu* was conducted by Gwilym Gwalchmai of Llanerfyl and Manchester, with Meirion Jones of Bala as President. The festival ended with a *Noson Lawen* compéred by Charles Williams, with Cassie Davies as President. Apart from its cultural and social contribution, the success of the entire project was reflected in the financial result. A surplus of £1,253 was the highest that any County Festival had achieved.

This was not the only festival held by the Urdd in 1961. The second occurred as a result of the direct initiative of the Breconshire County Committee. The members felt they needed some non-competitive activity not too ambitious in scale. The Urdd had no Organiser in Breconshire and the planning and organising were undertaken voluntarily by members of the County Committee. It was a one-day festival and included a féte opened by Lady Edwards, sports competitions and an exhibition of folk-dancing, followed in the evening by a children's concert. Though on a smaller scale than the usual *Gŵyl Sir*, it proved what a County Committee could achieve without help from a county organiser or from Headquarters. If it could be done in Breconshire, it could be done in any Welsh county. And it posed the question whether a less ambitious scheme held annually in a dozen counties would not attain far more, financially and otherwise, than one major county festival. It seemed that Breconshire had, unwittingly, provided a blueprint for the future. Incidentally, the festival had also paved the way for the appointment of a full-time County Organiser.

*   *   *   *

The demand for ' *Cymraeg* ' was continually increasing, largely because the editor, Ivor Owen, had linked it with the second-language scheme devised by the Glamorgan Education Authority. Ivor Owen himself was often called to serve on language panels and attend conferences, and it was generally recognised that he had much to contribute in the task of evolving second-language teaching-methods and techniques.

Among other duties, J. Cyril Hughes had already taken over the central organisation of the National Eisteddfod and County Festival. In addition, he now undertook the editing of *Yr Aelwyd*, partly in order to allow the Director more time for other schemes and partly because R. E. Griffith felt that, after twenty-one years, the imprint of a new editor would lend new life to the magazine.

Through the efforts of 62 Branches, a total of 10,304 volumes were sold in the 1961 Welsh Books Campaign and the record for the highest number of volumes sold was again held by *Adran Ysgol Frondeg*, Pwllheli. The Campaign had now been in progress for twenty-five years and the Urdd had several times declared its readiness to withdraw in favour of some organisation that had the sale of Welsh books as its main aim. The one possibility was the Union of Welsh Books Societies which had Alun R. Edwards as its Honorary Secretary. It was he who had stimulated the establishment of sixteen Welsh Books Societies and, together with Emlyn Evans, Secretary of the London-Welsh Book Club, he had welded these Societies into one national Union. Hitherto, however, the link between the Societies had been somewhat tenuous ; the Union had no office, no paid staff, and no financial resources. And when the Urdd announced its intention of withdrawing its support of the Welsh Books Campaign in 1961, Alun Edwards felt that the decision was premature. He had been striving to persuade Local Authorities to set up a body specifically designed to promote the writing, publishing and distribution of Welsh books, and he felt that, despite all difficulties, he was well on the way to achieving his aim. This, in his view, would be the body that could adopt the Welsh Books Campaign. But not just yet. The Welsh Books Council was established in 1962 and Alun R. Edwards became its Honorary Secretary. For 1961, however, a compromise was needed and this was reached with the help of the Union of Welsh Publishers and Booksellers. The administrative work of the Campaign was undertaken by *Gwasg Gee*, while the Urdd again circularised its Branches, urging them to continue for a little longer. Despite the achievements of twenty-five years, the Urdd knew that much more could be attained in this field by a body concentrating solely on the publication and distribution of books, a body that had the financial support of Local Authorities.

*   *   *   *

October 7 was more than an ordinary field day in Cardiganshire. On the invitation of the Urdd County Committee, a large crowd gathered at Llanarth to celebrate the fact that it was there, forty years earlier, that Sir Ifan ab Owen Edwards had written the article that brought the Urdd into being. There were old friends present who had supported the Urdd in its early years ; there were also young people who had joined the ranks in the forties and fifties. In the birthday celebrations, they were all one. What made it a singularly happy occasion was the fact that Sir Ifan was well enough to attend. It was obvious that tributes paid to the Urdd were also personal tributes to the Founder who had guided the movement through forty years of exciting developments.

President of the afternoon meeting was the Rev. Tegryn Davies of Aberporth, and no one was more deserving of the honour. One of the speakers, Gwenith Davies, chose to speak of the Eisteddfod —the artistry of movement, the purity of tone, the beauty of poetic expression, the skill of manual art. The Urdd had safeguarded this inheritance, and introduced each succeeding generation to the joy of participation.

Aneurin Jenkins-Jones spoke of the contribution made by the Urdd through its magazines on the one hand, and its recreational activities on the other—the mabolgampau, the organised games, the camps and other outdoor activities. These had brought a new dimension into the lives of Urdd members, a new joy from which had grown a love for Wales and which later led to a desire to repay their debt in loyalty and service.

Tributes were also paid by two younger members—Dic Jones of Aberporth and Eirlys Jones-Lewis of Lampeter. There were choral items from Lampeter, and the Aberporth *cerdd dant* group sang a *cywydd* specially composed by Dic Jones. Following this meeting, the audience gathered outside *Y Pandy* where a cairn of Arenig stone had been erected, inscribed in Welsh to indicate that it was in this house, in October 1921, that Ifan ab Owen Edwards wrote the historic article. The tablet was unveiled by Norah Isaac in a ceremony presided over by Alun Creunant Davies, Vice-Chairman of the County Committee. The day's events ended at Aberaeron with a feature-programme, presented by Sadie Jones of Gorsgoch, depicting the varied activities which the Urdd had introduced to its Adrannau and Aelwydydd.

Although Sir Ifan was not allowed to take an active part in the proceedings, he had been asked to write a message to be included in the printed programme. In it, he outlined some of the changes that had taken place in forty years and paid tribute to the men and women who had chosen the Urdd as a means of serving Wales—

> ' They have done this voluntarily although there were ample opportunities for them to use their leisure for personal gain. This is something for which I am particularly grateful. No movement has ever received more loyal service than the Urdd during its first forty years.
>
> What brings hope—and indeed certainty—for the future is the knowledge that young men and women continue to leave our schools and colleges fired with the same enthusiasm as their parents before them. It may be that the problems they will have to face will be more difficult than those which faced us, and that their methods of dealing with them will be different from ours. It may be that today's youth are more conscious of the nationhood of Wales than we were. Ours was a simple love of Wales ; for them, Wales is something very real . . .'

*   *   *   *

One result of the training courses in the building and handling of canoes at Glan Llyn was the canoe-camping expedition planned for July 1961. Led by Elwyn Huws, the nine canoeists set out from Glan Llyn, followed the River Dee as far as Llangollen, switched to the canal, and later followed the Shropshire Union Canal as far as Chester. This experience opened up a new sphere of opportunity and Elwyn Huws was already mentally exploring the possibilities of other British rivers and even considering continental expeditions.

This new interest in canoeing did not obscure the appeal of the mountains. After a week's walking in North Wales, a group led by

Iwan Bryn Williams could relate with some pride that they had succeeded in climbing *Y Cnicht, Y Moelwyn, Moel Siabod, Y Carneddi, Y Glyder Fawr, Tryfan* and *Yr Wyddfa.*

*   *   *   *

In 1959, members of *Aelwyd Llanuwchllyn*, led by Gwyn Williams, had joined a midnight procession to the *Friedenskreuz*— the Cross of Peace—at Bühl-Baden in Germany. And in presenting *Y Ddraig Goch* to be flown alongside the national flags that encircled the cross, Gwyn Williams had referred to the Goodwill Message of the youth of Wales to the youth of the world, whereupon the Germans decided that a special ceremony would be held at the Cross each year on Goodwill Day, May 18. In 1961, Gwyn Williams decided to join in that ceremony. The Goodwill Message was read in several languages, and the meeting ended with a group of German schoolchildren singing *Hen Wlad fy Nhadau*—in Welsh !

*   *   *   *

1961 was not without its changes in the Urdd staff. After five years as Organiser for Caernarfonshire and Anglesey, Iris Parry returned to the teaching profession, and her place was taken by John M. Hughes. Pembrokeshire Education Committee decided to offer a generous grant of 75% towards the salary and expenses of a County Organiser. The choice fell on Gwyn Griffiths of Tregaron, who had just completed his course at the Cardiff College of Education. Tecwyn Jones left his post as Organiser for Merioneth and Montgomeryshire and was replaced by Robin Hughes of Liverpool, who had recently left Trinity College, Carmarthen.

*   *   *   *

Prompted by Aneurin Jenkins-Jones, *Aelwyd Aberystwyth* embarked on a new scheme during the summer of 1961. It was felt that visitors to the town had little opportunity of sampling any form of Welsh entertainment. The Aelwyd, therefore, decided to present an all-Welsh programme under the title 'Welsh Serenade', compéred by Owen Edwards and introduced mainly in English.

At the end of the evening, the organisers were surprised at the enthusiastic comments of the visitors. It seemed that they had searched in vain for this kind of entertainment, something that was intrinsically Welsh, and they had found it, unexpectedly, at Aberystwyth.

Having proved the point, the next step was to convince the Borough Council that visitors to Wales were looking for something different, and that it would be to the town's advantage if this kind of entertainment were offered as one of the attractions of Aberystwyth. Once convinced, the Council became enthusiastic in its support of the 'Welsh Serenade', and ever since, the Aelwyd, in co-operation with the Council, has undertaken to organise a series of annual concerts. It is a service that other Aelwydydd could consider emulating and an attraction that the Wales Tourist Board could well be asked to sponsor.

*   *   *   *

The Annual General Meeting was held at Aberaeron on the morning of the Llanarth celebrations. Presenting the report, the Chairman, Cassie Davies, said that she was yet to hear of any movement, in any country, that had ventured and achieved so much as the Urdd. The Treasurer, Cynfab Roberts, said that the Urdd could report gains in every sphere except the financial one ! The accounts showed a deficit of nearly £515. Nevertheless, the movement had raised—and spent—a total of £65,000. Ten years earlier, in 1951, the expenditure amounted to £25,000. This meant an increase of £40,000 in ten years, an average of £4,000 per year. If this trend continued, it was imperative that there should be a proportionate increase in income. It was unlikely that grants would be correspondingly increased and this meant that some additional effort would be necessary if the Urdd was to maintain an even keel. The Treasurer closed his remarks by saying that, like the Chairman, he had no worries about the activities of the Urdd, but that he was a little concerned about the movement's finances. ' I feel,' he said, ' like the businessman who once said, "I have no worries except financial ones" ! '

16

THE Press was generous in the publicity it gave the Urdd on its fortieth anniversary. The unbiased views of outsiders were always welcome, and it was a satisfaction to find the Press unanimous that the life of Wales would be much the poorer had it not been for the Urdd and its activities. It was even more gratifying when one remembered that the Urdd had lacked adequate means of providing a constant flow of information regarding its activities. Officers and staff were overburdened with organisation, and publicity tended to be neglected.

Y Faner and the *Western Mail* may not always see eye-to-eye, but they both agreed that the Urdd's achievements over a period of forty years were worthy of comment. ' When one remembers,' said the editor of *Y Faner*, ' that the Urdd is a voluntary movement, largely dependent on a labour of love, those who are in any way connected with the movement have cause to rejoice and to feel proud of its achievement.'

Like *Y Faner*, the *Western Mail* had been generous in its coverage of Urdd activities for more than thirty years. Assessing its contribution to the life of Wales, an editorial had this to say on the occasion of the movement's fortieth birthday—

' Apart from a uniting burning desire to beat England at Rugby, Wales tends to live in a continual state of schism. It is, therefore, the finest possible tribute to Urdd Gobaith Cymru that the whole nation will wish it well on its fortieth birthday. Born of one man's vision, it has expanded and prospered beyond recognition during his lifetime. In fact, the Urdd has won the affection of many for widely differing reasons. Its annual eisteddfod has offered a challenge and the hope of success to children and young people through every county in Wales. At its summer camps, youth from the anglicised areas have met their Welsh-speaking counterparts, and realised the vitality of a language and way of life which were previously locked in the aridity of a textbook. In its publications, the Urdd has brought liveliness and enjoyment to those learning the language as well as to the fluent. Through its founder, it has also played a vital part in the growth of Welsh-medium schools. Aimed at fostering nationalism in the widest and finest sense, the Urdd has grown through its forty years without aligning itself to any cause other than this, and without great financial support from any official body. May it continue for many more years. *Pen-blwydd hapus i'r Urdd.*'

The Times too carried an article entitled ' They catch them young in Wales'. After a detailed analysis of the movement's aims and activities, the author concluded—

' The Urdd is national without being political in the party sense, and Christian without being tied to any denomination. It is also international in many of its interests and contacts. These three aspects of its philosophy are reflected in the three-fold pledge of ' loyalty to Wales, to fellow-man and to Christ ' which is taken by every member . . . The movement has done and is still doing much to foster in young people not only the use of the language, but also the sense of belonging to a living nation.'

Individuals too made the occasion an opportunity for appraisal. One of these was Goronwy O. Roberts, M.P. who summed up as follows—

' The Urdd has contributed much in perpetuating the Welsh language. Not only has it given the language dignity and distinction among Welsh-speakers, but it has inspired hundreds of non-Welsh-speakers to learn the language. Instead of alienating these members, the Urdd has welcomed and encouraged them. It went into the schools and inspired the teachers. It gave a lead in Welsh education by pioneering and establishing the Welsh Schools Movement. In addition, it believed in providing a balanced leisure education for the youth of Wales ; physical recreation was catered for as well as cultural activities. And I must emphasise the Urdd's valuable contribution to Welsh citizenship. The movement's aim is to promote Welsh Christian citizenship, and its threefold pledge of loyalty to Wales, to fellow-man and to Christ is one to which nothing can be added and from which nothing can be taken away.'

The celebrations which had begun at Llanarth in October 1961 moved to London in 1962 when the London Welsh Association invited the Urdd to be responsible for the major part of its St. David's Day concert-programme at the Royal Albert Hall. Three-hundred-and-fifty young people from eight centres in Wales were joined by London-Welsh youth to form a massed choir to perform under the baton of Dr. Terry James. Supporting the choir, and punctuating the script devised by Aneirin Talfan Davies, there were folk-songs, *cerdd dant*, mime, camp-songs, a ' Peace ' dance, and trampoline displays. At the end of the programme, a spotlight was beamed on Sir Ifan ab Owen Edwards, and the enthusiasm of the applause, especially from the Urdd members assembled on the stage, brought him to his feet in acknowledgement. It must have been a memorable moment for him, and well worth the effort he had made to attend.

*　　　*　　　*　　　*

It was in February 1962 that Saunders Lewis delivered his radio lecture entitled *Tynged yr Iaith* (The Fate of the Language). Forecasting the results of the 1961 census figures, he spoke as follows—

> ' I predict that the figures soon to be published will be a shock and a disappointment to those of us who consider that Wales will not be Wales without the Welsh language. I also predict that towards the beginning of the next century, if the present trend continues, we shall see the end of the Welsh language as a living language.'

He maintained that ever since the Act of Union in 1536 the ' English Government ' had deliberately and consistently striven to abolish the Welsh language in official, administrative and legal circles. ' With the exception of the schools, the fact remains that in every administrative post or office in Wales, English is the only essential language.'

Since 1536, the Welsh language, in the eyes of the Government, was a political issue. Within Wales, however, voices had periodically been raised in defence of the language. Such were the voices of Michael D. Jones and Emrys ap Iwan in the nineteenth century, both of whom considered the language to be the very essence of the nation. The resultant awakening, however, lost its impetus in the rapid social changes that took place at the beginning of the twentieth century. ' Today,' said Saunders Lewis, ' the Welsh language is in retreat ; it is the language of a minority, and that an ever-diminishing minority.' It was not only the Government that he blamed. He was even more critical of the Welsh Members of Parliament, of the political parties, of some Welsh institutions and of the Welsh Local Authorities. The Government had laid down its policy, and could now sit back and watch its allies in Wales annihilating the Welsh language.

> ' Is the situation without hope ? It is, if we allow ourselves to despair. Centuries of political tradition and the entire economic trends of today militate against the continuance of the language. Nothing can change this except determination, willpower, effort, struggle, sacrifice . . .
>
> The language could be saved . . . but the task must be undertaken steadfastly and without wavering ; it must be made impossible for local or central government to operate within Wales without the use of Welsh . . . This is not a policy for individuals, one here and one there ; it is a policy for a movement. It must be an organised effort, progressing step by step, giving notice of action and allowing time for change.
>
> I maintain that this is the only political issue that merits our concern at the present time. I am aware of the difficulties. There would be stormy opposition from all directions. Fines imposed by the courts would be heavy and the consequences of non-payment would be severe . . . I do not deny that it would be a period of hatred, of persecution, of contention. The restoration of the Welsh language in Wales will be nothing less than a revolution. Only revolutionary methods will succeed. The revival of the language might possibly lead to self-government ; I cannot tell. The language is more important than self-government . . .'

This radio lecture was a significant utterance in the life of Wales. It was a blow to Plaid Cymru that Saunders Lewis, of all people, should have declared self-government to be of secondary importance. One gathers too that the Urdd's forty years' service to Wales was in his view of little or no significance. In Saunders Lewis' opinion, a new and revolutionary movement was required if the Welsh language was to be restored. Before the end of 1962, such a movement had emerged. *Cymdeithas yr Iaith Gymraeg* (The Welsh Language Society) owes its existence to Saunders Lewis and the inspiration of his radio lecture. The movement quickly developed political undertones and set about challenging law and authority, using unconstitutional methods, revolutionary though non-violent. Its members showed, however, that they were prepared to face the consequences.

It is not necessary here to trace the development of this movement, but it is important to note its origin and background since it has been an important factor in the life of Wales during the past ten years and has created an awakening more potent than anything that occurred in the days of Michael D. Jones and Emrys ap Iwan. It appeals largely to the youth of Wales, particularly the Welsh-speaking youth, and has thus become active in the field in which the Urdd had already worked for forty years.

*　　　*　　　*　　　*

The early sixties were years of active development at Glan Llyn. Elwyn Huws sought every opportunity to improve its amenities and to increase outdoor activities. The centre was now in continuous use at weekends and there was a full-time programme during the summer months. The emphasis during the ' low season ' was on leadership-courses in lake and mountain-based activities. Boating had already been taken seriously, but little attention had been paid to mountaineering. Now leaders were discovering the challenge of rock-climbing and the discipline involved in the acquisition of these new skills. It was not long before we had a team of experienced climbers capable of passing on their expertise to the younger generation. Glan Llyn had acquired another new dimension.

Walking and canoeing expeditions were also linked with the centre. Two staff members, John M. Hughes and Elwyn Huws, agreed to lead two canoe expeditions in 1962, the one ' coming down the Wye,' and the other, which included 17 young men and women, exploring a section of the River Seine in France. These expeditions certainly added to the attraction of Glan Llyn, and it was not surprising that Christopher Chataway, Parliamentary Secretary to the Ministry of Education, should be impressed with the centre and its amenities when he visited Glan Llyn in 1962. With these new developments, it soon became necessary to appoint a full-time caretaker-warden, and the choice fell on R. G. Williams, a leading member of the Aelwyd at Llanfaethlu in Anglesey and a skilled craftsman.

Staff changes were apparently inevitable and the Magazines Department again seemed particularly vulnerable. Catrin Lloyd Rowlands left to take up a post with *Teledu Cymru*. Marian Rees, with four years' teaching experience, was chosen as a replacement, but as she had already accepted a year's appointment in Brittany, Gwenda Ellis Jones of Bangor University College was appointed for the interim period.

While the policy of reducing the number of independent Aelwyd premises was adhered to, it was a different story at Dyserth in Flintshire. Here a new extension to a centre built in 1939 was erected at a cost of £6,000. Generous grants had been received both from the Ministry of Education and from the Local Education Authority, and these, coupled with determined efforts on the part of the Aelwyd itself, meant that the total costs had been met by the time the new premises were officially opened.

Circumstances at Talgarreg in Cardiganshire were somewhat different but not less exciting. Here, T. Ll. Stephens, Headmaster of the Primary School, Aelwyd founder and undisputed leader of the local community, had acquired a disused woollen mill in the village, and converted it into a social, recreational and cultural centre for the Aelwyd. Later, an adjoining building was purchased and the extensions were opened when the Aelwyd celebrated its coming-of-age in 1962. T. Ll. Stephens did not live to see the opening ceremony, but he had ensured a permanent home for the Aelwyd by transferring this freehold property to Cwmni'r Urdd.

* * * *

The 1962 Urdd National Eisteddfod found a home at Rhuthun in the Vale of Clwyd. It was one of the happiest and most successful of Urdd Eisteddfodau, and this was largely due to the co-operation which existed between the two-hundred committee members led by T. Glyn Davies, Director of Education. Collaborating closely with these voluntary workers were a number of Urdd staff, each with his particular responsibility and led by J. Cyril Hughes. This had now become the established pattern in the organisation of the Eisteddfod—the staff helping to ease the burden while still leaving the control in the hands of the local committee.

The Eisteddfod Presidents were Menai Williams of Bangor, Frank Price Jones, and Hywel Davies, Head of BBC Programmes (Wales). Dr. Roger Webster presided over the official opening of the Arts, Crafts and Science Exhibition, in place of J. E. Daniel,

H.M.I., who had died earlier in the year. Sir Ifan ab Owen Edwards was present and, for the first time since his illness, he ventured to address the audience. It is no wonder that the Eisteddfod was a happy event.

For the previous seven years, D. Jacob Davies had been Master of Ceremonies in the Crowning and Chairing events. For this occasion, he had asked to be relieved of one of the two, and Jennie Eirian Davies was invited to conduct the Crowning ceremony. No better choice could have been made and the result was a most impressive ceremony. Incidentally, it was the women's day. The Crown was won by Enid Wyn Baines of Mynytho in Llŷn, while second and third respectively were Emily Hughes, a student at the Normal College, Bangor, and Marian Rees who had already won the Crown at Mold.

The Chair was won by Gerallt Lloyd Owen, a sixth-form pupil at Bala Grammar School. The adjudicator, James Nicholas, described the winner as an artist of first degree. Second was Edwin Brandt of Dolgellau, who had learnt Welsh sufficiently well to be able to compose in strict metre, while another sixth-form pupil, Peter Davies of Ardwyn School, Aberystwyth, was placed third.

The evening sessions too—the drama competitions, the public-speaking contest and the *Noson Lawen* competition—reached an unusually high standard and were well supported. Perhaps it was not surprising that an Eisteddfod held in the Vale of Clwyd—a district that had produced Tudur Aled, Bishop William Morgan, William Salesbury, Twm o'r Nant, Emrys ap Iwan and T. Gwynn Jones—should be a major success. And it was not irrelevant that the Eisteddfod accounts showed a balance of £2,848, the highest ever in a North Wales Urdd Eisteddfod.

For the second year in succession, Breconshire held its own Festival without the services of an Organiser and with very little help from Swyddfa'r Urdd. This time it was held at Brecon ; it included a concert, a féte, together with athletic sports and folk-dancing, and it had the full support of the county's Member of Parliament, Alderman Tudor Watkins.

The biennial *Gŵyl Werin* (The Folk-Song-and-Dance Festival) was held at the Sophia Gardens Pavilion in Cardiff. Twenty groups from South Wales took part in the massed dancing displays, and four counties provided exhibition teams. Those who had attended the first festival at Corwen four years earlier could not fail to be impressed by the progress made. The dancers were more confident, more skilled, and more ready to experiment with this new medium which they had now made their own. But while they were more disciplined, they had lost none of their vitality and spontaneity.

On this occasion, we had invited two groups from outside Wales— the Marlow Scottish Dancers and the Oxford Morris Dancers— who introduced new elements and greater variety into the programme. Interspersed with the group-dancing were folk-songs by Esme Lewis, a harp *ensemble*, and clog-dancing by Owen Huw Roberts. The afternoon session was followed by a *Noson Lawen* and, still later, a *Twmpath Dawns*. Despite heavy costs, the financial success of the venture was guaranteed, much to the relief of the Treasurer, Keri Harris Hughes. The surplus was £206.

The annual County Festival—*Gŵyl Sir*—was held in Caernarfonshire under the chairmanship of Ifor Hughes, one of the county's most dedicated leaders. With Alwyn Hughes Jones as Chairman of the Finance Committee, it is not surprising that the accounts showed a balance of £1,020, a worthy second to the record achieved by Montgomeryshire the previous year. The week's festivities included two performances of a feature-programme based on the life and work of T. Rowland Hughes, a *Cymanfa Ganu*, a *Noson Lawen*, and a concert featuring Richard Rees, John Stoddart, Gwen Parry Jones and the *cerdd dant* group from *Aelwyd Bro Cennin*. The festival féte was held in the Glynllifon grounds and opened by Marian Goronwy Roberts while, in the mansion, were held the diverse skill and knowledge competitions which had now become a recognised part of the Saturday programme.

The annual Goodwill Message Service was broadcast from Eglwys Dewi Sant, Cardiff, on the Sunday prior to Goodwill Day. This was planned in conjunction with the Cardiff Aelwyd, and the address given by the Rev. Canon R. M. Rosser.

*   *   *   *

Sir Ifan was not able to attend the Annual General Meeting at Aberystwyth, and it was presided over by the Council Chairman, Cassie Davies. The Treasurer's report disclosed that the year's expenditure amounted to £65,000, towards which just over £10,000 was received in grants. The Ministry grant had been increased from £6,500 to £7,500, while, for the first time, LEA grants exceeded the £2,000 mark. By its own efforts the Urdd had raised a total of £55,000, and with great satisfaction the Treasurer was able to report that at long last the Urdd was free of debt. This was not announced in any self-congratulatory spirit, but those acquainted with the facts knew to what extent the improvement was due to the Treasurer's own shrewdness and careful husbandry of the Company's resources.

The Rev. H. E. Jones, Rector of Garthbeibio in Montgomeryshire, believed that the Urdd should concentrate more on fundraising on a county level. He decided to set up his own fund, aimed at getting five-hundred Montgomeryshire persons to make an annual contribution of £1 to the Urdd. The scheme was immediately successful but before its completion he was transferred to Bala. His enthusiasm, however, was unabated, and ten years later, he found himself Chairman of the Finance Committee of the 1972 Urdd Jubilee Eisteddfod, with a £10,000 advance-fund as his target.

A radio appeal made by Dr. Wyn Griffith brought in a welcome total of £1,000, and with another £1,000 from the Pantyfedwen Trust, a total of £2,000 was available. It was decided that some of the more urgent improvements needed at Llangrannog could now be considered. An electric cooker and a number of new tents were purchased, stocks of blankets and mattresses were replenished, sick-bay facilities were improved and an assembly hut built for staff and leaders. The only snag was that all this meant an expenditure of £3,000 instead of £2,000 !

*   *   *   *

In the early fifties, R. E. Griffith had been approached confidentially as to whether he would accept the OBE. Having refused to serve in the armed forces and being unable to lend support to the concept of a British Empire with its imperialism and its militarism, he felt obliged to decline the offer. In 1961, he was again approached with a similar request. It was pointed out to him that much had happened in the past ten years. The British Empire as such was disintegrating and was being replaced by the Commonwealth of Nations, a very different concept of association. The OBE title as such was, therefore, largely obsolete, and the offer represented a genuine desire on the part of the Government to acknowledge the forty years' service given by the Urdd to the youth of Wales. Viewed in this light, R. E. Griffith found it somewhat easier to accept, and after considerable heart-searching he finally agreed. And judging by the messages he received when the Birthday Honours were announced in January 1962, he could have spared himself the torture of his dilemma.

The other honour bestowed upon him during that year was one he could accept without hesitation. It was an invitation to preside at the National Eisteddfod of Wales at Llanelli. In his address, he took up the cudgels on behalf of the young people of Wales and their jealous zeal for Wales and its language—

'. . . It is they who will decide whether the Welsh language is to live or die within the next forty years.

And what a noble generation they are . . . I believe that never was there a finer generation of youth than we see around us today. But let us not forget that we must meet them on their own ground. We who are older must be more flexible in mind and less conservative in spirit. We must not feel indignant if their thoughts are not our thoughts ; if they do not look the same or dress the same as we do . . . These young people have realised that the Welsh language must serve every facet of life . . . Through camping, mountaineering, sailing and dancing, they have created a new Welsh society. For them, the language is not a burden, not a problem, but an adventure of true and real joy.

But although leisure activities are important, this is not the only factor in the struggle to save the language. Some will see it as an educational problem. To others, it is a political issue. I believe, however, that the first essential is to instil a love of the language into the homes and hearts of our youth. The more help that is received from official sources, the better—from central and local government, from education authorities and law courts, from national bodies and movements. But a formal recognition of the language is useless—even if it were wrapped in self-government—without a love of the language in the heart and the active support of parents in the homes. We must guard against losing the essence in promoting the frills. Let us first win the homes of Wales, and these other aspects will inevitably follow.'

63   The Pantyfedwen Family Bowl—Eisteddfod County Trophy

64   The Orlyk Ukranian Dancers at Aberafan in 1964

65   Owen Huw Roberts
performing the Clog Dance

Looking back today, eleven years later, it is obvious that a new spirit was manifest in Wales in 1962. A young generation was growing up who felt just as intensely for Wales as the first generation of Urdd members had done in the twenties. And the Urdd, to a large extent, was responsible.

* * * *

It is doubtful whether the Urdd has displayed greater flexibility in any sphere than it has in connection with its publications. For many years, *Cymru'r Plant* was the one and only monthly publication. In 1955, *Cymraeg* appeared, the first magazine for Welsh learners. A year later, Ivor Owen was appointed editor, and 1957 saw the appearance of *Cymru*, a magazine for senior Welsh-speakers. To these, *Yr Anrheg* was added in 1959. This provided a wealth of pictures and light-reading material for primary school readers, and as its name implies, it was distributed as a free inset with *Cymru'r Plant* and *Cymraeg*.

By 1963, Ivor Owen had seven years' editorial experience, was ever ready to experiment, and prepared to work unreasonably long hours in order to achieve his aims. The annual Magazines Conference proved a boon, and as a result of recommendations made in 1963, yet another magazine was added, and the necessary adjustments made to allow it to fit into the existing pattern. The new magazine, *Deryn*, would provide for Welsh-speakers in the 5-8 age-group, thus leaving *Cymru'r Plant* free to concentrate on the 9-12 age-group. At the same time, it was decided to make *Cymru* more contemporary in content and format and the new title *Hamdden* (Leisure) was designed to conform with the new image. By the end of 1963, the combined monthly sales of the four magazines—*Deryn*, *Cymru'r Plant*, *Hamdden* and *Cymraeg*—amounted to 43,850.

* * * *

In five years, the skiffle bands had given way to pop groups. To older ears, the deafening notes of English and American pop music on radio and television were harsh and primitive, but the effect on the younger generation was stimulating and infectious, and the reaction of Welsh youth was no exception. There was a danger that this new cult would completely oust the traditional Welsh music and thus add to the already serious Anglicising influence of the mass media. It was this fear that led Glan Llyn campers to translate current pop-songs so that, if they must be sung, they could at least be sung in Welsh. This was admirable as a first move in coming to terms with the new trend. As a further step, the Urdd urged Aelwydydd members, and especially those who regularly assembled at Glan Llyn, to adopt a more creative approach and to write their own Welsh words to tunes of their choice, or better still, to compose both words and music. In adopting this new medium, it was important that Wales should aim at creating its own tradition rather than emulate a trend that was essentially alien. Soon Glan Llyn became the cradle for a new Welsh tradition with the guitar as its symbol. It is true that there was little expertise in the accompaniment, but the strumming helped to create the desired atmosphere and it lent support to the less experienced singers. What was significant was the fact that members were now renouncing the English and American songs, bent on creating their own tradition in words and music. Chief among the pioneers were Dafydd Iwan and Edward Morus Jones, followed later by Huw Jones and Dewi (Pws) Morris. Gradually, this new medium extended beyond the confines of Glan Llyn, and radio and television producers were quick to see its possibilities and to grant further opportunities to pop singers, many of whom had served their apprenticeship at Glan Llyn.

There were two main themes to the Welsh songs, or perhaps two aspects of the one theme which was Love—love of person and love of country. The patriotic songs were more numerous and showed greater vitality than the more personal love songs. The new Welsh pop tradition was characterised by a seriousness and earnestness not found in the light-hearted songs of the earlier generation of song writers—Idwal Jones, W. R. Evans, R. E. Jones, W. D. Williams and D. Jacob Davies. It is true that patriotic songs had been popular at the end of the nineteenth century, but they were sentimental and superficial, whereas those of the sixties reflected an element of challenge and rebellion. These young people cared deeply about the future of the Welsh language and the Welsh nation, and song was the natural medium through which they could express their feelings. They were not without their critics in this respect, and it may be true that, in their enthusiasm, they sometimes failed to distinguish between the general and the personal ; between satire and contempt. Their feelings, however, were genuine and the Urdd had helped to awaken in them this Welsh awareness, this sense of responsibility for the welfare of the nation. As Sir Ifan ab Owen Edwards had said at Llanarth in 1961 in referring to the new generation,—

' It may be that the problems they will have to face will be more difficult than those which faced us, and that their methods of dealing with them will be different from ours . . . It may be that today's youth are more conscious of the nationhood of Wales than we were. Ours was a simple love of Wales ; for them Wales is something very real.'

And from 1963 onwards, the pop song became a powerful weapon in the struggle to preserve, protect and promote the Welsh language; in creating a new sense of identification with Wales.

17

BRYNAMAN, or to give it its older name—*Y Gwter Fawr*—is a large village at the foot of the Black Mountain, just two miles on the Carmarthenshire side of the boundary between Carmarthenshire and Glamorgan. It is a village where 95% of its inhabitants express themselves through the Welsh language, not only in their homes and churches, but in all aspects of their everyday life. It is this Welsh tradition that accounts for the rich and varied contribution they have made to the cultural and religious life of the nation.

When one recalls that an Urdd Adran had existed at Brynaman since 1928, and that a flourishing Aelwyd had acquired its independent premises in 1939, it might seem surprising that the district had not invited the Urdd National Eisteddfod before 1963. But the festival had twice visited the neighbourhood, and on both occasions, Brynaman had been involved—at Gwaun-Cae-Gurwen in 1937 and at Amanford in 1957. Now, however, it was the turn of Brynaman itself. They had behind them a century of Eisteddfodic experience, and under the leadership of Emlyn O. Evans (Emlyn Aman), with Elfyn Talfan Davies at his elbow, the local committees took up their task with enthusiasm. For two years, the inhabitants of Brynaman ' lived ' the Eisteddfod, and with the help of neighbouring villages, leaving no stone unturned, it is little wonder that the Eisteddfod was one of the most successful and most memorable of Urdd Eisteddfodau. The Presidents were Stella Treharne, one of Carmarthenshire's untiring voluntary leaders, Dr. Stephen J. Williams of Swansea, Dr. D. Mathew Williams, H.M.I., and E. D. Jones, Head of the National Library at Aberystwyth.

The winning bard was chaired by proxy. He was Donald Evans of Talgarreg in Cardiganshire who was sitting his final examination paper at Aberystwyth. It must have called for considerable will-power to concentrate on that paper knowing that a large and enthusiastic audience was waiting to honour him in the Eisteddfod pavilion. However, he rushed from his examination to Brynaman, and was given a compensating welcome by the *Noson Lawen* audience in the evening.

D. Jacob Davies had asked to be relieved of the Chairing Ceremony, and his place at Brynaman was taken by Aneurin Jenkins-Jones, while Jennie Eirian Davies once again conducted the Crowning Ceremony. Out of twenty-four short-story writers, the Crown was won by David Wyn Davies of Tycroes. He too had sat his final examination the previous day, which explains why the two ceremonies could not have been interchanged. Emily Hughes of Caeathro, Caernarfon, shared second place with Nest Llwyd Williams of Amanford, while the third place went to John Meurig Edwards and Douglas V. Price, both of *Aelwyd Coleg y Drindod*, Carmarthen. In the final reckoning, perhaps it was natural that the South Wales counties should win the highest number of points, West Glamorgan winning the Royal Prize, with Carmarthenshire and Cardiganshire second and third respectively.

There was just one cloud that hung over the Eisteddfod Committee during the two years of preparation. An application had been made for permission to hold the Eisteddfod on the local rugby ground by arrangement with the Brynaman Welfare Committee. This committee, however, came under the control of the Coal Industry Social Welfare Organisation (CISWO) which opposed the application. Even within four months of the Eisteddfod, it was still not certain whether the permission initially given by the Brynaman Welfare Committee would not have to be withdrawn because of CISWO pressure. In desperation, the Urdd approached the Cwmaman Council to discover whether the Eisteddfod could be held on Cwmaman Park should CISWO persist in its opposition. The inhabitants of Brynaman felt they would be forever shamed if the Eisteddfod had to be moved to an outside venue, and they were almost unanimous in their indignation at CISWO's obstinacy. Finally, CISWO yielded, but only after imposing on the Urdd a legal contract in the most stringent and exacting terms. And when the Eisteddfod was over, a sum of £588 was claimed for alleged damage to the rugby ground. Finally, after a lengthy legal battle, it was proved that no permanent damage had been caused and that only a negligible sum was necessary to restore the field to its former condition. But what unnecessary bitterness and anxiety had been caused by this autocratic body.

It was mainly because of this possible contingency that the Eisteddfod Committee had sought to exceed the £2,000 advance fund that was requested of them. And as a result of this fund of £3,600, the highest total ever, a surplus of £3,400 was handed to the Urdd at the closing meeting. The Urdd officials felt it was a great privilege to be present at this meeting to express their gratitude to the people of Brynaman for their efforts and achievements, and particularly for their help and their tenacity in what had been an unnecessary crisis.

* * * *

For the second time, the Urdd Annual *Gŵyl Sir* was held at Corwen. But whereas the 1955 function had been a four-county effort, the 1963 event rested squarely on the shoulders of Merioneth. As always, however, there was no lack of willing workers. The committee elected Mathew O. Griffith as its Chairman, and once again the invincible Trefor O. Jones became Secretary. The Festival opened with a concert organised by the County Music Organiser, Arthur Hefin Jones, who conducted a choir of Penllyn and Edeyrnion pupils singing to a capacity audience in the Corwen Pavilion. The following evening, it was the turn of the county's Adrannau and Aelwydydd. Then, on the Saturday, the féte in the afternoon was followed by a *Noson Lawen* compéred by the Rev. Huw Jones. And for the third time that day, the pavilion was again packed for a *Twmpath Dawns* with Alice Williams as Caller. With so much activity, it was not surprising that a surplus of £978 was later handed to the Urdd Treasurer, F. Wynn Jones, himself a native of Llandrillo and proud to extol the virtues of Edeyrnion.

* * * *

Both domestic staff and camp leaders were loud in praise of the latest improvements at Llangrannog. Only seasoned campers like 'Bobi Gordon', who had known the primitive conditions at the first Llanuwchllyn camp in 1928, wondered whether the centre was not becoming too luxurious ! Everyone, however, approved of the new light-weight equipment which enabled small groups of campers, accompanied by a camp-leader, to set off carrying with them all the essential items for their overnight camping.

Electricity had not yet reached the Glan Llyn side of Penllyn, but there were indications that this would soon be remedied, and accordingly Glan Llyn was wired in anticipation. At the same time, a corrugated iron hut, attached to the mansion since the days of Sir Watkin, was demolished and replaced by a modern extension with its picture-windows overlooking the lake. This became the camp tuck-shop and social centre. The games-hut too was extended so that it could be used for folk-dancing and table-tennis ; kitchen equipment was improved ; several new boats were purchased, as well as other recreational equipment including a full-sized trampoline. In all, more than £5,000 was spent on improvements at Glan Llyn, towards which a grant was received from the Ministry of Education which, by then, had been re-named the Department of Education and Science.

Glan Llyn was used more extensively than ever and, during the Christmas vacation, more than a hundred young people attended a winter camp. The severe weather did nothing to curtail the activities or depress the enthusiasm of the members. Canoes moved bravely over the dark and icy waters of *Llyn Tegid* ; mountainwalking took place each day, and one group of enthusiasts shovelled away the snow on the slopes of Aran Benllyn so that they could pitch their tents for the night.

It was in similar conditions that a group of Urdd leaders from Flintshire brought forty primary school pupils to spend a weekend at Glan Llyn. Hitherto, the camp had been regarded as a centre for adolescents but this new departure was so successful that it became an annual event, with the full co-operation and financial support of the Flintshire Education Authority. The aim was to bring non-Welsh-speaking pupils into contact with the Welsh atmosphere of Penllyn and Glan Llyn. It would obviously not be possible to teach them more than a modicum of Welsh during a brief and full weekend, but something in the informal atmosphere gave them a new desire to learn the language and thus made the role of subsequent classroom teaching so much easier.

But in addition to the activities at Glan Llyn, there was still room for excursions further afield. Three mountain-walking expeditions were arranged in 1963—two to Snowdonia and the

Pumlumon range, while the third ventured into the Scottish Cairngorms. But perhaps the thrill of the year was the canoe-expedition during the Easter vacation along the Ardeche. Headed by Elwyn Huws, twenty-three young people set out from Glan Llyn, camping first at Arras and then on the banks of the Loire before unloading their canoes in the Ardeche Gorge. Here the wild waters with their whirlpools and cross-currents were very different from the rivers of Wales which seemed calm and serene by comparison. For those who struggled and triumphed, it was an unforgettable experience ; an adventure and an achievement. For the less experienced, there was another expedition down the Wye, following the river on its usually quiet but occasionally turbulent meandering from Glasbury to Hereford, and finally past Goodrich Castle and Tintern Abbey to Monmouth.

For some time, members of *Senedd yr Ifanc* had been pressing for the provision of a climbing-hut in Snowdonia. After the Executive Committee had agreed in principle, the members searched around and discovered a disused barn in Nant Gwynant which could be adapted to sleep 12-16 persons. A ten-year lease was obtained, and the cost of adaptation was met by contributions from some of the *Seneddau Sir* (County Youth Councils). Gradually, the interest grew and members found that *Sgubor Bwlch* was an excellent base for activities which varied from rock-climbing and mountain-walking to field studies and photography. It was obvious that there was need for small cells of this nature, where members planned and conducted their own activities, as well as for the larger units of Glan Llyn and Llangrannog.

While on the subject of recreational activities, it deserves mention that 203 Branches took part in the organised games tournaments of 1963, which included soccer, rugby, netball, table-tennis, darts and snooker; five counties held their own *mabolgampau* and the followers of the *Twmpath Dawns* were as numerous as ever. To relieve the pressure on the Department of Camps, Training and International Affairs, a new officer was appointed and designated Camps Organ-iser. He was J. Eric Williams, a trained teacher with specialist qualifications in Physical Education who had been Head of the P.E. Department at a residential secondary school in Liverpool.

* * * *

Since 1951, the Urdd Council had met annually at Pantyfedwen during the Christmas vacation. A severe snowstorm made it necessary to cancel the arrangements for 1962/63, and it was decided that future Council meetings would be held in October. At the Annual General Meeting that followed the Council meeting in October 1963, A. D. Lewis was elected Chairman of the Council to succeed Cassie Davies, with Aneurin Jenkins-Jones as Vice-Chairman. A. D. Lewis had already served as Vice-Chairman for six years as well as being Chairman of the Executive Committee. He was henceforth to act as Chairman of both bodies—'both sentences to run concurrently' as Tomos Bifan remarked in *Yr Aelwyd*! Fortunately, the Executive Committee elected Alun Creunant Davies, Headmaster of Llangeitho Primary School, as its Vice-Chairman, and in him A. D. Lewis found a loyal and able supporter.

On this occasion, the General Meeting complied with Cynfab Roberts' request that he be allowed to resign from the office of Treasurer, and it was with regret that he was released, after holding office for a difficult period of nine years. He had inherited a debt of nine-thousand pounds, and few would relish such an inheritance. Cynfab Roberts, however, in his loyalty to the Urdd, accepted the challenge, and it is a tribute to his astuteness and diligence that in nine years he had brought the Urdd safely out of acute financial difficulties. His place was taken by F. Wynn Jones, recently retired from a Ministry of Labour post, an ardent Welshman of wide cultural interests. Three new Vice-Presidents were elected—Cynfab Roberts, Dr. Emyr Wyn Jones of Liverpool and J. Clifford Thomas of London.

For two or three years, there had been a feeling among some Council members that there was a decline in the number of Aelwyd-ydd. A survey made in 1963, however, showed that, while it was inevitable in a voluntary organisation that there should be periodic ebb and flow due to changes in the availability of leaders, the previous three years had actually seen a slight increase in the number of Aelwydydd. In 1960/61, twenty-one new Aelwydydd had been formed, fourteen in 1961/62, and twenty-nine in 1962/63, making a total of sixty-four.

In his last report as Treasurer, Cynfab Roberts disclosed that the Company's annual expenditure was fast approaching the £70,000 mark. This was £25,000 more than had been the case five years earlier, an average annual increase of £5,000. Towards this total of £70,000, barely £12,000 was received in grants. In 1962/63, this left a total of £58,000 to be raised by the Urdd, and through some miracle, this had been achieved, even leaving a surplus of £279. But while rejoicing in this achievement, the Treasurer warned that the margin was extremely small, and with costs soaring at the current rate, one could not avoid a feeling of anxiety in forecasting the situation over the next five years. There was a limit to what a voluntary movement could achieve without placing undue emphasis on fund-raising at the expense of providing new and improved opportunities and programmes for the members. Grants received from education authorities, at both central and local levels, were totally inadequate. It was a case of paying lip-service to the voluntary organisations without granting them the financial support they needed and deserved.

The Treasurer's comments were felt to be amply justified. From a financial standpoint, the 1959 Albemarle Report was dead as a door-nail. It was obvious that the Urdd would have to struggle for its very existence, but struggle it would.

Glan Llyn claimed a good deal of time and attention during 1964. The Urdd had occupied the centre since 1949/50, first on an annual tenancy, and from 1959 on a twenty-one year lease. Shortly afterwards, it was announced by the Ministry of Agriculture that the entire Glan Llyn Estate was to be sold. This included a considerable number of farms and small-holdings, the camp centre leased to the Urdd, and the lake itself—*Llyn Tegid*. A local consortium was formed, and within three years, most of the tenants had been able to purchase their properties. In this way, the consortium not only safeguarded the rights of the tenants, but in so doing, it succeeded in perpetuating the Welsh character of the neighbourhood. *Llyn Tegid* became the property of the Merioneth County Council, and when Glan Llyn came to be sold in 1964, no-one was surprised that the Urdd should be given the first option. The Ministry was aware of the fact that the movement had spent more than £30,000 in improving the amenities of the centre, and bearing this in mind, Sir Ifan ab Owen Edwards was somewhat disappointed that £8,000 was being asked for the freehold. He realised, however, that Glan

Llyn had to be secured for the Urdd whatever the cost, and as the offer included the mansion itself, an adjacent house known as Glan Llyn Isaf, eight acres of land, jetties and boat-houses, and the right to forty-eight craft on the lake, it was too good an offer to be missed, and one that would probably never again come our way. The Founder decided to forget his disappointment and set himself the task of raising the necessary capital. At the time, Dr. Wyn Griffith was associated with the Pilgrim Trust, and with his support, Sir Ifan prepared an appeal for help from that Foundation. The result was a grant of £4,000, to which Sir Ifan himself generously added another £1,000 to make a total of £5,000. Within three months, the remaining £3,000 had been raised and the Urdd then owned one of the finest outdoor-pursuits centres in the country.

This shows how well Sir Ifan ab Owen Edwards had recovered from the seizure he suffered four years earlier. The possibility of purchasing Glan Llyn was more effective than any other form of therapy, and for two or three months, something of his old vigour returned, even though his physical strength had been impaired. And when the purchase had been completed, he was already campaigning for further improvements. His new development programme entailed a fresh expenditure of £10,000. This included re-designing the domestic block, widening and surfacing approach roads, clearing and surfacing a parking area, improving the sewerage system, and the purchase of equipment and other essentials. It was realised, of course, that some time would inevitably elapse before such a scheme would mature and this provided the much needed breathing-space in which to raise the Urdd's share of £5,000 in anticipation of a 50% grant from the Department of Education and Science. Meanwhile, the centre was continually gaining in popularity. During nine weeks of summer camps in 1964, nearly twelve-hundred young people in the 14-25 age-group had spent a week at Glan Llyn. Nor was its use confined to the summer months. Adrannau and Aelwydydd were booking more weekend periods, and schools and colleges were progressively discovering the centre's potential.

Partly because of the heavy commitments at Glan Llyn, improvements at Llangrannog were limited to what could be achieved by a small band of voluntary workers during the Easter vacation. The timber huts had now borne the brunt of westerly gales over a period of thirty years and were causing considerable concern, although the 2,161 campers in 1964 never spared the matter a moment's thought. Nevertheless, the Urdd could not ignore the fact that the lease on the land was due to expire in a few years' time, and that there was no guarantee that it would be renewed. Tentative enquiries were accordingly made regarding the possibility of purchasing two or three fields, but to no avail. It was obvious that the owner did not yet consider that the time was ripe.

*   *   *   *

It was in 1964 that Sir David James, the London-Welsh philanthropist, expressed a wish to present the Urdd with a special Eisteddfod trophy, and a spate of correspondence passed between him and Sir Ifan ab Owen Edwards. The Urdd already had the Royal Prize as its main Eisteddfod trophy, and it was difficult to see how another ' special ' trophy could be fitted into the pattern. Sir Ifan felt that it would be far better if Sir David James could forget the trophy and agree to help—as J. M. Howell did in the early days—by donating a substantial sum of money which the Urdd could use according to its discretion. Failing this, Sir Ifan and R. E. Griffith did their utmost to interest Sir David James in the rebuilding of the Llangrannog Camp. His one love, however, was the Eisteddfod, and he was not interested in a children's camp. Nor could he understand why the Urdd refused to offer prize-money to winning competitors. Even at that moment, he was preparing to make available an annual income to various Eisteddfodau within Wales to be allocated as prize-money in specific competitions, and these offers had been readily accepted. The Urdd, on the other hand, chose to reject his offer of prize-money, and was even reluctant to accept an Eisteddfod trophy, pleading instead the cause of a children's camp in a remote spot on the Cardiganshire coast ! It must have been an enigma to him, and he would doubtless have withdrawn his offer completely were it not for his personal respect for Sir Ifan ab Owen Edwards. And Sir Ifan was diplomat enough to know how to deal even with a personality so vastly different from himself.

Eventually, Sir David made an offer of a solid silver bowl valued at £2,000, to be known as *Cwpan Teulu Pantyfedwen*, which would be presented annually to the winning county along with the Royal Prize. There was reason to believe that the ' Pantyfedwen Family Bowl,' almost a yard in diameter, would be the largest in the world, and many felt it would be unsuitable for the Urdd Eisteddfod. With it, however, went a sum of £20,000 to be invested by the Catherine and Lady Grace James Foundation to provide an annual income of £1,000 which, in turn, the Urdd was required to invest so as to provide the winning County Committee with an annual income towards developing its activities. It was this that induced Sir Ifan ab Owen Edwards to accept the trophy, and with his usual promptitude, Sir David James arranged for the first £1,000 to reach the Urdd in time for its 1964 National Eisteddfod.

Even if it were not always possible to agree with Sir David James' ideas, one could not fail to admire him for his generosity to his native land. More than any other Welshman, he chose to share his wealth with his fellow-countrymen. Within a period of a few years, he had distributed a total of £2,000,000 to institutions and causes that he considered worthy of support, particularly bodies that fostered religious and cultural activities. Men of his benevolence are rare, and Wales is deeply indebted to him. What he would have valued most would be that his legacies should lead to the revitalisation of the religious and cultural life of his native country.

*   *   *   *

Throughout its thirty-five years' pilgrimage through Wales the Urdd National Eisteddfod did not reach Llŷn and Eifionydd in Caernarfonshire—until 1964. It is true that, on many occasions, the Urdd had cast an eye on the possibilities therein, but for some reason no-one seemed moved to offer the invitation. This, however, might be no more than a reflection of the unassuming character of the inhabitants, and the Chief Organiser decided to prod !

Porthmadog seemed to be the most likely venue and, unknown to anyone, R. E. Griffith and J. Cyril Hughes decided to call on some of the leading local councillors who they knew were sympathetic to the work of the Urdd. They found that no persuasion was necessary and that the Urban District Council and the people in general were likely to welcome the idea. Goronwy O. Roberts, M.P., was one of the speakers at a public meeting called to discuss the matter when it was enthusiastically decided to invite the Urdd Eisteddfod to Porthmadog in 1964.

With their Member of Parliament as Honorary President, a committee was formed with W. J. Hughes and William Rowland as Chairman and Vice-Chairman respectively, and with D. Keri Evans as Treasurer and R. D. Jones as Secretary. The first major event for which they were responsible was the Proclamation Festival which included a procession through the town led by the Penrhyndeudraeth Brass Band, a féte, a *Noson Lawen* and a *Twmpath Dawns*. This proved to be an effective means of giving publicity to the forthcoming Eisteddfod and a considerable impetus to the advance-fund.

By May 1964, all arrangements had been completed ahead of schedule. An advance-fund of £2,500 was requested, but the sum collected amounted to £3,795. Hospitality for 4,000 competitors was asked for, and many more places were offered. Involvement in the Eisteddfod was complete, and its success assured. The enthusiasm reached its climax with the announcement at the final session that the Royal Prize together with the Pantyfedwen Family Bowl and its accompanying gift of £1,000 had been comfortably won by the home-county with 350 points, well ahead of West Glamorgan which came second with 192 points. The Eisteddfod Presidents were chosen from amongst benefactors of the movement in various fields—Ivor Owen of Llanuwchllyn ; John Gwilym Jones of Groeslon ; Edward Rees, Principal of the Normal College, Bangor ; Dr. Elwyn Davies, Secretary for Education (Wales) ; and Gwyneth Evans, H.M.I.

The Crowning Ceremony was again in the competent hands of Jennie Eirian Davies, while Desmond Healy, Headmaster of *Ysgol Glan Clwyd*, Y Rhyl, who had himself been chaired at Maesteg in 1953, took charge of the Chairing Ceremony. There were fourteen contestants for the Crown, and the adjudicator, Glyn Evans, said he was greatly encouraged by the high standard. The Crown was won by Mary Hughes of Carmel, Caernarfon, with Emily Hughes of Caeathro and Eileen Wynne Williams of Botwnnog second and third respectively. Thus the first three places went to women competitors, and all three from Caernarfonshire.

The men, however, came into their own in the Chair competition. The adjudicator, R. E. Jones, predicted that Wales would hear a great deal more of the winning poet. He was twenty-two year old Geraint Lloyd Owen of Sarnau, Merioneth, recently appointed to a teaching post at Machynlleth. His brother, Gerallt, had won the same honour two years earlier at Rhuthun. Donald Evans, the Chaired bard of 1963, was declared second, while close on his heels came Geraint Eckley of Aberystwyth.

For several years, pop music had been clamouring for a place in the Eisteddfod programme. It had first crept into the *Noson Lawen* competition, and at Porthmadog, it was allowed to take another step forward. Instead of the usual Saturday evening concert, a *Twmpath Dawns* was held in the marquee, with a group pop-song competition as part of the programme. The marquee, with its many tent-poles was not ideal for a *Twmpath Dawns*, and the standard of the pop-song competition was mediocre. Experience, however, is the best teacher, and several valuable lessons were learnt from this innovation.

There were no two minds about the success of the Porthmadog Eisteddfod. And when, later, three representatives of the Urdd Council—A. D. Lewis, F. Wynn Jones and R. E. Griffith— attended the final meeting of the Executive Committee, they had no reservations in expressing their gratitude and their appreciation. In addition to the cultural and social success of the event, it was disclosed that, including the advance-fund, the total receipts amounted to £7,924, while costs had been kept to a minimal £3,846, an incredibly modest sum for a festival of such magnitude. The Treasurer proudly presented the Urdd with a cheque for £4,078, the highest surplus ever in the history of the Urdd Eisteddfod. R. E. Griffith must have felt justified in his initial prodding !

*   *   *   *

Ten years had elapsed since Cardiganshire had its last taste of the County Festival. There were, of course, many who recalled with pleasure the first Cilgwyn Festival in 1953, followed by the Tregaron Festival in 1954. Now, a decade later, there was a move to invite the festival to Llandysul. The Urdd was fortunate in having Edward Lewis of *Gwasg Gomer* as Chairman of the Committee, and he was ably supported by the Rev. J. Marles Thomas as Vice-Chairman, Hefin Williams of Pencader as Treasurer, and R. Alun

Evans and Alun T. Lewis as Honorary Secretaries. And from *Swyddfa'r Urdd*, J. Cyril Hughes placed all his experience at their disposal, while Evan Isaac, the County Organiser, added his intimate knowledge of the territory and its inhabitants.

The Festival, entitled *Gŵyl Glannau Teifi*, opened with a *Cymanfa Ganu* for Aelwydydd conducted by Edward Morgan of Llandysul, one of Cardiganshire's greatest benefactors of music in this century. Later in the week came the second *Cymanfa Ganu*, this time for Adrannau, conducted by D. Roland Morris, the County Music Organiser. Between these two sessions, there was an evening of one-act plays, when Aneurin Jenkins-Jones, as Vice-Chairman of the Urdd Council, took the opportunity of paying tribute to the pioneering work of the late Mary Lewis in the field of drama and choral-speaking.

Saturday's programme included a fête opened by Alun Williams of the BBC. Everything contributed to the festive atmosphere, from the laden stalls to the series of team contests in public-speaking, general knowledge and verse-making. The day ended with a *Noson Lawen* and *Twmpath Dawns*, while the Festival closed with a religious service for youth on the Sunday. The highlight, however, was '*Y Cwilt*', a feature-programme presenting episodes in the history and traditions of the Teifi valley. It was intended for the Friday evening only, but so great was the demand for tickets that two additional performances were staged during the following week.

In every respect, this was a memorable festival. No effort had been spared, and the people of Llandysul and the surrounding areas had been unstinted in their support and generosity. As a result, the 'Cardi', usually credited with being tight-fisted, was able to contribute to the Urdd a total of £1,955, seven-hundred pounds more than the surplus of any previous *Gŵyl Sir*, and even today, Llandysul still holds the record in this respect.

Gŵyl Glannau Teifi was not the only Urdd Festival in 1964, for it was also the turn of the biennial Folk-Song-and-Dance Festival. This was held at Aberafan, and no function could have received better support than the *Gŵyl Werin* was given by the Borough Council, by the Glamorgan Education Authority, and by the Governors, Headmaster and staff of the Sandfields Comprehensive School. Among the Honorary Officers were Alderman Llewellyn

Heycock, Col. Cennydd Traherne, John Morris, M.P., and Trevor Jenkins, Director of Education. The festival arrangements were entrusted to a committee headed by Gwynn Tudno Jones (Chairman), T. Glyn John (Vice-Chairman), Eleanor Davies (Secretary) and Owen Jones (Treasurer), aided as always by members of the Urdd staff.

Teams for the massed dancing were drawn from four South Wales counties, while the exhibition teams came from the Aberystwyth and Betws Aelwydydd, Llandyfri College, and the Pontardawe and Gwaun-Cae-Gurwen Secondary Schools. The guest dancers were the ' Orlyk ' Ukranian Dancers from Manchester. Their colourful costumes, the disciplined vitality of their dancing, and the exciting rhythm of their music captivated the audience, while they themselves were inspired by the Welsh atmosphere and gave what they judged to be their best performance ever, a standard that could only have been achieved through the utter dedication of every member. Equally appreciated was the superb clog-dancing of Owen Huw Roberts, while the folk-songs of Alwyn Samuel and Pat Shaw were interludes of pure joy.

The afternoon session was followed by a *Noson Lawen* and a *Twmpath Dawns*, and here one must mention the contribution of *Band y Gwerinwyr*. John Elfed Jones, Deputy Controller of the Rheidol Hydro-Electric Scheme, had established a flourishing Aelwyd at Llannon, Cardiganshire. At the close of a *Twmpath Dawns* in the Aelwyd, mention was made of the need for live music to replace dance records. The possibility of forming a band within the Aelwyd was considered, and within a very short time, instruments had been bought and an embryo band came into being. It was this group that the Urdd invited to provide music for the *Gŵyl Werin* massed dancing and the *Twmpath Dawns* at Aberafan. From then on, with the help and guidance of Llinos Thomas, a first-rate musician from Aberarth, the band settled down in earnest not only to master their instruments, but also to explore the possibilities of Welsh folk-tunes, gradually building up a wide *repertoire* of Welsh dance-music. Their second engagement was to provide music for the *Twmpath Dawns* in the County Festival at Llandysul. Following this, they were firmly established, and in West Wales, *Band y Gwerinwyr* became almost synonymous with a *Twmpath Dawns*. By

Christmas 1971, they had played for a thousand such functions and a Celebration *Twmpath* was held at Aberporth, when the Cardiganshire Aelwydydd and Young Farmers Clubs joined forces to pay tribute to the band for their service to folk-dancing, and especially for their part in ensuring that the *Twmpathau* had maintained their essential Welsh character.

To meet the demand for simple community dances for the use of Adrannau and Aelwydydd, and to serve as a handbook for new callers, a selection of community dances popularised by the *Twmpathau Dawns* was compiled by Swyddfa'r Urdd, and this, combined with the efforts of *Band y Gwerinwyr* and other dance bands, helped to promote and extend the interest in community dancing during the mid-sixties.

*   *   *   *

Among other 1964 events, the following merit a brief mention.

i.   Another canoe-camping expedition took place at Easter 1964 when 36 members, led by Elwyn Huws, ventured as far as Bordeaux in the South of France, and during the summer, Iolo ap Gwynn led a walking-expedition in Snowdonia, while Iolo Wyn Williams and his group made for the Republic of Ireland.

ii. The games tournaments were as popular as ever, with thirteen competitions attracting 270 Adrannau and Aelwydydd. On this occasion, it was *Aelwyd Trawsfynydd* that won the Pantyfedwen Soccer Cup.

iii. Five Urdd members from the Adran at *Ysgol Brynhyfryd*, Rhuthun, under the direction of R. Ieuan Griffith, won the Duke of Edinburgh's Gold Award in 1964. They were not the first Urdd members to gain this honour, but they were the first group from one Branch to win the Award simultaneously.

iv. A total of 19,958 volumes were sold by Urdd Branches in the 1964 Welsh Books Campaign, with *Ysgol Frondeg*, Pwllheli, again coming to the fore with a total sale of 2,076 to their credit.

v. *Aelwyd Caerdydd* hit the headlines during the National Eisteddfod of Wales at Swansea when the Aelwyd choir of more than a hundred young people in the 16-25 age-group, trained and conducted by Alun Guy, out-classed the established favourites and won the Chief Choral Competition. They also came second in both the Second Choral Competition and the Youth Choirs' Competition. This, despite the fact that—as Gwilym Roberts, the Aelwyd leader, bemoaned—the Urdd had no centre worthy of the movement in Wales' capital city.

vi. Cardiff was to be the home of the Urdd National Eisteddfod in 1965, and the Proclamation Festival in 1964 included a children's concert, a procession, a youth concert and an open-air *Cymanfa Ganu*. Altogether, a foretaste of things to come.

*　　*　　*　　*

1964 was not without its staff changes. The greatest loss was the departure of J. Cyril Hughes to take up a post with the BBC after eight years of outstanding service to the movement, especially in directing the Eisteddfod and the County Festival. To bridge the gap, John M. Hughes, Organiser for Anglesey and Caernarfonshire, who already had experience of the Eisteddfod at Porthmadog and the County Festival at Caernarfon, was appointed Eisteddfod and Festival Organiser. Ceredig Davies, Organiser for Denbighshire and Flintshire, was appointed Youth Officer for the LEA in Flintshire. His place as Urdd Organiser was taken by E. Alwyn Williams, then a teacher at Denbigh and one of the movement's most energetic voluntary workers.

Breconshire had been denied the service of a County Organiser for many years, and Urdd activities within the county depended almost entirely on voluntary efforts that were wholeheartedly supported by the Chief Education Officer, Deiniol Williams. Nevertheless, it was felt that given the aid of part-time organisers much more could be achieved, especially in connection with the post-school age-group. And in 1964, the Education Authority offered a grant of £250 towards an expenditure of £500 involved in the appointment of three part-time organisers. This was regarded

308

as a transitional arrangement until the Urdd could appoint a full-time Organiser.

When the Annual General Meeting was held at Pantyfedwen, Borth, in October 1964, F. Wynn Jones, in his first report as Treasurer, disclosed that the total expenditure for the year 1963-64 amounted to £72,000. Towards this sum, a total of £12,000 was received in grants, leaving £60,000 to be raised by the movement itself. It was almost incredible that this could have been achieved, leaving a margin of £702. It was not surprising, therefore, that the meeting continued in an optimistic mood. The officers felt they could face a new year with more confidence than had been possible for some time, and that they could bequeath to the future a movement anchored to the best in our past and yet forward-looking and progressive.

18

B Y 1965, the Welsh language issue had been brought into full focus and thereby assumed a new significance. Indeed, since the beginning of the decade, there were indications that both Parliament and people were concerned about the position of the language. The 1961 Census figures provided the first shock. They showed that the number of Welsh-speakers was no higher than 26% of the population, as compared with 28.9% in 1951, 36.8% in 1931 and 50% in 1901. This was a drastic reduction within a period of sixty years. Accordingly, the news was widely welcomed that the Council for Wales and Monmouthshire, under the chairmanship of Professor R. I. Aaron, was to devote itself to a study of the use made of the Welsh language in various spheres, and of ways and means of strengthening its position. The Council investigated to what extent the language was used in government and administration (including the law), in industry and commerce, in education, in the practice of religion, and in leisure activities. The report was presented to Parliament by the Minister for Welsh Affairs (Sir Keith Joseph) in November 1963, but like the majority of the Council's reports, it was shelved and forgotten. Such a comprehensive report, so intelligently and courageously conceived, should not have been ignored in this manner. It is regrettable that the new Labour Government, in 1964, did not grasp the recommendation which urged the establishment of a permanent body, scheduled to meet at least on a quarterly basis, and given responsibility for planning for the prosperity and well-being of the language. Had this step been taken in 1964, the story of the ensuing years might have been very different.

A few months prior to presenting the Council's report, the Minister for Welsh Affairs had announced his intention of setting up a committee under the chairmanship of Sir David Hughes Parry to clarify the legal status of the Welsh language and to consider whether any changes in the law were necessary. Following an enquiry lasting two years, a detailed report with specific recommendations was presented to the Secretary for Wales in October

1965. This advocated equal validity rather than bilingualism. The report and its recommendations were accepted by the Government, and this led to the passing of the Welsh Language Act through Parliament in 1967. It was generally agreed that the Hughes Parry Report had given the language greater dignity and a new legal status. Some felt, however, that it had not gone far enough and, moreover, that ' equal validity ' in itself was a vague principle.

By this time, *Cymdeithas yr Iaith Gymraeg* (The Welsh Language Society) had been in existence for three years and was already making itself heard. It, too, was concerned with the status of the language, and was already considering plans of campaign. It was a society of young people, mostly students and teachers, all enthusiastic, sincere, and intelligent. Many were members or former-members of the Urdd, and it is probable that the Urdd had helped to awaken in them an awareness of their Welsh heritage. They now felt, however, that the Urdd was not sufficiently militant to meet the urgency of the situation whereas the Welsh Language Society, on the other hand, advocated the kind of action they deemed essential. For this Society, the wheels of the constitutional machine turned far too slowly ; the Welsh language would be dead long before the committees of the ' establishment ' had ended their deliberations and before the Government had passed any laws that would be effective in halting the decline. For these young people, the only means of deliverance were those advocated by Saunders Lewis in 1962—a revolutionary movement prepared to challenge law and authority. They accepted his warning that this would mean contempt, suffering and sacrifice, and would lead to law-courts and even to prison.

From its inception, the Welsh Language Society was a protest movement ; this was its very essence. Nor did it have to look far to find matters about which to protest and campaign. Public reaction to their sit-ins was mixed, just as it had been in former times to the campaigns of the Suffragettes, the Rebecca Riots and the Tithe Wars. People resented being shaken out of their complacency even though they admitted that many of the rights which today are taken for granted were won by much the same methods. The Society stressed that their methods were to be non-violent ; nevertheless their actions created tensions, and were frequently condemned by those who overlooked the fact that the Society's aim was to draw attention to and campaign against injustice.

How was the Urdd to react to this development ? There was never any question regarding the Urdd's allegiance to the language, but what it had achieved had been done, not through protest or political action, but by providing the opportunity and encouragement that would create in its members an awareness of their Welshness and a pride in their heritage. In this, it had gained the support of people of diverse political opinions; it was an aim in which all could unite and all could help. It was admittedly sometimes a tight rope to walk, but the Urdd consistently sought to unite and to unify rather than to divide and separate. This was the method it had always adopted ; this was the policy it continued to pursue. But this did not mean that it should refrain from actively campaigning in matters relating to its own work. It was the Urdd, for example, that succeeded in 1965 in persuading the banks to produce bilingual cheques. The head offices of the major banks were obviously out of touch with what was happening in Wales, and the Urdd's request at first met with a flat refusal. Fortunately, the correspondence reached the hands of W. Emrys Evans, a high-ranking official in the headquarters of the Midland Bank in London. Not only did he persuade his own bank to accept the Urdd's first-ever bilingual cheque, but he successfully appealed to the other major banks and the clearing-house to do likewise. The Urdd followed this with an appeal to other Welsh bodies to make the same request. Eventually, the banks were persuaded to provide bilingual cheques for the general public as well, and it then depended on organisations and individual customers to insist on being allowed to make use of these facilities, however stubborn local branches might be. Quietly, without protest, but with unyielding tenacity, victory was won.

This, however, was a very minor struggle compared with the battle fought and lost in 1965. This was the year that saw the drowning of Cwm Tryweryn in Merioneth to provide water for Liverpool's growing population and developing industries. Despite the united efforts of the Welsh nation and the fact that the Members of Parliament for Welsh constituencies were united in opposing the Act that made the scheme possible, the battle was lost. Such oppressive action inevitably led to further tension within

Wales, and it needed no prophet to foresee that this tension would grow into open hostility and rebellion. It is hardly surprising that the younger generation, with their deep sense of loyalty to Wales and a genuine respect for their heritage, should now be convinced that the future of Wales could no longer be safeguarded through constitutional channels.

*   *   *   *

Arrangements were initiated by *Undeb y Cymry ar Wasgar* to celebrate the centenary, in 1965, of the establishment of the Welsh colony in Patagonia, and it was natural that the Urdd should be interested. During the ten years prior to 1939, the Urdd had close contacts with the leaders of Welsh life in Patagonia where the Urdd Branches were linked with the Welsh churches. But when contact was re-established after the war, it became apparent that the Argentinian Government was unsympathetic towards the existence of a Welsh colony. Furthermore, due to the influence of the schools, Spanish was already replacing Welsh as the language of the younger generation. Even Welsh Societies and Welsh churches were losing their grip, and gradually, the Urdd Branches deteriorated and were discontinued. Sir Ifan ab Owen Edwards was saddened to think that the brave little Welsh community was in danger of becoming an indistinguishable part of Spanish-speaking Argentina. Writing in 1945 to R. Bryn Williams, then of Rhuthun, he expressed his fears—

' I have thought a great deal about the Welsh community in Patagonia. I have tried hard to maintain contact with them, but I have failed. I cannot but conclude that they would now prefer to forget Wales and become fully integrated in Argentina, and that we in Wales can do no other but bid them farewell. How I wish that they would return to Wales, but I fear that this is no longer possible. And yet it is obvious that they would have greater freedom here in Britain than they are now allowed under the Argentinian flag. It is a sad story.'

Sir Ifan did not change his views during the following twenty years. Contrary to general opinion, he still maintained that it had been a mistake to emigrate in 1865 and it is possible that history has proved him right. Writing in *Yr Aelwyd* in April 1965, he traced the Urdd's connections with Patagonia and extended a warm

welcome to any young Welsh people who might visit Wales on the
occasion of the centenary celebrations—

> ' The doors of Llangrannog, Glan Llyn and Pantyfedwen
> would be wide-open to welcome them, and we would do every-
> thing in our power to help them. But we cannot conceal the fact
> that we would wish them to return to Wales and settle perm-
> anently in the 'old country'. The battle to save the soul and the
> language of Wales is to be fought here—not overseas. It was a
> tremendous loss to Wales when those valiant sons and daughters
> left on the *Mimosa* to seek their freedom on the distant prairies.
> Youth of Patagonia, come back to Wales for the very reason
> that led your ancestors to emigrate to Patagonia, to seek freedom
> to live as Welshmen and to speak the Welsh language. Come
> home to Wales, for it is only in Wales that opportunities can be
> found to keep alive the soul and the language of our nation.'

His was a voice in the wilderness, and it was lost in the excitement
of the celebrations. Representatives of various Welsh organisations,
and individuals who saw it as an opportunity to visit Patagonia,
were flown over for the centenary. The Urdd was represented by
Desmond Healy, Headmaster of *Ysgol Glan Clwyd*, Y Rhyl. He
returned convinced that it was still possible to strengthen existing
links and to forge new links between the people of Wales and their
kinsmen in this distant land.

Earlier in the year, a small group of young Patagonians came to
Wales on a brief visit. As part of their tour, they attended the
Urdd National Eisteddfod at Cardiff and spent some time at the
Urdd camps. The Argentinian Society in Wales presented the Urdd
National Eisteddfod with a trophy to be awarded annually to the
county that came second in aggregate marks.

The Urdd, naturally, rejoiced in being able to renew a measure of
contact with the Welsh community through the 1965 celebrations.
Nevertheless, it was obvious that the Patagonian youth were first and
foremost Argentinians. There was little hope that they would
return to settle in Wales as Sir Ifan would have liked. From time
to time, a few individuals have come, but they were rare exceptions.
For the majority, the Argentine was their home and Wales was
progressively becoming a foreign country. Sir Ifan may well have
been right when he said in 1945, ' We can do no other but bid them
farewell . . . It is a sad story'.

*   *   *   *

The Urdd National Eisteddfod had to wait thirty-five years before being invited to Cardiff. The opportunity came, however, in 1965, and the prime mover was Hywel D. Roberts, who was elected Chairman of the Executive Committee by virtue of his long association with the Urdd and his zealous support of all Welsh causes. His fellow-officers too were persons whose names were already familiar in Welsh life, and included W. R. Evans as Vice-Chairman, Keri Harris Hughes as Treasurer, and T. Gwynn Jones and Wynne Lloyd as Honorary Secretaries.

The Lord Mayor and the City Council gave the Eisteddfod their wholehearted support. This was no mere formality but resulted in a contribution of £5,000 towards the Eisteddfod Fund. It was also agreed that the Lord Mayor and the Director of Education should accept an invitation to become Honorary President and Vice-President respectively. But although the Eisteddfod was to be held at Cardiff, the whole of Glamorgan came into the picture and the Lord Lieutenant, Sir Cennydd Traherne, and Alderman Dr. Llewellyn Heycock, Chairman of the County Education Authority, became Patrons, while the Director of Education, Trevor Jenkins, joined R. E. Presswood as Honorary Vice-President. And as a gesture of its goodwill, the Glamorgan County Council contributed £1,000 towards the Eisteddfod Fund. The third Vice-President was Wynne Ll. Lloyd, and the invitation was as much a personal tribute to him as it was recognition of the continued support of the Department of Education and Science to the Urdd. These major contributions were followed by 500 guineas from TWW, and these early donations added up to more than £6,500. This was, of course, a source of encouragement to the Committee, but it might have been better had the big money arrived at a later date, since the news had the effect of creating a somewhat apathetic attitude to the committee's own fund-raising efforts. In fact, the total advance-fund raised was short of £9,500.

It was obvious that holding the Eisteddfod in a large city had many advantages. But it also had its disadvantages, and these too became apparent. In the first place, committee members were widely scattered throughout the city and at the same time committed to other Welsh activities. Furthermore, the Eisteddfod was only one of many events held in Cardiff during that week. Nevertheless, the arrangements were duly completed, and perhaps the greatest achievement was that of Mrs. R. M. Rosser and her committee, who succeeded in arranging home hospitality for four-thousand competitors.

The Eisteddfod was ideally sited in Sophia Gardens. An atmosphere of youthful excitement prevailed throughout, and adjudicators and visitors alike were impressed by the high standard of competition and the efficiency of the organisation. For the first time, the Arts, Crafts and Science Exhibition was held in a smaller marquee on the Eisteddfod ground, and it was opened by former Urdd member, Dewi Prys Thomas, Head of the Welsh School of Architecture. The Eisteddfod Presidents were Eirwen Humphreys, a native of Cardiff, who had given years of service to Wales as teacher and Urdd leader, and who had her own methods of inspiring pupils who were learning Welsh as a second-language ; Dr. Emyr Wyn Jones of Llansannan and Liverpool ; and the Rt. Hon. James Griffiths, Secretary of State for Wales, who had been a staunch supporter of the Urdd for more than thirty years.

There were eleven competitors for the Chair, offered for a collection of ten unpublished poems. It was won by Gerallt Lloyd Owen, a twenty-year old student who, three years earlier, had gained the honour at Rhuthun. Another anthology of his poems was placed second, while the third place went to Donald Evans, chaired bard of the 1963 Brynaman Eisteddfod. The Crown for the main prose competition was awarded to Robin Gwyndaf Jones from Llangwm in Denbighshire. Close on his heels were Enid R. Morgan (now of Aberystwyth) and W. Penri Jones (now of Tonypandy).

The Pantyfedwen Family Bowl for the winning county was exhibited in the Arts, Crafts and Science Exhibition and was the centre of attraction. ' Seeing is believing ' was the comment of one reporter who had previously been sceptical of its statistics ! No wonder the audience gasped when it was brought to the stage ! All, however, shared in the rejoicing of East Glamorgan when they were declared its winners, together with the £1,000 investment and a replica to be retained as a County trophy. They also received the Royal Prize which hitherto had been the sole trophy awarded to the winning county. West Glamorgan who were placed second became first winners of the Argentine Trophy, followed by Carmarthenshire, who were first winners of the Cardiff Aelwyd Cup.

When the time came to make a financial assessment, it was disclosed that the Eisteddfod receipts amounted to £13,350, expenses stood at £7,627, leaving a surplus of £5,828. All things considered, the officers and their committees could well feel proud of their achievement.

*   *   *   *

The 1965 *Gŵyl Sir* went to Flintshire, and one knew that some exciting highlights could be expected. The County Council and the Local Education Authority once more gave their wholehearted support. This was reflected in the choice of Dr. B. Haydn Williams as President, and Dr. Huw T. Edwards, Councillor Ethleen Williams-Thomas and J. Caradog Williams as Vice-Presidents. The Festival Committee elected Watcyn Jones as Chairman, Derwyn Roberts as Vice-Chairman, Mairwenna Williams as Secretary, and Howell Griffiths as Treasurer. In addition, the help and experience of the Urdd's Festival Organiser, John M. Hughes, and the movement's County Organiser, E. Alwyn Williams, were placed at the committee's disposal.

Flintshire seemed unchallenged in the art of producing a pageant. Many people still recalled the Urdd Pledge Pageant (*Pasiant yr Addunedau*) staged in 1958 and 1959, and looked forward eagerly to see what the 1965 festival would produce. *Pasiant y Diwydiannau* (Pageant of Industries), devised by Leslie Harries and Desmond Healy and produced by Elwyn Evans, certainly lived up to expectations. Four-hundred boys and girls drawn from fifteen schools participated, and this in itself was an indication of the scale of the project. Modern techniques were widely used, and of the many highlights, no one who witnessed the performance is likely to forget the three dances—*Dawns y Cysgodion* (Dance of the Shadows), *Dawns y Peiriannau* (The Machine Dance) and *Dawns y Sidanau* (Dance of Silks).

There was in addition the usual festival pattern—*Cymanfa Ganu*, one-act plays, a *Noson Lawen* and a *Twmpath Dawns*, not forgetting the fête organised by a committee headed by T. Wesley Hughes, E. M. Parry and Bethan Bebb. In opening the fête, Councillor Ethleen Williams-Thomas remarked—' This Festival is a symbol of the re-vitalisation of Welsh values that is today taking place in

Flintshire. We are in the process of re-establishing the Welsh character of the county, and the Urdd has a vital part to play in this enormous task.'

While preparations were in progress, one cloud weighed heavily on all concerned. This was the sudden death of the Festival President, Dr. B. Haydn Williams. Despite their loss, the Committee members were determined to win through as their President would have wished them to do. Ultimately, the Festival achieved two things—it brought the county's Welsh-speaking inhabitants closer together, and at the same time, it succeeded in creating a new interest in the non-Welsh-speaking section of the community. The importance of maintaining and extending this co-operation was emphasised during the final meeting of the Committee at which a total of £1,447 was received, with pride and gratitude, by A. D. Lewis, Chairman of the Urdd Council.

*   *   *   *

The Urdd's ' Skill and Venture Scheme ' was launched in 1965. It was a scheme of voluntary leisure-time activities not unlike the proficiency tests already operated by other youth organisations. Some Urdd members had already taken part in the Duke of Edinburgh's Award Scheme, but there was a feeling that a scheme more directly related to Wales might have a wider appeal. The ' Skill and Venture Scheme ' was, therefore, devised to cater for both boys and girls, and for both Welsh-speaking and non-Welsh-speaking members ranging from 9 to 21 years. There were four grades, each divided into sections, all of which offered a wide choice of challenging activities designed to test the skill, venture and perseverance of the individual.

Such a comprehensive scheme, presented as a cyclostyled schedule, was inclined to appear cumbersome and complicated, and apart from the First Grade, which could easily be integrated into the school curriculum or Adran programme, it has not met with the response that one would have wished. This is understandable, partly because of its bulky appearance and the fact that it demanded competent leadership to encourage and stimulate the interests of small groups or individuals. With the advent of more units meeting outside school-hours, and with greater emphasis on team-leadership, the ' Skill and Venture Scheme ' may perhaps be given the opportunity it needs and deserves.

* * * *

A random selection of 1965 news-flashes would include the following—

i. Dr. Huw T. Edwards, Chairman of the Wales Tourist Board, presented the Urdd with a certificate in recognition of the movement's contribution in bringing Wales to the notice of overseas countries, particularly through the Goodwill Message, the Inter-Celtic and International Conventions, the canoe-expeditions, and organised visits and exchanges.

ii. Three prominent Aelwydydd had been long enough in existence to claim the right to celebrate. The Chester Aelwyd could boast of 21 years of service to young Welsh people living in the city, while the Dolgellau and Llanelli Aelwydydd were both celebrating their Silver Jubilee.

iii. Former Urdd members continued to gain honours in the rugby world. Clive Rowlands was selected Captain of the Welsh team for the third consecutive season ; Dewi Bebb was adding to his stock of international caps, and Terry Price had won his first. In the Urdd's own games competitions, *Aelwyd Llanystumdwy* won the Pantyfedwen Soccer Cup.

iv. Sixty-five Branches sold 13,900 volumes in the Welsh Books Campaign, with *Ysgol Frondeg*, Pwllheli, in the lead for the ninth successive year, followed, on this occasion, by *Ysgol David Hughes*, Menai Bridge.

v. The summer camps had maintained their high level of popularity. A total of 2,325 attended camp at Llangrannog and 1,928 at Glan Llyn. There was a week's mountaineering in Snowdonia, and another in Skye. Two canoe expeditions were organised—one on the Wye, the other, for more advanced canoeists, in Spain.

vi.   *Senedd yr Ifanc* arranged for a group of twelve Aelwydydd members to spend three weeks in voluntary work-camps in West Germany.

vii. Urdd magazines came in for unexpected praise. Ronald L. Dice from Indiana, USA, wrote ' I have never seen such superb publications for youth, even in our big country.'

viii. *Aelwyd Aberporth* was proud to pay public tribute to the Rev. and Mrs. Tegryn Davies who were relinquishing the leadership of the Aelwyd after more than twenty-five years of dedicated service. The tributes included a *cywydd* by Dic Jones, who doubted whether he would have won the honours that had come his way had it not been for the help and encouragement of these two leaders.

*   *   *   *

Among staff changes, there were several new appointments. T. Prys Jones of Llangybi, with two years teaching experience, was appointed Organiser for Anglesey and Caernarfonshire. Merioneth and Montgomeryshire were given full-time Organisers in the re-organisation following the departure of Robin Hughes. Robert Gapper and Arfon O. Jones, both trained teachers, were given charge of Merioneth and Montgomeryshire respectively.

The Glamorgan Urdd County Committee had long been pressing for the appointment of a second full-time Organiser, and in 1965 Robin A. Davies, who had recently completed his course at the Cardiff College of Education, was appointed to take charge of East Glamorgan, allowing John R. Lane to concentrate on West Glamorgan. In another new appointment, Hywel Wyn Jones, a graduate of Swansea University College, became administrative assistant at Headquarters.

The departure of Elwyn Huws, Physical Recreation Organiser, was a sad blow. For more than six years, his pioneering work in developing Glan Llyn, in the training of leaders, in the planning of mountain-walking and canoe expeditions, had added new dimensions to the activities of the Centre, and enriched the experience of those privileged to take part. He left to take up an appointment under the Anglesey LEA as Warden of the Ourdoor-Pursuits

Centre at Beaumaris. He was replaced by J. Eric Williams, our Camps Organiser, who would henceforth be responsible for all aspects of Physical Recreation in addition to the administration of the Glan Llyn summer camps.

The outstanding feature of the Urdd Council meeting and Annual General Meeting held at Aberystwyth in October was the presence of a high percentage of young people. It was obvious that the young leaders of Adrannau and Aelwydydd were also eager and ready to play their part in the governing of the movement. This was a matter of great joy and satisfaction to Sir Ifan, for nothing pleased him more than seeing young people taking the reins.

In line with this development was the election of Prys Edwards as Joint-Honorary Secretary of the movement. He had completed his course at the Welsh School of Architecture in Cardiff and was now entering into partnership with a firm of architects in Aberystwyth. Sir Ifan was delighted ; this was a sphere in which he himself was greatly interested, and he was happy to think that one of his sons had taken to architecture with such enthusiasm. Moreover, Prys would now be in Aberystwyth and able to give the Urdd valuable service in many directions.

*   *   *   *

The Cardiff Aelwyd had been formed in 1958/59, and initially shared the amenities of *Tŷ'r Cymry* with other Welsh societies. As its membership increased, however, it became necessary to rent a larger building in Charles Street. This too proved inadequate, and another move was made to premises in West Grove, only to find, in 1965, that these were due for demolition. The guiding spirit behind the Aelwyd throughout this period was Gwilym Roberts, a dedicated and enthusiastic Cardiff teacher. He was torn between his desire to preserve the Welsh character of the Aelwyd and his sympathy with the *Dysgwyr* who had been members of Adrannau at school and were anxious to retain their contact with the Urdd by becoming members of the Aelwyd. The result was a compromise. They, for their part, agreed to learn Welsh if he could arrange for classes to be held in the Aelwyd. And thus, while continuing to act as voluntary leader ultimately responsible for the Aelwyd's activities, Gwilym Roberts took up the challenge.

One of the Aelwyd's most active groups was the mixed choir, first established by Owain Arwel Hughes, and on his departure, taken over by Alun Guy. The choir's success at the Swansea National Eisteddfod of Wales was followed by many other notable triumphs in later years. The Aelwyd could also boast of a choral-speaking group, a rugby team, and a folk-dance group which became one of the major groups pioneering in the interpretation of traditional Welsh dances. Members of the Aelwyd also played a prominent part in the summer camps at Llangrannog and Glan Llyn.

It was almost impossible to do justice to so much activity in cramped premises with a restricted time-table, and Gwilym Roberts seized every opportunity to convince Swyddfa'r Urdd that the movement should have a worthy home in Wales' capital city. ' Here,' he argued, ' we have three-hundred members meeting on four evenings a week in inadequate, rented premises. What we need is our own building, large enough to accommodate several groups simultaneously. Only thus can we do justice to the work we want to accomplish.' Eventually, the Director challenged him to find such a building and promised that he would help to find the money for its purchase.

Thus it was that in June 1966 the Urdd's Executive Committee was called to consider correspondence from the Cardiff Aelwyd. Through Don Richards, the City's Youth Officer, the Aelwyd Committee had learnt that premises in Conway Road, property of the English Methodist Church, were to be offered for sale. The Aelwyd considered the building suitable for conversion and asked Cwmni'r Urdd to purchase the premises on their behalf. Eventually, the freehold property was bought for £14,000, towards which grants of £9,375 were obtained.

The building was far from ideal as a youth centre, but the Aelwyd insisted on being allowed to move in immediately, and Gwilym Roberts felt like a king in his castle. Plans for adaptations and improvements were drawn up and it became evident that the project could mean an expenditure of £30,000. Such an outlay was, of course, dependent on a generous grant from the City's Education Authority and it was disappointing to learn that modified plans would have to be considered and the work phased over a period of years. Nevertheless, the first step had been taken in providing Urdd members in Cardiff with spacious freehold premises possessing endless possibilities. It was a bold step for a voluntary organisation, but an opportunity that could not be missed.

* * * *

At the Magazines Conference in March 1966, delegates paid generous tribute to *Cymraeg*, the second-language magazine initiated by Sir Ifan ab Owen Edwards eleven years earlier. Its monthly circulation had reached 25,000 copies, and Sir Ifan rightly gave credit for its success to Ivor Owen who had edited the magazine for ten years. In discussing the editor's main problem of providing for so wide an age-range—from primary school to adolescence—the Conference suggested that the Urdd should consider publishing two second-language magazines, one for primary schools and the other for secondary schools and adult evening classes. Such a dichotomy had already been carried out in the case of the first-language magazines with the addition of *Deryn* for infants/juniors and *Hamdden* for teenagers. If this development was deemed necessary to meet the needs of first-language readers, it followed that the same principle should be applied to second-language needs. In considering this request, the Executive Committee, although recognising the desirability of the proposed arrangement, had to pay due regard to its financial implications. The cost of producing two magazines would be almost double the cost of one while there was no guarantee that the combined sales of two magazines would equal the current circulation. Moreover, the Committee feared that an additional magazine would place an impossible burden on the shoulders of the editor and his assistant. In his enthusiasm, however, the editor belittled the extra work, and eventually the Committee agreed. In September 1966, *Cymraeg* was replaced by *Bore Da* and *Mynd*, and within three months, it was obvious that the change had been welcomed. The combined December sales totalled 26,600. Tributes to the new magazines were numerous, including praise by overseas visitors who had their own problems of bilingualism and came to see how Wales was facing the situation. One of these, in a letter of appreciation to the editor, said, ' We have searched everywhere for this kind of help, but we had to come to this corner of Wales and to a voluntary body to find it.'

The magazines were not the only contribution made by the Urdd to Welsh-learners. *Dysgwyr* had, of course, for many years been accepted at Llangrannog and Glan Llyn camps, and separate weeks allocated to them. During these weeks, English was the main medium of communication, and apart from a few simple phrases, no serious attempt was made to teach Welsh. In 1963/64, however, we became aware that a number of campers, mainly from Glamorgan, would welcome the opportunity of extending their knowledge of the language. Consequently, under the direction of Islwyn Jones, a lecturer at the Glamorgan College of Education, experiments in informal group-tuition were made in 1964 and 1965. Then, for an Easter course for school-leavers, we were persuaded by Alun Jones of Pontypridd Boys' Grammar School, to include Welsh Conversation in the choice of subjects. It was anticipated that a dozen members might opt for this group with Alun Jones himself acting as tutor. Instead of the anticipated dozen, we found that of the ninety-two members accepted for the course, forty-five had opted for Welsh Conversation, and hurried arrangements were made to find additional tutors. It was gratifying to find that not only were there pupils eager to grasp the opportunity, but also that there were teachers enthusiastic enough to sacrifice part of their vacation in order to give those pupils the practice that was not possible within the limitations of a school curriculum. The emphasis at the Llangrannog course was entirely on speaking the language, and due to the concentrated practice on the one hand, and the informal atmosphere on the other, the pupils found no difficulty in breaking through the language-barrier. At the end of the course, it was obvious that the Urdd had a hitherto undiscovered contribution to make in the task of teaching Welsh as a second-language.

In this new development two factors had coincided. Firstly, teachers in schools were experimenting successfully with new techniques of second-language teaching, with much greater emphasis on the spoken word. Secondly, there was a new interest in learning the language, especially amongst young people. This was linked with the heightened Welsh awareness largely generated by the urgency of the language situation ; it was reflected in the response to BBC and TWW Welsh-language lessons, in the increasing demand for adult evening classes, and in the growing support for Welsh-language courses at Coleg Harlech.

Within this general awakening, the Urdd had obviously something valuable to offer, and it would be wrong to withhold it. The 1965 Easter course was only the beginning. Gradually, the courses were extended to include various age-groups of pupils ranging from primary schools to sixth forms. Teaching techniques were crystallised and improved ; teaching material was revised, tested and graded ; the team of teachers gradually grew, and special courses were held to explain and demonstrate the methods and techniques to newcomers. Initially, planning and directing the courses was entrusted to Alun Jones of Pontypridd and Gwilym Roberts of Cardiff, but as the scheme developed, other experienced teachers were called in to assist.

To a certain extent, these language courses replaced ordinary camping-weeks, and there were some who feared that members who had neither the ability nor the desire to learn Welsh were being deprived of the thrill of camp-life which, after all, is not confined to language-courses. While striving to maintain a reasonable balance, such was the progressive demand, that, by 1972, a series of seven courses were held, in addition to an introductory course for college students and a supplementary course for experienced teachers. In this way, the Urdd is making a positive contribution to the teaching of Welsh by supplementing the work so admirably done by language teachers, restricted as they are by the limitations of curriculum and classroom. The Urdd provides the facilities, the organisation and the inspiration ; the scheme is operated by the teachers themselves, acting in a voluntary capacity and in close co-operation with the Urdd staff.

* * * *

From Cardiff in 1965, the Eisteddfod moved to Holyhead in 1966. Cledwyn Hughes, M.P., was elected Honorary President, and despite the demands of his office as Minister for Commonwealth Affairs, he usually succeeded in reaching Holyhead on a Friday evening in time for the monthly meeting of the Executive Committee ; and it was his wife who headed the team responsible for arranging free hospitality for competitors from afar. While preparations were in progress, the Eisteddfod lost one of its Vice-Presidents in the death of the Director of Education, D. Jones Davies.

It had been agreed from the start that the Eisteddfod should not be the monopoly of Holyhead ; it belonged to the whole of Anglesey, and the entire population rallied to its support, especially in matters of finance and hospitality. The Finance Committee had a target of £3,500, but the advance-fund exceeded £5,200. The choice of T. Hywel Thomas as Chairman was at once a tribute to his active support of the Urdd as club and camp leader, and an assurance that the Eisteddfod Committee would be given wise and enthusiastic leadership. Unfortunately, however, he was taken ill during the preparatory period, and much of the burden was borne by the Vice-Chairman, R. T. D. Williams, Deputy Clerk to the County Council. He had the full support of the Honorary Secretary, Elwyn Puw Jones, and the Treasurer, Trefor Lloyd Jones, both of whom were energetic and meticulous in their tasks. As usual, these officers knew they could rely on a strong body of committee members and an experienced team of Urdd staff.

One innovation at Holyhead was the Science Exhibition organised by the Science Sub-Committee led by Alwyn R. Owens, a University lecturer. It was designed partly to show how science and technology had affected the lives of the people of Anglesey, even in the more remote areas, and partly to demonstrate how the Welsh language could be adapted to the demands of complicated technical terminology.

Adjudicators and visitors alike commented on the high standard of competition. Their only complaint was that one could not leave the marquee for more than a few minutes without missing one of the many highlights ! Two of the Eisteddfod Presidents were television personalities—Owen Edwards, who for five years had introduced the BBC programme *Heddiw*, and Wyn Roberts, TWW Programme Director for Wales. Saturday's President was the Rt. Hon. Cledwyn Hughes who by then was Secretary of State for Wales. He referred to the Government's intention of introducing an Act of Parliament based on the Hughes Parry Report and designed to give equal validity to the Welsh language. He warned, however, that the language could not be saved by Acts of Parliament alone, but by creating the desire and the will to use it. ' Welsh must be the language of the home as well as of the college ; of industry and commerce as well as of culture and literature.' While he spoke, a murmur of disapproval could be heard amongst a section of the audience ; it seemed that members of *Cymdeithas yr Iaith Gymraeg* were present who felt that the Welsh Office was dragging its feet in matters of paramount importance to Wales. A little later, speaking as Guest of Honour, Sir Ifan ab Owen Edwards appealed to the young people to be tolerant for a little longer. ' Give the Welsh Office a chance, give Mr. Cledwyn Hughes and his team a year, and if they have not made a good job of it in a year's time, well, out they go, boys !' The tension was eased and the Eisteddfod proceeded in the usual even tenor.

The Chair, awarded for five poems each portraying a different character, was won by Peter Davies of Goginan, Cardiganshire, a student at Trinity College, Carmarthen. The adjudicator found in the work a measure of maturity that one would not have expected in a person under 25 years of age. The Master of Ceremonies was Aneurin Jenkins-Jones and it came as a surprise to him that he was to chair one of his own students. Next in merit was Geraint Lloyd Owen (chaired at Porthmadog in 1964), and the third was Ieuan Bryn Jones of *Ysgol Alun*, Mold.

John Gwilym Jones was the adjudicator in the main prose competition and, of the twenty competitors, the Crown was awarded to Mair Gibbard of Llannerchymedd. Master of Ceremonies was R. Alun Evans, but the real star of the show was the little lad who walked ceremoniously across the stage to present a replica of the crown to the winning prose-writer ! That little lad was Robin ab Emyr ap Cynan, who had obviously inherited his grandfather's flair for ceremony ! The second place went to Nan Lloyd Roberts of Dinbych, with John Glyn Ifans of *Ysgol David Hughes*, Menai Bridge, third.

The Holyhead Eisteddfod began in a heatwave and ended in a deluge. This, however, did nothing to impair the enthusiasm when it was announced that the home-county had won the Royal Prize and the Pantyfedwen Family Bowl, together with the £1,000 investment. Financially, the Eisteddfod was a notable success, and the balance of £5,051 was surpassed only by that of the Cardiff Eisteddfod, and even here the lead was no more than £776.

The Pembrokeshire *Gŵyl Sir* had at first promised to be no more than a modest event, but in the course of preparation it grew into a nine-day function. The activities were widely diversified, from the opening concert at Haverfordwest to the 'Vagabond Dance' at Crymych ; from a bonfire on Crug yr Hwch to a devotional service at Cilgerran. Other attractions included drama performances at St. David's, a *Cymanfa Ganu* at Dinas and Fishguard, and a féte at Crymych, opened by Desmond Healy of Rhyl, former teacher at the Preseli School. These varied activities were made possible by the tireless efforts of the organising committee, the energetic initiative of *Senedd y Sir* (Youth Council) and the generous support of the County Council and Education Committee. The Director of Education, Wynford Davies, was Honorary President, and his Assistant, J. Dewi Davies, was Chairman of the Executive Committee. When one adds the names of Glenys Lewis and Tonwen Davies as Joint Secretaries, and Geraint Davies of Fishguard as Treasurer, it is little wonder that the programme was comprehensive and the financial result secure. A balance of £1,738 was handed to the Urdd Officers, and they could well salute the team that had produced a festival that was as joyous as it was successful.

Nor was this the only festival of the year, for it was once again the turn of the biennial *Gŵyl Werin*. For the first time since it was initiated at Corwen in 1958, the Festival was to return to North Wales, this time to Wrexham. With D. T. Morgan as Chairman, R. J. Owen as Vice-Chairman, Mair E. Jones and Andrew R. Jones as Secretary and Treasurer respectively, the Committee set out to prove that they could equal the high standard achieved by the South Wales festivals—and they succeeded. The *Gŵyl Werin* was held at the Technical College and the massed dancers filled the stage with colour and movement. Exhibition teams were provided by the Dewi Sant and Bryn Offa Schools in Wrexham, Machynlleth Secondary School and the Pendorlan School, Colwyn Bay, together with the Mold and Penrhyndeudraeth Aelwydydd ; and interspersed with the dancing, came folk-songs by Olwen Lewis and clog-dancing by Owen Huw Roberts.

To add to the variety and to give the Welsh teams an opportunity of assessing their progress, we had invited Josef Baracsi's group of Hungarian Dancers from London. They had already distinguished themselves during visits to France, Italy and Portugal and had won awards at Llangollen in 1959 and Edinburgh in 1964. Their dances, like those of the Ukranian dancers at Aberafan in 1964, were less restrained than the Welsh dances, and allowed individual dancers to vie with one another in acrobatic skills.

Once more, the Festival had reached a high standard and the Officers could well feel proud of their achievement. But they would be the first to acknowledge that this would not have been possible without the support of the Borough and County Councils, the County Education Committee and the Principal and Governors of the Denbighshire Technical College, Wrexham.

*   *   *   *

Of other 1966 events, the following merit a brief mention.

i. It was not unusual during this period for Aelwydydd to celebrate the reaching of a special milestone, and in 1966, the Aelwydydd at Morriston and Llanfair Caereinion announced their twenty-first anniversary, while those at Cwmlline and Llanbrynmair celebrated their Silver Jubilee.

ii. For Rhuthun Branches, 1966 was a 'Triple Crown' year. Rhuthun Aelwyd won the Pantyfedwen Soccer Cup; fourteen members of the Adran at the Brynhyfryd School gained the Duke of Edinburgh's Gold Award and together with two Urdd staff members—J. Eric Williams and E. Alwyn Williams—the Brynhyfryd Adran leader, Ieuan Griffith, gained the Mountain Leadership Certificate at a Plas-y-Brenin Leaders' Course.

iii. In October 1966, the nation was shocked by the Aberfan disaster. The Pantglas Junior School was engulfed by the moving coal-tip and 116 children were among the 144 who lost their lives. Some Urdd leaders were among those who rushed to offer their help in the rescue operations. A few days later, Swyddfa'r Urdd opened a fund towards which Urdd Branches, not contributing through their schools, raised a total of £1,225 towards the Appeal Fund opened by the Mayor of Merthyr Tydfil.

66   Sir Ifan ab Owen Edwards at 70 years of age

iv. The summer camps were more crowded than ever. A total of 3,933 boys and girls spent a week at Llangrannog or Glan Llyn. This was made possible through improvements undertaken at Glan Llyn by a work-camp of 70 members during the Easter holiday.

*   *   *   *

During the course of the year, the Urdd had lost three of its former Vice-Presidents—Sir Emrys Evans, Lady Megan Lloyd George, M.P., and Dr. Griffith Evans of Caernarfon. The same year saw the death of W. Mitford Davies, the artist who had illustrated the Urdd magazines over a period of forty years.

It was now the end of a triennial period, and the Annual General Meeting at Aberystwyth in October was the occasion for the election of new Officers and Council members. There was no question of electing anyone other than Sir Ifan ab Owen and Lady Edwards as Presidents. Dr. Emyr Wyn Jones, Cynfab Roberts and J. Clifford Thomas joined the ranks of Ex-Vice-Presidents. In their place were elected Emlyn Hooson, M.P., the Rt. Hon. Cledwyn Hughes, M.P., and F. Wynn Jones. The latter's place as Treasurer was taken by J. Elfed Jones, Deputy Controller of the Rheidol Hydro-Electric Scheme, who was previously Chairman of the Camps Sub-Committee. The other Officers were re-elected for a further three years—A. D. Lewis (Chairman) ; Aneurin Jenkins-Jones (Vice-Chairman) ; Owen Edwards and Prys Edwards (Joint Honorary Secretaries) ; Prof. D. J. Llewelfryn Davies (Honorary Counsel) and T. Ivor Jones (Honorary Solicitor). A special tribute was paid to A. D. Lewis who, as Chairman of the Executive Committee, had shouldered the main burden since 1957, a period of nine years.

The Council decided to grant ' County ' status to the Urdd Cardiff administration. Although the new ' County ' would be composed of only two Districts, it already had more than a hundred Adrannau attached to schools, an Uwch-Adran and Aelwyd meeting in the new Urdd centre, as well as College Branches. In itself, it was a large enough administrative unit to merit ' County ' status and such devolution would be to the benefit of both Cardiff and East Glamorgan.

The item that evoked the greatest interest, however, was a memorandum from *Senedd yr Ifanc* expressing concern regarding the effectiveness of the Urdd's field work. The document pointed out that while central administration was exceptionally competent in the organisation of national and regional events, too little attention was paid to work on the local level and to the effectiveness of District and County administration. The Council agreed to undertake an enquiry and stressed that it should be as objective and searching as possible. Two Commissions were to be set up, the one investigating the day-to-day life and work of the movement and the other reviewing its organisation and government. The composition and exact terms-of-reference were left to the Executive Committee. The first Commission was formed without delay and made responsible for directing the enquiry and deciding on the method of collecting and collating relevant material. A special committee was set up in each county to collect data and supply the information required. Such an extensive and thorough investigation was a major task and meant that A. D. Lewis as Chairman, and myself as Secretary, were sentenced to almost four years' hard labour ! It was, however, cheerfully undertaken in the knowledge that it was essential that the movement should operate as effectively as possible and that any defects discovered should be speedily eradicated.

*   *   *   *

As a training centre, Glan Llyn had begun to feel the need for a full-time Principal (*Pennaeth*) and it was decided that a new appointment be made. The choice fell on Owain Owain, a scientist and Senior Lecturer at the Normal College, Bangor, who had wide cultural interests and strong convictions on Welsh affairs. Plans were later made to convert Glan Llyn Isaf into two flats for the use of the residential staff. In another appointment, Audrey Davies, who had recently completed her course at Swansea College of Education, became Public Relations Officer, a post which had remained vacant for some time. On the debit side, the Urdd lost the services of Eirlys Charles who had given four years of outstanding service as Organiser, first for Carmarthenshire and then for Pem-

brokeshire. She left to take up a teaching appointment in her old
school at Haverfordwest.

*   *   *   *

Improvements at Pantyfedwen during 1965/66 had cost in the
region of £8,000, including an extended central-heating system.
The question of a third camping centre was discussed, and premises
near Brecon were considered. They were, however, not entirely
suitable, and moreover, the capital required was not immediately
available. During the financial year, the cost of running the
movement had risen from £74,000 to £80,000. It was difficult to
believe that ten years earlier the annual expenditure had been only
£30,000. If this rate of increase continued into the seventies, the
Urdd could be faced with an annual outlay of £150,000, and the
thought, if not a nightmare, was a source of great concern.

One ray of sunshine, though not affecting the movement's
finances centrally, came from the Foundation set up by Sir David
James in memory of his father and brother. The Foundation was
intended mainly to enable local Eisteddfodau to offer better prize-
money. The Urdd, however, offered no monetary prizes, and it was
feared that its regional Eisteddfodau would not benefit. However,
the Foundation Secretary, Tom Jones, pointed out to Sir David
James that prize money was normally used to offset travelling
expenses, and that the organisers of the Urdd Eisteddfodau could
be helped to contribute towards competitors' travelling expenses.
Consequently, Sir David agreed to include the Urdd District and
County Eisteddfodau within the terms of the John and Rhys
Thomas James Foundation. The news was greatly welcomed by
Urdd leaders, and the annual contribution, though not large, has
proved a boon, especially to those Branches for whom the Eisteddfod
previously meant a serious drain on their financial resources.

With mixed feelings, the Urdd was at last able to hand over to
another body a scheme for which it had been responsible for almost
thirty years. This was the Welsh Books Campaign initiated in
1936/37. During this period, Urdd Branches had sold nearly half a
million Welsh volumes. But, as in other fields, the Urdd felt that its

part was to pioneer, to prove that a scheme was practicable and viable, and then to hand over to a body that possessed better facilities and greater resources. The Welsh Books Council had been in existence for four years. Alun Creunant Davies had been appointed Organiser and lost no time in adopting the Campaign as part of the Council's programme for promoting the sale of Welsh books. The Council's first Campaign came in 1966, and the Urdd was happy to see the seed it had sown in 1936/37 and carefully nurtured for thirty years, now transplanted into new ground and richer soil.

19

THERE were still many people who vividly recalled the 1935 Carmarthen Eisteddfod and hailed it as the greatest of pre-war Urdd Eisteddfodau. And when it became known that the Eisteddfod was to return to the town in 1967, many were prepared to predict that this would be the major Eisteddfod of the post-war period. In inviting the nation to Carmarthen, the Chairman of the Executive Committee, Aneurin Jenkins-Jones, referred in Welsh to the sequence of recent Eisteddfodau—' Caerdydd, Caergybi, Caerfyrddin : these three, and the greatest of these will be Caerfyrddin.' Nor did it seem an idle boast. Had not the Lord Rhys been patron of the Cardigan Eisteddfod in 1176 ? Was it not at the Carmarthen Eisteddfod of 1451 that Dafydd ap Edmwnd was awarded a trophy for his classification of those strict metres that could be deemed worthy of an *Awdl* ? And was not the Carmarthen Eisteddfod of 1819 renowned for the achievements of Iolo Morganwg and Gwallter Mechain ? Nor were the honours by any means confined to the town of Carmarthen ; for three or four centuries, the entire county had excelled in musical and bardic tradition. Based on such a past, the organisers were determined to plan a contemporary Eisteddfod designed to meet the mood of the sixties. Ernest Evans, who had been Joint Secretary of the 1935 Eisteddfod, was this time elected Vice-Chairman. With Dewi Thomas as Secretary, assisted by Eireen Thomas, and B. O. D. Griffiths as Treasurer, they were a team that could well make the success prediction come true.

The Proclamation Festival in 1966 raised £1,000 which brought the advance-fund to £3,000. The Chairman then declared that the target of £4,500 was far too low and should be raised to £7,000. With this as their new aim, the committee embarked on a *Tramp a Thwmp*—a sponsored walk followed by a *Twmpath Dawns*. Charity organisations in England had for some time been experimenting with sponsored walks, but the idea was relatively new to Wales. With meticulous organisation, the backing of the press, and the aid of the police and other services, the scheme was an unqualified success. A thousand boys and girls set out to walk ten miles to Carmarthen, converging on the town from various directions. And, as a result, another £2,000 was raised towards the new target of £7,000.

All other Eisteddfod arrangements were tackled with the same enthusiasm and it seemed as though everything contrived to reward the efforts of the workers. Carmarthen Park was an ideal site ; the weather was perfect ; the standards higher than ever. Opening the Arts, Crafts and Science Exhibition, the President, Iorwerth Howells, said—

> ' In this troubled world of ours, it is worth taking pains to discover the good and the beautiful, and thus to be able to distinguish between the true and the false, the genuine and the fake, the pure and the adulterated.'

The Eisteddfod Presidents were Hefina Thomas of Llanfair Caereinion who had given a life-time of voluntary service to the Urdd, Lady Parry-Williams, an early member of the movement, and Gwynfor Evans, President of *Plaid Cymru* and recently elected MP for Carmarthenshire. Both Lady Parry-Williams and Gwynfor Evans bemoaned the fact that the youth of Wales were forced to leave their country in search of employment. Gwynfor Evans went on to urge the young people to remain in Wales ' even if it means foregoing a successful career, wealth and fame. Our country needs us ; the fate of our nation must be decided by us, and by us alone.' The response of the audience to the patriotic appeal in each address reflected the new awakening already afoot, and it was obvious that a new national consciousness was already beginning to emerge. The Eisteddfod Chair was won by Peter Davies of Goginan, near Aberystwyth, who had chosen as his theme the Irish Rebellion of 1916. Second came Elan Closs Roberts, a student at Oxford, and the third was John Hywyn Edwards, a student at the Normal College, Bangor.

The Eisteddfod Crown offered for a dramatic composition was won by Dafydd Huw Williams of Llandegfan in Anglesey. Once again, R. Alun Evans was Master of Ceremony and he was delighted to crown one who not only had been a fellow-student at Bangor but was currently a colleague on the BBC staff. Despite this coincidence, the secret was well guarded, even from the BBC !

One interesting experiment was the introduction of ' Studio C ' where fringe activities in the modern idiom were presented by young people. There were professional performances by the Jane Phillips Caricature Theatre ; a feature-programme in word and mime by Carmarthen Trinity College students ; a preview of *Dan y Wenallt*, the new Welsh version of 'Under Milk Wood', and a programme of patriotic and satirical songs by Welsh pop singers. There was never any doubt about the success of this experiment and it is regrettable that later Eisteddfod Committees have not been able to achieve the same measure of success.

The one cloud over the Carmarthen Eisteddfod was the absence of Sir Ifan ab Owen Edwards. For some time, he had been in poor health, and old and young alike missed the inspiration he invariably provided. He would be the last, however, to allow his illness to mar in any way the record-breaking achievements of Carmarthen,— records in standards, in attendance, in organisation, and in the Welsh atmosphere of the festival. These combined to bring about a record financial success as well. The advance-fund had reached £10,861, the total receipts were £16,845 and the balance stood at £8,026— all record-breaking figures. The Chairman's claim that ' the greatest of these will be Carmarthen ' seemed to have been amply justified.

*   *   *   *

It was not the first time that an Urdd festival had been held in Breconshire, but this was the first occasion for the county to be the home of the *Gŵyl Sir*. Initially, we were a little apprehensive lest such an undertaking should prove too great a burden in a largely Anglicised county, but we found the Committee enthusiastic and the Adrannau ready for action, while the scheme also had the support of the Education Authority and of the Headmasters. The Honorary President was Alderman Tudor Watkins, M.P., and the Vice-Presidents were the Director of Education, Deiniol Williams, and Councillors David Lewis and John Hughes. With D. Gwenallt Rees as Chairman, Katie Williams as Treasurer, and Edgar Humphreys as Secretary, the directing team was complete.

The five sub-committees recruited into their ranks Welsh-speaking and non-Welsh-speaking supporters, some of whom had no previous connection with Urdd activities. Thus the two sections of the community worked harmoniously in a common cause. The activities were divided between Ystradgynlais and Brecon and included a pageant, an opera, and a *Cymanfa Ganu*, as well as athletic sports and folk-dancing. Opening the fête on the final day, Mary Middleton of the BBC explained that she was one of those who had learnt Welsh as a second-language, and that it was through the Urdd that she first realised that the language was the key to full participation in Welsh life. The week's activities had their own intrinsic value ; that financial considerations had not been forgotten was reflected in the balance of £1,476 later presented to the Urdd as tangible evidence of the achievement of the promoters.

* * * *

By 1967, the language issue provided regular headline reading. This was the year in which the Welsh Language Act became law. Despite a measure of disappointment regarding some of its aspects, objective observers found a marked change of climate when they compared the new Act with the 1536 Act of Union and the Blue Books of 1847. It was, however, one thing to place the Act on the Statute Book and quite another to ensure that the spirit of the Act was observed in public life, and in administrative and legal circles.

On the political front, there was a marked increase in national awareness. Gwynfor Evans had won his seat as Member of Parliament for Carmarthenshire and lost no opportunity in the House of Commons of raising matters of particular relevance to Wales. *Plaid Cymru* election campaigns were keenly fought and Council seats were won in the counties of Glamorgan, Monmouth, Pembroke, Carmarthen and Brecon. It was only by a narrow margin that the party lost the Parliamentary seat in the West Rhondda By-election in March 1967. It may well be that these successes spurred the other political parties to pay more attention to Welsh affairs than they had done hitherto. It may also be true that some within those parties who genuinely had the welfare of Wales at heart were not always given credit for their efforts. In our enthusiasm, we sometimes forget that the complete vision is not given to one person or one party, and that Wales needs the co-operation of all its people.

67   Pony-trekking at Llangrannog Camp

68   The new boat-house at Glan Llyn, 1972

69   A. D. Lewis   70   Alun Creunant Davies

71   At the Urdd Council meeting, October 1969

Despite its successes, *Plaid Cymru* was not without its problems. Perhaps the greatest of these was the emergence of the Free Wales Army, a small group who proclaimed their intention of gaining freedom for Wales by violent and revolutionary methods. There was, of course, no connection between the handful of Free Wales Army members and *Plaid Cymru*, but since they both aimed at political independence, the uninitiated were inclined to assume a link and to tar both movements with the same brush. This, naturally, was detrimental to a political party that had respect for political standards and constitutional means, and in an attempt to dissociate itself from the rebel group, *Plaid Cymru* decided to expel from its ranks members of the Free Wales Army as well as members of an equally vague group—The Patriotic Front.

Nor were the activities of the Welsh Language Society always conducive to *Plaid Cymru*'s progress. It was natural that the party should sympathise with the objects of the Society, but their direct methods were often a source of embarrassment to *Plaid Cymru* leaders whose aim was to win votes, which meant gaining support by persuasion. And if the activities of the Society meant that people became estranged from the national cause, it made the progress of *Plaid Cymru* more difficult and even endangered the ground already won, especially among the non-Welsh-speaking section of the community.

Cymdeithas yr Iaith, on the other hand, had nothing to lose by its protest campaigns. Indeed, the Society's efforts during its first five years had brought a measure of success. In mid-1966, official forms began to appear in Welsh and gradually the number increased until the Welsh Office felt the need for a panel of linguists and legal experts to translate dozens of monolingual English forms and certificates. This battle was largely won before the end of the decade, but it is still debatable whether full use is made by the Welsh public of the facilities provided. This is partly due to the fact that people have been conditioned into accepting and completing English versions, but it is also true that, even when certain forms are available in Welsh, they are deliberately neither offered nor displayed, and only the most ardent will take the trouble of returning the English form and demanding a Welsh or bilingual version.

The Society's next campaign was aimed at securing bilingual road-signs. In addition to demonstrations, the Society constitutionally appealed to the Government through the Welsh Office, and to Local Authorities. The response was agonisingly slow. Official policy seemed to be minimum concessions belatedly granted. It became obvious that the apathy of authorities and the determination of the Society could lead to confrontation that might have undesirable results.

What effect did all this have on the Urdd ? A national awakening was happening in a generation that had largely grown up through the Urdd, and in the case of many, it was the Urdd that had aroused in them their first sense of pride in their Welsh heritage. Some of these chose to devote themselves to the activities of *Cymdeithas yr Iaith*. On the other hand, there were many active Urdd members who felt they could express their loyalty to Wales through the usual channels and who did not feel they could align themselves with the political activities of the Welsh Language Society. For them, it was more important to work continuously with Adrannau or Aelwydydd, in language classes, in camps and courses. There was room for both groups and both methods, but the situation was bound to cause some tension and division of loyalties.

* * * *

There were other significant developments in the Welsh scene during 1967. St. David's Day saw the opening of the new BBC centre at Llandâf. TWW was soon to be replaced by Harlech Television. A new movement—*Merched y Wawr*—was formed when a group of women broke away from the National Federation of Women's Institutes following an argument over the status of the Welsh language in the activities of that movement. Other Welsh movements that came to the fore were *Undeb y Gymraeg Fyw* led by John L. Williams of Llanfairpwll ; *Pwyllgor Cydenwadol yr Iaith Gymraeg* under the presidency of the Rev. Dr. E. Lewis Evans of Pontarddulais ; the Glyndŵr Foundation, established by Trefor Morgan of Ystradgynlais, partly to set up and maintain two-hundred Welsh Nursery Schools; and UCAC under the presidency of Dafydd Kirkman of Dolgellau.

* * * *

339

For Sir Ifan ab Owen Edwards, 1967 was a depressing year. He
was taken ill in May and was hardly aware that the Carmarthen
National Eisteddfod had been held. He had been invited to preside
at the National Eisteddfod of Wales at Bala, but was unable to
attend, and his message was delivered by Lady Edwards. It was
natural that it should contain some reference to nearby Llanuwchllyn—

> ' I remember my father,' he said, ' sixty years ago, pointing to
> the old Llanuwchllyn School—the school of Sir Watkin and the
> "Welsh Not"—and saying that what had given him greatest
> satisfaction was to be able to close that school and re-open it
> again 'under new management'.   Today Llanuwchllyn is a
> natural Welsh school.   And if closing Sir Watkin's old school
> gave my father so much satisfaction, I felt a similar delight in
> re-opening Sir Watkin's mansion, Glan Llyn, as a permanent
> centre for the youth of Wales.'

Shortly afterwards, Sir Ifan was moved to Llandough Hospital.
Once more, there was cause for anxiety, and at one period it was
doubtful whether he would recover.   But once again his spirit
triumphed, and the doctors were amazed at his determination to
live.   And once the corner was turned, there was no holding him
back. Not only did he want to know of everything that was happening in the Urdd, but he was interested in all that went on around
him.   He was missed from his bed one day to be discovered in the
hospital kitchen discussing the latest equipment and making notes
of those items he felt the Urdd camps should possess !
Those who knew Sir Ifan knew of his sense of humour and his
fondness of leg-pulling.   While at Llandough Hospital, he shared a
ward with a person who had a habit of praying aloud so that Sir
Ifan was never sure whether his fellow-patient was talking to him or
to the Almighty.   One day, Sir Ifan turned to him and said, ' Look
here, my friend, before you start praying, you should say ' Trunk
Call ', and when you want to talk to me, say ' Local Call ' !'

*   *   *   *

J. Eric Williams was already Physical Recreation Organiser and
it was natural that he should be invited to take over as Principal
Officer of Glan Llyn when Owain Owain left to take up a teaching

post in 1967. Glan Llyn, however, had to be closed during the winter months to allow for building work. This was completed at a cost of £8,000, towards which a DES grant of 50% was received. Even so, the Urdd was hard pressed to find the required balance.

*　　　*　　　*　　　*

When the Pantglas School at Aberfan was destroyed by the moving coal-tip in October 1966, the Urdd had offered to provide a week's holiday for those children who, though they had escaped with their lives, were still scarred by the memory of the tragedy. The offer was taken up during the summer of 1967, and at the beginning of September, 64 children in the 7-11 age-group together with four mothers and two teachers arrived at Llangrannog to be joined by a team of Urdd leaders and staff. They were days of carefree re-creation in new surroundings followed by nights of untroubled sleep. It was the first time some of the children had laughed for almost a year. The Urdd leaders deemed it a special privilege, and no thanks were needed. The people of Aberfan, however, insisted on expressing their gratitude, and before they left Llangrannog, a £400 trampoline was presented to the camp on behalf of the people of Aberfan.

*　　　*　　　*　　　*

There were, as usual, a number of staff changes in 1967. Some, like Arfon O. Jones, Robin A. Davies and Hywel W. Jones, had been with us for no more than two years, but each had contributed something of value to the movement. Marian Rees had served as assistant magazines editor for four years and left a gap that would not easily be filled. She had volunteered for work with the VSO and had been allocated for service in the Fiji Islands. Her place was taken by Megan Tudur, a graduate and an experienced teacher. Other new appointments included Delyth Rees, a graduate of Swansea who took over the administration of training schemes and became Secretary to the International Affairs Committee. John Japheth of Pwllheli, another experienced teacher, was appointed Assistant Eisteddfod and Festival Organiser.

*　　　*　　　*　　　*

It was a matter of great rejoicing that Sir Ifan ab Owen Edwards had recovered sufficiently to attend the Annual General Meeting at Aberystwyth in October. At this meeting, the Treasurer reported that the company's turnover for 1966/67 amounted to £90,000, towards which no more than £15,000 was received in total grants. The death of three Vice-Presidents was recorded—Dr. William George of Cricieth who died in his 102nd year, Sir David James, the Welsh philanthropist, and the Rev. Dr. E. Tegla Davies. Three Urdd supporters lost in the prime of life were the Rev. Dewi Jones of Llangefni, the Rev. Walter P. John of London, and T. J. Jeffreys Jones, Warden of Coleg Harlech. Wales was the poorer for their passing.

*　　*　　*　　*

Those who had witnessed the vicissitudes of the Llangrannog Camp since it was first opened in 1932 heaved a sigh of relief when Cefn Cwrt Farm was finally bought by the Urdd in 1968. The annual tenancy basis had given way to a twenty-one year lease in 1938. This made the camp-field together with certain rights of way secure until 1959. Then a further fourteen-year lease was granted, but without giving much hope that an extension beyond 1973 would be considered. It was natural, therefore, that by the mid sixties the Urdd should view the situation with concern if not apprehension.

After thirty-five years, the camp buildings were rapidly deteriorating, and indeed the entire campus needed to be designed and constructed anew. But the possibility that the site might not be available after 1973 meant that any such expenditure could not even be considered. Upon approaching the owner, R. E. Griffith was told that the lease would not be further renewed. Nor would the owner consider selling the camp-field together with sufficient adjacent land to allow for growth and development. More in jest than in earnest, R. E. Griffith said that the only alternative was for the Urdd to buy the entire farm. The owner replied that this was something he was prepared to discuss. No price was named and no offer made, but at least the matter was now open to negotiation. The Executive Committee gave the Director the authority to negotiate up to £15,000, and over and above that figure to use his discretion. The freehold property, consisting of 160 acres, a large farmhouse and numerous outbuildings was finally bought for £18,000. Sir Ifan was, of course, delighted. The Urdd already owned Glan Llyn as an outdoor-pursuits centre for its older members and now Llangrannog was secured for generations of younger members. As in the case of Glan Llyn, the Urdd did not seek grant-aid towards the purchase price. It was as though Welsh land had a sacred quality and had, therefore, to be paid for from the Urdd's own investments. A grant towards reconstruction costs would be an entirely different matter.

It was now possible to dream of the 'new Llangrannog'. It could still be a camp-centre for younger members during the summer months while becoming a study and recreation centre during the remainder of the year. The farm too could become a basis for ecological and environmental studies. The first step, however, was for the campus to be professionally planned and this was entrusted to our architect, Prys Edwards. One realised, of course, that it would take several years before the 'new Llangrannog' would become a reality, but at least there *was* a future. In the meantime, expert guidance was sought regarding the use to be made of the farm land, and steps were taken to implement those plans.

*   *   *   *

Llanrwst in the Conwy Valley would be an ideal venue for the Urdd National Eisteddfod but for one fact. The annual *Dyffryn Conwy* Eisteddfod was of long standing and the tradition was zealously guarded. Urdd supporters in the area were also pillars of this Eisteddfod, and the organisation of two major events within the same period would jeopardise the success of both. Thus, it seemed that Llanrwst could not be host to the Urdd Eisteddfod, at least in the foreseeable future. But tentative enquiries revealed that the *Dyffryn Conwy* Eisteddfod officials were most sympathetic and the Committee readily agreed to lay aside their own event for one year and to give all possible support to the Urdd National Eisteddfod.

Llanrwst and the Conwy Valley had their own claims to fame, their own gallery of famous men. The three persons chiefly responsible for translating the Bible into Welsh had connections with the district—Bishop William Morgan of Wybrnant, Bishop Richard Davies, a native of Conwy, and William Salesbury who had lived at Plas Isa, Llanrwst. *Llywelyn Fawr* (Llywelyn the Great) was born in Dolwyddelan Castle and he and his wife, Siwan, worshipped at Llanrhychwyn Church. Llywelyn himself later found sanctuary at Aberconwy and at Maenan Abbey. Nearer our time, there were famous names like Ieuan Glan Geirionnydd, John Jones Tal-y-Sarn, John Evans Eglwysbach, Robert Roberts *y Sgolor Mawr* (The Great Scholar), John Lloyd Jones and J. Lloyd Williams. It was to this district, rich in past glory, that the Urdd Eisteddfod was invited in 1968.

Robert Jones, Headmaster of a Llanrwst school, was shortly to retire and this made him an even more obvious choice to lead the team of officials that included William Thomas as Vice-Chairman, T. Vaughan Jones as Treasurer, and Arthur Vaughan Williams as Secretary. Together with their numerous colleagues, they kept the wheels moving smoothly and efficiently, and gave us one of the happiest of Urdd Eisteddfodau. They did not attempt to emulate or to vie with anyone else; they knew what they could achieve, and they set out to accomplish it with dignity and pride.

Sir Ifan ab Owen Edwards was given a rousing welcome when he arrived at the Eisteddfod with Lady Edwards. It was good to see him back in public life after his illness the previous year. Robert Jones had been elected President of Thursday's session, not as Chairman of the Executive Committee, but in recognition of a life-time of service to the Urdd, to his own neighbourhood and to Wales. The other Presidents were Alun Creunant Davies of Aberystwyth and the Rev. E. Gwyndaf Evans, then Archdruid of the Gorsedd of Bards. In his address, ' Gwyndaf ' spoke of the debt the National Eisteddfod of Wales owed to the Urdd Eisteddfod—

> ' It is the Urdd that provides the National Eisteddfod with generation after generation of competitors, adjudicators and compéres. That Eisteddfod would today be immeasurably poorer were it not for the Urdd, and it is only right that we should publicly acknowledge our debt.'

The Arts, Crafts and Science Exhibition was opened by the Director of Education, T. Glyn Davies. The Rt. Hon. George Thomas, M.P., the new Secretary of State for Wales, was present at the Eisteddfod and gave a brief address in Welsh.

Yn Ieuenctid y Dydd (When the Day is Young) was the subject set for the Chair competition and it drew a record of twenty-four entries. A poem in memory of the children of Aberfan won the Chair for John Hywyn Edwards, a student at the Normal College, Bangor. The Crown was offered for a story based on a series of letters. There were eleven entries, and the winning competitor had based his story on imaginary letters that had passed between two monks— Father John, who had set himself the task of rebuilding the Priory on Tudwal Island as penance for a quarrel, and Father Andrew in Dublin who urged him to return to the Fraternity. The author was John Clifford Jones, another Normal College student and a close friend of John Hywyn. Little did Rhiannon Davies-Jones, a lecturer at the College, think that she was awarding the Crown to one of her own students. Richard Morris Jones of Cardiff was placed second, and equal third, in what had proved an excellent competition, were Eiflyn Roberts of Conwy and Nan Lloyd Roberts of Dinbych.

It is fairly commonplace for the county acting host to the Eisteddfod to win the final laurels. This is simply because, in their enthusiasm, they usually make a greater effort than their opponents. No-one was unduly surprised, therefore, when it was announced that Denbighshire had won the Royal Prize, the Pantyfedwen Trophy and the £1,000 investment. Nor was the honour gained by a narrow margin, for they had scored a total of 330 points as opposed to their nearest rivals, Carmarthenshire, with a score of 195, and Flintshire with a total of 190. Like that of Carmarthen the previous year, the Llanrwst Eisteddfod had attracted enthusiastic audiences, and the financial surplus of £6,469—excelled only by Carmarthen— was ample proof of the support it had received. Llanrwst had scored a great triumph.

* * * *

From its modest beginnings at Glan Llyn ten years earlier, the Welsh pop-song had gathered momentum as light entertainment in local halls throughout the country and had found its way into radio and television programmes. The idea that the Urdd should embark on a national pop-festival came from the Chairman and Secretary of the 1969 Eisteddfod Committee—Peter Hughes Griffiths and

John Garnon of Aberystwyth. Under the title *Pinaclau Pop*, it was held in the Pantyfedwen Pavilion at Pontrhydfendigaid, and despite the fact that the building could seat two-and-a-half thousand, all tickets were sold well in advance. It had been anticipated that the audience would be mainly young people, but to everyone's surprise, the middle-aged and the elderly were almost as numerous and equally enthusiastic. The inimitable Ryan Davies acted as compére, and supporting him were Dafydd Iwan, Edward, Mari Griffith, Meinir Lloyd, Heather Jones, Helen Wyn, Huw Jones, *Tony ac Aloma, Aled a Reg, Y Cwiltiaid, Y Diliau, Y Derwyddon, Y Pelydrau* and *Hogiau Llandegai*. Where else could such a galaxy of talent be found? It is little wonder that the three-hour session seemed far too short. Furthermore, it had proved to be a financial success, and with all expenses paid, it added £800 to the advance-fund being raised for the 1969 Aberystwyth Eisteddfod.

West Glamorgan became host to two Urdd Festivals in 1968— the *Gŵyl Sir* and the *Gŵyl Werin*. The original intention was to conserve effort by merging the two under the control of one executive committee. But when it was decided that the County Festival would be based on the Cwm Tawe and Abertawe Districts whereas the *Gŵyl Werin* demanded the facilities of the Gwaun-cae-gurwen Welfare Hall, the two festivals began to operate independently. The County Festival, spearheaded by the Rev. T. Burgess Jones, included concerts by primary and secondary school Branches, a *Cymanfa Ganu*, and on the final day, a féte followed by a concert at Pontardawe given by the choirs of *Aelwyd Caerdydd* and *Aelwyd Treforys*. Eventually, a surplus of £1,405 was presented to the Urdd following a memorable festival.

The *Gŵyl Werin* Executive Committee was headed by William Samuel as Chairman, with Handel Thomas and Margaret Roberts as Treasurer and Secretary respectively. At the time, Gwaun-cae-gurwen Hall was rarely used except for cinema and bingo sessions and needed cleaning and redecorating before the festival. These tasks were undertaken voluntarily by committee members and were performed with the same dedication as was shown in all the other aspects of the preparations.

The guest dancers on this occasion were a group of young Yugoslavs from Cardiff, and the ' Dungeer Mummers ' from

Wexford, Ireland, who had won awards at Llangollen. Nor were
the Welsh dancers eclipsed in any way by their excellent performance. The afternoon session was followed by a *Noson Lawen* and
later by a *Twmpath Dawns* in true Urdd tradition. By its very nature,
the *Gŵyl Werin* is not expected to be a viable financial proposition
and on this occasion it would not have been possible without the
support of the Glamorgan Education Authority and the local
Councils. The modest balance of £484 later presented to the Urdd
in no way reflected the efforts of the committee, the generosity of
the artistes who received no more than a nominal contribution
towards their travelling expenses, or the support of the entire
neighbourhood. It is a festival recalled with much pleasure and
satisfaction.

*   *   *   *

Other 1968 news-flashes included the following :

i.   The Annual Goodwill Service was broadcast from Llandysul
     on the Sunday prior to Goodwill Day, May 18, and arranged
     by the Rev. John G. E. Watkin and his wife, Cathryn Watkin.

ii. A total of 168 teams had participated in the Urdd games
     contests during the 1967/68 session and the finals of the
     nine competitions were centred on Glan Llyn and Bala.

iii. For the third time, the Urdd welcomed the Bielefeld Youth
     Choir from Germany. Still under the same conductor,
     Friedrich Feldmann, the choir enjoyed hospitality at
     Morriston and Newcastle Emlyn and gave concerts at these
     two centres and at Maesteg, Tenby, Carmarthen and
     Lampeter.

iv. A highly successful festival was held at Aberystwyth to
     herald the 1969 Urdd National Eisteddfod. The proclam-
     ation ceremony was part of a feature-programme, and the
     week's events also included a carnival, a féte, a sacred
     concert, a *Noson Lawen* and a *Twmpath Dawns*.

v.   In co-operation with the Rhondda Youth Action and
     Community Service Volunteers, groups of Urdd members,
     led by Aled Wyn Jones of Cardiff, took part in a series of

work-camps in the Rhondda, redecorating the homes of the elderly, and clearing industrial waste to make room for an adventure playground for children.

*   *   *   *

It was realised that four or five years would not be too long a period in which to make adequate preparation for the Urdd's fiftieth anniversary in 1972. The Director, R. E. Griffith, was asked to submit to the Council a memorandum outlining those aspects that he considered essential. Two schemes appeared to stand out clearly. One was that the story of the Urdd during its first fifty years should be written. The other was the need to raise a substantial fund that would enable the movement to step boldly into a new era. A minimum of £50,000 was suggested and at the Council's request, R. E. Griffith agreed to undertake this task in addition to all the other work for which he was already responsible. Planning an appeal was no new experience for him, and as long as he could rely on the support of the Urdd's voluntary workers throughout Wales, he felt sure the target could be reached. The Jubilee Fund was officially opened in a BBC radio appeal made in Welsh by I. B. Griffith, Mayor of Caernarfon, on March 3.

I. B. Griffith had been a keen supporter of the Urdd for more than thirty years, and making this appeal was something he did with relish—

' This is an appeal to debtors ! And every living soul in Wales is deeply indebted to the Urdd—for its vision, its achievements, its dedication and its joyousness. To prove this, try to imagine what Wales would be like if it were possible to eradicate the Urdd completely. It would be a Wales without the Urdd Eisteddfodau and their thirty-thousand annual competitors. Would you like to live without these events ?

The Urdd Camps ? Years ago, our Sara returned from Llangrannog black as soot, but happy as a lark ! "Fabulous" was her verdict ! And like Glan Llyn, it is still fabulous for hundreds of children and young people. Would you like to be without these camps ?

Then, the Welsh Schools. By today they have swept like wildfire throughout Wales, but it was the Urdd that initiated the first Welsh School. When everyone else since the time of Llywelyn the Last Prince had failed to create a Welsh aristocracy, the Urdd succeeded. Would you like the nation to be without this new sense of pride in its Welshness ?

And what about Welsh books ? Urdd members became packmen and pedlars going from door to door, from Anglesey to Gwent, selling nearly half-a-million Welsh books. And Gruffydd Jones of Llanddowror was on tip-toe in heaven, shouting his "Bravo" !

But there was also need for magazines equal to and better than those of England. And *Cymru'r Plant* gave birth to six more magazines—colourful, absorbing and contemporary. Would you like to be without these ?

What will the Urdd do with its anniversary fund, this debt that we all owe, coupled with the expression of our goodwill? The movement needs it to provide better opportunities for our children, to turn visions and dreams into realities. Every penny will be paid out to Wales, to fellow-man and to Christ. The Urdd exists to serve these. Please send your birthday gift today, this very minute. And having paid your debt, having expressed your gratitude and your goodwill, you will sleep like a log ! '

It was an off-beat but earnest appeal that went straight to the hearts of those who knew that everything the speaker had said was true. Contributions poured in, not from the rich, but from ordinary men and women who knew that if Wales was to live, the Urdd must live too. The total amounted to £4,176/3/11 which seems to have been a record for a Welsh radio appeal.

A novel response came from a group of BBC artistes who were former members of the Urdd—Alun Williams, Ryan Davies, Ronnie Williams, Mari Griffith and Bryn Williams. They offered their services for a whole week for no more than their expenses. The offer was readily accepted and we immediately planned a new-style *Noson Lawen* to be held at Crymych, Aberystwyth, Llanrhaeadr-ym-Mochnant, Cricieth, Bangor and Llangefni. Each night, they played to packed audiences who were thrilled with their perform-ance. And at the end of the week, £317 had been added to the Jubilee Fund.

*   *   *   *

Having served as a member of staff for twenty years, Evan L. Isaac was promoted Chief Field Officer responsible for supervising new County Organisers. His place as Organiser for Cardiganshire was taken by Aneurin V. Thomas. John Japheth replaced Robert Gapper as Organiser for Merioneth, and his post as Assistant Eisteddfod Organiser went to Gareth O. Gregory, a former student of Bangor University College who later served for three years in a London bank. Pressure of work in the Magazines Editorial Department necessitated the appointment of a second assistant editor, and the choice fell on Eurwen Booth, a Welsh graduate of Aberystwyth.

There were also several changes among the clerical staff. In a town like Aberystwyth, wages paid by a voluntary movement can hardly keep pace with those of government departments and other direct-grant institutions, and it is understandable though regrettable that staff trained by the Urdd should be lost to these establishments. Throughout the years, however, there have been notable exceptions who have turned a blind eye to better financial inducements because they felt that, through the Urdd, they were able to serve Wales more directly. These have always been salt of the earth, and the movement could hardly have functioned without them.

As usual, the Annual General Meeting was held at Aberystwyth in October. It came as something of a shock for members to learn that since 1964/65, the annual expenditure had increased, on average, by £10,000 per year. In 1967/68, the figure stood at £103,000, and at this rate of growth, one could foresee an expenditure of £150,000 in five years' time. Hitherto, the money raised by the Urdd had just kept pace with expenditure, but the increase in grants was pitiably low. If this growth-trend in costs continued, it was obvious that the Urdd would soon have to give serious consideration to other ways of increasing its income.

*   *   *   *

Turning to the broader Welsh canvas, the Gittins Report on Primary Education in Wales recommended that every child in the primary schools of Wales should have the opportunity of learning Welsh. This in turn gave a new impetus to the Schools Council and its experimental scheme of bilingual teaching in Anglicised areas. A Language Unit was set up at Trefforest, mainly to provide aids to those teaching Welsh as a second-language. *Ysgol Glyndŵr*, an independent Welsh residential school, was established at Bridgend by Trefor Morgan of Ystradgynlais. The BBC and Harlech

Television continued their series of Welsh lessons, and there was also a substantial increase in the number of Welsh-language evening classes for adults. The Faculties of Education at Aberystwyth and Bangor were experimenting with crash courses for adult Welsh learners, and there was an ever-growing demand for more places and more courses for children and adolescents at Llangrannog and Glan Llyn. There were 77 voluntary Welsh nursery classes providing for 750 children, most of whom came from non-Welsh-speaking homes. There was little doubt that the teaching of Welsh as a second-language was gaining impressive momentum.

On the political front, too, interest in Welsh affairs seemed to be on the upgrade. The Queen's Speech in October announced the setting up of a Royal Commission (which later became known as the Crowther/Kilbrandon Commission) to consider the question of devolution. It was obvious that politicians were at last yielding to pressure for a greater measure of self-government, and were ready to discuss the degree and form of possible decentralisation.

It is significant too that *Plaid Cymru* came within two-thousand votes of winning the Caerffili Parliamentary By-election. The Welsh Liberal Party had already published its manifesto with plans for the establishment of a Federal Welsh Parliament. George Thomas, Secretary of State for Wales, had reconstituted the Council for Wales under the Chairmanship of Dr. Brinley Thomas, but it was a disappointment to learn that its deliberations were to be confined to economic and industrial affairs to the exclusion of matters relating to the language and culture of Wales.

Despite these indications that Wales was approaching some form of self-government, there was no discernible official move to recognise and to preserve the Welsh language as such, and 1968 was a year of constant struggle and confrontation. There was little evidence that the governing authorities—central or local—were prepared to implement the Welsh Language Act. This led to numerous protests and demonstrations by *Cymdeithas yr Iaith* in a bid to achieve for the language the status granted by the Act. It was only after much campaigning that the various Welsh or bilingual documents demanded were eventually obtained—car discs, radio and television licenses, tax-forms, birth certificates, etc. Young people were fined and even imprisoned for their part in these campaigns, but eventually government departments would yield to pressure. In the words of one politician—' Governments always tell us that they will never yield to force. History tells us, however, that they never yield to anything else.'

When it felt that the campaign for Welsh forms was as good as won, *Cymdeithas yr Iaith* turned its attention to English road-signs and appealed to the authorities for bilingual versions. When constitutional approaches had failed, they began a campaign of daubing English signs with green paint. Once again, there was prosecution, punishment and imprisonment. The Society's other target was the BBC ; members marched to the Corporation's centre at Llandâf to present a petition calling for more Welsh programmes and demanding an independent television channel for Wales. In their criticism of Aneirin Talfan Davies, Head of Programmes, they were criticising one who had given outstanding service to the Welsh language. Whatever of the rank and file, the leaders of a responsible Society should realise that there are many serving within establishments such as the BBC who have the cause of Wales at heart and who have laboured against many odds on behalf of the Welsh language.

The linguistic-political battles were not without their effects on the Urdd. On the one hand, they helped to strengthen the national awareness, thus creating a climate in which the Urdd could operate. On the other hand, there were people who resented the methods used by *Cymdeithas yr Iaith* and who wrongly included the Urdd in their condemnation. There were signs that tensions were mounting, and before the end of the year the Urdd found itself in the fiercest battle of all—the opposition to plans for the Investiture of Prince Charles as Prince of Wales in July 1969.

20

THE forthcoming investiture of Prince Charles as Prince of Wales in 1969 had been officially announced in May 1967. The ceremony would take place at Caernarfon on July 1, and be followed by a tour of Wales. The arrangements were entrusted to a committee headed by the Duke of Norfolk, the Earl Marshal, and including many prominent Welshmen, among whom was Sir Ifan ab Owen Edwards. In addition to these official plans, it was envisaged that, throughout the summer of 1969, the occasion would be celebrated by a great variety of special events organised on local and national levels. With this in view, the Welsh Office had asked the Wales Tourist Board to form a National Committee to encourage and promote a variety of events to be included in the ' *Croeso 69* ' programme. Here, too, it was felt that the Urdd should be represented, and the Director, R. E. Griffith, was invited to serve on the committee. The Urdd Executive Committee had agreed that the Founder and Director should serve on these bodies with the proviso that any invitation to the Urdd to play an official part in the celebrations should be referred to the Executive Committee.

As far as *Croeso* 69 was concerned, a circular to Urdd Branches outlined the plans envisaged, but left it to Adrannau and Aelwydydd, and to District and County Committees to decide what part, if any, they wished to play in local celebrations. On the national level, however, it became clear, as early as the beginning of 1968, that events connected with Prince Charles would affect the Urdd in three directions—at the Urdd National Eisteddfod to be held in Aberystwyth, at Glan Llyn following the investiture, and in connection with the investiture itself.

By this time, however, the investiture and everything associated with it had become an emotive and inflammatory subject throughout Wales. The nation was deeply divided on the issue; indeed, there was a strong element of opposition to the whole idea, especially amongst young people. Those who opposed, however, were far from unanimous in their reasons for their opposition. Some were anti-royalist ; some were opposed on political grounds ; and others

72   Prince Charles at the Aberystwyth Urdd
Eisteddfod, 1969

73   John Garnon

74   The Royal Prize—
gift of the Queen, 1960

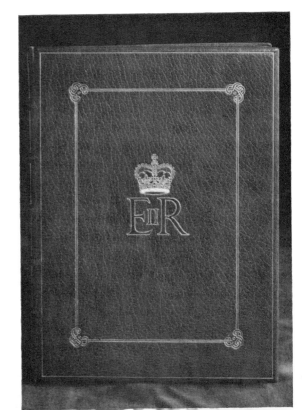

75 F. Wynn Jones

76 John Elfed Jones

77 Prys Edwards

78 Owen Edwards

objected to the pomp and unnecessary expenditure that would be incurred. It was natural that the cleavage of opinion should be reflected within the Urdd, a movement whose members and leaders belonged to various political parties and held widely different opinions. Many leading Urdd members were sincerely opposed to the investiture ; there were some who welcomed it ; others held that it should be accepted as no more than a traditional ceremonial event, and that the Urdd should not waste its energy arguing about it.

On the broader Welsh front, however, opposition to the investiture was much more fierce, and sometimes led to violent action. There were a number of explosions, some of which were aimed at pipelines carrying water to England ; another occurred in the Temple of Peace, Cardiff, on the eve of a conference to launch the *Croeso* 69 project. ' Welsh extremists ' and ' saboteurs ' were terms that constantly crept into English press reports. A small band of men belonging to the self-styled ' Free Wales Army ' channelled their frustration into a game of make-believe, proclaiming that their aim was 'to free Wales from the tyrranical English'. Their antics were magnified beyond reason, and they were eventually brought to task in a trial that ended on Investiture Day and cost £100,000 of public money. There was no evidence that these men were in any way connected with the bombing incidents, but the authorities seemed to have decided that their conviction might serve as a warning to others. However, on the morning of the Investiture, two men at Abergele were killed by a bomb they were carrying. If the Free Wales Army were playing at being soldiers, there were others to whom violence was a reality. One of these was John Barnard Jenkins, leader of a group that called itself *Mudiad Amddiffyn Cymru*. Jenkins was charged with offences involving explosives and was imprisoned for ten years. In a letter written in prison, he said, ' Of course, it can be said that violence is unnecessary and that *Plaid Cymru* have the answer. My proviso is that by the time independence arrives, the Wales we know now will have long gone ; the Wales we wanted free and Welsh will be absolutely unattainable.'

Three days before the investiture, *Cymdeithas yr Iaith Gymraeg* held a rally attended by more than a thousand people at Cilmeri, where stands the memorial to Llywelyn, the last native Prince of Wales. A satirical song entitled ' Carlo ' and aimed at Prince Charles and his investiture was recorded by Dafydd Iwan. It angered some people who regarded it as a personal attack on the Prince; the record, nevertheless, became a best-seller.

Plaid Cymru decided that the question of the investiture be left on the table. The President, Gwynfor Evans, declined to attend the Caernarfon ceremony, though some people felt that, had he accepted, he would have publicly dissociated himself from the activities of such movements as the Free Wales Army, *Mudiad Amddiffyn Cymru* and the Patriotic Front.

Those responsible for the investiture arrangements were, of course, well aware of the tension that existed within Wales ; it was part of the duties of the Secretary of State for Wales to keep the authorities informed of reactions and developments. In view of the growing tension, it was decided that the Prince should spend part of the 1969 summer term as a student at the University College in Aberystwyth. This would lend more meaning to the investiture, and Welsh people would be more ready to accept him if he were to associate himself with Wales and become acquainted with the language and history of the nation. And under expert and concentrated tuition, it was not long before he had gained a basic knowledge of the language.

It happened that the Urdd National Eisteddfod was to be held at Aberystwyth at the time the Prince would be a student there. Under the circumstances, it would seem inappropriate not to inform him of the Eisteddfod which, after all, was the premier cultural festival of the youth of Wales. This was agreed by both the Urdd Executive Committee and the Eisteddfod Committee. It was further decided that should the Prince attend he should be asked to present the Royal Prize to the winning county at the final Eisteddfod session, on the clear understanding that he would do so in Welsh. It was then left to the Principal, Dr. Thomas Parry, to discuss the matter with the Prince and to inform the Urdd of his decision.

In the meantime, Dr. R. H. Jones, Secretary to the Investiture Committee, had been in correspondence with the Director, R. E. Griffith, regarding the part the Urdd was desired to play in connection with the Prince's tour of Wales following the Investiture on July 1. Apparently, the Prince had expressed a wish to spend some time amongst young people and had indicated Glan Llyn as his first choice. The request was granted by the Urdd Executive Committee, with the proviso that the visit should be private, informal, and free of pomp and ceremony.

It was when the question of sending Urdd representatives to attend the Investiture at Caernarfon that the real crisis arose. Though no official invitation had yet been received, it was understood that one would be forthcoming. When the matter was discussed by the Executive Committee, there was a sharp divergence of opinion. Some argued that to accept would be to lose the allegiance of the many who sincerely opposed the investiture. Others held that this was a matter of policy, and that in such matters, it was the duty of the Urdd to lead and not to be led by its members. Faced with such a cleavage of opinion, the Committee decided to refer the matter to the Urdd Council. But that body too found itself facing the same dilemma. A memorandum stating the pros and cons of the situation had been prepared by the Director, though he himself was in hospital when the Council met to consider the matter. In the discussion that followed, those who opposed the investiture argued that it was a political stunt, an attempt to bind Wales more closely with England and to strengthen the psychological ties that seemed lately to have become frayed and insecure. On the other hand, it was pointed out that the Urdd had always accepted the Monarchy and its government, and had pursued a policy of trying to influence and enlighten the ' Establishment ' from within rather than adopting a negative attitude from without. It was thus that it had won the support of the Department of Education and Science which recognised the movement as an educational organisation—patriotic but non-political. To decline to play any part in the investiture would be contrary to the Urdd's tradition and character, and would be interpreted either as an indication that the Urdd was rejecting Royalty, or as a political act, both of which would be contrary to the normal policy of the movement.

Eventually, a motion proposed by Sir Ifan ab Owen Edwards— 'That, should an invitation be received, a small contingent representing the Urdd would be allowed to attend the Investiture'— was carried by 31 votes to 21, with 2 abstentions. Two Council members resigned in protest. They agreed, however, to continue serving as Chairman and Vice-Chairman of the Urdd Eisteddfod

Executive Committee so as not to jeopardise in any way the success
of the festival to be held at Aberystwyth in May 1969. There were
others who felt uneasy about the decision, including three or four
staff members, who were not present at the Council meeting.

At the following meeting of the Executive Committee in
November, reaction to the Council's decision was reported and
analysed and it was decided to re-convene the Council to consider
the whole issue anew. In the meantime, the views of the Urdd
County Committees were sought and found to be almost equally
divided.

At the extra-ordinary meeting of the Council on December 14, on
a motion proposed by the Officers, it was decided—

   i. To rescind the decision taken by the Council at its previous
      meeting regarding sending representatives to Caernarfon.

  ii. To confirm the Urdd's readiness to welcome Prince Charles
      to visit Glan Llyn according to his wish, and to attend any
      other Urdd function of his choice.

The two resolutions were voted upon separately and both were
carried by a majority vote. The following day, a press headline
read—' Urdd boycotts Investiture.' One leading Council member
resigned in protest against the new decision.

R. E. Griffith, whose illness for four months had prevented him
from taking any part in the deliberations, felt that having second
thoughts over the matter was a mistake. In his view, to re-convene
the Council was an error of judgement, and he held that members
had allowed themselves to be influenced by personal feelings and
had failed to think in terms of the Urdd as a movement. Although
naturally respecting the Council's decision, the Director reserved
the right to make it known that he disagreed with it, and maintained
that he represented the views of many Urdd members and supporters.

There were, naturally, some official and statutory bodies who
disapproved of the Urdd's decision which they saw as contradictory
to what could be expected of a non-political organisation. Ironically, it fell to R. E. Griffith, who had had no share in the tight-rope
decision, to explain to these bodies the dilemma in which the Urdd
had found itself and the crisis with which it had been faced. It was

left to him to explain that the tension, heightened by the investiture, was in reality part of the crisis of a nation's survival, and that, faced with such a crisis, one could understand that there should be a sense of urgency and sometimes a feeling of anger and desperation.

*　　　*　　　*　　　*

The Prince came to the Urdd National Eisteddfod at Aberystwyth on the final day, and like everyone else, he arrived unceremoniously in his Wellington boots ! For four hours, he sat listening to the proceedings and was obviously impressed by the high standard and by the zest of the competitors. The last competition over, the compére called on Lady Edwards to present the trophies to the counties that had won second and third places ; on Tom Jones, Secretary of the Pantyfedwen Trust, to present the Pantyfedwen Trophy and investment to the winning county ; and on Prince Charles to present the Royal Prize. As soon as the Prince stepped on to the stage, however, about a hundred young people stood up and walked out of the marquee carrying banners and posters protesting against his visit. It was a silent and non-violent protest by members of *Cymdeithas yr Iaith*, but there were many who disapproved of their action. The compére waited until the last demonstrator had left the marquee and then remarked that he was glad to see that many more had stayed in than had gone out ! This relieved the tension and when the Prince stepped to the microphone to make his first public speech in Welsh, the welcome he was given seemed as though those who remained wished to make up for those who had left. The Prince spoke with confidence and ease and with a sprinkling of humour. He referred slyly to the fact that the Urdd would not be at Caernarfon, and to the song 'Carlo'. He obviously knew how to reach his audience, and if some of those who listened disapproved of the Investiture, it was obvious that it in no way constituted a dislike of the Prince.

*　　　*　　　*　　　*

On the day following his Investiture, the Prince arrived at Glan Llyn accompanied by Col. J. F. Williams-Wynne, Lord Lieutenant of Merioneth. Sir Ifan ab Owen and Lady Edwards were there to

greet him and to introduce to him some of the movement's officials
and staff. During lunch in the camp dining-hall, Lady Edwards
presented the Prince with an Urdd badge as a memento of his
visit, and the Lord Lieutenant presented Glan Llyn with a visitors'
book which the Prince was requested to sign. Altogether, it was,
perhaps, as informal an occasion as a royal visit could be expected to
be.

*   *   *   *

There was, of course, a great deal more to the 1969 Urdd National
Eisteddfod than the visit of Prince Charles. The festival had not
been held at Aberystwyth since 1938 and the decision to invite the
1969 Eisteddfod was greeted with enthusiasm not only in the town
itself but throughout North Cardiganshire in general. One noticeable feature was the fact that a high proportion of young people
were given key positions within the Executive Committee. Among
the chief officers were Peter Hughes Griffiths (Chairman), William I.
Griffith (Vice-Chairman), John Garnon (Secretary) and Glyn T.
Jones (Assistant Secretary). Not only did they bring with them the
energy and enthusiasm of youth, but they could also draw upon a
fount of experience and ability. Add to these the astuteness of T. O.
Gregory as Treasurer, and one had a team equal to any that had
been entrusted with the task of directing the preparations for the
Urdd Eisteddfod. R. E. Griffith was elected Honorary President,
and the Officers knew that in him they had a great deal more than a
figurehead, and that they could turn to him for advice and guidance
on any problems that might arise. The advance-fund reached a
record total of £10,344 so that the financial success of the venture
was never in question. No less praiseworthy were the efforts of the
Hospitality Committee in ensuring free accommodation for five
thousand competitors, and this despite the demands of seasonal
visitors.

Plas Crug recreation ground provided an ideal site for the Eisteddd-
fod, but unfortunately, the abnormally heavy rains on the opening
day and the cloudburst the following day turned the whole field into
a quagmire. It seemed as though the Eisteddfod was doomed. But
competitors and public alike cheerfully accepted the disastrous
conditions, donned their Wellingtons or plastic boots, or even tied

plastic-bags over their shoes, and returned triumphantly to session after session throughout the three-day period. It was a triumph of will, enthusiasm and good humour in the face of adversity.

Aneurin Jenkins-Jones of Carmarthen presided over the first Eisteddfod session. In inviting him, the committee wished to acknowledge the debt the Urdd owed to one who had contributed so freely and so ably to the life of the movement over a period of fifteen years. In his address, he referred to the awakening that had become apparent in Wales during the sixties, and the part played by the Urdd in this development. Had it not been for the Urdd, he said, it is unlikely that any young person in Wales would be concerned about the fate of the language, or about the nation's right to its dignity and pride. He went on—

> ' If there be any credit for the uneasiness that stirs the Wales of today, the Urdd can claim part in that credit. And if it is to be condemned, the Urdd must bear a share of the condemnation. The movement cannot escape responsibility for nurturing a generation of youth independent in spirit, dissatisfied with the *status quo*, fervent and proud.'

At the same time, the speaker went on, the Urdd had stressed, and must continue to stress, the importance of tolerance and understanding, of responsible action based on the principles and the life of Christ.

It was Elystan Morgan, M.P. for Cardiganshire, who presided over Friday's session. He too made an appeal for tolerance—tolerance towards one another and towards other nations—

> ' We must aim at the patriotism of Thomas Davies which is ' a love of country that is untainted by hatred of any other '. Tolerance is not a sign of weakness, but a symbol of strength.'

Saturday's President was Dr. Goronwy H. Daniel, Permanent Secretary at the Welsh Office, and Principal-elect of the University College at Aberystwyth. He knew well of the Urdd's dilemma regarding the Investiture, and although he disagreed with the Council's decision to refrain from participating, he had shown that he understood the crisis the movement had faced.

The Chair was won by Gerallt Lloyd Owen of Sarnau, Merioneth, for a poem entitled *Cymru Heddiw* (' Wales Today '). This was his third triumph at an Urdd Eisteddfod, and the adjudicator, T. Llew Jones, considered the work to be of a very high standard. Second and third respectively were John Hywyn (who had won the Chair at Llanrwst) and Ieuan Wyn Evans, a student at the Normal College, Bangor. In the main prose competition there were ten competitors for the Eisteddfod Crown, and it was won by Nan Lloyd Roberts of the Dinbych Aelwyd, who had been placed second and third on previous occasions.

The Eisteddfod ground was no more than a stone's throw from Bryneithin, home of Sir Ifan ab Owen and Lady Edwards, and despite the weather and his failing health, the Founder was determined to make the effort to attend. It was exactly forty years since the first Eisteddfod was held at Corwen in 1929 and to mark the occasion, Sir Ifan was presented with an album made at the National Library and inscribed by Hywel Harries. Lady Edwards received a silver brooch whose design was based on the Urdd badge ; this she wears regularly and treasures greatly.

There is no doubt that the Aberystwyth Eisteddfod is one that will linger long in the memory. It was beset by more than one kind of storm, but it also had its moments of sunshine and triumph. And despite unanticipated expenses there was still a balance of £9,840. This was indeed a record, and one that might not be challenged for many years to come.

*   *   *   *

Three years had passed since the Urdd Council had decided to set up a Commission to inquire into the day-to-day life and work of the movement. It was appropriate that a movement that had existed for almost half a century should look critically at its aims, its activities and its achievements. One could expect to find some weak links which should either be strengthened or replaced in order to achieve maximum efficiency. Led by A. D. Lewis, Council Chairman, the Steering Committee drew up its plans for collecting the relevant data. Special county committees were set up, composed mainly of leading Urdd workers, but also including persons having a special interest in the youth service but not directly concerned with Urdd activities,—educationists, probation officers, clergy, social workers, councillors, etc. In this way, we hoped to obtain an

unbiassed assessment and a wide variety of suggestions and recommendations. Branch leaders, as well as a cross-section of individuals, were also asked for their criticism and comment. As
secretary to the Commission, it fell to my lot to collect, analyse and
collate the information received from all sources, to prepare a report
and present it to a special meeting of the Council in September 1969.
A staff conference was later held to study some aspects of the report
in detail, and this was followed by another meeting of the Council
in April 1970.

Broadly speaking, the findings were classified under four main
headings.

1. AIMS AND IDEALS

There was unanimous agreement that the threefold Urdd Pledge
was adequate and acceptable and that no change was required. It
should be regarded as an ideal always to be aimed at, rather than
as a once-and-for-all pledge of loyalty ; an ideal for the Urdd as a
movement and for members as individuals. These objectives were
further defined in a statement released upon the adoption of the
Commission's report—

> ' Urdd Gobaith Cymru is a patriotic youth movement based on
> the ideal of service to Wales, to fellow-man and to Christ. The
> aim of the movement is to inspire the youth of Wales, both
> Welsh-speaking and non-Welsh-speaking, to take pride in their
> heritage, to promote the Welsh language and the life of the
> Welsh nation, to serve their fellow-man, whoever he may be,
> and to do all this in the Christian spirit.'

Within this broad outline, the Urdd's immediate aim was to
provide its members with the opportunity and the encouragement
to 'live life more abundantly'. This meant helping individuals—

- i.   to develop their potential skills and abilities in the cultural,
  recreational and social fields.
- ii. to achieve a happy relationship with one another and with
  society in general.
- iii. to acquire a sense of identity with and responsibility for the
  community in which they live, on the local, the national and
  the international levels, thus aiming at the ultimate ideal of
  'service to Wales, to fellow-man and to Christ'.

2. The Urdd as a Youth Movement

Attention was paid to its relationship with the LEA's ; to its county administration and activities ; to its local units—their place within the movement, their problems, their shortcomings and their possibilities.

On the first point, it was agreed that the Urdd should continue to operate in partnership with the LEA's in every possible way, but without sacrificing its independence in favour of grants and other facilities.

On the second point, it was recommended that there should be only one governing body within each county, with sub-committees responsible for stimulating and co-ordinating various aspects and activities. This meant that some means would have to be found of integrating the present County Youth Council with the County Committee.

With regard to local units, some concern was expressed regarding the imbalance between the number of Adrannau attached to schools and those operating outside school hours and school premises. It was urged that, despite problems of depopulation and the scarcity of trained leaders, greater emphasis should be laid upon units having no direct connection with schools.

3. Leaders and their Training

Here there were two main recommendations :

i. That a leaders' handbook be prepared, offering suggestions of activities and guidelines on the administration of Adrannau and Aelwydydd.

ii. That far more training courses should be provided, both on a national and county level, based mainly on the presentation of activities, on ways of dealing with problems of behaviour and discipline, and on advising members on personal matters. The rapid development of courses for members learning Welsh as a second-language was universally acclaimed, and the Urdd was urged to consider extending this provision still further.

4. COMMUNICATION AND PUBLICITY

It was here that the Commission was most critical. The Urdd had, in the past, concentrated on the organisation of its activities and paid too little attention to communicating with the general public through the mass media. Looking back today, one sees a vast improvement in this direction following the Commission's recommendations.

Many of the Commission's recommendations were implemented without delay, others followed later ; some still await attention. The overall effect was to make everyone concerned—both voluntary workers and full-time staff—more fully aware that there was always room for reappraisal and improvement, and that we all had something to learn when setting the stage for the second half-century.

*   *   *   *

In the international field, the usual arrangements were made regarding the Goodwill Message of the youth of Wales, and the annual Goodwill Service was broadcast by the BBC from Penrhyndeudraeth. Three Urdd members were selected to attend an international youth conference in Berlin—Gwenno Lloyd Price of Penygroes, Heulwen Hughes Jones of Corwen, and Peter Thomas of Llanelli. An attempt to re-introduce an Inter-Celtic Conference, this time at Glan Llyn, was only partially successful in attracting young people from the other Celtic territories. But if young people in general seemed less ready to attend conferences, Urdd members showed a growing readiness to take part in practical, humanitarian service. Many Uwch-Adrannau, Aelwydydd and County Youth Councils contributed in various ways towards providing for the needs of others. Some raised money for charitable organisations such as Oxfam, The Save The Children Fund, Christian Aid, Cancer Research, etc.; some held carol services in hospitals and homes ; invalid chairs were bought for homes for the aged ; £700 raised for the Children's Home at Bontnewydd ; a guide dog provided for a blind person ; Christmas dinners for senior citizens ; music programmes for patients were presented in hospitals, and a few senior members helped on weekends to relieve the staff at the Handicapped Children's Holiday Home at Aberthin, near Cowbridge. Those who gave their services in this manner deserve credit for their initiative. But in view of the crying need for humanitarian service in our society, the ideal would be that every single Branch should include some scheme of community service in its annual programme.

The finals of the organised games in which 180 teams had taken part were again centred on Glan Llyn and Bala. The main interest was the Pantyfedwen Soccer Competition. For the fourth time, the Porthmadog Aelwyd had reached the final, but once again they were robbed of the coveted prize which, on this occasion, was won by the Cardiff College of Education Aelwyd.

When it became known that the Rev. and Mrs. Tegryn Davies were to retire from the leadership of the Urdd at Aberporth, it was locally decided to present to the movement the hut which had been the home of the Adran and Aelwyd for many years. This would now be equipped as a small residential centre for groups of twelve, and would be ideal for language groups or for field and environmental studies. Another gift received was that of two ponies presented to Llangrannog Camp by the West Glamorgan Urdd Committee who were anxious that riding and trekking should be part of the activities that the camp would one day be able to offer.

*   *   *   *

During the autumn of 1968, the Urdd Executive Committee had agreed to the appointment of a Deputy Director. Since Sir Ifan's illness, R. E. Griffith had shouldered an ever-increasing burden of responsibility. To this was now added the task of raising a £50,000 Jubilee Fund, and Sir Ifan had already expressed a personal wish that the story of the Urdd during its first fifty years should be written by the Director. The Committee realised that these tasks would only be made possible when a Deputy had been appointed. The choice fell on J. Cyril Hughes, who for the previous four years had served as Assistant Information Officer with BBC Wales. Prior to that, however, he had for eight years been a member of the Urdd staff as Personal Assistant to the Director. He rejoined the staff in January 1969 and brought with him the added experience he had gained during his four years at Cardiff.

During the year, the Staffing Committee had to face a number of changes. Having served for four years as Organiser for Anglesey and Caernarfonshire, T. Prys Jones left to take a degree course at Bangor. It had long been recognised that this was far too large a territory for one person, and it was decided to allow each county a full-time Organiser. John Clifford Jones, a teacher of one year's standing, was appointed to Anglesey, and Gwilym Charles Williams to Caernarfonshire. John Japheth returned to Swyddfa'r Urdd as Public Relations Officer with the added responsibility of organising the Llangrannog camps. His place in Merioneth was taken by John Hywyn, who already had a year's teaching experience. Other new appointments included Wynne Melville Jones of Tregaron as Organiser for Carmarthenshire, and Andrew Russ as Organiser for East Glamorgan and Monmouthshire.

*   *   *   *

In the death of T. Ivor Jones, a London solicitor, the movement lost a loyal supporter. A childhood friend of Ifan ab Owen Edwards, he had shown an early interest in the Urdd and was one of those responsible for establishing an Incorporated Company to govern the movement. When the first Officers were elected in 1932, he became the Company's first Honorary Solicitor, an office he held for 37 years until his death in 1969. It was to him that the Urdd had turned for expert legal advice throughout this long period, and never once did he accept any remuneration for his services.

Miss S. J. Hughes of Nantymoel was another whose contribution to the Urdd could never be truly measured. A native of Montgomeryshire, she had moved to Glamorgan and, for many years, was Head of the Welsh Department at the Ogmore Grammar School. It was there, in that Anglicised area, that she quietly performed miracles, not the least being her annual efforts in organising flag-days for the benefit of the Urdd. When Sian Hughes died in 1969, some part of the movement seemed to have been lost for ever.

*   *   *   *

1969 was the end of a triennial period in the Urdd calendar, and new Officers and Council members were elected. The Annual General Meeting considered it a privilege to ask Sir Ifan ab Owen and Lady Edwards to continue as Presidents. Three Vice-Presidents had completed their term of office—Emlyn Hooson, M.P., the Rt. Hon. Cledwyn Hughes, M.P., and Francis Wynn Jones of Aberystwyth. On this occasion, however, it was decided to elect only one Vice-President for the period 1969-72. This was perhaps the highest tribute the Urdd could pay to A. D. Lewis who had served the movement with unique loyalty for twelve years, first as Vice-Chairman and then as Chairman of the Council, and throughout the period as Chairman of the Executive Committee, quite apart from additional responsibilities he had shouldered from time to time.

It was intended that Aneurin Jenkins-Jones, Vice-Chairman since 1963, should follow A. D. Lewis as Council Chairman, but in 1969, unfortunately, his health did not allow him to undertake any extra duties. Owen Edwards was therefore elected Chairman, with Alun Creunant Davies as Vice-Chairman of the Council and Chairman of the Executive Committee. Prys Edwards, who had shared the duties of Honorary Secretary for four years, became Treasurer. It was a source of great satisfaction to Sir Ifan not only to see his two sons taking an active interest in the Urdd, but also accepting responsibility with others for governing the movement. This was no light undertaking at a time when the annual expenditure was close on £110,000 and likely to escalate even more alarmingly in coming years. The choice of Honorary Secretaries fell on two young people who had already given the movement outstanding service—John Garnon of Aberystwyth and Ann Lloyd Lewis of Cemaes, Montgomeryshire. After twenty-five years, Professor D. J. Llewelfryn Davies was relieved of his duties as Honorary Counsel and his place was taken by Hywel Moseley, a Cardiff barrister who later became a Professor of Law at Aberystwyth. The death of T. Ivor Jones necessitated the appointment of a new Honorary Solicitor and the Urdd was again fortunate in obtaining the services of Emyr Currie-Jones of Cardiff, a native of Caernarfon and an Urdd member from the early thirties. One notable feature of the 1969 Annual General Meeting was the election of a high proportion of young people as members of the Council. There had been a trend in this direction for some time, and the County Committees too had been urged to include young members among their representatives to the Council. It was most encouraging to find the younger members ready and eager to share the responsibilities.

Now that Jubilee Year was on the horizon, it was decided to set up a national committee to be responsible for planning the major events of that important year. The new Vice-President, A. D. Lewis, was unanimously elected Chairman of the Jubilee Committee, and Evan L. Isaac, Chief Field Officer, was seconded to act as Organising Secretary. Thus, at the beginning of 1970, the Urdd was preparing to launch into a period that would prove to be one of unusual and exciting activity.

*   *   *   *

As 1969 drew to its close, it became clear that Sir Ifan ab Owen Edwards was fighting a losing battle. During the first weeks of the new year, his condition gradually deteriorated, and he died on January 23.

It was, of course, not unexpected. He had been spared for ten years after his first major illness, and there had been several occasions when his life seemed to hang precariously in the balance. When the end did come, however, it was no less of a blow to those who had known him well. It was a sudden and shattering realisation that he was no longer with us. It was just as though we had transcended time and had shared in the experience of the people of Gwynedd when they learnt of the death of Llywelyn Fawr in 1240. Messages of sympathy poured into Bryneithin from all over Wales ; from young and old. They expressed the deep sorrow of a nation.

Salem Presbyterian Chapel at Aberystwyth was full to capacity half an hour before the funeral service was due to begin. In addition to the Rev. H. R. Davies, who had been the Founder's Minister and friend for many years, tributes to Sir Ifan were paid by Dr. Thomas Parry, R. Alun Evans, Norah Isaac and R. E. Griffith. They paid homage to the idealist, the realist, the optimist, and above all, the indomitable leader, undaunted by difficulties, criticism or ill-health. R. Alun Evans spoke of Sir Ifan as one who had provided Urdd members with the opportunity and the tools so that they could themselves accomplish the task. ' He gave us the

opportunity to know our own country, and to meet young people
from other lands as equals. And, as citizens of Wales, we acquired
a new dimension of self-confidence, self-discipline and self-respect.'
In his closing remarks, R. E. Griffith said—

> ' Urdd Gobaith Cymru will never be quite the same again, but
> the Founder's inspiration will help us to shoulder the burdens
> without feeling the weight. Sir Ifan had been granted his last
> wish ; he had seen a new generation of leaders emerging,
> young men and women ready to walk in his footsteps, ready
> to give of their service and to promote his ideals with complete
> loyalty. That generation is here today, ready to grasp the handles
> of the plough. It is with this certainty that Sir Ifan slipped
> away over the horizon—quietly, contentedly, peacefully, just as
> the mist rises from the valley.'

Later that day, Ifan ab Owen Edwards was buried in his native
Llanuwchllyn.

On February 21, a memorial service was held at Cardiff when
the Cardiff Aelwyd Choir sang *Angau, Ni'th Ofnaf* (Bach). This was
followed by a tribute in Welsh by Hywel D. Roberts who referred
to Sir Ifan as the greatest friend of youth that this century had
produced. In a tribute in English, Sir Ben Bowen Thomas regretted
that the young people of today were not given the opportunity of
knowing Sir Ifan in his prime. He went on—

> ' Sir Ifan had an eye for an opening, the kind of eye that we
> expect of our halves and centre-three-quarters in rugby football.
> He also had the gift of taking other people along with him. He
> could share a vision and rouse within others enthusiasm for a
> common task. In his autobiography, John Masefield describes
> Rosetti as a *kindling man*—one who kindles fire in other people's
> hearts and minds. Such a man was Sir Ifan. He kindled, and the
> flame, once lit, spread into the lives of a host of our young people.
> And the flame still burns.'

Press and radio were equally generous in their tributes. Under
the title ' A Great Welshman ' the *Western Mail* editorial said—

> ' The death of Sir Ifan ab Owen Edwards will be mourned by
> Welshmen everywhere . . . He will be mourned but not forgotten.
> His permanent memorial is the organisation he founded and
> which has done so much for the youth of Wales.'

Frank Price Jones, writing in *Y Faner*, ended with a word of advice to the youth of Wales today—

> 'The present generation of youth, anxious to serve Wales, could learn from Sir Ifan's example. Many of his ideas were new and unorthodox, but he succeeded in presenting them in a manner that would not antagonise unduly the 'establishment' of his day. Sir Ifan knew how to combine ardour and enthusiasm with patience and courtesy.'

In *Heno* (Tonight), a poem written on the night Sir Ifan died, Aneurin Jenkins-Jones ended with the following verse—

> 'Heno mae'r hebrwng ; cydymdeithiwn mewn afiaith ;
> Nid cymwynas â'r teithiwr mo'n hochain a'n cwynfan ;
> Mae'r optimist heno'n cadw oed â'r Gobaith,
> A dyma nhw'n cwrdd. Nos da, Syr Ifan.'

> (Tonight we accompany him ; let us walk together joyfully ;
> Moaning and sorrowing befit not this pilgrim ;
> Tonight the optimist has an appointment with Hope ;
> Now they have met. Goodnight, Sir Ifan.)

And on the threshold of the seventies, thousands of admirers all over Wales echoed the adieu—'Goodnight, Sir Ifan'.

*   *   *   *

A year later, a memorial was erected to mark his grave at Llanuwchllyn. It was designed by his son, Prys, and inscribed by Hedd Bleddyn Williams of Llanbrynmair. The unpolished slate rests obliquely on a metal pillar, with an upright rod passing through to support a three-dimensional Celtic Cross in wrought-iron. The inscription reads simply—

> Syr Ifan
> ab Owen Edwards
> 1895—1970
>
> Sylfaenydd Urdd Gobaith Cymru.
>
> Cymru
> Cyd-ddyn
> Crist

*   *   *   *

It was not easy to envisage the future without Sir Ifan ab Owen Edwards at the helm. It was even more difficult to think of Jubilee celebrations now that the Founder was no longer with us. Yet, ironically, this was the very first decision that had to be faced. The initial meeting of the National Jubilee Committee had been called for Saturday, 24 January, and Sir Ifan had died the previous evening. But the Officers knew that the Founder would have wished them to carry on, and one sensed a new determination that others must now bear a greater share of the burden that the Founder had borne for forty-eight years.

21

THE Urdd National Eisteddfod had twice been held in Montgomeryshire, first in 1932 and then in 1952, and on both occasions at Machynlleth. It returned in 1970, and was welcomed to Llanidloes with the support of the entire county. The Director of Education, Dr. J. A. Davies, was elected Chairman of the Executive Committee, but his services were lost when he left on his appointment as Principal of the Normal College, Bangor. Fortunately, there were two Vice-Chairmen, and it was decided that one of these, Arwel Jones, should step into the breach. Although not a native of the county, he had lived and taught at Llanidloes for many years.

No-one knew the Urdd better than he, and in his preface to the Eisteddfod programme, he referred to the death of Sir Ifan ab Owen Edwards—

' It would be wrong of us to succumb to grief, since the vital element in Sir Ifan's vision was not sadness but joy. To be true to that Christian and patriotic vision, this Eisteddfod should be an anthem of joy and of thanksgiving for the fact that our small nation should have been given so great a man, and that he should have dedicated his life to the service of its youth.'

He went on to refer to the current problems of Wales—

' In many respects, we are a divided nation. It may well be that only a movement such as the Urdd can bridge these gaps . . . Let us endeavour to understand and to get closer to those with whom we do not always agree.'

The Chairman was ably supported by his fellow-officers—Islwyn Lewis as Vice-Chairman, and his daughter, Ann Lloyd Lewis, as Secretary ; and on the financial side, by I. H. Edwards as Treasurer and R. T. D. Williams as Chairman of the Finance Committee. A target of £6,000 had been set for the Eisteddfod fund. That sum was exceeded and it was encouraging to find that a very substantial part of this fund was raised by members of Aelwydydd and *Senedd y Sir*.

Competitors flocked to Llanidloes from far and near ; for many, it was their first experience of *mwynder Maldwyn*—the gracious hospitality of Maldwyn. But despite the challenge of visiting competitors, Montgomeryshire held its own, winning both the Royal Prize and the Pantyfedwen Trophy and investment. Audience support of the Eisteddfod was not what the organisers would have wished, but one has to remember that Montgomeryshire had suffered severely from depopulation and that Llanidloes itself was a small town with a high proportion of non-Welsh-speaking inhabitants.

The Eisteddfod Presidents were Marged Jones of Llanfyllin, one of the county's indefatigable workers, Emlyn Hooson, M.P., and the Rev. Gwilym R. Tilsley, a native of Montgomeryshire and current Archdruid of the Gorsedd of Bards. An especially warm welcome was accorded to Dr. J. A. Davies when he returned to open the Arts, Crafts and Science Exhibition. It was disappointing to learn that there would be no Crowning ceremony. This had happened only once before in the history of the Urdd Eisteddfod, and while sympathising with the audience who were denied the most exciting feature in the day's programme, one had to agree that the adjudicator was right in insisting on the standards expected at Urdd Eisteddfodau. The Chair, however, was won by Ieuan Wyn Gruffydd, a sixth-former of Preseli School, Crymych, for a poem entitled *Y Deffro* (The Awakening) in which he had chosen to extol the virtues of the patriarch, D. J. Williams of Abergwaun (Fishguard), who had died at the turn of the year. Second and third places went to Sion Eirian of Ysgol Maesgarmon, Mold.

Financially, the Maldwyn Eisteddfod coincided with a crucial period of contract renewals. The Urdd's five-year contracts had ended with the Eisteddfod at Aberystwyth in 1969, and Llanidloes were the first to bear the brunt of the inflationary tendencies in the renewed contracts. Ground and marquee expenses that had amounted to £3,984 at Aberystwyth reached a total of £7,152 at Llanidloes, with the result that of the total receipts of £12,855, more than £11,164 was needed to meet actual running expenses, leaving a balance of no more than £1,721. It was something of a shock to realise that the cost of holding the National Eisteddfod would soon amount to £15,000. This was a situation that would call for careful consideration in the near future.

*   *   *   *

After ten years, it was again Anglesey's turn to be host to the annual *Gŵyl Sir*. It was decided to confine the effort to one area and the choice fell on the *Glannau Menai* District. R. Arwel Jones, Head of the Welsh Department at *Ysgol David Hughes*, Menai Bridge, was elected Chairman, and this alone was sufficient to guarantee the success of the venture. His fellow-officers were Ella Owens, Vice-Chairman; Dr. Marian Thomas, Secretary; and J. Medwyn Hughes, Treasurer.

Not for a long time had so much activity been stimulated within this particular catchment area. Each village set up its committee, and for months in advance, these bodies were a hive of activity, vying with one another in friendly rivalry. The Festival itself was largely centred on *Ysgol David Hughes*, and it was here that eleven Adrannau gave two performances of a pageant devised by Bedwyr Lewis Jones and Dafydd Huw Williams, and produced by J. O. Roberts. It was here too that the fête, opened by Mrs. Cledwyn Hughes, was held on the Saturday. The programme also included a *Cymanfa Ganu* for children at Menai Bridge and one for adults at Brynsiencyn. The *Noson Lawen* at Llangefni, however, fell somewhat short of the standard expected. *Gŵyl Glannau Menai* proved to be much more than a fund-raising effort. It brought new life to the Adrannau and introduced new leaders who were not only ready to help with existing Branches, but also prepared to set up new units where none existed.

The biennial *Gŵyl Werin* was also due in 1970—the seventh in the series begun in 1958—and for the third time it found a home in West Glamorgan, this time at Maesteg. With the patronage of the local Council and its Chairman, Brinley Richards, it also had the generous support of the Glamorgan County Council whose Chairman, Ald. E. Gwynfryn Davies, had never turned a deaf ear to appeals on behalf of Welsh cultural organisations. The Festival Chairman and Vice-Chairman were Gerallt C. Jones and Gwynfor Davies, with Lewis Watts and Dilys Richards as Treasurer and Secretary respectively.

Aelwydydd teams from Aberystwyth, Brynaman, Cardiff and

Morriston took part, as well as secondary school groups from Pontardawe, Cymer Afan, Rhydaman and Bae Colwyn. The guest dancers
were the *Scoleon Apostolos Andreas* Group, exiles from Greece living in
London. In a three-hour programme, twenty dances were exhibited,
interspersed with items by Ann Griffiths and her Harp *Ensemble*,
folk-songs by Dafydd Edwards and clog-dancing by Owen Huw
Roberts. The afternoon session was followed by a concert and later
by a pop-festival. It was a full day's programme, and certainly not a
day to be easily forgotten by those who were present.

*   *   *   *

Two years had elapsed since Cefn Cwrt farm at Llangrannog had
become the property of the Urdd. The precise use to be made of the
' new Llangrannog ' was still being discussed, and the subsequent
planning was entrusted to an Aberystwyth firm of architects—E.
Francis Jones, Prys Edwards and Associates. Eventually, the Urdd
Council decided on an ambitious and contemporary scheme
estimated to cost £120,000, in the hope that a 50% grant would be
made by the Department of Education and Science. Even so, it
would mean an outlay of £60,000 for the Urdd, but it was argued
that we were building for the future and that coming generations
needed—and deserved—the best that could be offered in facilities,
in leadership, in training and in inspiration.

The next step was to convince the Department of Education and
Science of the need for and the feasibility of a dual-purpose centre at
Llangrannog, envisaged not only as a summer camp for 300
children, but also as a full-time residential training and recreation
centre for 150 young people during the greater part of the year.
Detailed plans were submitted and the schemes discussed with
representatives of the Department. But although the validity of the
case was admitted and the high standards envisaged were approved,
there were still no indications that grant-aid would be forthcoming.
Frustrated by the seemingly endless delay and realising that building
work should be started without further procrastination, it was
decided in 1970 to submit a modified scheme estimated to cost
£70,000. Again there was no response, and it now seemed as
though the Department was unable to come to a decision.

Meanwhile, the Government had changed its method of distributing grants to voluntary organisations. Broadly speaking, it meant

that these bodies would first submit applications to Local Education Authorities, and that the Department would only undertake to bring the total grant up to 50% of the cost. In the case of Llangrannog, this could only mean further delay. Nor was there any guarantee that the LEA's would be able to grant-aid a new scheme of this nature which could add to their existing expenditure. In view of this, and having already waited two years for a firm reply from the Department, the Urdd decided to proceed alone. This would, of course, mean further curtailment of the scheme, but it would at least enable work to commence immediately on those buildings most urgently needed for the 1973 summer camps. However, in August 1972, when all hope had been abandoned, it was learnt that the Department was prepared to reconsider the application. Consequently, in October 1972, a grant of £30,000 was offered towards a scheme limited to a maximum cost of £60,000. It was gratefully accepted, and within a month work had commenced on laying the foundations for new camp buildings that would constitute the first phase in the development. But how much more could have been achieved, and how much better the premises that could have been built, had even the same grant been made available two years earlier.

In complete contrast to the delay in dealing with Llangrannog, the Department had always been sympathetic towards any application in respect of Glan Llyn. While appealing on behalf of the 'new Llangrannog,' we had simultaneously applied for a grant towards the cost of erecting a new boat-house and landing-stage at Glan Llyn at an estimated cost of £14,000. In this case, not only was a grant of £7,000 readily made available, but the scheme was advanced to enable the work to be included in the 1971/72 building programme. This gesture was greatly appreciated and the new facilities served to improve considerably the challenging activities that made Glan Llyn so acceptable to the older age-group.

*   *   *   *

In July 1970, the Urdd wrote to the Secretary of State for Wales, asking that a recommendation be made to the Government urging the appointment of a permanent Royal Commission to safeguard the interests of the Welsh language and to promote the cultural life of Wales by all possible means. This would not be another Advisory

Council, but a body with power to act and the resources to operate efficiently on a broad basis. A superstructure of this nature and stature would crystallise the needs of Wales, make detailed and regular investigations, and act on the highest level. This would eliminate the need for continuous confrontations and protests, bitterness and resentment, resulting in piecemeal concessions.

It was recognised that such a recommendation would demand considerable research and investigation before it could be put to the Government. Nevertheless, it was hoped that the Secretary of State and the Welsh Office would accept it in principle, and be prepared to study its implications and feasibility. The Urdd was not alone in feeling strongly on this matter ; similar suggestions had been made by other bodies, and some Members of Parliament had expressed their support. The request, however, did not evoke any expression of urgency from the Welsh Office. Several further approaches were made, and two years later the Secretary of State asked for a memorandum outlining the aims and the terms-of-reference of such a Commission. Although this was no task for laymen, the Urdd agreed to outline the ideas which it felt should from the basis of the envisaged recommendation. We were convinced that this was a proposal that all sections of the Welsh community should be able to support ; here was an opportunity for political parties, religious bodies, local authorities, cultural organisations and voluntary movements—an opportunity to present a united front on behalf of everything we mean by ' Wales '. This was not a matter for any one movement—the destiny of the nation could depend on it—and if the major bodies were to stand united behind such a recommendation, no Government would dare refuse.

*   *   *   *

Other events in the Urdd calendar for 1970 included the following.

    i. The publication of a new 80-page Handbook for Urdd Leaders. This not only dealt with administration and organisation, but also included programme suggestions that would enable leaders to offer varied and stimulating activities, especially in Aelwydydd. The Handbook was produced in response to one of the main recommendations of the Urdd Commission.

ii. A proclamation festival was held at Swansea to stimulate interest in the 1971 Urdd National Eisteddfod and to further the financial efforts of the Eisteddfod Committee.

iii. The finals of the organised games were once again centred on Bala and Glan Llyn. Aelwyd Llanuwchllyn proved to be second-time victors in their bid for the Pantyfedwen Soccer Cup.

iv. In conjunction with Christian Aid, the Urdd arranged through its Branches for the collecting of woollen materials to be sold towards providing a school and medical clinic for needy Indian settlements in Patagonia.

v. A critical memorandum was sent to the Department of Education and Science following the publication of ' Youth and Community Work in the 70's,' the report of the Milson and Fairbairn Committees on behalf of the Youth Service Development Council. Although, in general, it contained some very valuable suggestions, it was felt that the report had completely ignored Wales and its special problems, despite the fact that, according to its own terms-of-reference, it purported to deal with 'England and Wales'. The recommendations, however, were not accepted by the Government, and little more was heard of the report.

Due to the additional duties connected with the Jubilee celebrations, the Director felt that he could no longer edit the light-hearted magazine, *Blodau'r Ffair*, which had appeared regularly since 1953. It would henceforth be the responsibility of the Urdd editorial staff. It was in this same editorial department, however, that the Urdd saw the major staff changes of 1970. The two assistant editors—Megan Tudur and Eurwen Booth—both left during the summer, and the editor, Ivor Owen, had announced his retirement to take effect from the end of the year. To replace a person of Ivor Owen's calibre was no easy task, but we were fortunate in securing the services of Ieuan Griffith, a native of Llŷn and a graduate in Welsh who had experience of second-language teaching both in the Rhondda and Llandrindod. It was arranged that he should commence in September, thus allowing for an overlap of four months with Ivor Owen before he was due to retire.

At the same time, two new assistant editors took up their duties—
Nan Lloyd Williams of Dinbych and Eirian Mai Hopcyn of Glyn-
arthen, Cardiganshire, both experienced teachers.

Ivor Owen had given fifteen years' dedicated service to this aspect
of Urdd work, and he had always approached his task with incredible energy and devotion. When he left his office in the evening,
it was only to begin another 'day', and he allowed himself no
respite even for brief holidays. Convinced that the existing pattern
could not do justice to the wide age-range of first and second-
language readers, he added *Deryn* to *Cymru'r Plant*, changed *Cymru*
for *Hamdden,* and replaced *Cymraeg* with *Bore Da* for juniors and
Mynd for adolescents. His expertise in the teaching of Welsh as a
second-language was widely recognised and acclaimed. It would be
no small task for anyone to take over from a man so dedicated and
possessing so much experience and creative ability, but Ieuan
Griffith was to prove himself fully capable of accepting the challenge.

Other staff changes included the overdue appointment of a full-
time Organiser for Breconshire. With the aid of a grant from the
County Education Committee, Dylan Evans, who had just completed his course at the Normal College, Bangor, was appointed to the
post.

*   *   *   *

It is doubtful whether there had been within living memory a
year of such heavy losses in the life of Wales. More than twenty
eminent Welshmen died during the year, several of whom had been
prominent within the Urdd. In addition to the Founder himself,
there were Hywel Huws of Bogota, one of the original sixteen
Vice-Presidents elected in 1931/32 ; Dr. Huw T. Edwards, similar
in stature and in personality, and elected Vice-President in 1957 ;
Cynfab Roberts of Aberystwyth who had been Vice-Chairman of
the Urdd Council and Chairman of its Executive Committee for
six years, only to be given new responsibilities as Treasurer for a
further period of nine years until he became Vice-President in 1963.
His death in December 1970 was followed two days later by that of
Francis Wynn Jones who had taken over from him as Treasurer.
They were close friends and loyal in their support of the movement.
Equally shattering was the sudden death of Meirion Jones of Bala,

an ideal headmaster, a far-sighted and progressive educationist, who, in his limited leisure, found time to work for every cause that contributed to the enrichment of Welsh life. Other Welsh losses included such prominent people as D. J. Williams of Abergwaun, Cynan, Trefor Morgan, Gwilym Gwalchmai, T. I. Ellis, J. E. Jones, Alun Ogwen Williams, Professor J. R. Jones, F. G. Fisher, Iorwerth Roberts, Nan Davies and Gwyneth Alban Jenkins. Of all these, it would be true to say that Wales was interwoven in the very marrow of their bones, and their support of the Urdd had been unstinted.

These sad losses were referred to by Alun Creunant Davies at the Annual General Meeting in October. Paying tribute to Sir Ifan ab Owen Edwards, he referred also to the homage paid by the Vice-President, A. D. Lewis, in the printed Annual Report—

> ' The most outstanding feature of Sir Ifan's personality was that he combined the virtues of the visionary and the man of action ; the prophet and the realist. It was this, to my mind, that made him one of the nation's giants. His ability to clothe his dreams in flesh and blood was characteristic of the pioneer and leader. There are many who can dream dreams and see visions, and who can even crystallise those ideals ; there are some who can translate their ideals into plans. Few, however, have the ability to bring together and inspire individuals of like mind to form a movement. Sir Ifan ab Owen Edwards was one of these.'

The office of President had remained vacant for nine months following the death of Sir Ifan ab Owen Edwards, and the Annual General Meeting had no hesitation in asking Lady Edwards to assume the duties of President for the remaining two-year period. She graciously consented, and no-one doubted that she would perform those duties with meticulous care and natural dignity.

*   *   *   *

Financial problems can well present voluntary organisations with a dilemma. On the one hand, the lack of adequate resources prompts one to be cautious ; on the other, there can be no real progress without the courage to venture. One needs a large measure of faith, but one also needs to be able to distinguish between faith and recklessness. Thanks to Sir Ifan, the Urdd had never lacked faith, never been afraid to venture, and it was this that had made it possible to achieve so much during the first half-century. Even so, there were times when the movement had been forced to cut the coat according to the cloth.

It was this kind of dilemma that faced the Urdd at the beginning of the seventies as one became acutely aware of the rapid increase in expenditure. In a brief eight-year period, costs had almost doubled.

1964/65	£73,994	1968/69	£109,875
1965/66	£80,480	1969/70	£111,396
1966/67	£89,524	1970/71	£122,283
1967/68	£103,716	1971/72 est.	£135,000

This was an average annual increase of £7,500, but with a tendency towards progressive escalation. If the annual income were to show a corresponding increase, there would be no great cause for anxiety, but this was far from being the case. It was not surprising, therefore, that the Treasurer and his committee should devote themselves to the task of finding a solution to the problem. They felt that an annual income of £250,000 should be aimed at, but realised that such an achievement would demand an entirely new approach and could not be attained through the ordinary established channels of fund-raising efforts. The only solution was for the Urdd to venture into the business world. A beginning could be made with Panty-fedwen, and plans outlined by the Treasurer seemed both practicable and exciting. The first essential, however, was to discover whether the Company's Constitution would allow it to trade in the manner envisaged. Here the Urdd sought the guidance of its Honorary Counsel, Professor Hywel Moseley, its Honorary Solicitor, Emyr Currie-Jones, and Cennydd Howells, a London barrister specialising in Company Law. It was also necessary to consult the Department of Education and Science and the Department of Trade and Industry. As a result of these enquiries, it became clear that minor changes in the Constitution could be made, and a scheme devised whereby the status of the Urdd as a charity and an incorporated body would not be jeopardised.

These constitutional changes were the prerogative of the Commission appointed by the Urdd Council, under the chairmanship of Owen Edwards, to review the organisation and control of the movement. Any comprehensive review of organisational matters, however, was inevitably linked with the pending restructuring of Local Government, and this meant that changes in the Urdd Constitution could not be finalised until 1973/74.

*   *   *   *

It was forty years since the Urdd National Eisteddfod had been held at Swansea. During that period, a highly organised Eisteddfod system had been devised and the festival had grown in complexity. Costs too had increased, and in 1971 they were ten times as high as in 1931. Swansea and Cwm Tawe had an abundance of enthusiastic workers, and it was not difficult to find the requisite number of officers and committee members. The Chairman of the Executive Committee was the Rev. Trebor Lloyd Evans, one-time Chairman of the Urdd Council, and for nearly twenty years leader of the Morriston Aelwyd. The two Vice-Chairmen were the Rev. T. Burgess Jones of Pontardawe and Professor T. J. Morgan of Swansea, and the secretarial duties were shared by the Rev. and Mrs. D. Islwyn Davies. Harry Clarke Jones, with his magnetic personality, held the office of Treasurer, and with a man of Evan Morris' calibre as Chairman of the Finance Committee, one could rest assured that the advance-fund of £10,000 would not present insurmountable difficulties. The Committee had already succeeded in enlisting the support of the City Council, who had promised a grant of £2,500 and agreed that a site in Singleton Park be made available for the Eisteddfod.

One could hardly imagine any major Urdd event being held in Glamorgan without the wholehearted support of the Lord Lieutenant, Sir Cennydd Traherne. At Swansea, he had agreed to be Honorary President, and it was he who later officiated at the opening ceremony of the Arts, Crafts and Science Exhibition. Equally popular was the choice of the four Vice-Presidents— Dr. Stephen J. Williams, Mrs. J. T. Morgan, Ifor Davies, M.P., and Tillie Thomas. Collaborating with the officers were the several committees who worked tirelessly for two years, but perhaps the greatest credit should go to the Hospitality Committee, led by Mrs. Trebor Lloyd Evans, who arranged hospitality in homes for five-thousand competitors. This is one of the Urdd's annual miracles.

The major disappointment was the lack of public support for the Eisteddfod sessions. Was it due to lack of publicity and communication ? Did the Eisteddfod lack the spectacle and pageantry that alone could draw the crowds ? Were the people of the area becoming less conscious of their Welsh identity ? Or, in our affluent society, has the interest in culture yielded to more mundane and less demanding entertainment ? These were questions which inevitably occupied the minds of the organisers. Fortunately, the seeming lack of public support did not worry the competitors, and the usual high standards were evident. At the close of the proceedings, it was West Glamorgan that won the chief laurels and it was their representatives who received custody of the Royal Prize and the Pantyfedwen Trophy and investment.

The Eisteddfod Chair for a sequence of poems portraying historical characters was won by a young schoolteacher, Arwel John, a native of Pontyberem. Second and third were Ieuan Wyn Gruffydd of Crymych (chaired at Llanidloes) and Islwyn Edwards of Pontrhydygroes. The Crown, in the main prose competition, went to Sion Eirian, a seventeen-year old pupil at Ysgol Maesgarmon, Mold, who had already been placed second and third in the Chair competition at a previous Eisteddfod. Second place was shared by Yvonne Davies of *Aelwyd Caerfyrddin* and Gwenda Owen of *Aelwyd Llangefni*, with Nan Lloyd Williams, who had been crowned at Aberystwyth, third.

The President on the Thursday was Edward Morus Jones, pop-singer idol of the younger generation, camp leader and tutor at the Urdd language-courses. A native of Llanuwchllyn, it was natural that he should invite the audience to the Urdd Eisteddfod at Bala the following year, and he did so in an original song entitled *Eisteddfod y Jiwbili*. Friday's President was Huldah Bassett, former Headmistress of Gowerton Girls' Grammar School, who testified to the value of a school Branch of the Urdd for those members privileged to benefit by its activities.

Welsh was a second-language for the Most Reverend Dr. Glyn Simon who presided over Saturday's session. Like Edward Morus Jones, he referred to members of *Cymdeithas yr Iaith Gymraeg* found guilty in their trial at Swansea a fortnight earlier, and deplored the obstinacy of the authorities in refusing to recognise the rightful place of the Welsh language in the life of Wales. These remarks were approved by many and resented by others, and once again, the cleavage of opinion on the language question became evident.

As at Aberystwyth, the Eisteddfod at Swansea was one that triumphed over difficulties. It was the most costly of all Urdd Eisteddfodau, and despite total proceeds of £18,380 including an advance-fund of £12,271, expenses reached £13,782, leaving a balance of only £4,600. The alarming prospect was the possibility that costs could further escalate at a rate of £2,000 a year, which meant that by the mid-seventies they would reach a figure of £20,000. It was clearly a matter needing urgent attention.

*　　　*　　　*　　　*

Only once since the idea was first mooted in 1953 had the *Gŵyl Sir* visited Caernarfonshire. That was in 1962, when it was confined to the Arfon District. Early in 1971, it was announced that the Llŷn and Eifionydd District would be prepared to act as hosts. Meirion Parry of Porthmadog was elected Chairman of the Executive Committee, with Robin W. Hughes as Vice-Chairman, and Elwyn Owen as Treasurer, while the duties of Secretary were undertaken by Bettie Jones. Twenty village committees were set up; branches of *Merched y Wawr* and the Women's Institutes, schools and even churches became involved. New village Adrannau sprang up as a result of this involvement, and this was more important than the Festival itself, if only because of its more permanent nature.

The week opened with a *Cymanfa Ganu* at Porthmadog and closed with another at Edern the following Sunday. In between the two, there were a *Twmpath Dawns*, a *Discotec*, a *Noson Lawen*, a féte, and a pageant entitled *Y Môr a'r Glannau* (The sea and its coasts) devised by Councillor Glyn Roberts, Mayor of Pwllheli, and welded into a quick-moving colourful and artistic whole by the producer, the Rev. Canon Huw Pierce Jones. The task of co-ordinating and stimulating the festival was in the competent hands of the County Organiser, Gwilym Charles Williams, supported by Gareth Gregory from Swyddfa'r Urdd. But the main honours must surely go to the scores of voluntary workers who together created a model festival that left its mark on the entire area. It seemed incredible that expenses could have been limited to £73 and it was with a large measure of justifiable pride that a cheque for the balance of

£1,320 was handed to the Urdd Treasurer at the final meeting of the Executive Committee.

*   *   *   *

Other matters given publicity during the year included the following.

i. A festival was held in the Penllyn area of Merioneth to proclaim and publicise the Jubilee Eisteddfod to be held at Bala in 1972 and to further its financial appeal.

ii. The first volume of the story of Urdd Gobaith Cymru (1922—1945) by R. E. Griffith was published on 1 May 1971. By this time, the author realised that it would not be possible to do justice to the remaining period, 1945—1972, in one volume, and that a third volume would, therefore, be necessary.

iii. The policy of re-publishing, in book form, material that had first appeared in Urdd magazines was continued, and 1971 saw the publication of *Storiau Meic Ifans* by R. Gordon Williams, *Cymdogion Lôn Goch* (for Welsh learners) by Ina Tudno Williams, and *Lle yn yr Haul*, a volume of nature articles by E. Breeze Jones.

iv. The 1971 Goodwill Message was the fiftieth in the annual series. The first draft of the Message was prepared by a small group of students at the City of Cardiff College of Education, and on the Sunday prior to Goodwill Day, a special service was televised by the BBC from the Llandâf Cathedral, the address being given by Hywel D. Roberts.

v. An annual grant of £100 was offered by the National Westminster Bank towards furthering schemes of humanitarian or social service by Urdd members. The first grant was awarded to Aelwyd Gwyddelwern, Merioneth, that had undertaken to convert a building into a social centre for the youth of the village.

vi. Once again, the Cardiff College of Education Aelwyd were victors in the Pantyfedwen Soccer Competition. Incidentally, it was a source of great pride that so many former

79   The Barry John XV at the Urdd Jubilee Game

80   Barry John's famous last try

81 *Gŵyl y Gobaith*—Festival of Hope—at Llanuwchllyn, September 1972

82 Speakers at the Jubilee Celebration

members of the Urdd were included in the Welsh Rugby XV that won both the Triple Crown and the Rugby Championship in 1971.

vii. The Urdd Executive Committee expressed its dissatisfaction at the tardiness of the Government and the Welsh Office in granting its rightful status to the Welsh language. It was resolved to protest against the decision to distribute to Welsh homes an all-English booklet explaining the change to decimal currency. At the same time, Urdd Branches and County Youth Councils voluntarily undertook to distribute thousands of copies of the Welsh version which otherwise would be reluctantly produced on demand from under the counter.

The Urdd also submitted a memorandum to the Roderic Bowen Committee, set up by the Secretary of State for Wales to advise the Government on the matter of bilingual road-signs. The memorandum maintained that the provision of bilingual road-signs in a bilingual country was a matter of elementary justice and common-sense, and little did we think that eighteen months would elapse before any announcement would be made. It was frustrating delays of this nature that made the Urdd still more convinced of the need for a permanent Royal Commission to keep a watching brief over the well-being of the language.

viii. Following the success of its annual series of Welsh-language courses at Glan Llyn and Llangrannog, the Urdd sought to persuade the Welsh Joint Education Committee to make it possible, through the Local Education Authorities, for the Urdd to appoint four or five specialist teachers as full-time tutors for school groups released during term-time to attend short residential courses at Glan Llyn. Unfortunately, too few Authorities supported the scheme to make it viable, and an opportunity that would have been a boon to teachers and pupils alike was irretrievably lost.

22

U NTIL 1970, the word ' retirement ' had not entered into the vocabulary of members of the Urdd staff. Many had resigned to take up other posts, but Ivor Owen was the first to 'retire'. Others were to follow in 1971. In February, it was the turn of Dafydd Jones, who over a period of thirty-one years had held various posts, first as field officer and as part-time Organiser of the Urdd Eisteddfod, and later as member of headquarters staff at Aberystwyth. During the whole of his service, no-one had shown greater willingness to shoulder new responsibilities, or greater loyalty both to his colleagues and to the movement.

August saw the retirement of Maldwyn W. Jones after twenty-five years as Manager of Pantyfedwen. He was entrusted with an arduous task, but his complete devotion ensured its success. Panty-fedwen had become the property of the Urdd in 1947, and although used during vacation periods for the Urdd's own needs—the International and Inter-Celtic Conventions, Staff conferences and Council meetings, courses and reunions—it was never possible to make full use of the premises. Consequently, during term-time, it was let to schools and colleges and used later as a hostel for Aberystwyth students. For part of the summer vacation, it was run as a hotel, with some weeks reserved for Welsh-speaking visitors. Many of these lived across the border, and welcomed the opportunity of renewing their acquaintance with Wales and with their fellow-countrymen at Pantyfedwen. Its closure was naturally a disappointment to those who had enjoyed its amenities, but there were several factors that led to this decision, and when it was learnt that the College of Librarianship would not require its use as a students' hostel after 1971, it was decided that Pantyfedwen be offered for sale and the capital used to develop the 'new Llangrannog'.

At the time, however, the demand for such a building was slight, and it was as an alternative that the Treasurer, Prys Edwards, proposed a scheme which included converting the greater part of the building into flats and utilising the remainder as a craft-shop and restaurant. Plans were submitted and it was learnt that grants of £36,000 would be available towards the necessary adaptation. By the end of 1971, however, contractors' fees had increased to such an extent that the total costs would amount to more than £90,000. Even with the available grant-aid, it meant an expenditure of almost £60,000 for the Urdd, and even though much of this could be recovered in a few years, the Council did not feel justified in investing so much capital in a centre that was not really fulfilling the Urdd's own need , when the money was so urgently needed elsewhere. For this reason, it was reluctantly decided to abandon a scheme that was at once ambitious and exciting, and to make further efforts during 1972 to dispose of the property to someone who was blessed with greater financial resources.

This decision meant that other members of the Pantyfedwen staff became redundant. Two of these had served the movement loyally for twenty-four years. Ann Lloyd had shared managerial duties with Maldwyn Jones and was a model of efficiency ; her secretarial experience would now be invaluable at Swyddfa'r Urdd, if only on a part-time basis. The other key person was the Chef, Fred Keall. He too had been exceptionally conscientious, and though he had reached retirement age in 1971 he was in good health and agreed to continue in a part-time capacity until the fate of Pantyfedwen was finally decided.

There were, inevitably, other changes in the Urdd staff, especially in the ranks of County Organisers. Alwyn Williams could claim seven years' service as Organiser for Denbighshire and Flintshire— long enough to have left his mark on his 'parish'. He had also played a prominent part in the running of Glan Llyn, becoming one of its most experienced activity leaders. When he left to take up a teaching appointment at *Ysgol Glan Clwyd*, St. Asaph, it was decided, following the offer of increased grants from the Education Authorities, to appoint a full-time Organiser for each of the two counties. John M. Hughes had been a member of the staff for ten years, first as Organiser for Caernarfonshire and Anglesey, and later as Head of the Eisteddfod and Festival Department. He resigned to take up another administrative post, and was replaced by his assistant, Gareth Gregory. Wynne Melville Jones, Organiser for Carmarthenshire, was transferred to the post of Public Relations Officer at Headquarters. This aspect had never been given adequate attention, and the new appointment would be a step in the right direction, and would allow John Japheth to devote all his time to the organisation and development of the Llangrannog centre.

Death, as ever, had taken its toll of persons who had given distinguished service to the movement. Notable among these were Dai Williams of Tregaron and Elfyn Talfan Davies of Brynaman. Perhaps the greatest loss, however, was that of Dr. Gwenan Jones, whose help in the development of *Yr Ysgol Gymraeg* during the period 1931—1951 had been inestimable. When Ifan ab Owen Edwards was elected President of the Urdd in 1944, Dr. Gwenan Jones took over as Council Chairman and continued in office until 1948 when she became a Vice-President. She had also been Chairman of the O. M. Edwards Centenary Committee. The Urdd was indeed privileged to have had the benefit of her strong character, her wealth of experience and her brilliant intellect for more than thirty years.

*   *   *   *

It was inevitable that the Jubilee celebrations should overshadow the year's regular events, but from the outset, it had been emphasised that, as far as possible, the special functions should not be allowed to obstruct the normal activities of the movement. There were ten weeks of summer camping at Glan Llyn and eleven at Llangrannog. At the latter centre, three weeks were allocated to non-Welsh-speaking members, in addition to the three weeks' language-courses. Another week was reserved for Welsh-speakers who yet felt the need to improve the quality of their spoken language. Altogether, a total of 2,722 campers were accepted ; another 700 had to be disappointed through lack of accommodation. A total of 1,348 spent a week at Glan Llyn, and these included third and fourth year secondary school pupils taking part in the two language courses. Glan Llyn, however, was open throughout the year, and outside the camping period, a total of 3,791 had attended courses and conferences at this centre.

Even while the camps at Llangrannog were in progress, work was started on improving and adapting Cefn Cwrt farmhouse, so that accommodation would be available for the resident staff required for the centre. Shortly afterwards, work was begun on new camp dormitories, with toilets and washing facilities, and on a new dining-hall and kitchen complex. The scheme also allowed for a spacious building to house an instructional swimming pool and an indoor arena for the teaching of pony riding techniques. The other existing buildings are not to be replaced until the second phase of development can be implemented. One still hopes, however, that a complete new campus will have been erected by 1976.

The Urdd Camps Committee, under the chairmanship of Hywel W. Jones, supervised these developments and were also required to keep an eye on two other group-centres—one at Aberporth and the other at Nant Gwynant in Caernarfonshire. The hut at Aberporth, despite its many advantages, did not achieve the popularity one would have wished, primarily because it lacked separate accommodation for leaders. But because of its proximity to Llangrannog, the Committee hesitated to recommend the expenditure required for its development, and its fate was uncertain. The other centre, *Sgubor Bwlch* in Nant Gwynant, had been consistently used by small groups since 1963, but the expiration of the lease in 1973 prompted the owner not only to demand a much higher rent, but also to stipulate that the Urdd should undertake structural improvements at considerable cost. The committee decided that these demands were excessive and that the property should be abandoned. However, as one door closed another seemed to open. A disused power-house near Croesor in Caernarfonshire was purchased for £850, and although dilapidated, the property was freehold and offered many possibilities of development. The Jane Hodge Foundation made a grant of £500 towards the cost of purchase, and more than £200 was contributed by the Junior Urdd Club at Aberystwyth whose members had been *Sgubor Bwlch* supporters and now wished to ensure that an alternative centre would speedily be provided. It was realised that the cost of reconstruction and adaptation would be substantial and applications for grant-aid were made to five Local Education Authorities in North Wales. When *Blaen y Cwm* becomes operative—one hopes by 1974—it should prove an ideal mountain-centre for adventure-groups wishing to plan their own activities and cater for their own needs.

The 1972 organised games tournaments claimed their usual quota of supporters, and altogether more than 1,500 members participated. Teams from six Welsh counties took part in the final contests, and for the first time, the Pantyfedwen Soccer Cup was won by *Aelwyd Myrddin*—the Urdd group at Trinity College, Carmarthen.

* * * *

1972 was not an easy year for the Magazines Department, and in their first year the new editorial staff had to cope with several problems without the help of any committee other than the Magazines Conference. When that body met in March 1972, the monthly sales figures were quoted as follows—

First Language		*Second Language*	
' Deryn '	6,452	' Bore Da '	16,407
' Cymru'r Plant '	5,986	' Mynd '	9,407
' Hamdden '	2,135		

This meant that the combined monthly sales were as high as 40,387, despite the fact that, over a period of fifteen years, prices had more than doubled in a vain attempt to keep pace with production costs. The circulation figures would, of course, present quite a different picture were it not for the requisitions of the Local Education Authorities, but they were the first to admit that the magazines were invaluable to schools.

Hamdden, however, had had a chequered existence. Its sale had dropped from five-thousand to just over two-thousand, and during the previous five years, it had been published at a loss. It was not intended mainly for classroom use, and was therefore not directly requisitioned to the same extent by the Education Authorities. Furthermore, bookshop sales had proved inadequate, either because of lack of appeal or lack of publicity. Faced with this situation, the Urdd decided to discontinue *Hamdden* and to replace it in 1973 with a new and different kind of magazine that would have a more direct appeal for teenagers. A welcome grant of £700 towards the launching of *I'r Dim* was received from the Catherine and Lady Grace James Foundation as a gesture to the Urdd in its Jubilee year.

Faced with such problems and pressure of work generally, it was clear that the editorial staff could not cope with the additional task of editing *Blodau'r Ffair*. The obvious solution was to appoint an

editor from outside, and one did not have to look far to find Dan
L. James, a University lecturer, an editor and author, a specialist in
second-language teaching, and one of the Urdd's most ardent
workers. The magazine reappeared in 1972, bubbling over with
originality and humour. *Blodau'r Ffair* had been given a new lease of
life. March 1972 saw the publication of R. E. Griffith's second
volume, continuing the story of the Urdd (1946—1960). Other
publications were *Storiau Aelwyd Brynclyd* (Brenda Wyn Jones) and
Helyntion Jac y Gofalwr (W. Morgan Rogers), both of which had
appeared in serial form in *Mynd*, the second-language magazine for
adolescents.

One can hardly mention the publication of Welsh books without
being reminded of the enormous contribution made by the Welsh
Books Council. Brought into being in 1962 through the far-
sightedness and perseverance of Alun R. Edwards, County Librarian
for Cardiganshire, its growth and development have been phenomenal and its contribution to the production and distribution of
Welsh literature inestimable. Through its various departments—
editorial, publicity, and design—it has given Welsh publishers the
kind of professional help they had all wanted. This is in addition to
establishing a National Books Centre at Aberystwyth ; arranging
annual Book Festivals and other exhibitions ; translating selected
volumes for library use ; producing large-print books and cassettes ;
and providing remuneration for Welsh authors. Indeed, the
Council has completely revolutionised the Welsh book-trade
during the past ten years. This could not have been achieved
without the aid of grants from the Welsh Arts Council and the
Local Authorities, but the dynamic figure behind the overall
achievement is the Council's Director, Alun Creunant Davies.
Some would even argue that the Council could claim to have made
the most positive contribution to the cause of the Welsh language
during the past decade.

*　　*　　*　　*

The Urdd Council's Eisteddfod Committee, under the chairmanship of John Garnon, kept a watchful eye on forthcoming Eisteddfodau and Festivals, ready to help or offer advice when required.
These events included the Proclamation Festival at Pontypridd in

anticipation of the Eisteddfod to be held in 1973. The Executive
Committee there was led by Eric Evans, and it elected Sir Geraint
Evans Honorary President, and Brynmor John, M.P., and Leslie
Jones, Secretary for Education (Wales), Vice-Presidents. The
Eisteddfod Patrons were Sir Cennydd Traherne and the Rt. Hon.
The Lord Heycock, two who had been constant supporters of the
Urdd over many years. The Committee were alert to the financial
implications, and given a target of £12,000 for the advance-fund,
their immediate reaction was to raise it to £15,000, and by the end
of 1972 they were already within £2,000 of their goal. This would
be the first Eisteddfod in the Urdd's second half-century and this
in itself was an added incentive on all fronts.

Meanwhile, Flintshire was on the move with its plans for the 1974
Eisteddfod to be held at Rhyl. With J. Howard Davies, the county's
Director of Education, as Chairman of the Executive Committee,
they lost no time in coming to grips with their tasks which included
raising a reserve-fund of £15,000. The fact that they decided to
extend the event to be a four-day festival was in itself an indication
of their enthusiasm, and possibly a pointer towards future trends.
This will be the last Urdd Eisteddfod to be based on the present
County administration ; by 1974, Flintshire as such will have
ceased to exist and will have become merged into the new County
of Clwyd.

In October 1972, the Urdd Executive Committee gratefully
accepted an invitation to hold the 1975 National Eisteddfod at
Llanelli, and there were already rumours that some North Wales
towns were considering the possibilities for 1976.

*　　　*　　　*　　　*

The Urdd Council had already given considerable thought to the
urgent need for better provision in Welsh-language radio and
television programmes, especially for children and young people.
It had expressed deep dissatisfaction with the disparity in the
number of hours allocated to Welsh and English programmes and
the consequent effect on the Welsh child's attitude to his language as
well as on the standard of the spoken word. Accordingly, a memorandum outlining the situation and expressing the anxiety felt by
Welsh-speaking parents was sent to the Broadcasting Council for

Wales (BBC) and to the Welsh Committee of the IBA. Both bodies welcomed deputations from the Urdd, but although these were sympathetically received, it was abundantly clear that little improvement could be expected unless more funds were released for the purpose. A further deputation met Charles Curran, Director General of the BBC, and once again, the question of availability of funds was stressed. Since it was categorically stated that the Corporation did not have adequate finance to meet the demands of Wales—which meant trebling the hours and improving the standard of Welsh language programmes, and ensuring satisfactory reception in all parts of the country—there was no alternative but to take the matter direct to the Government. So long as Wales remains an integral part of Britain, the Government bears a major responsibility for the promotion of the language and culture of the Welsh people, not only through schools and colleges, but also through the media of radio and television.

The Urdd was not alone in pressing the need for improvement in this direction. A committee elected by the University of Wales Council made a detailed investigation of the situation and considered possible solutions. Resolutions passed by various bodies called for an independent Welsh channel, while many individuals expressed their dissatisfaction through non-payment of television licence fees. Both *Plaid Cymru* and the Welsh Language Society had long advocated that the hitherto unused Fourth Channel be given exclusively to Wales. There was indeed a large measure of agreement in favour of this plan, though opinions differed as to how the channel should be administered, and whether it should be used for bilingual or all-Welsh programmes.

The Urdd too believed that the desired results could best be achieved by allocating to Wales the available Fourth Channel. Priority should be given to programmes in Welsh, but with provision also for a substantial number of English-language programmes of special interest to Wales. This would, therefore, be a channel reflecting the whole spectrum of Welsh life and providing a service that could unite the nation. Naturally, it could not be maintained without a substantial Government subsidy, but this would be no more than the Government's legitimate obligation to Wales.

*　　　*　　　*　　　*

Like most other Welsh movements, the Urdd welcomed the Bowen Committee Report on Bilingual Road-signs and the Government's favourable reaction as expressed by the Secretary for Wales. Nevertheless, it must be recognised that Welsh or bilingual road-signs alone will not save the language. There are many other needs clamouring for serious and urgent attention. Adequate provision in radio and television programmes has already been referred to. There is an urgent need for many more Welsh nursery schools and a further development in teaching through the medium of Welsh along the lines already explored by the Schools Council. This in turn would lead to a demand for more bilingual secondary schools. There is an upsurge of desire, hitherto unknown, among non-Welsh speakers anxious to learn the language, and the facilities available could well be multiplied. Furthermore, at the time when it was announced that £3,275,000 would be needed for the provision of bilingual road-signs, Welsh publishers were urging the Government to increase its annual grant of £12,500 towards the publication of Welsh books. A grant of £50,000 p.a. over a period of five years would amount to no more than a quarter of a million. As long as these other demands continue to be ignored, how much can bilingual road-signs in themselves achieve ? Without the means of safeguarding the living culture—especially through the media of broadcasting, education and literature—bilingual road-signs, important though they are, could become the tombstones of a dead language.

There is, therefore, a dire need for a comprehensive study and continuous survey of all the factors affecting the wellbeing of the language and culture of the nation, and it is for this that the Urdd had pressed, urging the setting up of a permanent Royal Commission that would examine the situation in its entirety and have power to act on a broad basis. It would operate in many spheres and have a built-in capacity to evolve according to the needs that arise. The language problem is a complex one, and the various needs are often inter-related and cannot be treated in isolation. It is surely time to view the cultural and linguistic needs of Wales in a comprehensive, intelligent and sympathetic manner, and to introduce the kind of measures that will meet those needs—before it is too late.

*   *   *   *

Long before 1972 had drawn to its close, R. E. Griffith and I had deemed it wise to inform the Urdd Executive Committee of our intention to retire in 1973. It was necessary to give the Staffing Committee ample time to review the pattern of administration and to decide on any changes that might be necessary to meet the needs of the new era, an era that would be deprived of the guiding hand of R. E. Griffith. It would be foolish to attempt in a few words to evaluate the part played by R. E. Griffith in the development of the Urdd, or his influence on the movement. Over a period of forty years—first as Chief Organiser and later as Director—he had worked side-by-side with the Founder, knowing of every move and partaking of every decision. But this was by no means all. He was a born administrator, a meticulous and systematic organiser, a proverbially hard worker who yet found time to acquaint himself with departmental developments and, when necessary, to discuss even minor problems with his colleagues. He could, of course, draw upon a wide and diversified experience, and he had a unique gift of diplomacy and persuasion. But his greatest strength lay in his meticulous planning. With the far-sighted strategy of a general, he would plan every move, and anticipate possible difficulties so that he would meet them armed with as many alternative solutions as the circumstances might demand. This was largely the secret of his success and a measure of his greatness. And now, in an official capacity at least, the Urdd was to lose his leadership. Fortunately, however, J. Cyril Hughes was already Deputy Director and the next step was to appoint him Director Designate. He had given twelve years' service as a member of staff and, during his four years as Deputy Director, had proved himself an excellent administrator. He had kept himself informed of developments in every department and had grasped every opportunity to meet workers in the field. He had achieved a happy working relationship with the statutory authorities and was alert to every development within the Youth Service. It was felt, therefore, that he had the ability and the experience to enable him to take over the Directorship in October 1973.

At the Committee's request, the Director Designate outlined the staffing pattern he would like to aim at in the near future. He foresaw the need for three key appointments—Administrative Secretary, Finance and Business Officer, and Chief Organiser. The first would have to claim priority due to my departure in 1973, having achieved my ambition of devoting myself to the service of Wales through a movement in whose ideals I could wholeheartedly believe. The new post of Administrative Secretary went to Gwilym Charles Williams who had been Organiser for Caernarfonshire for nearly four years.

Delyth Lewis and I had collaborated closely for more than five years and her departure in the autumn of 1972 meant that short-courses for school-leavers, and the Welsh-language courses in particular, would be deprived of her expertise. This was also true of the Goodwill Message and other aspects of international, religious and social affairs for which she was mainly responsible. To fill the immediate gap, responsibility for the short-courses was given to John Japheth, while Evan L. Isaac agreed to add the duties of Secretary to the International, Religious and Social Affairs Committee to those of Chief Field Officer, now that his duties as Organiser of the Jubilee Celebrations were drawing to an end.

The Urdd would thus face the new era with J. Cyril Hughes as Director, Gwilym C. Williams as Administrative Secretary, and a Finance/Business Officer and a Chief Organiser to be appointed later. Elsi Williams would continue as Head of the Finance Department, and here it is appropriate to record that she has given more than forty years' exemplary service to the Urdd and has identified herself completely with the movement. The Estates Officer, Huw Cedwyn Jones, has a record of thirty-two years of unbroken service. His skill as a designer, his craftmanship and his knowledge of building techniques have made his contribution unique. Elvey Macdonald replaced Gareth O. Gregory as Head of the Eisteddfod and Festival Department, and together with Ieuan Griffith as Magazines Editor and Wynne Melville Jones as Public Relations Officer, this would complete the team of Headquarters administrators. And with John Japheth and J. Eric Williams as Principal Officers of Llangrannog and Glan Llyn respectively, one could rest assured that the two centres would be operated in accordance with the aims and ideals of the movement. The twelve County Organisers would, for some time yet, be able to benefit by the experience of Evan L. Isaac as adviser and liaison officer. His twenty-five years' service to the movement have covered a wide range of activities, not the least being his interest in Llangrannog Camp, sharing the main responsibility with John R. Lane, who has given seventeen years' service as Organiser in Glamorgan.

Added to these are the team of secretarial and clerical staff, headed by Morwena Jones with twenty-two years' loyal service. Altogether, the movement can well feel proud of its staff, many possessing years of experience, some even having turned a blind eye to more remunerative opportunities. With these as the mainstay of the movement, the Urdd can face the new era with confidence and courage.

Two former Vice-Presidents who had been staunch supporters of the movement died during the year. They were Dr. Iorwerth Hughes Jones of Swansea, one-time Chairman of the Urdd Council, and Sali H. Davies of Lampeter. Two other prominent Council members who died during the year were Keri Harris Hughes of Cardiff and the Rev. T. Alban Davies of Ton Pentre.

*   *   *   *

To mark the Jubilee year, R. E. Griffith and I were honoured by being admitted to the Druid Order of the *Gorsedd* at the National Eisteddfod of Wales in Haverfordwest. In the same year, R. E. Griffith was made a Deputy Lieutenant of Cardiganshire.

*   *   *   *

The Company's financial position at the end of the first half-century was something of a paradox. On the one hand, the cost of running the movement in 1971/72 had reached a record total of £135,942, no small undertaking for a voluntary movement. On the other hand, the Company's investments amounted to £70,000 which could be redeemed if necessary. In addition, the Urdd owned land, buildings and other property that could be valued in excess of £200,000. Although by no means a wealthy movement, it was certainly in a healthier state in 1972 than it had been in 1952 or in 1932. Much of the credit for this was due to the Company's Treasurers, and especially to W. J. Williams who had laid the foundations during his period of office, to Cynfab Roberts for his careful husbandry between 1954 and 1963, and to Prys Edwards for his detailed supervision and bold initiative during the three years 1969-72. One cannot forget, of course, that from the very beginning until his death in 1970, the Founder's interest in this aspect of the work had been a source of encouragement to every Treasurer in the difficult task of making ends meet ; even in the darkest hour, they knew that Sir Ifan's genius for ' breaking through' was at hand.

It was obvious that building the new Llangrannog centre, developing Glan Llyn, together with the possibility of providing a smaller residential centre in Glamorgan, would use up a considerable share of the Company's investments. One realised, however, that such expenditure would in itself be a form of investment, although not primarily a financial one. The gains from the above centres would, at best, be long-term benefits, and without some imaginative and more lucrative schemes to offset the expenditure, the Urdd could find itself facing another period of lean years as it approached the eighties. Even in recent times, it had been a continuous struggle to meet day-to-day expenses. And as the cost of living continues to escalate, without substantially increased grants, it is becoming increasingly difficult for a voluntary organisation to offer salaries comparable with other educational establishments. It would not be unreasonable to ask that the grants received from the Department of Education and Science and the Local Education Authorities be doubled from £20,000 to £40,000 per annum. This and more is paid in salaries to the staff of any one secondary school !

23

ALTHOUGH the Urdd's fiftieth birthday fell on New Year's Day, it was deemed advisable that the whole of 1972 be designated 'Jubilee Year'. It opened with a special supplement of *Y Cymro* tracing facets in the development of the movement. In his leading article, the editor summed up his assessment—

' The story of the growth of the Urdd, from being a movement for a handful of youngsters to being a youth movement for a whole nation, is an inspiration and a lesson for others. It has displayed characteristics not usually associated with our national character : efficient organisation—combining the professional and the voluntary—and perseverance arising out of an un-wavering vision. It has embraced the non-Welsh-speakers without sacrificing any of its own Welshness . . .'

And beginning on New Year's Day, scores of messages were received expressing the congratulations, appreciation and good wishes of all sections of the Welsh community.

In a New Year's press-message to Urdd members, the President, Lady Edwards, appealed to those ' non-Welsh-speakers ' referred to in *Y Cymro*—

' We need your co-operation and your wholehearted support if the nation is to be united, content and harmonious. We depend on you to help us in our efforts to close any gaps and heal any breaches that may occur between us as Welsh people . . .'

On the threshold of a new era, it was felt that a new official Urdd song was required to replace the well-known and well-worn *Dathlwn glod ein cyndadau*. The tune was retained, but new words, written by Aneurin Jenkins-Jones, were adopted, the verses dealing respectively with the Wales of the past, the present and the future.

*   *   *   *

Among the London-Welsh community, no one has his fingers more closely on the pulse of Wales than John Williams. Early in 1971, anticipating Jubilee Year, he had persuaded the London-

Welsh Association to invite the Urdd to be responsible for the 1972 St. David's Day Concert programme in the Albert Hall, and we were pleased to accept. The content of the programme was, of course, entirely in Welsh, but it was agreed that the narration should be mainly in English so that the non-Welsh-speaking members of the audience could appreciate the significance of the items in relation to the ideals and the activities of the movement as it stepped into the seventies. The Urdd was asked to devise the programme, select the artistes and prepare the narration script ; the presentation of the programme was entrusted to the Association's experienced production-team led by Peter Morley Jones, Mervyn Evans and John Thomas. Altogether, some five-hundred members took part, including a massed choir of nearly four-hundred voices drawn from Adrannau and Aelwydydd and blended into a cohesive whole by the conductor, Dr. Terry James. There were also folk and classical songs, *penillion* singing, harp *ensemble*, folk-dancing, pop songs, and a camp scene in which the massed choir joined in the hilarity of the camp songs. Linked by the narrator, Alun Williams of the BBC, the selected items conveyed something of the discipline, the vitality, and the spontaneity of the movement. As the programme drew to its close, three colourful tableau-groups portrayed the Urdd pledge of loyalty—to Wales, to fellow-man and to Christ. Then, as the stage lights were dimmed, a spotlight picked out the huge photograph of Sir Ifan ab Owen Edwards with the dates 1922—1972. Simultaneously, the narrator continued—

' We close our tribute to Urdd Gobaith Cymru and its glorious record of service to the youth of Wales for the past fifty years. And let us now acknowledge that nothing of this would have happened were it not for one man—Sir Ifan ab Owen Edwards, who founded the Urdd in 1922 and led and inspired the movement until he died two years ago . . . He was, without doubt, one of Wales' most brilliant sons. He was a visionary, a prophet, an idealist, a dreamer of dreams. But he was also a realist, a practical man who set about doing things rather than talking about them. We mourn his loss tonight, but we feel that he is here in spirit—here amongst the boys and girls he loved so much and for whom he laboured without counting the cost. The Urdd is a living memorial to Sir Ifan ab Owen Edwards. He will never die so long as the Urdd goes marching on. Let us wish the movement God speed during its next fifty years. *Bendith Duw fo ar Urdd Gobaith Cymru.*'

83 The unveiling by Lady Edwards

84 Officers of the N.U.T. presenting a cheque for £500 for the Jubilee Fund

85   R. E. Griffith

86   J. Cyril Hughes

87   Elsi Williams

88   Maldwyn W. Jones

89   Dafydd Jones   90   Huw Cedwyn Jones

91   The 'unofficial' Jubilee Stamp

92   The Jubilee postal franking

The choir and audience then joined in singing *Hen Wlad fy Nhadau*, and it is doubtful whether the National Anthem was ever sung in the Albert Hall with so much meaning and so much fervour as on that occasion.

Part of the programme was later broadcast by the BBC on radio and colour television, and the response of listeners and viewers who had not been able to attend the concert was fantastic. The occasion was a unique opportunity of presenting the Urdd to the non-Welsh-speaking community and this released a fount of goodwill towards the movement. Financially, the Urdd did not stand to gain anything from the Festival and the participants received only a small proportion of their expenses. Soon afterwards, however, John Williams and W. Emrys Evans, through personal approaches to patriotic London Welshmen, were instrumental in adding more than a thousand pounds to the Urdd Jubilee Fund.

*   *   *   *

Two music compositions were commissioned by the Urdd to mark Jubilee Year. The first was a choral work by Professor Alun Hoddinott for which words, entitled *Ieuenctid y Dydd* (Youth of Today), were written by Sir Thomas Parry-Williams. It was first performed in the Llandâf Festival on June 5 by the Cardiff Aelwyd Choir under its conductor, Alun Guy. The other was an orchestral work by Professor William Mathias entitled ' Celtic Dances ' and included in the *repertoire* of the National Youth Orchestra of Wales in a concert at Haverfordwest during the National Eisteddfod week. Both commissioned works were subsidised by the Welsh Arts Council.

March saw the publication of a bilingual supplement by the *Cambrian News*, and articles in Welsh and English appeared in various other newspapers and periodicals. The second volume of R. E. Griffith's story of the Urdd was published, and the University of Wales Press had taken Sir Ifan ab Owen Edwards as the subject of their St. David's Day bilingual booklet. It was written by Norah Isaac, with an English translation by Aneurin Jenkins-Jones.

The *Western Mail* in its editorial listed Wales' debt to the Urdd—

'. . . First, its practical contribution towards preserving and revitalising the culture that makes Wales Welsh ; . . . it was the Urdd which pioneered the Welsh schools from its own funds at Aberystwyth in 1939 . . . Not only has the movement helped the Principality's native tongue hold its own with English as an educational medium, but it has also released the language from the aridity of text-books . . . Perhaps the biggest tribute on its Golden Jubilee is to say that in an era when it has become commonplace for youth to drop out, the Urdd has constantly encouraged 47,000 children and teenagers to opt in.'

In his final assessment, the editor of *Y Faner* struck a similar note—

' One cannot measure the influence the movement has had on the lives of our children and our youth during the impressionable years.'

Sir Goronwy Daniel, writing in the *Western Mail*, traced the Urdd's contribution in various fields, emphasising its value not only to the individual, but also to young people in relation to the society in which they live. He concluded—

' High priority should be given to encouraging non-political organisations like the Urdd which promote the physical and mental health of the individual, engage him in voluntary service to the community, and interest him in the culture of his country.'

In *Y Ddraig Goch*, Cassie Davies paid her own tribute and that of *Plaid Cymru*. Viewing the scene objectively as an educationist, no-one was better qualified to assess the movement's contribution to the life of Wales.

It was in much the same vein that Dr. R. Tudur Jones wrote in *Y Cymro*—

' If one had to express the Urdd's contribution to the life of Wales in one word, that word would be *llawenydd* (joyousness) . . . Generation after generation have come to associate their national heritage, not with despair and despondency, but with vitality and joyousness . . . One can only wonder at the quantity and the variety of the Urdd's achievements throughout the years . . . and in all that it did, it succeeded in combining the best in our traditional life with the demands and interests of the twentieth century . . . This is just another way of saying that Ifan ab Owen Edwards was one of the most powerful and creative influences in our nation's history. He was like the shelter of a rock in a storm, at the very time when so many of Wales' religious and political leaders had lost their faith and their vigour.'

Such tributes could only make those closely linked with the movement more determined than ever to strive their utmost to justify the
nation's trust.

*　　　*　　　*　　　*

The credit for organising the star-studded rugby match at Cardiff
on 26 April must go to a group of Urdd supporters in the city who
immediately took up a suggestion proposed by Robin Jones. The
organising panel had Dewi Bebb as Chairman, Bob Roberts as
Treasurer, David Meredith as Publicity Officer and John Evans as
Organising Secretary. Everything seemed to favour such an
enterprise in 1972—the Welsh International team had won both
the Triple Crown and the Rugby Championship in 1971, and many
Welsh players were among the British Lions that beat the All
Blacks in New Zealand. Two persons were considered vital to the
success of the Urdd scheme—Carwyn James and Barry John.
Both had connections with the Urdd and readily agreed to co-
operate. Barry John would select his team mainly from the Welsh
XV, while Carwyn James' XV would be drawn mainly from the
English, Scottish and Irish 'Lions'. They had no difficulty in
enlisting the necessary players.

It was originally intended that the game should be played on the
Cardiff Rugby Club ground in the Arms Park. Within two weeks,
however, all available tickets had been allocated and orders were
still pouring in. It was realised that only the National Stadium
could accommodate the huge crowd of would-be spectators. An
application was quickly made to the Welsh Rugby Union, and the
organisers held their breath until it was learnt that the Stadium
would be made available. John Evans shed tears of joy ! BBC
Wales televised part of the game in colour with a Welsh commentary
by John Evans. Later that evening, highlights of the match, with
an English commentary, were shown on BBC I network in the
' Sportsnight with Coleman ' programme.

It was a mild April evening. Welsh flags fluttered in the breeze,
and the ground was in perfect condition. The teams were evenly
matched, and at half-time the score stood at 16-16. Both teams
played hard but without tension ; it was not a battle, but an
exhibition of how rugby could be played at its best. Fifteen minutes

from the end, Carwyn James' XV took the lead with a score of 28-26. Then the miracle happened. With three minutes to go, Barry John scored a classic try and the game was theirs. Few people that night knew that Barry was to retire from rugby and that this famous try was to be his last ever.

The proceeds of the game exceeded £21,000, and even with costs at more than £7,000, there was a balance of £14,500. Like every festival ever organised by the Urdd, the surplus would have been far less were it not for the voluntary efforts of those directly concerned. And, since it was intended that part of the Jubilee Fund should be earmarked towards adapting and renovating the Urdd Centre in Cardiff, £11,500 was immediately paid into the account of the Cardiff Urdd Council.

A venture of this magnitude could well have sufficed as the Jubilee event of the year, but the Urdd had several other schemes in mind and it was no time to rest on one's oars.

* * * *

From the outset, the 1972 Eisteddfod had adopted the title *Eisteddfod y Jiwbili*. It was no mere accident that it was held in Merioneth. The Founder was born at Llanuwchllyn, and it was here that he sited the first Urdd Camp in 1928, returning to nearby Glan Llyn in 1950. It was at Corwen that the first Urdd Eisteddfod was held, and it had returned to Merioneth more often than to any other county in North Wales. Nothing could be more fitting than that the Urdd should turn again to Merioneth in its Jubilee year. The credit for seeing that it did so belonged to Meirion Jones of Bala, and although he did not live to see his dream come true, he had tilled the soil and sown the seed and could safely leave the harvest to his fellow-workers.

The Rev. Huw Jones was elected Chairman of the Executive Committee and there could not have been a happier choice. He was ably supported by two Vice-Chairmen, Iolo ab Eurfyl and Gwylfa Roberts, while the Secretary's duties were quietly and efficiently carried out by Penri Jones. R. O. Humphreys was elected Treasurer, and when he left the area, his duties were taken over by T. G. Bellis, while the Chairman of the Finance Committee was none other than the Rector, the Rev. H. E. Jones. The target

for the advance-fund was fixed at £8,000, but it was decided to add
to it the county's £2,000 contribution to the Jubilee Fund, and thus
aim at a total of £10,000. In an area rich in Eisteddfodic
tradition, there was no problem in assembling a team of workers to
share in the organisation. The Honorary President was Lady
Edwards ; this was the fortieth Urdd National Eisteddfod and
Lady Edwards held the record of being the only person who had
attended each one. The five Vice-Presidents were as closely
identified with the Urdd as they were with Merioneth—Trefor O.
Jones ; Elena Puw Morgan; Mrs. L. E. Morris; J. F. Owen; and
W. D. Williams. The three Patrons were Col. J. F. Williams-Wynne,
Lord Lieutenant of Merioneth; W. E. Jones, Director of Education;
and Sir David Hughes Parry, President of the National Eisteddfod
Court.

R. Alun Evans had been in charge of the Crowning ceremony
since 1965. His aptitude of speech, his unobtrusive manner and his
lively personality had made him, in a true sense, Master of Ceremonies. It was not surprising that at Bala he again took care of both
the Crowning and the Chairing, and few knew at the time that this
would be his last appearance in this capacity. The Crown was won
by Catrin Beynon Davies who hailed from Aberystwyth but
currently held a teaching post at Cardiff. Next in order of merit
came Delyth Beasley of *Ysgol Rhydfelen*, and equal third, Yvonne
Davies of Carmarthen, and Nan Lloyd Williams of Aberystwyth
who had won the Crown in 1969. As at Swansea the previous year,
the Chair was won by Arwel John of Pontyberem. Second and
third were Islwyn Edwards of Pontrhydygroes and Dylan Iorwerth
Jones of Waunfawr, Caernarfonshire.

Lewis Hywel Davies of Machynlleth had been chosen to open the
Arts, Crafts and Science Exhibition, but illness prevented him from
attending, and his place was taken by Lady Edwards. The Eisteddfod Presidents were Jennie Eirian Davies, Carwyn James and Dr.
Osian Ellis. Jennie Eirian Davies took the Jewish Jubilee, an
occasion for the releasing of prisoners, as the theme of her address.
She felt that, in the Wales of today, the Welsh language lacked the
freedom to grow, to expand and to develop simply because its use
was limited by habit, by tradition and by external influences.
Could not the Urdd Jubilee be the occasion for setting the language
free ?

Carwyn James naturally turned to the rugby field for his theme. He referred to two celebrated players, very different in temperament and in technique, who had played an outstanding role in Welsh rugby and were complementary to one another—Gareth Edwards and Barry John. No compromise was required on the part of either ; their success lay in their mutual understanding and their complete co-operation. This was the spirit Wales needed today. There was room for swift, brilliant break-through on the one hand, and for calm, calculated, unyielding perseverance on the other. There would be times when the Urdd would be required to voice its opinion clearly on matters of importance relating to the future of the nation ; there would also be occasions when it should act calmly, consistently and unostentatiously.

Dr. Osian Ellis deviated from the orthodox pattern of Eisteddfod presidency. He made no speech ; instead he played a piece of 17th century harp music. As he took the harp for the second time in response to the enthusiastic applause, he slyly remarked that he had never before heard of an Eisteddfod President being given an *encore* !

On the occasion of the Jubilee, the Committee had asked R. E. Griffith, as Director of the movement, to address the audience. He too referred to present-day Wales—to the language crisis and the tensions involved. He expressed his belief that there was still room for a movement that was patriotic yet non-political, that promoted spiritual values and was yet non-sectarian. The Urdd should not be blamed for being non-political ; it was not within its terms of reference to be otherwise. It should not be condemned for not being a protest movement ; this would not be compatible with its policy. What Wales needed today was mutual tolerance and understanding.

Two facets of the Eisteddfod bore a special relation to the Jubilee year. One was a pageant presented in the Eisteddfod pavilion by Merioneth schools and Aelwydydd, portraying—in word and song, mime and dance—the various dimensions that the Urdd had added to the experience of its members. The other was an exhibition planned and arranged by Harlech Television Company as a tribute to the Urdd on its fiftieth anniversary. This was a visual presentation of the movement's development during the years 1922—1972 and it was perhaps the most popular attraction on the

Eisteddfod ground. The Urdd greatly appreciated this gesture, and especially the care and interest shown by members of HTV staff responsible for the planning and exhibiting.

It was no doubt a disappointment to Urdd members and leaders in Merioneth not to have won the Royal Prize and the Pantyfedwen Trophy and investment. By a margin of just seven points, this honour went to Flintshire, with Caernarfonshire in third place. But Merioneth folk were able to derive some satisfaction from the knowledge that the victory would provide a new impetus to the county that was to stage the Eisteddfod at Rhyl in two years' time. At the final meeting of the Eisteddfod Executive Committee, Urdd officials were privileged to receive a balance of £6,700 which included the County's £2,000 contribution to the Jubilee Fund. It was felt by all that the Bala Eisteddfod would rank among the happiest and most successful of Urdd Eisteddfodau.

*   *   *   *

While mainly concerned with the organisation of special events, the Jubilee Committee had also advocated the setting up of a development fund that would help the movement to meet its immediate commitments at the beginning of the new era, more particularly the long-overdue expenditure in connection with the Llangrannog centre. A target of £50,000 was suggested and it was realised that this could not be achieved without adequate and efficient planning. The obvious choice for undertaking such a task was the Director himself, and despite pressure of other duties, he readily agreed to assume responsibility for the project. In addition to appealing to outside grant-aiding bodies, it was decided that the movement itself should make a substantial effort, and every county was set a target of £2,000. In this way, it was hoped that a total of £25,000 would be raised by Urdd County Committees, and it was gratifying to note that, by the end of 1972, the total had exceeded £36,000.

Individual donations and covenant subscriptions brought in £24,000, including contributions from voluntary societies and organisations. Appeals were made to County and County Borough Councils for grants from Welsh Church Funds, and with the exception of Monmouthshire and Radnorshire all responded readily and generously. There were also contributions from the major Banks and from a number of Trusts. From all these sources, another £20,000 was added to the Fund. A most welcome gesture came from the National Union of Teachers ; a contribution of £500 was received, earmarked towards the cost of publishing this story of the Urdd. Later, another £300 towards the same project was received from the Catherine and Lady Grace James Foundation.

In October, the BBC allowed a bilingual television appeal on behalf of the Urdd. It was made by Garry Nicholas of Llanelli, who had been a prominent member of the Urdd from early childhood and was currently joint-leader of *Senedd yr Ifanc*. Speaking on behalf of his fellow-members, he said—

> ' I think I speak for every member of the Urdd when I say that, as Welshmen, our lives would have been poorer but for the vision of one man fifty years ago . . . Over the years, the Urdd has welcomed the support of both Welsh and English speakers, and the companionship of Aelwyd and Camp has done much to bridge the gap between those who speak Welsh and those who do not . . . '

His words obviously fell on good soil, and as a result of his appeal, another £3,000 was added to the Fund.

And so, the Jubilee Development Fund reached not £50,000 but £80,000. And just as important as the financial result was the evidence it bore of the nation's faith in its own youth organisation. Nothing could be more encouraging to those whose hands would hold the reins at the beginning of the new era.

The BBC and HTV were generous in their coverage of the year's events. In addition, they arranged their own special programmes, either featuring the movement's development or assessing its contribution to Welsh life. The BBC gave us *Y Gadwyn Aur*—a programme for children by Aneurin Jenkins-Jones; and *Jiwbili*—a programme devised by Geraint Stanley Jones and presented by Ednyfed Hudson Davies. HTV featured the Urdd in one of its ' Outlook ' series, chaired by Lord Chalfont, who was joined by Robert Presswood, former Director of Education for Cardiff ; Charles Quant of the *Liverpool Daily Post* ; Trevor Fishlock, Welsh Correspondent of *The Times* and author of *Wales and the Welsh* ; William Edwards, M.P., Carwyn James and J. Cyril Hughes.

This ready co-operation was greatly appreciated, but it would be too much to expect that *all* would go the Urdd way during Jubilee Year. Despite appeals by the Urdd Council, the Welsh Office, Elystan Morgan, M.P., and many others, the Post Office Board refused to issue a commemorative 50th Anniversary stamp. The result was that thirty MP's and more than fifty Local Authorities voiced their protest and called on the Board to reconsider its decision. Meanwhile, the Urdd had produced its own unofficial stamp of which nearly 100,000 were sold. A commemorative cover was also designed and arrangements made for a special franking at Llanuwchllyn on 23 September, when the main Jubilee event—*Gŵyl y Gobaith*—would be held in the village.

By this time, the Post Office Board had realised that it had misjudged the issue and, through the Rt. Hon. Cledwyn Hughes, M.P., offered to provide a commemorative cover and place at our disposal their facilities for publicity and distribution. The offer, however, came too late and we were obliged to decline. But the Welsh Office still considered that the initial refusal of the Board to issue a stamp had been a slight on the Urdd and on Wales, and by way of recompense, it asked the Urdd to accept an offer by the Board whereby some seventy Local Authorities in Wales would forego their own postal franking for the period 10-16 September in favour of one advertising the Urdd event—*Gŵyl y Gobaith*. The cost—which amounted to more than £1,000—was met by the Welsh Office as a mark of their appreciation of the Urdd's contribution to Wales.

*   *   *   *

July brought a visit by a children's choir from Valencia, Spain— *Pequeños Cantores de Valencia*. This was not their first visit to Wales ; in 1970, they had won a choral trophy at Llangollen, and were competing again in 1972. So, from Llangollen, they travelled to Llangrannog where they spent a week as guests of the Urdd. During their stay, they gave concerts at Cardigan, Aberporth, Felinfach Arts Centre, Aberystwyth and Cross Hands, performing works in Spanish, Catalan, Latin, English and Welsh. Arrangements for their visit were made in conjunction with R. Bryn Williams who acted as their interpreter and compére throughout their stay.

A month later, at the National Eisteddfod of Wales at Haverford-west, the authorities set aside a ten-minute interlude on the Thursday to greet the Urdd on the occasion of its Jubilee. Greetings were extended by Professor Idris Ll. Foster on behalf of the Eisteddfod Council and by W. J. Philipps Williams, Chairman of the local Executive Committee. A special Jubilee poem was sung to harp accompaniment by Aled Lloyd Davies. These greetings were acknowledged by Lady Edwards, and no sooner had she ended her brief remarks than a sudden uproar was heard at the back of the pavilion and all heads were turned as some thirty boisterous children ran shouting towards the stage. They were Llangrannog campers dressed in everyday jeans and camp shirts, determined to be part of the event. Having squatted on the stage, they decided it was their turn to respond, and as they sang, the audience supplied the beat to their camp songs, and a ceremony that had begun in formal dignity had suddenly come alive!

On the same day at Haverfordwest, the Most Reverend Dr. G. O. Williams, Archbishop of Wales, addressed the Honourable Society of Cymmrodorion on the subject *Brwydr yr Iaith* (The Language Struggle). Referring to the movements and individuals that were contributing towards the well-being of the language, he said—

' In this struggle to win people's hearts—to persuade them to adopt the language and feel responsible for its continued existence —I feel sure that the best advocates are the poets, the dramatists, the novelists and creative artists of all kinds, not because they are propagandists for the language, but because it is through them that our culture lives and grows and wins our allegiance. Let them have no misgivings about their function. It is through them that the enchantment of the language is conveyed to us . . .
Next to them, I would rate Urdd Gobaith Cymru and the schools. If I were asked what would be of greatest benefit to Wales in the next decade, I think I would say that what would be most profitable would be to pour prodigious sums into the Jubilee Fund so that the Urdd would be fully armed to continue its mission of winning hearts and minds in support of the language. The age of fifty is no doubt a critical one for a movement just as it is for people. For a voluntary organisation, entirely dependent on its ability to stimulate enthusiasm in generation after generation, one of the main dangers lies in an unwarranted disillusion amongst its followers. It is natural that, in retrospect, we should

ask whether the Urdd's policy has been the right one. Was it a mistake to trust in the inherent ability of Welsh culture to make people willing and ready adherents ? Would it not have been better to have concentrated on changing those institutions that condition our attitude towards Wales and the Welsh language, in such a way that they would use their influence in favour of the language rather than against it ? I believe both methods are necessary—to create the personal response, and also to change the conditions that determine the place of the language in society. And because of this, I believe it would be a colossal mistake to belittle the importance of the Urdd in the present struggle on behalf of the language.'

Towards the end of his address, the Archbishop referred to the tensions associated with the language question—

' I think I can understand how the language crisis weighs on people to such an extent that it makes them reject the methods of persuasion we once trusted. What makes me doubt the value of direct action—quite apart from the question of law-breaking—is the evidence of hatred and viciousness that emerges . . . I shudder in my heart lest this hatred should increase. We, Welsh-speaking Welshmen, however honest our aims, are not immune to it, for anger, by its very nature, begets anger. One must, therefore, refrain from any action that could increase antagonism. To my mind, it is far better to rely on constitutional methods, appealing to reason and conscience, and creating within Wales a united desire to solve the delicate problems and practical difficulties which today threaten the very life of the nation . . .'

*   *   *   *

It would be unpardonable to convey the impression that the only notable Jubilee celebrations were those organised on a national level. Each County Committee had its own ideas for celebrating the event. Many of these were original, colourful and contemporary, but it would be impossible here to do more than select a few of the highlights.

In Anglesey, R. Ieuan Griffith and three of his colleagues under-took a sponsored weekend climb of fourteen peaks in Snowdonia. Despite atrocious weather conditions which forced a group of military cadets to abandon a similar task, the four teachers survived the gales and returned triumphant. The county also had a pilgrimage of ' saints '—Alwyn Owens and J. Elfed Jones—who trod the paths of Saint Seiriol and Saint Cybi, the one traditionally walking from Penmon and the other from Holyhead, meeting at Ffynnon Clorach and joining in prayers at Llandyfrydog. Dressed as monks, the 1972 ' saints ' covered the same journey and arrived at Llandyfrydog Church to be welcomed in a service conducted by the Rev. W. R. Hughes of Amlwch and the Dean of Bangor, Bishop B. N. Y. Vaughan.

Caernarfonshire hit on the idea of creating a pyramid, each side representing the triangular Urdd badge, and conveyed to Caernarfon by wheelbarrow from four points fifteen miles distant. Despite torrential rains, the four sections were duly received by the Mayor, Ald. R. T. Cemlyn Williams, and the pyramid erected.

E. Alwyn Williams, Organiser for Denbighshire and Flintshire, made a solo sponsored pilgrimage, following the Pilgrims' Way from Holywell to St. David's. The 164-mile journey was covered in eight days, and more than £1,000 raised towards the county targets. Pride of place in Flintshire's calendar, however, went to the village of Treuddyn where the first Urdd Adran was formed in 1922. At a Jubilee concert, a silver salver was presented to Lady Edwards to be used as a trophy at the Urdd National Eisteddfod. Marian E. Williams, who had been the first ' General ' and who founded the first Adran, was unable to attend due to illness. She died shortly afterwards, and in memory of her a contribution from Treuddyn was sent to the 1974 Rhyl Eisteddfod Fund.

Cardiganshire had its own relay race, converging on Llanarth, the village in which was written the letter that gave birth to the movement. Thirty couriers ran in relay from Llangybi, Llandysul, Ysbyty Ystwyth and Pont Llyfnant. Pembrokeshire stalwarts loaded a pillar of Preseli stone on a hand-trolley and moved it, not to Stonehenge this time, but to Glan Llyn, where it was erected as a permanent record of Jubilee Year. Carmarthenshire events would need a volume to themselves. They ranged from a barbecue and dance at Cydweli Castle to the publication of traditional Carmarthenshire recipes and to the selling of more than seven-hundred pounds of home-made marmalade !

West Glamorgan decided that something tangible and lasting was called for, and produced a booklet, edited by Dr. Prys Morgan, tracing the movement's development within the region. But this was by no means all. A very different enterprise was embarked upon by the fourteen trekkers and their three leaders who mounted their horses at Cwmafan and trekked the 120 miles to arrive at Bala on the opening day of the Jubilee Eisteddfod. Incidentally, Cwmafan had also arranged for the reconstructed Aelwyd premises to be opened in Jubilee Year. The county's celebrations ended in a special religious service held at Tabernacl Chapel, Morriston, the address being given by the Rev. J. Gwilym Jones of Bangor. East Glamorgan and Monmouthshire had their own versions of sponsored walks, the one around the periphery of public parks and the other exploring the intricacies of forest walks. Breconshire had adopted the 1972 County Festival. This included a Concert at Brecon, a *Twmpath Dawns* at Builth and a *Discotec* at Pontsenni. Most of the events, however, were concentrated on Ystradgynlais, and included a religious service, a *Cymanfa Ganu*, a concert, a féte and a *Noson Lawen*. There was also a sponsored canoe expedition along the canal from Gilwern to Brecon.

*   *   *   *

When plans for the Jubilee Year were first considered, it was agreed that the climax of the celebrations should be at Llanuwchllyn. This event was given the title *Gŵyl y Gobaitn* (Festival of Hope). It was envisaged, not as a nostalgic event, but as a joyous jamboree of forward-looking optimism.

Shortly before the Founder's death, R. E. Griffith had told Sir Ifan ab Owen Edwards that he would like to see a statue of him placed alongside that of his father at Llanuwchllyn. ' Would you be willing ? ' And with a sad smile Sir Ifan replied, ' Yes, but that is something for you to decide.' No more was said, but it was decided to approach Jonah Jones, who had made the statue of Sir O. M. Edwards in 1959. Rather than add a separate statue, he suggested a new composite sculpture of father and son. This meant depicting two generations, and conveying the relationship between the two figures.

With the concept thus clarified, an application was made to the Welsh Arts Council for grant-aid towards the cost of the commission. For a whole year we were led to believe that a sum in the region of £1,000 could be expected, but eventually we were informed that the Council could not make a contribution due to the fact that a sculptor had been selected without first discussing the choice with the Arts Council. It was not that they objected to the choice as such ; indeed they would readily have approved, but they had not been consulted in the first place, and that was that. We were not aware of such a stipulation ; we had inadvertently transgressed on a technical point, and apparently, the red tape could not be cut. The fact that the artist selected by the Urdd was one of Wales' most brilliant sculptors made the decision even more disappointing. Fortunately, however, a sum of money was held by the Trustees of the O. M. Edwards Centenary Fund. It was partly earmarked for the completion of the Llanuwchllyn *Cilfach Goffa* (memorial-recess), and an appeal to the trustees resulted in the balance of this fund being transferred to the Urdd Jubilee Fund.

The arrangements for *Gŵyl y Gobaith* were greatly facilitated by the ready co-operation of the Merioneth County Council and its Education Authority. Numerous committees were set up at Llanuwchllyn to deal with the local arrangements and the generosity of Penllyn was again made manifest in their whole-hearted support. There was no doubt that *Gŵyl y Gobaith* was eagerly anticipated.

A marquee with a seating capacity of two-thousand had been erected on the school field, and by 23 September all was set to make Llanuwchllyn the Mecca for Welsh people of all ages. *Senedd yr Ifanc* had organised a colourful motorcade from each county, converging on Llanuwchllyn just before the afternoon session. In warm September sunshine, the crowds arrived early, not only to ensure their seats for the afternoon meeting, but also to enjoy a leisurely reunion with old acquaintances. There seemed to be a prevailing air of festivity ; it was a family home-coming.

The afternoon session was chaired by A. D. Lewis, Vice-President of the Urdd and Chairman of the Jubilee Committee. His first task was to call on the representatives to present scrolls bearing the greetings of their County Committees. These were received by Owen Edwards, Chairman of the Urdd Council. Thanking the representatives and their Committees, he remarked, ' Fifty years ago, my father's message went out from Llanuwchllyn to all the counties of Wales. Today, half a century later, the youth of those counties have brought their replies to Llanuwchllyn.'

The theme of the meeting was ' Yesterday, Today and

Tomorrow.' It was R. Gordon Williams of Penygroes who spoke of ' Yesterday ' and he was able to draw on his personal reminiscences of the pioneering days. He brought out the vintage of the twenties and thirties and shared it joyously with the youth of the seventies. He then appealed to them to assume responsibility for the Urdd. ' It is your movement ; take the reins and lead it.'

' Today ' was represented by two young people—Welsh-speaking Ann Lloyd Lewis, and Philip Masson who had learnt Welsh as a second-language. For Ann Lloyd Lewis, Wales had reached a crisis, and following from a distance was not enough. There was no deliverance except through complete commitment and total responsibility. Philip Masson had learnt Welsh at Pontypridd Boys' Grammar School and was currently a student at Oxford. Speaking in fluent Welsh and referring to Dafydd Iwan's song, *Mae'n wlad i mi, ac mae'n wlad i tithau*, he maintained that, above all else, he wanted to belong to Wales, and in order to identify oneself completely with a nation, one had to learn its language.

It was left to Aneurin Jenkins-Jones to raise the curtain on the movement's 'Tomorrow'. He felt that being present at the half-centenary celebration was a great privilege, but he predicted that an even deeper experience would be the lot of those who saw the Urdd's centenary—' when service to one's country, to fellow-man and to Christ will have reached a level that today is beyond our comprehension. There are already signs that this is beginning to happen.'

The brief addresses were interspersed with music items by the Cardiff Aelwyd Choir, Bala Primary School Choir, *Y Diliau*, Ysgol O. M. Edwards, Llanuwchllyn, and Carys Vaughan Jones of *Aelwyd Llandudno*. The meeting ended as Richard Pugh of Aberystwyth, echoing the final words in Aneurin Jenkins-Jones' address, sang *Mor Fawr yw'r Iôr* (How Great Thou Art).

The audience then moved to join those already assembled at the *Cilfach Goffa*. Here, the proceedings were in the charge of the Director, R. E. Griffith, and the unveiling ceremony was performed by Lady Edwards. With brevity and dignity, she referred to Sir Owen and Sir Ifan as two sons of Penllyn who had dedicated themselves to the service of Wales. She hoped the Memorial would be ' an inspiration to all of us, and to future generations, to follow their example.' When the two bronze statues were unveiled it was

416

obvious that they met with the approval of the crowd. They saw
the figure of O. M. Edwards, at the height of his career, standing
slightly behind his son as though urging him on to greater things
than he himself had accomplished. For the sculptor, Jonah Jones,
standing unobtrusively aside, that moment must have been one of
memorable satisfaction.

The evening session was a *Noson Lawen* with a difference. Entitled
Hwyl Hanner Canrif, it had brought together some of the unique
talent that had entertained Welsh audiences over a period of some
forty years. To have assembled so many of the stars together on the
same platform was something of a miracle, and one that may never
be repeated. They included Meic Parry, Huw Jones (Bala), Tomi
Scourfield, Alwyn Samuel, Gwyn Williams, Aled Lloyd Davies and
Meibion Menlli, Islwyn Jones, John Garnon, Glan Davies, Hywel
Gwynfryn, Elfed Lewis, Eiry Palfrey, Olwen Lewis, Huw Jones and
Edward Morus Jones, together with groups from the Aelwydydd at
Aberystwyth, Morriston and Llandudno, Machynlleth High
School, *Triawd y Coleg*, *Parti'r Ffynnon* and *Côr Godre'r Aran*.

This three-hour variety programme was to end with *Côr Godre'r
Aran* singing *Caru Cymru* to harp accompaniment. Then, unannounc-
ed, between the first and second verses, Arwel Jones of Llanidloes
read a tribute to the Urdd and its Founder—perhaps the finest piece
of prose ever written by Islwyn Ffowc Elis and given here in
translation—

'When darkness faced our nation ; when Wales was only a
name for a strip of land, without succour, without purpose,
without hope ; when our old men dreamt dreams of what had
been but our young men saw no visions of what would be ; when
there was no respect for our language ; no lustre in our education ;
no place for our history :
It was then that Ifan ab Owen of Llanuwchllyn raised a cry :
a cry against the extinction of our nation, against the death of
our language. It was not to the old that he spoke, nor to the
middle-aged, but to the very young : 'It is we who must do
something, for we are the hope of our land.'
That gentle cry was not a sound, but a silver light which moved
from valley to valley, from hill to hill, to village and town and
city, to every place where young Welsh hearts were waiting for it.
And by the hundred and the thousand, those hearts were set
alight, kindled into glowing witnesses to the greatness of the
past, tireless missionaries for the glory of tomorrow. In the silver

93 'Good Night, Sir Ifan'

gleam of the cry, all was made new. Despair was turned into
hope; instead of death came life ; fruitless dreams were replaced
by the Urdd.

Today, half a century after the voicing of the cry and the
kindling of the silver ray, there stands a new Wales. Not a free
Wales, but a Wales which *can* be free ; not a Welsh-speaking
Wales, but a Wales where the ancestral language is fast raising
its humble head. Here, in this corner of the earth, instead of a
nation resigned to die, there is a nation determined to live.

This is the feat of Ifan ab Owen, this is the achievement of the
Urdd. We owe it to his vision and to the dedication of his
movement that today there is here a small nation whose language
is still alive, that is not now ashamed to stand among the nations
of the world, equal with each and every one. And if the Founder's
silver cry has been silenced in death, its message rings on : as we
defend our own language and our very soul, let us be gracious
towards our fellow-man, let us be true to Christ.'

The words were spoken with feeling and sincerity, and one could
almost have heard a pin drop. It was so unexpected, so devastatingly
effective in its simplicity. There was a moment's complete silence,
and then *Côr Godre'r Aran* sang the second verse of *Caru Cymru*. The
words now seemed to have acquired a new meaning, a new dimension. It was almost an act of dedication in which the audience
silently joined. ' And here, in this corner of the earth, instead of a
nation resigned to die, there is a nation determined to live.'

*   *   *   *

Throughout the year's celebrations, we had endeavoured to
project the ideals, the principles and the values of the movement.
The Urdd had so much for which it could be thankful—for the
vision of Ifan ab Owen Edwards in his youth, and his inestimable
service to Wales throughout his life ; for the movement's thousands
of voluntary self-sacrificing leaders ; for the dedication of a host of
young people who had served as members of staff ; for the public
support of rich and poor alike. ' Freely we have received, let us
freely give.' Such gratitude could best be expressed in a religious
service, a service of thanksgiving for what had been received, and of
dedication on the threshold of a new era. It would be a service that
would include a variety of media—in word, in music, and in
dance—and this meant that the choice of venue was important

When His Grace The Archbishop of Wales, the Most Reverend Dr. G. O. Williams, was approached regarding the possibility of holding such a service in the Cathedral at Bangor, he warmly welcomed the suggestion and assured us of his personal support and the fullest co-operation of the Dean, the Rev. Bishop B. N. Y. Vaughan, and the Education Director, the Rev. Alwyn Rice Jones. A steering committee was set up and a service based on the theme ' Wales, Fellow-man and Christ,' was devised by the Rev. J. Gwilym Jones of Bangor and produced by the Rev. Canon Huw Pierce Jones of Pwllheli.

The service was recorded for television by the BBC. The church was full to capacity, and the spirit of devotion shown by the participants was as impressive as the excellence of their performance. In a brief address, the Archbishop appealed to Urdd members and leaders to stand firm by their faith, to re-dedicate their talents, to vow anew to follow in the footsteps of the Founder, offering their whole life to the service of Wales, of fellow-man and of Christ.

This service was the final episode of the Jubilee year. Its basis and inspiration was the Urdd Pledge ; it was a service in which young people dedicated themselves anew, and were not afraid to be committed. It was on this note that the curtain was lowered on the first half-century in the story of the Urdd. May the movement created by Ifan ab Owen Edwards march forward without losing any of its faith, its vitality, its hope or its joyousness. And may each new generation build on the past to meet the needs of the future.

Appendices

APPENDIX 1

CWMNI URDD GOBAITH CYMRU

OFFICERS

Former-Presidents

Mr. J. M. Howell (1929—1944)
Sir Ifan ab Owen Edwards (1944—1970)

Former Vice-Presidents

Sir John Cecil-Williams
Capt. Geoffrey Crawshay
Miss Cassie Davies
The Rev. Dr. E. Tegla Davies
Miss Gwendoline E. Davies
The Rev. Dr. Gwilym Davies
Dr. Jenkin Alban Davies
Mrs. L. M. Tegryn Davies
Miss Margaret S. Davies
Mr. O. Picton Davies
Miss Rachel Davies
Miss Sali H. Davies
The Rev. Dr. G. A. Edwards
Dr. Huw T. Edwards
Sir D. Owen Evans
Principal Ellen Evans
Sir Emrys Evans
Dr. Griffith Evans
Dr. Gwynfor Evans
The Rev. Trebor Lloyd Evans
Lady Megan Lloyd George
Dr. William George
The Rt. Hon. James Griffiths
The Very Rev. Dr. W. T. Havard
Mr. Emlyn Hooson
The Rt. Hon. Cledwyn Hughes
Mr. D. R. Hughes
Mr. Hywel Huws

Miss Norah Isaac
Sir David James
Dr. E. D. Jones
Dr. Emyr Wyn Jones
Mr. F. Wynn Jones
Dr. Gwenan Jones
Mrs. Hilton Jones
Dr. Iorwerth H. Jones
The Very Rev. Dr. J. C. Jones
Mr. J. R. Jones
Dr. T. Gwynn Jones
Mr. A. D. Lewis
The Rev. Dr. H. Elvet Lewis
The Rt. Hon. Sir Herbert Lewis
Mr. Wynne Ll. Lloyd
Mrs. Hopkin Morris
Sir David Hughes Parry
Lady Hughes Parry
Dr. Thomas Parry
Mr. Evan Phillips
Dr. T. Ifor Rees
The Very Rev. Dr. Timothy Rees
Mr. Robert Richards
Mr. Cynfab Roberts
The Rt. Hon. Goronwy O. Roberts
Sir Eric O. Skaife
Mr. T. D. Slingsby-Jenkins

Sir Ben Bowen Thomas
Mr. J. Clifford Thomas
Mr. J. R. Thomas
Dr. William Thomas
Mr. W. P. Thomas
Sir Percy Watkins
Sir Wyn Wheldon
Dr. Emlyn Williams

The Most Rev. Dr. G. O.
   Williams
Y Fonesig Mallt Williams
Mr. R. Gordon Williams
Mr. R. R. Williams
Mr. W. J. Williams
Mrs. W. J. Williams

Former-Chairmen of the Urdd Council

Mr. Ifan ab Owen Edwards (1931-44)
Dr. Gwenan Jones (1944-48)
Professor D. Hughes Parry (1948-54)
Dr. Iorwerth H. Jones (1954-57)
The Rev. Trebor Lloyd Evans (1957-60)
Miss Cassie Davies (1960-63)
Mr. A. D. Lewis (1963-69)
Mr. Owen Edwards (1969-72)

Former Vice-Chairmen

Miss Rachel Davies (1931-42)
Dr. Gwenan Jones (1942-44)
Professor R. I. Aaron (1944-45)
Dr. Iorwerth H. Jones (1945-48)
Mr. Cynfab Roberts (1948-54)
Dr. E. D. Jones (1954-57)
Mr. A. D. Lewis (1957-63)
Mr. Aneurin Jenkins-Jones (1963-69)
Mr. Alun Creunant Davies (1969-72)

Former-Treasurers

Mr. W. J. Williams (1931-42)
Professor D. Hughes Parry (1942-48)
Dr. Jenkin Alban Davies (1948-54)
Mr. Cynfab Roberts (1954-63)
Mr. F. Wynn Jones (1963-66)
Mr. J. Elfed Jones (1966-69)

Former-Secretaries

Mrs. Ifan ab Owen Edwards (1931-45)
Mr. Hywel D. Roberts (1945-48)
Dr. E. M. Job (1948-54)
{ Dr. Mary Clement (1954-57)
{ Mr. Iolo Francis Roberts (1954-57)
{ Mr. Dafydd Morris Jones (1957-60)
{ Miss Menai Williams (1957-60)
Mr. Owen Edwards (1960-69)
Mr. Prys Edwards (1965-69)
{ Mr. John Garnon (1969-72)
{ Miss Ann Lloyd Lewis (1969-72)

Former-Counsels

Professor D. Hughes Parry (1931-42)
Professor D. J. Llewelfryn Davies (1944-69)

Former-Solicitor

Mr. T. Ivor Jones (1931-69)

Current Officers

President	Lady Edwards (1970)
Vice-Presidents	Mr. Elfed Roberts (1972)
	Mr. Gwilym Roberts (1972)
Council Chairman	Mr. Alun Creunant Davies (1972)
Vice-Chairman	Mr. Arwel Jones (1972)
Treasurer	Mr. Prys Edwards (1969)
Secretaries	Mr. Sulwyn Thomas (1972)
	Miss Gaenor Edwards (1972)
Counsel	Professor Hywel Moseley (1969)
Solicitor	Mr. Emyr Currie-Jones (1969)

APPENDIX 2

URDD NATIONAL EISTEDDFOD

A. LOCATION

1929	Corwen	1953	Maesteg
1930	Caernarfon	1954	Y Bala
1931	Swansea	1955	Abertridwr
1932	Machynlleth	1956	Caernarfon
1933	Caerffili	1957	Amanford
1934	Old Colwyn	1958	Mold
1935	Carmarthen	1959	Lampeter
1936	Blaenau Ffestiniog	1960	Dolgellau
1937	Gwaun-cae-gurwen	1961	Aberdâr
1938	Aberystwyth	1962	Rhuthun
1939	Llanelli	1963	Brynaman
1940	Y Rhyl	1964	Porthmadog
1941-5	Gap during war years	1965	Caerdydd (Cardiff)
1946	Corwen	1966	Holyhead
1947	Treorci	1967	Carmarthen
1948	Llangefni	1968	Llanrwst
1949	Pontarddulais	1969	Aberystwyth
1950	Wrexham	1970	Llanidloes
1951	Fishguard	1971	Swansea
1952	Machynlleth	1972	Y Bala

B. WINNING COUNTIES

It was during the war years that the County became a separate unit in the Urdd system, and the County Trophy was first awarded at the Corwen National Eisteddfod in 1946. Later, the County Trophy was to include the Royal Prize, together with the Pantyfedwen Family Bowl and Investment. The winning Counties during the period 1946-72 were as follows :

1946	Merioneth	1953	West Glamorgan
1947	Denbighshire	1954	Carmarthenshire
1948	Caernarfonshire	1955	Cardiganshire
1949	Carmarthenshire	1956	Caernarfonshire
1950	Denbighshire	1957	Carmarthenshire
1951	West Glamorgan	1958	West Glamorgan
1952	West Glamorgan	1959	Cardiganshire

1960	Merioneth	1967	Carmarthenshire
1961	West Glamorgan	1968	Denbighshire
1962	Denbighshire	1969	Cardiganshire
1963	West Glamorgan	1970	Montgomeryshire
1964	Caernarfonshire	1971	West Glamorgan
1965	East Glamorgan	1972	Flintshire
1966	Anglesey		

Total County wins—

West Glamorgan	7	Merioneth	2
Carmarthenshire	4	Anglesey	1
Denbighshire	4	East Glamorgan	1
Caernarfonshire	3	Flintshire	1
Cardiganshire	3	Montgomeryshire	1

APPENDIX 3

URDD FESTIVALS

A. ANNUAL FESTIVALS

1953	Dyfed Three-County Festival	Newcastle Emlyn
1954	Cardiganshire Festival	Tregaron
1955	Four-County Festival (Counties of Merioneth, Montgomery, Denbigh and Flint)	Corwen
1956	Carmarthenshire Festival	Llanelli
1957	Pembrokeshire Festival	Fishguard
1958	Glamorgan and Monmouthshire Festival	Neath
1959	Denbighshire Festival	Denbigh
1960	Anglesey Festival	Llangefni
1961	Montgomeryshire Festival	Llanfyllin
1962	Caernarfonshire Festival	Caernarfon
1963	Merioneth Festival	Corwen
1964	Teifi Valley Festival	Llandysul
1965	Flintshire Festival	Mold
1966	Pembrokeshire Festival	Crymych
1967	Breconshire Festival	Brecon
1968	Cwm Tawe Festival	Pontardawe
1969	Monmouthshire Festival	Newbridge
1970	Menai District Festival	Menai Bridge
1971	Llŷn and Eifionydd Festival	Pwllheli
1972	Breconshire Festival	Ystradgynlais

B. FOLK-SONG-AND-DANCE FESTIVALS

1958	Corwen
1960	Haverfordwest
1962	Cardiff
1964	Aberafan
1966	Wrexham
1968	Gwaun-cae-gurwen
1970	Maesteg

APPENDIX 4

OUT-DOOR ACTIVITIES

A. CAMP CENTRES

1928	Llanuwchllyn	1932	LLANGRANNOG (still operating)
1929	Llangollen	1934-48	Porth Dinllaen
1930	Llangollen	1946-52	Cricieth
1931	Llangollen	1950	GLAN LLYN (still operating)

Camps were held in hired premises at Llanmadog in Gower during the summer of 1942 and 1943 ; from 1943 to 1947, the Caernarfon Aelwyd was used as a camping centre. The first International Camp was held in 1948 in the Aberystwyth Aelwyd centre, and following this they were held annually from 1949 to 1960 at Pantyfedwen, Borth ; Inter-Celtic Camps were held from 1949 to 1954, also at Pantyfedwen.

B. MABOLGAMPAU (YOUTH GAMES)

1932	Llanelli	1938	Pontypridd
1933	Swansea	1939	Neath
1934	Swansea		Bangor
1935	Aberystwyth	1940	Mountain Ash
1936	Cardiff		Porthmadog
	Machynlleth	1951	Cardiff
1937	Bridgend	1954	Mountain Ash
	Bangor		

The Mabolgampau were discontinued following a change of policy with regard to physical education in schools and colleges. Athletic contests were, however, continued on a District and County basis. Folk-Dancing was catered for at the Gŵyl Werin (from 1958), while from 1959, organised games tournaments were included in the Urdd's annual programme.

APPENDIX 5

OVERSEAS VISITS

A. EARLY CRUISES

1933 NORWAY—The Norwegian Fiords
1934 BRITTANY, together with Spain, Portugal and North Africa.
1935 FRANCE, together with Belgium, the Netherlands, Denmark and Norway.
1936 MADEIRA, Casablanca, Lisbon, La Rochelle.
1939 YUGOSLAVIA—The Dalmatian Coast, together with Corfu, Rome, and Monte Carlo.

B. EARLY PILGRIMAGES

1930 Geneva (Boys)
1931 Geneva (Girls)
1936 Geneva
1937 Lugano and Lucerne (Two pilgrimages)
       Geneva and Montreux
1938 Geneva
1949 The Republic of Ireland
       South of France
       Bielefeld, Germany
1950 Bavaria and Oberammergau
1951 Northern Spain
1952 Bielefeld, Germany
       Plochingen, Germany
       Yugoslavia

In later years, overseas visits were more frequently organised locally by the County Youth Councils (*Seneddau Sir*). There were also pilgrimages within Wales itself, concentrating on places of historic or literary interest.

428

APPENDIX 6

BOOKS AND MAGAZINES

A. WELSH BOOKS CAMPAIGN

1937—	1,025	1952—	8,114
1938—	3,545	1953—	9,031
1939—	3,063	1954—	12,281
1940—	3,545	1955—	9,217
1941—	7,584	1956—	9,680
1942—	17,378	1957—	10,875
1943—	39,625	1958—	14,265
1944—	54,043	1959—	11,301
1945—	43,678	1960—	11,575
1946—	26,570	1961—	10,304
1947—	17,115	1962—	8,414
1948—	17,326	1963—	9,034
1949—	14,352	1964—	10,958
1950—	9,242	1965—	13,900
1951—	8,289		

TOTAL SALES : 415,329

After a pioneering effort that lasted almost thirty years, the Urdd was able to hand over the Campaign to the Welsh Books Council, and this Council has assumed responsibility for its organisation since 1966.

B. URDD MAGAZINES

CYMRU'R PLANT—Initiated by O. M. Edwards in 1892. Became closely linked with the Urdd in 1922. Publication continues.

CYMRAEG (1955-66). Later gave way to two second-language magazines—BORE DA and MYND.

BORE DA (1966). Publication continues.

MYND (1966). Publication continues.

YR ANRHEG (1959-63). A free supplement that led to the publication of a first-language magazine—DERYN, for the younger readers.

DERYN (1963). Publication continues.

CYMRU, later given a new title—HAMDDEN (1957-72). This in turn gave way to I'R DIM.

YR AELWYD (1940—1969).

BLODAU'R FFAIR (1953). Publication continues.

APPENDIX 7

FINANCIAL

A. LEGACIES

Legacies received by the Urdd from its inception are listed below. The money was invested in property and shares, and the legacies thus perpetuated. Any friends who would like to support the movement in this manner may note that the full title for legal purposes is ' CWMNI URDD GOBAITH CYMRU (The Welsh League of Youth [Incorporated])', and the address of its registered office is SWYDDFA'R URDD, ABERYSTWYTH.

		£
1934	Sir Herbert Lewis, Penucha, Caerwys	25.00
1940	Mrs. M. J. Griffiths, Swansea	200.00
1942	Mrs. W. J. Williams, Gwynfa, Latchford, Warrington	500.00
1944	Miss M. E. Samuel, Mona House, Aberystwyth	180.00
1945	Mrs. R. Lloyd Phillips, Bryneithin, Llanfarian, Aberystwyth	200.00
1945	Miss Mair Jones, Llanwrda (formerly of Blaendulais)	25.00
1947	Miss Anna M. Roberts, Bryneithin, Llanfarian, Aberystwyth	100.00
1947	Dr. T. Benson Evans, Prestatyn	25.00
1948	The Rev. J. D. Evans, Talybont, Cardiganshire : property, 4, Epworth Terrace, Aberystwyth	450.00
1948	Dr. Erie Evans, Bangor	1,000.00
1948	Mrs. J. M. Evans, Talybont, Cardiganshire	100.00
1949	Mr. J. R. Thomas, Aberystwyth (formerly of Glyn Ceiriog)	100.00
1949	Mrs. E. J. Evans, Queensferry	100.00
1949	Mr. 1. D. Hooson, Rhosllannerchrugog	9,663.59
1952	Miss Mary Jones, Bwlchgwyn, Wrexham	5.00
1952	Mrs. M. Hughes Williams, Hazelmount, Colwyn Bay	50.00
1953	Mr. David Jones, Plas Drain, Llanddoget	300.00
1953	Mr. T. D. Jones, London	500.00
1954	Mrs. M. J. Evans, Brixton Hill, London	100.00
1955	Mr. David Williams, Maerdy, Y Rhondda	402.07
1955	Mr. O. P. Hughes, Caernarfon	100.00
1957	Mr. R. H. Davies, Llandrillo	1,000.00
1957	Mr. Thomas Owen (Hesgin), Swansea	200.00

1957	Mr. R. Ll. Jones, Machynlleth	.. ..	100.00
1957	Dr. Gwyn Williams, Llandudno Junction	..	7,090.79
1958	Mr. Lewis Edwards, Pentre Clawdd, Rhiwabon		100.00
1958	Miss M. A. Davies, Cardiff	.. ..	25.00
1959	Mr. Ifor Ll. Griffiths, Ffairfach	.. ..	50.00
1959	Mrs. Mary Pugh, London ..	.. ..	200.00
1960	Miss Margaret Morris, Aberdâr	.. ..	100.00
1961	Mr. Gwilym E. Hughes, Penarth	.. ..	1,000.00
1961	The Rev. Dr. Gwilym Davies, Aberystwyth	..	3,529.55
1963	Mr. T. Lloyd Roberts, Y Rhyl	.. ..	10.00
1963	Mr. and Mrs. H. Iorwerth Hughes, Liverpool..		1,000.00
1963	Professor W. E. Williams, Bangor	.. ..	2,000.00
1964	Mr. Tudor Price Howells, Penygraig, Rhondda		2,000.00
1965	Dr. T. Alwyn Lloyd, Cardiff	.. ..	6,690.93
1965	Mrs. E. A. James, Pontypridd	.. ..	100.00
1965	Mr. Evan Thomas, Utica ..	.. ..	440.60
1965	Miss Annie Williams, Colwyn Bay	.. ..	16.65
1966	Mrs. M. J. Rees, Swansea ..	.. ..	30.00
1966	Lady Hughes Parry, Llanuwchllyn	.. ..	100.00
1966	Mrs. A. M. Hughes, Birmingham	.. ..	100.00
1966	Miss M. G. Parry Powell, Letterston..	..	224.44
1967	Mr. James Davies, Old Colwyn	.. ..	100.00
1967	Mrs. M. A. Lewis, Fochriw	.. ..	100.00
1967	Mrs. M. Benson Evans, Aberystwyth	..	25.00
1968	Mr. Edwin Owen Jones, Weston, Hitchin	..	200.00
1969	Mr. Walter Jones, Aberystwyth	.. ..	437.91
1969	Mrs. C. M. Williams, Llanrwst	.. ..	50.00
1969	Miss Mary Elizabeth Parry, Old Colwyn	..	1,302.47
1970	Mr. D. J. Jenkins, Porthcawl	.. ..	1,511.82
1971	Mrs. M. E. Davies, Aberaman, Aberdâr	..	100.00
1971	Mr. William Devonald Griffiths, Whitland	..	510.00
1971	Mr. Cynfab Roberts, Aberystwyth	.. ..	25.00
1972	Miss M. A. James, Porthcawl	.. ..	200.00

B. GIFTS ' IN MEMORIAM '

From time to time, gifts in memory of Urdd members and supporters are received for investment. Gifts already received are listed below.

In Memory of

		£
1954	Mr. Arthur Jones, Glyn Ebwy (Ebbw Vale) ..	100.00
1954	Mr. and Mrs. Stanton Roberts, Gellifor ..	50.00
1954	Mr. George Bowen, Maesteg	50.00
1955	Mr. W. P. Thomas, Porthcawl	100.00
1956	Mrs. Elizabeth Ann Thomas, Bangor ..	100.00
1959	Mr. and Mrs. J. Orton Jones and Mr. John Rosser Jones, Glyn Ebwy (Ebbw Vale) ..	100.00
1960	Miss Carol Lewis, Ton Pentre	200.00
1961	Mr. D. O. Roberts, Aberdâr	100.00
1966	Mrs. Elizabeth Watkin Jones, Nefyn ..	1,000.00

C. EXPENDITURE INCREASES

The following table shows the enormous increase in the expenditure of Cwmni'r Urdd within a period of nine years : 1964/65—1972/73.

1964/65	:	£73,994
1965/66	:	£80,470
1966/67	:	£89,524
1967/68	:	£103,716
1968/69	:	£109,875
1969/70	:	£111,396
1970/71	:	£122,283
1971/72	:	£135,942
1972/73	:	£157,621

Index

Folk Festivals : 1958 (Corwen), 238-39; 1960 (Haverfordwest), 259-60 , 285-6 ; 1962 (Cardiff), 285-6 ; 1964 (Aberafan), 304-5, 328 ; 1966 (Wrexham), 327-8 ; 1968 (Gwaun-cae-gurwen), 345-6 ; 1970 (Maesteg), 373-4
Folk-dancing : 105, 159-60, 185, 192, 210, 218, 228, 237-9, 273, 286, 305-6
Foreign Office : 149
Free Wales Army : 337, 353-4
Friends Ambulance Corps : 121

G

Gaelic League : 162, 183, 186
Games Banner : 35, 63
Gandhi, Mahatma : 5
Gapper, R. L. : 85, 109, 140, 197
Geneva : 23, 28, 38, 55, 58, 66, 124, 163
George VI : 218
George, David Lloyd : *see* Lloyd George, David
George, Lady Megan Lloyd : *see* Lloyd George, Lady Megan
George, W. R. P. : 129, 202
George, William : 129, 202, 341
Girls' Section : *see* Adran y Merched
Gittins Report : 349
Glyn Ceiriog : 9-10
Goodwill Message : 13-14, 23, 32, 43, 53, 62, 68-69, 79, 120-21, 132, 146, 151, 159, 213, 230-31, 262-3, 277, 286, 318, 346, 363, 384, 396
Grand Hotel, Borth : 131 ; *see also* Pantyfedwen (Borth)
Gregynog Press : 21
Griffith, Alwyn : 121
Griffith, I. B. : 347-8
Griffith, Ieuan : 377-8, 396
Griffith, J. H. : 25, 50
Griffith, Ll. Wyn : 1, 170-71, 287, 299
Griffith, Olwen : 98, 133
Griffith, R. E. : 11-12, 37-38, 40, 44, 46, 50, 54, 56, 65, 69, 74-76, 79, 82-85, 91-92, 99, 103, 106, 110, 113-4, 118, 126, 128, 130, 134, 136, 145-6, 155, 159, 163, 167, 173, 175, 195-6, 199, 200, 205, 213, 216-8, 228, 235, 239, 241, 244, 246, 255, 257, 274, 287-8, 300-1, 303, 321, 341, 347, 352, 354-6, 358, 364, 367-8, 377, 384, 391, 395, 397, 406-7, 413, 415
Griffiths, James : 78, 89, 95, 101-2, 140, 315
Griffiths, T. Elwyn : 109

Gruffydd, W. J. : 2, 119, 173, 197, 245
Gŵyl Werin : *see* Folk Festivals
Gymnastic Displays : *see* Mabolgampau

H

Hamdden : 289, 322, 378, 390
Harlech Television : 338, 349-50, 406-8
Harlinghausen, Harald : 151
Harries, Hywel : 200, 209, 360
Harries, Leslie : 119, 241, 316
Hauteluce : 163
Hermann, Rudolph : 36, 149-50, 163, 173, 226
Hitler Jugend : 104
Home Exchanges : 147
Honourable Society of Cymmrodorion : 194, 252, 410
Hooson, I. D. : 119, 156, 167, 173, 197, 210
Howell, J. M. : 15, 17-19, 22, 24-25, 35-36, 39, 44, 47-48, 59, 77, 90-91, 101, 115, 118-9, 148, 211, 300
Hughes, J. Cyril : 229, 241, 259, 274, 284, 301, 304, 307, 364, 395-6, 408
Hughes, John M. : 277, 283, 307, 316, 387
Hughes, Richard (Jerusalem) : 110
Hughes, S. J. : 365
Hughes, T. Rowland : 54, 119, 173, 286
Hughes & Son (Publishers) : 5, 245
Hughes Parry Report : 309-10, 325
Humphreys, James : 87, 133, 169, 176, 182, 213
Huws, Elwyn : 255, 263, 276, 283, 296, 306, 319-20
Huws, Hywel : 21, 267, 378

I

Independent Broadcasting Authority : 393
Inter-Celtic Conventions : 162, 173, 185, 192, 202, 209, 213, 318, 363
International Conventions : 142, 149-51, 161, 164, 174, 185-6, 192, 202-3, 209, 214, 226-7, 231-2, 242, 250, 261-2, 318
International Relations : 120, 132, 142, 146, 171, 213, 340, 396
Investiture (1969) : 352-9
I'r Dim (magazine) : 390
Isaac, Evan L. : 155, 187, 234, 249, 304, 348, 367, 396
Isaac, Norah : 50, 57, 76, 98, 124, 127, 134, 153, 157, 167, 189, 196, 236, 245, 261, 276, 367, 401